SEMANTICS OF JAY

$\sigma = \{\langle v_1, val_1 \rangle, \langle v_2, val_2 \rangle, \ldots, \langle v_m, val_m \rangle\}$

$M(Program\ \text{p}) = M(\text{p.body}, \{\langle v_1, undef \rangle, \langle v_2, undef \rangle, \ldots, \langle v_m, undef \rangle\})$

$ApplyBinary(Operator\ op,\ Value\ v1,\ Value\ v2)$

$$\begin{aligned}
&= v1 + v2 && \text{if } op = + \\
&= v1 - v2 && \text{if } op = - \\
&= v1 \times v2 && \text{if } op = * \\
&= floor\left(\left|\frac{v1}{v2}\right|\right) \times sign(v1 \times v2) && \text{if } op = / \\
&= v1 < v2 && \text{if } op = < \\
&= v1 \le v2 && \text{if } op = <= \\
&= v1 = v2 && \text{if } op = == \\
&= v1 \ne v2 && \text{if } op = != \\
&= v1 \ge v2 && \text{if } op = >= \\
&= v1 > v2 && \text{if } op = > \\
&= v1 \wedge v2 && \text{if } op = \&\& \\
&= v1 \vee v2 && \text{if } op = \|
\end{aligned}$$

$ApplyUnary\ (Operator\ op,\ Value\ v) = \neg v \qquad \text{if } op = !$

$M(Expression\ e,\ State\ \sigma)$

$$\begin{aligned}
&= e && \text{if } e \text{ is a } Value \\
&= \sigma(e) && \text{if } e \text{ is a } Variable \\
&= ApplyBinary(e.\text{op}, M(e.\text{term1}, \sigma), M(e.\text{term2}, \sigma)) && \text{if } e \text{ is a } Binary \\
&= ApplyUnary(e.\text{op}, M(e.\text{term}, \sigma))) && \text{if } e \text{ is a } Unary
\end{aligned}$$

$$\begin{aligned}
M(Statement\ s,\ State\ \sigma) &= M((Skip)s, \sigma) && \text{if } s \text{ is a } Skip \\
&= M((Assignment)s, \sigma) && \text{if } s \text{ is an } Assignment \\
&= M((Conditional)s, \sigma) && \text{if } s \text{ is a } Conditional \\
&= M((Loop)s, \sigma) && \text{if } s \text{ is a } Loop \\
&= M((Block)s, \sigma) && \text{if } s \text{ is a } Block
\end{aligned}$$

$M\ (Skip\ \text{s},\ State\ \sigma) = \sigma$

$M(Assignment\ \text{a},\ State\ \sigma) = \sigma\ \overline{U}\ \{\langle a.\text{target}, M(a.\text{source}, \sigma)\rangle\}$

$$\begin{aligned}
M(Block\ \text{b},\ State\ \sigma) &= \sigma && \text{if } b = \varnothing \\
&= M((Block)b_{2\ldots n}, M((Statement)b_1, \sigma)) && \text{if } b = b_1 b_2 \ldots b_n
\end{aligned}$$

$$\begin{aligned}
M(Conditional\ \text{c},\ State\ \sigma) &= M(c.\text{thenbranch}, \sigma) && \text{if } M(c.\text{test}, \sigma) \text{ is } true \\
&= M(c.\text{elsebranch}, \sigma) && \text{otherwise}
\end{aligned}$$

$$\begin{aligned}
M(Loop\ \text{l},\ State\ \sigma) &= M(l, M(l.\text{body}, \sigma)) && \text{if } M(l.\text{test}, \sigma) \text{ is } true \\
&= \sigma && \text{otherwise}
\end{aligned}$$

Programming Languages

Programming Languages
Principles and Paradigms

Allen Tucker
Bowdoin College

Robert Noonan
College of William and Mary

Boston   Burr Ridge, IL   Dubuque, IA   Madison, WI   New York   San Francisco   St. Louis
Bangkok   Bogotá   Caracas   Kuala Lumpur   Lisbon   London   Madrid   Mexico City
Milan   Montreal   New Delhi   Santiago   Seoul   Singapore   Sydney   Taipei   Toronto

McGraw-Hill Higher Education

A Division of The McGraw-Hill Companies

PROGRAMMING LANGUAGES: PRINCIPLES AND PARADIGMS

Published by McGraw-Hill, a business unit of The McGraw-Hill Companies, Inc., 1221 Avenue of the Americas, New York, NY 10020. Copyright © 2002 by The McGraw-Hill Companies, Inc. All rights reserved. No part of this publication may be reproduced or distributed in any form or by any means, or stored in a database or retrieval system, without the prior written consent of The McGraw-Hill Companies, Inc., including, but not limited to, in any network or other electronic storage or transmission, or broadcast for distance learning.

Some ancillaries, including electronic and print components, may not be available to customers outside the United States.

This book is printed on acid-free paper.

International   1 2 3 4 5 6 7 8 9 0 QPF/QPF 0 9 8 7 6 5 4 3 2 1
Domestic   1 2 3 4 5 6 7 8 9 0 QPF/QPF 0 9 8 7 6 5 4 3 2 1

ISBN 0–07–238111–6
ISBN 0–07–112280–X (ISE)

General manager: *Thomas E. Casson*
Publisher: *Elizabeth A. Jones*
Developmental editor: *Emily J. Lupash*
Executive marketing manager: *John Wannemacher*
Senior project manager: *Jayne Klein*
Production supervisor: *Kara Kudronowicz*
Coordinator of freelance design: *Michelle D. Whitaker*
Freelance cover/interior designer: *Rokusek Design*
Cover images: *Photographed by Allen Tucker*
Supplement producer: *Brenda A. Ernzen*
Media technology senior producer: *Phillip Meek*
Compositor: *Interactive Composition Corporation*
Typeface: *10/12 Times Roman*
Printer: *Quebecor World Fairfield, PA*

Library of Congress Cataloging-in-Publication Data

Tucker, Allen B.
   Programming languages : principles and paradigms / Allen B. Tucker, Robert E. Noonan.—1st ed.
      p.   cm.
   Includes index.
   ISBN 0–07–238111–6 — ISBN 0–07–112280–X (ISE)
   1. Programming languages (Electronic computers). I. Noonan, Robert E. II. Title.

QA76.7 .T83   2002
005.13—dc21   2001044137
                                                   CIP

INTERNATIONAL EDITION ISBN 0–07–112280–X
Copyright © 2002. Exclusive rights by The McGraw-Hill Companies, Inc., for manufacture and export. This book cannot be re-exported from the country to which it is sold by McGraw-Hill. The International Edition is not available in North America.

www.mhhe.com

To Anatoly Sachenko and our friends at
  Ternopil Academy of National Economy
  Ternopil, Ukraine.

Allen Tucker

To Debbie and Paul.

Robert Noonan

Brief Contents

Contents

The study of programming languages at the advanced undergraduate or graduate level usually covers two main areas: principles of language design and two or three different programming paradigms. Texts for this study tend to fall into either of two categories: 1) concept-based surveys of a wide range of language design topics and paradigms; and 2) interpreter-based treatments of the design principles presented in a functional language.

APPROACH

This text attempts to unite the best features of these two approaches into a single and coherent framework. Like the interpreter-based texts, we include a rigorous, complete, and hands-on treatment of the principles using a formal grammar, type system, and denotational semantics, including an interpreter that implements the formal model. In contrast with these texts, we use Java as the language of illustration rather than a functional language. Like the concepts-based texts, this text presents and contrasts the major language design topics and programming paradigms. Unlike the concepts-based texts, we hope to cover this material in a more modern and coherent fashion.

Our approach is based on the belief that a formal treatment of syntax and semantics, a consistent use of the mathematical notations learned in discrete mathematics, and a hands-on treatment of the principles of language design are centrally important to the study of programming languages. This approach is advocated, for instance, in the design of the Programming Languages course in the *Liberal Arts Model Curriculum* [Walker 1996], and is also consistent with the recommendations of *Computing Curricula 2001* [CC 2001]. The concepts-based texts seem to have foregone such rigor in recent years in favor of surveying an increasingly wide variety of topics and languages. The topics that should be central to a student's understanding of language principles and paradigms, such as the formal treatment of semantics, are usually presented late in these texts, as one of many unrelated topics, and in a way that encourages instructors to skip them altogether. We think that a study of programming languages principles should integrate these topics in a more compelling way.

With regard to *Computing Curricula 2001* [CC2001], the material in this text covers all the topics (PL1 through PL11) in the Programming Languages section of the core body of knowledge. It also covers other topics in that core body of knowledge, such as event-driven and concurrent programming (PF6), memory management (OS5), and functional and logic programming (IS). However, this text generally treats these topics in greater depth than that suggested by *Computing Curricula 2001*.

Our treatment of syntax and semantics includes the use of BNF grammars and a formal denotational approach to type systems and semantics. This approach is fully illustrated, so that the theory can be explored by students with the aid of a Java interpreter that directly implements the formal semantics. This approach allows students to study all the dimensions of language design using the available formal tools: BNF grammars, abstract syntax, recursive descent parsing, and functional definitions of type systems and meaning. A small imperative language that we call "Jay" is used as a basis for illustrating the principles of language design and formal methods. Java is used throughout Chapters 2–5 as the implementation language for exercising the syntax, type-checking, and semantics functions of Jay.

Another point of departure from the concepts-based texts is that we have tried to focus on a single language per paradigm. We believe that a deeper understanding of each paradigm is more important than a survey of the many languages that support it. Often the same problem is solved in each paradigm so that an instructor can better illustrate the differences between the paradigms.

Java is ideally suited to supporting most of the topics in this text. It is a widely popular language, designed in a more principled way and containing a richer collection of features than most of its predecessors. This versatility allows Java to be used in most of the lab exercises and illustrations that accompany this text. So we use Java for the imperative, object-oriented, event-driven, and concurrent programming paradigms. We use Scheme and Haskell for the functional paradigm, and Prolog for the logic programming paradigm. Why two languages for functional programming? Scheme represents a more traditional, widely used Lisp-like functional style which cannot be summarily overlooked. However, Haskell contains several contemporary features—lazy evaluation, list continuations, and a strong and versatile type system—that set it apart from the traditional functional programming style, and thus merit its separate inclusion. As a practical matter, we recommend that instructors cover only one of these two languages in the functional programming part of the course.

We have extended the discussion of formal semantics into some of the paradigm chapters as well. That is, the run-time semantics of Jay are reimplemented in the object-oriented, functional, and logic programming chapters. This strategy provides more coherence for the book overall by working out a single substantial example in each of several different programming styles.

Another *thread* that can be followed through the book is formal correctness of programs. Axiomatic correctness of imperative programs is treated in Chapter 3. Both the chapter on object-oriented programming and the one on functional programming contain a section on formal correctness.

Beyond the "standard" paradigms—imperative, object-oriented, functional, and logic programming—this book identifies two other paradigms: *event-driven programming* and *concurrent programming*.

Event-driven programming characterizes programs that respond to events arriving in an unpredictable sequence, rather than controlling *a priori* the sequence in which these events occur. The most dramatic current examples of the event-driven paradigm are those programs written for Web-based interactions—online registration and electronic commerce applications, for example. But event-driven programming is a more mature paradigm than these recent applications suggest. It also appears in programs that are embedded in vehicles, operating systems, networks, and home alarm systems. We are convinced that this paradigm is sufficiently mature and distinctive from the others that it can no longer be ignored in any study of programming languages that presumes to cover the major paradigms.

Concurrent programming is a sixth paradigm treated in this text. Parallelism is central in modern computing, and is seeing increasing visibility at the programming language and application level, especially in scientific computing. Combining this emergence with traditional applications at the operating system and hardware levels, concurrent programming now requires first-class attention in a programming languages text. Thus, the book has a chapter on concurrent programming, including the related concepts of parallelism and nondeterminism that occur at the systems and applications levels.

COURSE ORGANIZATION

This text contains more material than can be covered in a one-semester course. Our experience shows that there are at least two different paths through the text for a 14-week semester. There are definitely more, as the following diagram suggests:

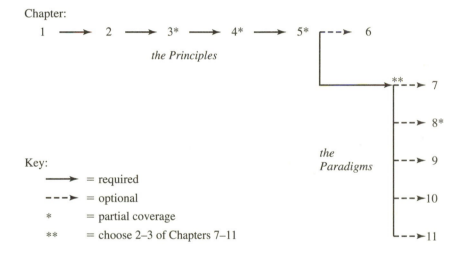

The chapter sequence divides the course into two major parts: a study of the principles of programming languages (Chapters 1–6) and a study of two or three major paradigms (separate from the imperative paradigm). Which paradigms to cover, of course, will vary with the preferences of the instructor and the content of other courses in the curriculum. For instance, if the curriculum regularly offers a course in parallel computing, Chapter 11 might not be covered in this course.

Some of the chapters are marked for partial coverage, again depending on local conditions. Coverage of Chapter 3 (semantics) should include type systems and denotational semantics, but operational and/or axiomatic semantics may be skipped. Some sections of Chapters 4 and 5 may also be skipped, depending on the preferences of the instructor for depth in the imperative paradigm. We do recommend that, as a minimum, the complete syntax and semantics of Jay, along with the syntax and semantics of methods and parameters that appear in these chapters, not be excluded.

Moreover, coverage of Chapter 8 (functional programming) will normally include either Scheme or Haskell and omit the other. We have intentionally designed the "paradigms" chapters to be mutually independent. However, they do revisit topics in syntax

Table 1

Two feasible
1-semester course
outlines

Bowdoin	William and Mary
Introduction 0.5	Introduction 0.5
Syntax 2	Object-oriented programming 2
Semantics 2	Syntax 1.5
Imperative Programming 2	Semantics 2
Memory Management 2	Imperative Programming 1.5
Object-oriented programming 1	Exception Handling 1
Functional Programming 2	Functional Programming 2
Logic Programming 2.5	Event-driven Programming 2
	Concurrent Programming 1
Total weeks = 14	Total weeks = 13.5

and semantics that are introduced in the first four chapters, so these four should normally be covered early in the course.

Table 1 shows two sample course outlines that we have used at Bowdoin and William and Mary while class-testing this material. The numbers beside the topics indicate the approximate number of weeks in a semester devoted to each topic.

We note that Chapter 6 on Exception Handling is somewhat problematic. Logically it belongs with Chapters 2–5 which cover the syntax and semantics of imperative languages. However, unlike these chapters, Chapter 6 is more conceptual in nature (like the paradigm Chapters 7–11) in that exceptions are not modeled formally. Also, because exceptions in Java are objects, some knowledge of the object-oriented paradigm is needed to present the material on exceptions. This option of covering Chapter 7 before Chapter 6 is reflected in the William and Mary course outline.

PREREQUISITES

Knowledge of Java is normally a prerequisite for using this text, since Java is the language of illustration in most chapters. However, at William and Mary we have used this material in a course where students had only C++ and imperative programming experience. In this case, we covered the Java Tutorial appendix and the object-oriented programming chapter immediately after Chapter 1, and Table 1 shows that it is a workable alternative. In any event, we recommend that students in this course have access to a good Java reference which will provide language-specific information beyond what appears in the Java Tutorial appendix.

On the other hand, we do expect that students in this course will bring some mathematical skills, as would be found in a discrete mathematics or discrete structures course. We assume that students are familiar with the basic notions of functions, sets, and logic, as well as some exposure to the basic ideas of recursion and proof. Such a course, along with a data structures course (i.e., familiarity with linked lists, stacks, flexible arrays, and hash tables), will normally be prerequisites for this type of programming languages course. Notions and notations for functions, sets, logic, and related mathematical topics are used throughout this text. A summary of these notations appears in Appendix A.

Familiarity with the Java realizations of these ideas is helpful, but not necessary since they are explained as they are used in the text and are also summarized in Appendix C. The software for this text can be used with any implementation of Java 1.1 or higher. We have implemented the Java software for this book using both Sun's JDK Java and Metrowerks' Codewarrior Java.

WEBSITE AND PEDAGOGICAL SUPPORT

We have also developed a considerable suite of software to accompany this text. You should use the website **www.mhhe.com/tucker** as a source for downloading that software and communicating with the authors as you teach the course. This website contains the following specific pedagogical support materials:

- A complete Java implementation of the formal syntax, type system, and semantics of Jay, as discussed in Chapters 1–4 and summarized in Appendix B. Specific references to this software are made in many examples and exercises throughout the text.
- A set of tools for "animating" various syntactic and semantic functions that are discussed in this text. Algorithm animation is an active area of research in computer science education, and we encourage instructors to experiment with these tools to help students visualize the semantic features of programming languages.
- A set of downloadable transparency masters for all figures and tables in the text.
- Answers to the exercises; available to instructors via a secure password.

ACKNOWLEDGMENTS

Many persons have helped guide us in the development of this text. James Lu was a key collaborator in the early conceptualization of this text. Colleagues Bill Bynum at the College of William and Mary and Laurie King at the College of the Holy Cross contributed to Chapters 4 and 8, respectively. The students at Bowdoin and William and Mary patiently worked through early versions of this material as we developed and class-tested it. Notably, Doug Vail developed solutions to some of the more challenging problems. We also appreciate the work of colleagues Eric Chown (Bowdoin) and Jack Wileden (University of Massachusetts, Amherst) for class-testing a complete draft of this text in Spring 2001, when they provided extensive and detailed suggestions. We thank all of our reviewers:

Manuel E. Bermudez	*University of Florida*
Sanjay Chawla	*University of Minnesota*
Charles Dana	*California Polytechnic University, San Luis Obispo*
Robert Van Engelen	*Florida State University*
Arthur Fleck	*University of Iowa*
Peter N. Gabrovsky	*California State University, Northridge*
Roger T. Hartley	*New Mexico State University*

Alan Kaplan   *Clemson University*
Srini Ramaswamy   *Tennessee Technological University*
Jack C. Wileden   *University of Massachusetts, Amherst*
Salih Yurttas   *Texas A&M University*

for their careful readings and constructive recommendations throughout the development of this text. Most of their recommendations have been incorporated in this final revision, and the text is greatly improved by their collective insight.

Finally, the cover design uses several photographs of Western Ukrainian cathedrals, which were taken in Spring 2001 by Allen Tucker. This design could convey the idea that overlaying a rigorous language design methodology (the quilt pattern) on top of many different languages (the cathedrals) can help dispel the idea that programming languages are no more than a modern Tower of Babel. If this seems like an over-interpretation, readers can simply enjoy the cover design for its sheer artistry!

Allen B. Tucker   **Robert E. Noonan**
Bowdoin College   *College of William and Mary*

Overview

1

". . . the tools we are trying to use and the language we are using to express or record our thoughts are the major determining factors determining what we can think or express at all!"

Edsger W. Dijkstra [1972]

CHAPTER OUTLINE

Programming languages, like our "natural" languages, are designed to facilitate the expression and communication of ideas between people. The ideas expressed in natural languages cover the whole spectrum of human expression, including prose and poetry, as well as a wide range of subject matter. However, programming languages differ from natural languages in two important ways. First, they have a narrower expressive domain, in that they facilitate only the communication of *algorithmic* ideas between people. Second, programming languages also enable the communication of algorithmic ideas between people and computing machines. Thus the design of a programming language must respond to different requirements than a natural language. We shall explore these requirements and design alternatives for programming languages in this text.

In this study, we will see that there are many similarities between the features of programming languages and the analogous features that characterize natural languages. We will also see that there are fundamental differences, brought on by the special computational environment in which a program must function. We explore these differences in a fairly rigorous way. This study includes a formal treatment of the principles of programming language design and a hands-on examination of the major programming paradigms that these languages support.

The programming languages of tomorrow's computers will be designed by those who understand not only the features, strengths, and weaknesses of the programming languages of today, but also the new application needs and programming potential that can be offered by the computers of the future.

1.1 PRINCIPLES OF LANGUAGE DESIGN

Language designers need to have a basic vocabulary about language structure, meaning, and other pragmatic features that aids in the understanding of how languages work with computers to help programmers express algorithmic ideas. This vocabulary most naturally expresses itself in the form of language design *principles,* many of which are borrowed from linguistics and mathematics. The principles that underlie the design of programming languages fall into the following categories:

- Syntax.
- Type systems and semantics.
- Memory management.
- Exception handling.

These areas are the principal topics of Chapters 2, 3, 5, and 6 respectively, and they are briefly summarized below.

Syntax This design category helps us understand what constitutes a correctly written program. That is, what is the grammar for writing programs in the language, and what is the basic vocabulary of words and symbols that programmers use to form syntactically correct programs. Programming language designers have borrowed strongly from the work of linguists in this area. We shall see that the syntactic structure of modern programming languages is defined using the linguistic formalism called a *context-free grammar.* This is done both for simplicity and clarity and to enable a more rigorous treatment of the concepts.

Type Systems and Semantics This area addresses the types of values that programs can manipulate and the meaning (semantics) of these programs. We shall see that type systems and semantics are also best understood using a formal approach. When we write a program, we are interested in understanding such ideas as the exact effect that an assignment has on the state of the computation, the impact of executing a sequence of steps, and the definition of what it means to execute a loop or a conditional statement. If we can learn this in a way that is independent of any particular machine or operating system architecture, we have a fully abstract definition of the language. Portability is fundamentally important in language design because machines and operating systems change; tying a language definition too closely to the features of a single machine automatically ensures its early obsolescence.

Memory Management This subject addresses the collection of techniques that help us understand the mapping of values, data structures, and program structures to the memory in which these entities ultimately reside. A modern view of memory and its use requires that we distinguish between static and dynamic memory, the stack and the heap, the lifetimes of various kinds of objects, and techniques for garbage detection and reclamation. The study of programming languages is incomplete without an appreciation for the algorithms and strategies for memory management that come into play during the execution of a program whose data and control structures are very complex.

Exception Handling Some events occur unexpectedly during the run of a program, such as an unexpected input error, an unexpected division by zero, or an unexpected unsuccessful attempt to create a new block of space in the heap. Together, these kinds of events are called *exceptions,* and programs written in modern languages must not only trap exceptions but also respond to them in a way that the entire computation is not brought to its knees. Exception handling is a fundamental principle of programming languages, and so we treat it in a separate chapter in this text.

At this point, it is fair to ask, Why treat these principles formally? That is, why can't we simply survey a few current languages and point out the similarities and differences among their syntax, type systems, semantic features, and strategies for managing memory and handling exceptions?

A short answer is: Because it's a very valuable exercise! This is not meant to be a glib answer; we really do believe that it is more valuable to utilize rigorous and mathematical tools for studying programming languages than it is to survey them haphazardly from an arbitrarily selected collection of features and examples. A formal study can more clearly identify common themes among languages. It can also add rigor in a field that needs to be treated rigorously. After all, compiler-writers do not design compilers from sample program fragments hastily contrived. Instead, they use the formal definition of a language's syntax and semantics so that the compiler reflects exactly the intentions of the language designer—no more and no less.

A slightly longer answer is: Because a formal treatment allows us to think about language design in a broader time/space spectrum. That is, a formal treatment frees us from the bonds of today's particular technology, applications, and languages that will eventually find the scrap heap as computing evolves in the 21st century. The study of programming languages should not be reduced to the study of *today's* programming languages; we can always learn about new features, but that in itself provides little inspiration or insight into *tomorrow's* possibilities for language design.

1.2 PROGRAMMING PARADIGMS AND APPLICATION DOMAINS

Programming languages are designed to communicate ideas about algorithms between people and computers. With such a constrained domain of discourse, the expressive features of programming languages are necessarily limited, focussing on the computationally pragmatic rather than the ephemeral or the esoteric. Programming languages are not for writing poetry!

Yet programming languages allow a surprisingly wide range of algorithmic expression, which supports a variety of computing applications across several *application domains,* such as scientific computing or management information systems. In order to achieve such versatility, different communities of programmers in these domains have developed special and different ways, or *paradigms,* for expressing algorithms that appeal especially well to their own application area.

The major programming paradigms that have evolved out of these communities' application domains are identified and briefly defined below. (More elaborate presentations and discussions of these paradigms are offered in Chapters 4, 7, 8, 9, 10, and 11 of this book.)

- *Imperative programming*—the program is a series of steps, each of which performs a calculation, retrieves input, or produces output. Procedural abstraction is an essential building block for imperative programming, as are assignments, loops, sequences, and conditional statements. Major imperative programming languages are Cobol, Fortran, C, and C++.

- *Object-oriented (OO) programming*—the program is a collection of objects that interact with each other by passing messages that transform their state. Object modeling, classification, and inheritance are fundamental building blocks for OO programming. Major object-oriented languages are Smalltalk, Java, C++, and Eiffel.

- *Functional programming*—the program is a collection of mathematical functions, each with an input (domain) and a result (range). Functions interact and combine with each other using functional composition, conditionals, and recursion. Major functional programming languages are Lisp, Scheme, Haskell, and ML.

- *Logic (declarative) programming*—the program is a collection of logical declarations about what outcome a function should accomplish rather than how that outcome should be accomplished. Execution of the program applies these declarations to achieve a series of possible solutions to a problem. Logic programming provides a natural vehicle for expressing nondeterminism, since the solutions to many problems are often not unique but manyfold. The major logic programming language is Prolog.

- *Event-driven programming*—the program is a continuous loop that responds to events that are generated in an unpredictable order. These events originate from user actions on the screen (mouse clicks or keystrokes, for example), or else from other sources (like readings from sensors on a robot). Major event-driven programming languages include Visual Basic and Java.

- *Concurrent programming*—the program is a collection of cooperating processes, sharing information with each other from time to time but generally operating asynchronously. Parallelism can also occur within an individual process, such as the parallel execution of the different iterations of a loop. Concurrent programming languages include SR [Andrews 1993], Linda [Linda 1980], and High Performance Fortran [HPF 1995].

Some programming languages are intentionally designed to support more than one paradigm. For instance, C++ is a hybrid imperative and object-oriented language, while the experimental language Leda [Budd 1995] is designed to support the imperative, object-oriented, functional, and logic programming paradigms. These languages are reminiscent of earlier efforts (notably, PL/I, Algol 68, and Ada) to design a single language that was general-purpose enough to absorb the interests of various communities by embracing all reasonably well-developed paradigms. Historically, these languages have failed to attract interest from across different programming communities, mainly because they failed to run as efficiently as single-paradigm languages in any single domain.

The programming communities that represent distinct *application domains* can be grouped in the following way:

- Scientific computing
- Management information systems
- Artificial intelligence
- Systems
- Web-centric

These communities' goals, major programming paradigms, and preferred programming languages and styles are briefly summarized below.

Scientific The scientific programming community evolved early in the history of computing; the first programs were written in the 1940s to predict the trajectories of missiles during World War II, using the well-worn physics formulae that characterize bodies in motion. These programs were first written in machine and assembly language by specially trained mathematicians. The first scientific programming language, Fortran I, was designed by John Backus at IBM in 1954 [Backus 1954].

Scientific programming is primarily concerned with making complex calculations very fast and very accurately. The calculations are defined by mathematical models that represent scientific phenomena. They are primarily implemented using the *imperative programming* paradigm. The more complex the scientific phenomena become, the greater the need for sophisticated, highly parallel computers and programming languages. Thus, the *parallel programming* paradigm is strongly motivated by the needs of scientific applications like modeling weather systems or ocean flow. Modern scientific programming languages include Fortran 90 [Chamberland 1995], C [K&R 1988], and High Performance Fortran [Adams 1997].

Management Information Systems (MIS) Programs designed for use by institutions to manage their information systems are probably the most prolific in the world. These systems include an organization's payroll system, accounting system, online sales and marketing systems, inventory and manufacturing systems, and so forth. Traditionally, management information systems have been developed in programming languages like Cobol, RPG, and SQL. Cobol supports an *imperative* programming style, while RPG and SQL are *declarative* programming tools for file definition, report generation, and database information retrieval.

More recently, businesses have developed a wide range of electronic commerce applications. These applications often use a "client-server" model for program design, where the program interacts with users at remote sites and provides simultaneous access to a shared database. A good example of this model is an online book ordering system, in which the database reflects the company's inventory of books and the interaction helps the user through the database search, book selection, and ordering process. *Event-driven programming* is essential in these applications, and programmers use languages like Java and Tcl/Tk to implement them.

Artificial Intelligence The artificial intelligence programming community has been active since the early 1960s. This community is concerned about developing programs that model human intelligent behavior, logical deduction, and cognition. Symbol manipulation, functional expressions, and the design of logical proof systems have been central tools in this ongoing effort.

Thus, the paradigms of *functional programming* and *logic programming* have evolved largely through the efforts of artificial intelligence programmers. Prominent functional programming languages over the years have included Lisp, Scheme, ML, and Haskell. Prominent logic programming languages include Prolog and CLP.

Systems Systems programmers are those who design and maintain the basic software that runs systems—operating system components, network software, programming language compilers and debuggers, virtual machines and interpreters, and so on. These types of software are intimately tied with the architectures of specific machines, such as the Sun Sparc, Intel Pentium, Power Macintosh, and the SGI machine.

Some of these programs are written in the assembly language of these machines, while many others are written in a language specifically designed for systems programming. Systems programming is typically done using the *imperative* design paradigm. However, systems programmers must also deal at a fundamental level with the *parallel* and *event-driven* paradigms. The primary example of a systems programming language is C, which was designed in the early 1970s in part to support the coding of the Unix operating system. In fact, about 95 percent of the code of the Unix system is written in C.

Web-centric The most dynamic area of new programming community growth is the World Wide Web, which is the enabling vehicle for electronic commerce and a wide range of applications in academia, government, and industry. The notion of Web-centric computing, and hence Web-centric programming, is motivated by an interactive model, in which a program remains in an infinite loop waiting for the next request or event to arrive, responding to that event, and returning to its looping state.

Programming languages that support Web-centric computing require a paradigm that encourages system-user interaction, or *event-driven* programming. Web-centric computing also benefits from the *object-oriented* design paradigm, since various entities that exist on the user's screen are most naturally modeled as objects which send and receive messages among each other. Programming languages that support Web-centric computing include Perl, Tcl/Tk, Visual Basic, and Java.

1.3 **PRAGMATIC CONSIDERATIONS**

Surrounding the study of programming languages is a collection of related practical concerns, which need to be briefly introduced. The following considerations provide a specific set of constraints that affect all programming language designs.

- Architecture constraints.
- Contextual constraints.
- Virtual machines and interpreters.
- Standards.
- Legacy systems.

Architecture Constraints Programming languages are designed for computers. This fact is both a blessing and a curse to language designers. It is a blessing because a well-designed and implemented language can greatly enhance the utility of the computer in an application domain. It is a curse because most computer designs over the past several decades have followed the "von Neumann" model, which is explained in Chapter 4. Many languages, like Fortran, Cobol and C, are well-matched with that architecture; others, like Lisp, are not.

For a few years, it was attractive to consider the idea of computer architecture as a by-product of language design, rather than as a precursor. A most notable design effort along these lines produced the genre of Lisp machines that emerged in the early 1980s. These machine architectures were configured so that Lisp programs would run optimally on them, and they enjoyed a degree of success for a few years. However, Lisp machine architectures were eclipsed in the late 1980s by the advent of RISC architectures (a variant of CISC architectures and fundamentally different way of designing von Neumann machines), on which Lisp programs were quickly proved to run more efficiently. Moreover, RISC architectures have been shown to be superior to other architectures in their support of Lisp and other programming languages, and thus became the architecture of choice for most applications.

So when we consider the virtues of various language design choices, we are always constrained by the need to implement the language efficiently and effectively within the constraints imposed by today's (RISC) variations of the von Neumann model. The notion that a good language design can lead to a radically new and commercially viable computer architecture is probably not in the cards.

Contextual Constraints Not only are languages designed to fit the constraints of a family of computer architectures, they are also designed to satisfy other constraints imposed by the context in which they are used: the application area, the operating system, the network, and preferences of the programming community. For example, Fortran is implemented on different platforms by different compilers to suit the needs of scientific programmers. These programmers work in various professions that use their own software design styles, tools, and (above all) their own natural languages for communication among themselves. This larger picture of the complex setting for language design is summarized in Figure 1.1.

Figure 1.1 **Levels of Language in Computing**

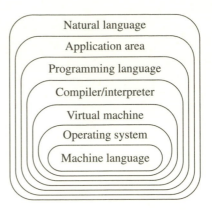

Some languages are intentionally more *general-purpose* in their design, opting to serve the interests of a wide range of applications. For instance, Ada [Ada 1983] was designed to be useful for all applications supported by the Defense Department, while Cobol was designed to support all business-oriented applications. While Cobol was moderately successful in this goal, Ada has been far less successful. Other languages are designed to be more *special-purpose* in nature. For instance, Prolog was designed to serve the narrow interests of natural language processing, theorem proving, and expert systems. C was designed primarily to support the interests of systems programming, although it has since been adopted by a broader range of applications.

Some programming languages are implemented using a *compiling* process, in which the program is translated, or "compiled," into the language of the target machine, and then run on the machine as a second step. Other languages are implemented using an *interpretive* process, in which the source program (usually in an intermediate form) is interpretively executed using software or hardware. Lisp and Prolog, for instance, are often implemented using interpreters (although they have compiled versions too), while Fortran and C are typically compiled languages. Java is a sort of hybrid in this sense, since it is compiled to an intermediate form called "Java byte code," and this form is then interpretively executed (see the discussion of virtual machines and interpreters) by the "Java Virtual Machine," or JVM for short. A *virtual machine,* in general, is any abstract model of a computer that is implemented in software, but not in hardware.

There are advantages and disadvantages when compiling is compared with interpreting. A major advantage of compiling a program is that its run-time performance is usually more efficient (in time and space) than that of its interpreted performance. On the other hand, the quality of interaction that the programmer enjoys with the system is typically better with an interpreter than with a compiler. Since program development is interactive, individual program segments (functions) can be tested as they are designed, rather than waiting for the entire program in which they are to be embedded to be complete. In this book, we illustrate this interactive development activity when we explore the functional and logic programming paradigms.

Virtual Machines and Interpreters Sometimes a language is designed so that the compiler is written only once, using a *virtual machine* as the target machine, and then that

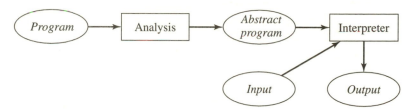

| **Figure 1.2** **Virtual Machines and Interpreters Used in this Text**

virtual machine is implemented by an interpreter on each of the different real machines of the day. As noted in the discussion of contextual constraints, that is the case for Java. When making this design choice, the Java language designers gave up a bit of efficiency (since interpreted code generally requires more resources than native code) in favor of flexibility and portability. That is, any change in the Java language specification can be implemented by altering a single compiler rather than a family of compilers.

Moreover, the virtual machine concept is valuable for other reasons that can offset its inherent loss of efficiency. For example, it is expedient to implement a language and its interpreter using an existing virtual machine for the purpose of design or experimentation with the language itself. Similarly, it is useful to study language design principles and paradigms by using an available *interpreter* that facilitates experimentation and evaluation of programs in that language. The general interpreter model is summarized in Figure 1.2.

In this text, we use as a virtual machine model a collection of functions that define the semantics of a program, and an interpreter written in Java that implements that collection of functions. We will see that this approach is useful to facilitate the study of language design principles because it eliminates machine-specific details that usually obfuscate rather than clarify the discussion.

Standards When a programming language receives wide enough attention and use among programmers, the process of *standardization* usually begins. That is, an effort is made to define a machine-independent standard language definition to which all implementors of that language must adhere.

The two major organizations that oversee and maintain standards for programming languages are the American National Standards Institute (ANSI) and the International Standards Organization (ISO). Several languages have been standardized over the years since the language standardization process began. Some of these, along with their most recent dates of standardization, are

ANSI Cobol (1985)

ISO Fortran (1997)

ISO Prolog (1995)

ANSI/ISO C (1999)

ANSI Basic (1989)

ANSI/ISO Ada (1995)

ANSI Smalltalk (1998)

ISO Pascal (1990)

The language standardization process is complex and time-consuming, with a long period of community involvement and usually a voluminous definition of the standard language as its outcome.

The value of standardization to the community is that software and hardware designers play a role in the process and commit their implementations of compilers and interpreters to conform to the standard. Such conformity is essential to maintain portability of programs across different compilers and hardware platforms.

Some have argued that the downside of language standardization is that it inhibits innovation in language design. That is, standard versions of languages tend to last for long periods of time, thus perpetuating the obsolescent or poorly conceived language features alongside the most valuable features.

More information about specific language standards and the standardization process itself can be found at the website **www.ansi.org.**

Legacy Systems It has been estimated that 90 percent of a programmer's time is spent maintaining existing applications, or *legacy systems,* that were designed and implemented by others, and 10 percent is spent developing code for new applications. The largest body of code for legacy systems is probably written in Cobol, a relatively venerable programming language.

In order to support the ongoing maintenance of legacy code, updated and improved versions of old languages must be "backward compatible" with their predecessors. That is, old programs must continue to compile and run when new compilers are developed for the updated version. Thus, all syntactic and semantic features, even the ones that are less desirable from an aesthetic point of view, cannot be thrown out without disrupting the integrity of legacy code.

For this reason, languages like Cobol become increasingly ponderous in their features as new versions evolve; they rarely become more compact. This is also true for C++, which was designed as a true extension of C in order to maintain backward compatibility. The design of Java, although a lot of its features are reminiscent of C++ features, departed from this tradition. As a central theme, Java designers wanted to free their new language from having to support the less desirable features of C++, so they simply cut them out of their new language. The result was a more streamlined language for new application development, but any legacy C++ system that needs to be converted to Java must be recoded before it can compile or run.

How does a programming language emerge and later evolve? Some programming languages are designed by individuals while others are designed by committees. The language design process in either case is complex, though the product of an individual effort is often a cleaner and simpler language than that of a committee effort. Notably, the languages Cobol and Ada were designed by committees, while the original versions of C and Lisp were designed more or less by individuals.

A more careful summary of the history of programming languages is the subject of Section 1.4. There, we shall see more clearly how languages and language styles have evolved over the last several decades.

1.4   **A BRIEF HISTORY OF PROGRAMMING LANGUAGES**

The first programming languages were the machine languages of the earliest computers, designed in the 1940s. Several hundred programming languages and dialects have been developed since that time. Most have had a limited life span and utility, while a few have enjoyed widespread success in one or more application domains. Many have played an important role in influencing the design of future languages. A general overview of the history of a few of the most influential programming languages is summarized in Figure 1.3.

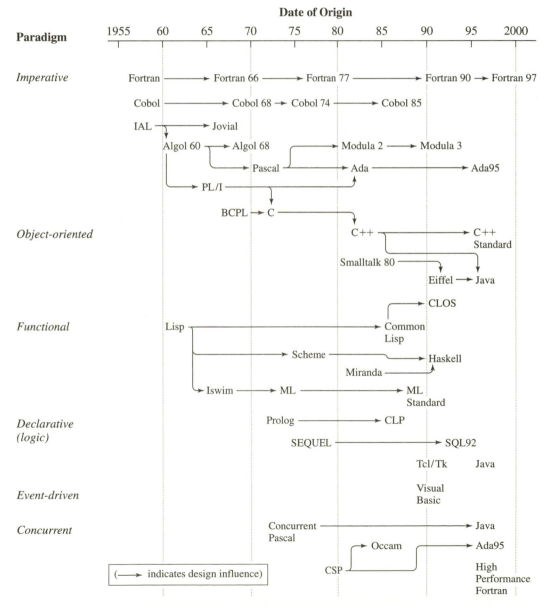

I Figure 1.3   A Brief Historical Lineage of Some Key Programming Languages

No single figure can capture the rich history of programming languages and the evolution of features across languages and paradigms. The languages, dates, and paradigms characterized in Figure 1.3 provide only a general overview of this history and most of the major players in the design of programming languages.

Notably, Cobol and Fortran have evolved greatly since their emergence in the late 1950s. These languages built a large following and have remained fairly autonomous in their evolution and influence on the design of other languages over the last 40 years. On the other hand, the Algol language design has had a tremendous influence on the development of several of its successors, including Pascal, Modula, Ada, C++, and Java. Jay, the experimental language developed for this text, is Algol-like in nature.

In the functional programming area, Lisp was dominant in early years and continues its influence to the present day, motivating the development of more recent languages such as Scheme, ML, and Haskell. In the logic programming area, only one language, Prolog, has been the major player, but Prolog enjoys little influence on the design of languages outside that area. The event-driven and concurrent programming areas are much earlier in their evolution, and only a few languages are prominent. Some of these, like High Performance Fortran (HPF), derive their features by extending those of a widely used base language (Fortran, in this case).

Finally, notice that the language Java appears several times in Figure 1.3—once for each of the object-oriented, concurrent, and event-driven paradigms. Java offers strong support for programming in each of these styles, as we shall see in later chapters of this book. That is one of the reasons why language designers find Java such an interesting programming language.

New languages will undoubtedly emerge in the near future as the younger programming paradigms evolve and their demands for computational power and versatility continue to expand.

1.5 PROGRAMMING LANGUAGE QUALITIES

It is often tempting during the study of programming languages to kick back, rest your head in your palms, and wonder aloud about what would make the ideal programming language. (Surely the current crop of languages has a long way to go before any claims of perfection can be made!) In this exercise, you quickly come to the point of needing some *design criteria* to help motivate and concretize your musing. The following criteria for language design have often been suggested in the literature, and have had a variety of different realizations over the years:

- Simplicity and clarity
- Binding
- Orthogonality
- Reliability of programs
- Applicability
- Abstraction
- Efficient implementation

Simplicity and Clarity How easily can a programmer write a program in this language? How intelligible is that program to the average reader? How easy is the language to learn and to teach?

Some languages, like Basic, Algol, and Pascal in the past, were intentionally designed to facilitate clarity of expression. Basic, for instance, had a very small instruction set. Algol 60 had a "publication language" which provided a standard format for typesetting programs that appeared in published journal articles. Pascal was explicitly designed as a teaching language, with features that facilitated the teaching and learning of structured programming principles.

Other languages appear to have been designed to minimize the total number of keystrokes that one would need to express an algorithm. Surely, the designers of languages like C and APL valued this economy of expression, sometimes it seems to the peril of persons who were trying to read these programs.

Binding A language element is *bound* to a property at the time that property is defined for it. For example, a variable is bound to its type at the time it is declared, as in the declaration

```
int x;
```

which binds the variable x to the type int. The principal binding times for elements to properties are the following:

- Language definition time: When the language is defined, basic data types are bound to reserved words that represent them. For example, integers are bound to int, and real numbers are bound to float in the language C.
- Language implementation time: When the compiler or interpreter for the language is written, values are bound to machine representations. For example, the real value 1.5 is bound to its IEEE 754 standard floating point representation, which is supported by modern computer architectures.
- Program writing time: When programs are written in some languages, variable names are bound to types, which remain associated with those names throughout the run of the program. The declaration of variable x above is a good example.
- Program compile/load time: When programs are compiled/loaded, the "static" variables are assigned to fixed memory addresses, the run-time stack is allocated to a block of memory, and the machine code itself is assigned to a block of memory.
- Program run time: When programs are running, variables are bound to values, as in the execution of the assignment x = 3.

Sometimes, an element can be bound to a property at any one of a number of alternative times in this continuum. For example, the association of a value with a constant may be done either at program compile/load time or at the beginning of run time. When such choices are possible, the notion of *early binding* means simply that an element is bound to a property as early as possible (rather than later) in this time continuum. *Late binding* means to delay binding until the last possible opportunity.

A language design must take into account these options, and we shall see in our study that (1) binding decisions must be made by the language designer, and (2) sometimes early binding is preferred, while at other times late binding is preferred.

Orthogonality Does a symbol or reserved word always carry the same meaning, regardless of the context in which it is used? Does the language contain a small number of basic features that interact in a predictable fashion no matter how they are combined in a program?

One example of orthogonality occurs when a particular name is bound to a type when the program is written and that binding cannot be changed throughout the runtime life of the program. A counterexample of orthogonality can occur with an inappropriate overloading of an operator. For instance, the meaning of + may convey an arithmetic operation when used with arithmetic values and something different when used with other values.

Reliability of Programs Does the program behave the same way every time it is run with the same input data? Does it behave the same way when it is run on different platforms?

Especially pertinent to these questions is the need to design appropriate exception handling mechanisms into the language. Moreover, languages that restrict aliasing and memory leaks, support strong typing, have well-defined syntax and semantics, and support program verification and validation have the reliability edge.

Applicability Does the language provide appropriate support for applications in the domain in which it is being used? For example, a language designed especially to support logical deduction in artificial intelligence research may be useless for client-server applications in electronic commerce.

Abstraction Abstraction is a fundamental aspect of the program design process. Programmers spend a lot of time building abstractions, both data abstractions and procedural abstractions, to exploit the reuse of code and avoid reinventing it. A good programming language supports data and procedural abstraction in such a way that it is a preferred design tool in the programming process.

Libraries that accompany modern programming languages attest to the accumulated experience of programmers in that domain at building abstraction. For example, Java's class libraries contain implementations of basic data structures (e.g., vectors and stacks) that, in earlier languages, had to be explicitly designed by programmers themselves. How often have we reinvented a sorting algorithm or a linked list data structure that has probably been implemented thousands of times before?

Efficient Implementation Do a language's features and constructs permit its practical and efficient implementation on contemporary platforms?

For example, Algol 68 was an elegant language design, but its specifications were so complex that it was (nearly) impossible to effectively implement. Early versions of Ada were criticized for their inefficient run-time characteristics since Ada was designed in part to support programs that run in "real time." Programs embedded in systems like airplanes had to respond immediately to a sudden change in input values, like wind speed, and Ada programs stood at the intersection of the sensors that provided the readings and the mechanisms that were to respond to them. Early implementations of Ada fell far short of these ambitious performance goals. The harshest critics of Ada's performance were known to utter, "Well, there's 'real time' and then there's 'Ada time'!"

Initial implementations of Java have been criticized on this same basis, although recent refinements to the code generation strategies of Java compilers have begun to improve its run-time performance.

1.6 **WHAT'S IN A NAME?**

Some programming languages have strange names. While we have a sense of familiarity with the origin and purpose of some languages, like Java, it is interesting to study the origins of other not-so-familiar language names. Here are a few of our favorite language names and their real (or imaginary) meanings:[1]

> Ada: named after the woman who is thought to be the first computer programmer in the 1800s, Ada Lovelace. She was assistant to the inventor Charles Babbage and daughter of the poet Lord Byron.

> Algol: short for "Algorithmic Language," designed by an international committee in 1959, and originally named the "International Algebraic Language" (IAL).

> APL: designed by Kenneth Iverson in the 1960s to facilitate the rapid programming of matrix algebraic and other mathematical computations, and named "A Programming Language," or APL for short.

> Basic: designed by John Kemeny in the early 1960s to facilitate the learning of programming and time-sharing principles. Basic enjoyed great popularity over the years, especially as a teaching language in secondary schools and university science programs.

> C: designed in the 1970s primarily to support the implementation of the Unix operating system. Revised, widely used in systems programming and other applications, and standardized by ANSI in 1988.

> C++: designed as an extension of C in the 1980s to provide new features that would support object-oriented programming.

> (*) C–: named for the grade received by its inventor when submitting it as a class project in a graduate programming languages course. C– is best described as a "low-level" programming language. In general, a C– program requires more statements than machine code instructions to execute a given task. In this regard, it is very similar to Cobol.

---

1. Some of these language names are contrived; we have borrowed the contrived names from the article "Languages to Look Out For," which first appeared in a DEC APL SIG Newsletter and has been circulating on the Web. The contrived names are marked by an asterisk (*) in the list to distinguish them from the names of real languages.

Cobol: stands for "*C*ommon *B*usiness *O*riented *L*anguage" and uses English as a basis for its syntax. Thus, Cobol programs are constructed out of clauses, sentences, and paragraphs, and generally tend to be more wordy than comparable programs in other languages. First designed in 1960, Cobol is arguably the most widely used programming language in history.

(*) Dogo: designed at MIOT (*M*assachusetts *I*nstitute of *O*bedience *T*raining), heralding a new era of computer-literate pets. Dogo commands include SIT, HEEL, STAY, PLAY-DEAD, and ROLLOVER. An innovative feature of Dogo is "puppy graphics," a small cocker spaniel that leaves deposits as it travels across the screen.

Fortran: designed by IBM in 1954 for scientific programming, "Fortran" is an abbreviation for "Formula Translator" and is probably the most widely used scientific programming language.

Jay: designed for use in this text as a simple language for studying the principles of syntax, semantics, and type systems.

Jovial: designed by Jules Schwartz in the 1960s to refine and augment the features of IAL. Hence the name "*J*ules' *o*wn *v*ersion of the *I*nternational *A*lgebraic *L*anguage."

Logo: designed at MIT as a medium for teaching elementary school children about problem solving, using a graphical user interface called "turtle graphics."

Lisp: short for "List processor" and designed by John McCarthy in 1960 as a tool for writing programs for symbol manipulation and list processing in the field of artificial intelligence.

(*) Lithp: a language distinguished by the absence of an *s* in its character set. Programmers and users must therefore substitute *th* where *s* would normally appear. Lithp is thaid to be utheful in proceththing lithtth.

(*) Sartre: named after the late existential philosopher, Sartre is an extremely unstructured language. Statements in Sartre have no purpose; they just are. Thus, Sartre programs are left to define their own functions, and Sartre programmers tend to be boring, depressing, and no fun at parties.

(*) Simple: an acronym for "*S*heer *I*diot's *M*onopurpose *P*rogramming *L*inguistic *E*nvironment." Simple was designed to make it impossible to write code with errors in it. Therefore, its only statements are BEGIN, END, and STOP; no matter how you arrange these statements, you cannot make a syntax error.

(*) Slobol: this language is best known for its lack of compiling speed. Although many compilers allow you to take a sip of coffee while they compile your program, the Slobol compiler allows you to travel to Colombia to pick the coffee! Programmers are known to have died of boredom waiting for their programs to compile.

(*) Valgol: designed in the San Fernando Valley, this language has commands that include REALLY, LIKE, WELL, and Y*KNOW. Variables are assigned values using the =LIKE and =TOTAL operators. Other operators include the California Booleans and NOWAY, and loops are specified using the FOR-SURE statement. Here is a sample Valgol program:

```
LIKE Y*KNOW (IMEAN) START
IF PIZZA=LIKE BITCHEN AND GUY=LIKE TUBULAR AND
    VALLEY GIRL=LIKE GRODY**MAX(FERSURE)
THEN
    FOR I=LIKE 1 TO OH*MAYBE 100
      DO*WAH-(DITTY*2)-DUM-DITTY-DO
    SURE
LIKE BAG THIS PROGRAM
REALLY
LIKE TOTALLY (Y*KNOW)
IM*SURE
GO TO THE MALL
```

1.7 GOALS OF THIS STUDY

Before moving on, we need to elevate this study above the level suggested by the foregoing section! We expect that you will gain the following insights and skills during your coverage of the material in this book.

- A formal approach to language design. This approach will help you see that mathematical subjects are, indeed, an integral part of the serious study of computer science in general and programming languages in particular. Using mathematical tools is a natural activity for this study, not one to be feared or avoided.
- A careful examination of the key programming paradigms. This will provide fresh insights into the wide range of problems that programmers in different communities solve, along with the special problem solving strategies that can be brought to bear on these problems.
- A hands-on laboratory experience. This provides an experimental medium in which to study both the formal theory of syntax and semantics and the realization of different paradigms by solving really different problems in really different languages from the ones with which you are now most familiar.

The programming language Jay is our own invention for linking the formal theory with the practice of language design. You will encounter Jay early and often during your study of the principles of syntax, semantics, type systems, and memory management. A complete formal definition of Jay's syntax, semantics, and type system is given in Appendix B. Jay provides a concrete vehicle that will allow you to play the role of language designer and critic. You will implement the language Jay from its formal specifications, and then you will have an opportunity to extend Jay so that it is more like the "real" languages that you have used in your other courses.

Feel free to visit the book's website given in the Preface for additional information and software that you can download while using this text. Enjoy!

EXERCISES

1.1 The site **www.yahoo.com/Computers_and_Internet/Programming_Languages** provides an index of links to major information sources for most of the contemporary programming languages. For each of the following languages, use this resource to learn something about it. Write, in your own words, a brief (one paragraph) summary of its features, paradigms, and relationship with other languages that preceded or followed it.

(a) Java

(b) Scheme

(c) Prolog

1.2 After learning what you can from the Java website **www.javasoft.com** and other sources, what can you say about the status of the Java standardization effort by ANSI and ISO at this time, if anything?

1.3 Find the C++ standard on the Web. What is meant by *nonconformant* when the standard discusses a language feature supported by a particular compiler? For the C++ compiler on your computer, are there nonconformant features?

1.4 Find the Fortran 90 standard on the Web. What version of Fortran does your computer support? If it is different from Fortran 90, identify three different features of Fortran 90 that are not supported by your version.

1.5 How many different ways can you write the assignment $x=2*x$ in C? What are the advantages and disadvantages of this flexibility?

1.6 Two different implementations of a language are *incompatible* if there are programs that run differently (give different results) under one implementation than under the other. After reading on the Web and in other sources about early versions of Fortran, can you determine whether or not Fortran had incompatible versions? In what specific form (statement type, data type, etc.) did this incompatibility appear? What can be done to eliminate the opportunities for incompatibility between two different implementations of a language?

1.7 The standardization effort for the language C began in 1982 with an ANSI working group, and the C standard was completed in 1989. This work was later accepted as an ISO standard in 1990. Read enough on the Web about ANSI and the ISO to explain briefly why this process took so long, and why C wasn't immediately standardized by ANSI and ISO working together.

Syntax

2

". . . a language that is simple to parse for the compiler, is also simple to parse for the human programmer."

Niklaus Wirth [1974]

CHAPTER OUTLINE

The *syntax* of a programming language is a definition of what constitutes a grammatically valid program in that language. Syntax is specified as a set of rules, just as it is for natural languages. For instance, the rule that an English sentence must end with a proper terminator (a period, question mark, or exclamation mark) is a matter in the domain of English syntax. A clear, concise, and formal definition of syntax is especially important for programming languages; without it, language implementors and programmers would be unable to function.

Formal methods for defining syntax have been used for several decades. These methods were first introduced in the definition of Algol syntax in the early 1960s [Naur 1960], and have been used for defining the syntax of most languages ever since.

In this chapter, we explore the use of formal methods for defining the syntax of a programming language, both at the concrete level and at the abstract level. The *concrete level* of syntax refers to the actual representation scheme for programmers to write programs in a language. The *abstract level* describes the actual information that is carried by a program, without concern for idiosyncrasies of presentation like whether or not the condition in an if statement is parenthesized. Abstract syntax is an enormously useful tool for linking the syntactic expressions in a language with their actual meaning, or semantics. One use of abstract syntax is as a tool for formally specifying a language's type system. Another is to provide a basis for the formal definition of a language's semantics. We shall explore these links in Chapter 3.

To motivate our study of syntax, semantics, and imperative programming, we introduce the simple imperative minilanguage Jay, which is used here and in later chapters as a vehicle for examining the syntactic and semantic properties of programming languages. We use Jay instead of a real language, such as C++ or Java, because real languages contain so many features that they tend to obscure the fundamental concepts in language design. Jay is a simple language, and hopefully its simplicity will provide a sound basis for clarifying the issues rather than obfuscating them.

2.1 FORMAL METHODS AND LANGUAGE PROCESSING

The language used to define other languages is often called a *metalanguage*. Several different metalanguages have been successfully used to formally define the syntax of programming languages. One, in particular, is particularly widespread, and we introduce it in this section.

2.1.1 Backus-Naur Form (BNF)

In order to describe precisely the strings that are legitimate programs and separate all the others (those which contain syntax errors of various sorts), the BNF formalism has been extraordinarily useful. BNF is a metalanguage based on a formal theory developed by the linguist Noam Chomsky [Chomsky 1957].[1] A BNF *grammar* is a set of rewriting rules ρ, a set of terminal symbols Σ, a set of nonterminal symbols N, and a "start symbol" $S \in N$. Each rewriting rule in ρ has the following form:

$$A \rightarrow \omega$$

where $A \in N$ and $\omega \in (N \cup \Sigma)^*$. That is, ω is a string of nonterminal and terminal symbols.

When used for defining programming language syntax, the words in N identify grammatical categories (like *Identifier, Integer, Expression, Loop,* and *Program*), and the start symbol S identifies the principal grammatical category being defined by the

---

1. BNF was adapted from Chomsky's formal model by John Backus and Peter Naur in 1960 when they used it to develop a formal syntactic definition for the programming language Algol [Naur 1963]. The term "BNF" thus stands alternately for "Backus-Naur Form" or "Backus Normal Form." BNF grammars constitute one class among the four that were originally defined by Chomsky. These classes are known as *regular, context-free, context-sensitive,* and *unrestricted* grammars. BNF is a synonym for context-free grammars. Regular grammars are the simplest class, and are analogous to so-called *regular expressions* and *finite-state automata* in their expressive power. Context-sensitive and unrestricted grammars are more powerful, and hence more complex than BNF grammars, and are not widely used in formal treatments of programming language syntax.

grammar. The symbols in Σ form the basic alphabet (for example, the ASCII or the Unicode character set) from which programs are constructed. Here is a pair of rules that defines the syntax of a grammatical category called *binaryDigit*.

binaryDigit $\rightarrow$ 0

binaryDigit $\rightarrow$ 1

This pair of rules says that the notion of a *binaryDigit* is either a 0 or a 1, but nothing else. The form below is often used to abbreviate a series of rules that share the same nonterminal symbol on their left-hand sides.

binaryDigit $\rightarrow$ 0 | 1

In this form, the alternatives are separated by the vertical bar (|), which means "or," so the interpretation remains the same as the original pair of rules.

The right-hand side of a BNF rule can be any sequence of terminal and nonterminal symbols, allowing a variety of interesting constructs to be concisely defined. Consider the following BNF grammar, which defines the meaning of the grammatical category *Integer* as any sequence of *Digits*.

Integer $\rightarrow$ *Digit* | *Integer Digit*

Digit $\rightarrow$ 0 | 1 | 2 | 3 | 4 | 5 | 6 | 7 | 8 | 9

The first rule allows an integer to be either a *Digit* alone or an *Integer* followed immediately by a *Digit,* while the second defines the usual decimal digits. This is a simple example of the recursive style that is used to define all sorts of sequences of entities that occur in programming languages. Effectively, this particular recursive rule allows an integer to be composed from any sequence of digits.

For example, suppose we want to justify that 352 is an *Integer*. To do this, we must derive this string from the above rules in a sequence of steps, beginning with the start symbol $S = Integer,$ as shown below.

1 Form the string *Integer Digit* as a particular kind of *Integer,* from the second alternative in the first rule.
2 Substitute *Integer Digit* for *Integer* in our string, again using the first rule, gaining the string *Integer Digit Digit*.
3 Substitute *Digit* for *Integer,* using the first alternative in the first rule, gaining *Digit Digit Digit*.
4 Substitute 3 as a particular kind of *Digit* from the second rule, achieving 3 *Digit Digit*.
5 Substitute 5 for *Digit* in our string, achieving the string 3 5 *Digit*.
6 Finally, substitute 2 for *Digit* in our string, achieving the string 352.

Formally, what we just did was *parse* the string 352 as an instance of the grammatical category *Integer*.

Since this parsing process is often used in the design and analysis of programming language syntax, it is useful to have a clearer style than English for expressing this sequence of steps. One way to do this is to describe the parse graphically in the form of a *parse tree*. A parse tree for the string 352 is shown in Figure 2.1.

Figure 2.1 **Parse Tree for 352 As an *Integer***

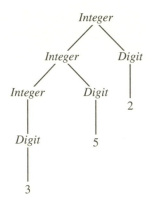

Here, we see that the root node of the parse tree is the particular grammatical category of interest, and every internal node is a grammatical category (in this case, *Integer* and *Digit*). There are the same number (6) of internal nodes in the parse tree as there are steps in the English-language parse of the string discussed above. Further, each internal node has as its direct descendants the elements that appear on the right-hand side of a grammar rule, reading these descendants from left to right. Finally, reading the leaves of the parse tree from left to right reconstructs the string being parsed.

Another useful method for describing the parse of a string is to develop a derivation for the string, again using the rules of the grammar. A *derivation* is a simple linear representation of a parse tree, and is often more helpful when the string being derived has a simple grammatical structure, like an *Integer*. Here is a derivation of 352, which describes, when read from left to right, the same sequence of steps that are described above in English and in the parse tree of Figure 2.1.

Integer ⇒ *Integer Digit* ⇒ *Integer Digit Digit* ⇒ *Digit Digit Digit*

⇒ 3 *Digit Digit* ⇒ 3 5 *Digit* ⇒ 3 5 2

Here, each instance of a double arrow ⇒ denotes the application of a single grammar rule to bring the string being derived one step closer to the final goal, which is at the right end of the derivation.

Each string on the right of a double arrow is called a *sentential form,* and generally contains terminal and nonterminal symbols. For example, the sentential form 3 *Digit Digit* occurs to the right of the fourth arrow in this derivation. At the left end of the derivation is the start symbol *S* which defines the grammatical class of objects for which we are trying to derive this goal as a member. In this case, *S* = *Integer*. Each intermediate step creates a sentential form that results from replacing the left-most nonterminal symbol A in the sentential form by the string ω of terminals and nonterminals that appears on the right-hand side of some rule that has the symbol A on its left-hand side.[2]

---

2. Strictly speaking, this is called a *leftmost derivation*. A *rightmost derivation* is one in which the right-most nonterminal in the sentential form is replaced at each step.

The *language* defined by a BNF grammar is that set of *all* strings that can be parsed, or derived, using the rules of the grammar.[3] For instance, the language defined by the above grammar is the set of all strings that are finite sequences of decimal digits, thus forming the syntactic category *Integer.*

2.1.2 BNF and Lexical Analysis

The lexicon of a programming language is the set of all grammatical categories that define strings of nonblank characters, called *tokens,* from which programs are written. The lexicon of a programming language typically contains the grammatical categories *Identifier* (variable names, function names, etc.), *Literal* (integer and decimal numbers), *Operator* (+, −, *, /, etc.), *Separator* (;, ., {, }, etc.), and *Keyword* (int, main, if, for, etc.). Each of these categories is defined by a simple BNF grammar like the one discussed above for *Integer*s.[4]

Together, this set of grammatical categories defines the *lexical syntax* of the language, which is the simplest level from the viewpoint of the compiler. These categories allow the compiler to look at a program as a stream of *tokens,* each one a member of a particular grammatical category, or *token class,* and separated from the next token by either *whitespace* (a series of blanks or carriage returns) or a *comment.* The program fragment in Figure 2.2 is annotated to illustrate these ideas.

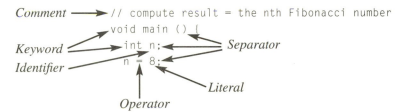

```
// compute result = the nth Fibonacci number
void main () {
    int n;
    n = 8;
```

| **Figure 2.2   A Program Fragment Viewed As a Stream of Tokens**

At the beginning of this C-like program there is a comment, an opening main function definition, a declaration, and an assignment statement. The individual tokens on each of the lines that follow the comment are members of the token classes indicated by the arrows. For instance, C programs begin with a line that has the *Keyword* main followed by the three *Separators* (,), and {.

Notice that whitespace separates many adjacent pairs of tokens, such as int and n in the second line. This isn't always necessary, as indicated by the absence of whitespace between n and ; on the same line. Whitespace is needed to separate any pair of

---

3. The parsing process can be a top-down or a bottom-up analysis of a string to obtain a parse tree (or, equivalently, a derivation). Various parsing strategies are used in the analysis of programs by a compiler. However, a detailed study of these strategies is beyond the scope of this text.

4. This simple form of BNF is an instance of Chomsky's "regular grammar" class, and is particularly useful for defining and parsing the individual tokens in a program.

tokens that could be interpreted as a single token if the whitespace were omitted. For instance, the absence of whitespace between `int` and `n` would leave the string `intn` interpretable as an *Identifier* rather than two distinct tokens, which in this context would be incorrect.

A simple BNF syntax that supports the definition of token streams in languages like the one shown in Figure 2.2 is given in Figure 2.3.

InputElement → *WhiteSpace* | *Comment* | *Token*
  WhiteSpace → `space` | `\t` | `\r` | `\n` | `\f` | `\r\n`
    Comment → `//` any sequence of characters followed by \r, \n, or \r\n
      Token → *Identifier* | *Keyword* | *Literal* |
              Separator | *Operator*
   Identifier → *Letter* | *Identifier Letter* | *Identifier Digit*
     Letter → `a` | `b` | `. . .` | `z` | `A` | `B` | `. . .` | `Z`
      Digit → `0` | `1` | `2` | `. . .` | `9`
   Keyword → `boolean` | `else` | `if` | `int` |
             `main` | `void` | `while`
    Literal → *Boolean* | *Integer*
   Boolean → `true` | `false`
    Integer → *Digit* | *Integer Digit*
  Separator → `(` | `)` | `{` | `}` | `;` | `,`
  Operator → `=` | `+` | `-` | `*` | `/` |
          `<` | `<=` | `>` | `>=` | `==` | `!=` | `&&` | `||` | `!`

| Figure 2.3 A Simple Lexical Syntax for a Small Language, Jay

Here, we see the familiar BNF definition of *Integer* that was introduced earlier, along with some BNF definitions of the various other syntactic classes that were discussed informally above. Together, these definitions cover the major token classes that would appear in a typical C-like program.

This lexical syntax defines *Identifier* as a sequence of letters and digits, the first of which must be a letter. That is, `n` and `n2` are identifiers, but not `2n` or `+n`. It allows a *Literal* to be either *Boolean* (`true` or `false`) or *Integer*. It defines several types of *Keyword, Separator,* and *Operator.* We shall see later that these token classes together support the definition of an interesting and reasonably robust imperative programming language.

2.1.3 Lexical Analysis and the Compiling Process

All programs must be parsed and analyzed for syntactic correctness before they are translated to machine code or interpreted. At the most elementary level, a lexical analysis process separates the program's individual characters into a stream of tokens that is passed on, one token at a time, to a higher level of analysis.

The larger *compiling process* in which lexical analysis takes part is summarized in Figure 2.4. Here, a program is initially viewed as a stream of individual characters in a common character set (such as ASCII or Unicode).

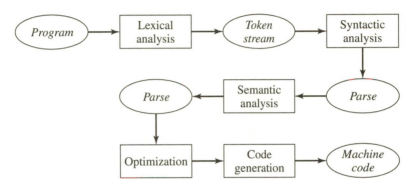

| Figure 2.4 Major Stages in the Compiling Process

Lexical analysis basically translates that sequence of characters which is the program text into a stream of tokens, passing the individual tokens one-by-one to the syntactic analysis stage as they are needed. *Syntactic analysis* develops an abstract representation or *parse* for the program, detecting syntactic errors along the way. Absent syntactic errors, the *semantic analysis* and *optimization* stages analyze the parse for semantic consistency (for example, checking consistent use of operators and data types) and transform the parse so that it can efficiently utilize the architecture where the program will run. Finally, the *code generation* stage uses the resultant abstract representation as a basis for generating executable machine code.

The lexical analysis process is governed strictly by the BNF rules that define the language's lexical syntax. The simple nature of these rules allows lexical analysis to be defined in a straightforward and efficient manner. That is, each new character that appears in the program provides a clue to the specific token class to which the next token belongs. For instance, the appearance of a slash (/) may indicate the beginning of a comment or a division operator, while the appearance of a letter may indicate the beginning of an *Identifier* or a *Keyword*. The end of each token is signaled clearly by the presence of whitespace, the beginning of a comment (comments are skipped by the lexical analysis process), or the beginning of a new token.

For example, consider the program fragment that appears in Figure 2.2, but strictly as a sequence of characters rather than as a stream of tokens. Figure 2.5 shows a skeleton lexical analysis method, written in Java, that will return the next token in the input stream each time it is called. This method would be part of the `TokenStream` class, whose instance variables are two: a token `type` (*Identifier, Keyword, Literal, Separator,* or *Operator*) and a token `value` (the string that was found in the scan of the next significant series of characters in the program).

```
public Token nextToken() { // returns next token type and value
    Token t = new Token();
    t.type = "Other";
    t.value = "";

// First check for whitespace and bypass it
    while (isWhiteSpace(nextChar)) {
        nextChar = readChar();
    }
// Then check for a comment and skip it (but remember that / is
// also a division operator
    if (nextChar=='/') {
        ...
    }
// Then check for an Operator; recover 2-character operators
// as well as 1-character ones
    if (isOperator(nextChar)) {
        t.type = "Operator";
        ...
    }
// Then check for a Separator
    if (isSeparator(nextChar)) {
        t.type = "Separator";
        ...
    }

// Then check for an Identifier, Keyword, or Literal
    if (isLetter(nextChar)) { // get an Identifier
        t.type = "Identifier";
        ...
    }
    if (isDigit(nextChar)) { // check for Integer
        t.type = "Literal";
        ...
    }
    ...
    return t;
}
```

| Figure 2.5   Skeleton Lexical Analysis Method That Returns Tokens

This skeleton uses several auxiliary methods to accomplish its task. These are easily written, given the BNF definitions for the various token classes in Figure 2.3. For instance, the method `isSeparator` can be written as follows:

```
private boolean isSeparator(char c) {
    return (c=='(' || c==')' || c==':' ||
        c=='{' || c=='}' || c==';' || c==',' || c=='.');
}
```

Completion of the `nextToken` method and the `TokenStream` class for the syntax shown in Figure 2.3 is left as an exercise.

2.1.4 Regular Expressions and Lexical Analysis

There is an alternative to BNF for formally specifying and analyzing a language at the lexical level. This is called the *regular expression,* and is a widely used tool in language design for formally specifying each token class in the language. The language of regular expressions is summarized in Figure 2.6.

Figure 2.6 **Conventions for** **Writing Regular** **Expressions**	**Regular Expression**	**Meaning**
	x	A character (stands for itself)
	"xyz"	A literal string (stands for itself)
	M | N	M or N
	M N	M followed by N (concatenation)
	M*	Zero or more occurrences of M
	M+	One or more occurrences of M
	M?	Zero or one occurrence of M
	[a-zA-Z]	Any alphabetic character
	[0-9]	Any digit
	.	Any single character

With these conventions, we can define the lexical syntax of various syntactic classes in Figure 2.3. For instance, here is a regular expression defining the class *Integer:*

```
[0-9]+
```

This literally means "one or more occurrences of a digit." Moreover, a regular expression to define the meaning of an *Identifier* is similarly constructed:

```
[a-zA-Z][a-zA-Z0-9]*
```

which means "a letter followed by zero or more occurrences of a letter or a digit."

Other regular expressions corresponding to elements of the syntax described in Figure 2.3 are

```
"//"[a-za-Z ]*("\r" | "\n" | "\r\n")
"true" | "false"
```

The first of these describes a *Comment* as a series of characters followed by a return. The second describes a *Boolean* value.

Regular expressions have become a very popular tool in language design because they admit readily to automatic generation of lexical analyzers. That is, rather than writing code for a lexical analyzer like that outlined in Figure 2.5, one would submit the regular expressions directly to a generic lexical-analyzer generator. Two commonly used generators are known as "Lex" (generating C code) and "Jlex" (for generating Java code). More information about this process can be found in various texts on compiler design [Aho 1986; Appel 1998].

It is important to emphasize that, while regular expressions are useful for defining the lexical syntax of a language, they are not as powerful a mechanism as BNF for defining more complex syntactic structures. In particular, regular expressions are incapable of generating the language $\{a^n b^n\}$ where the number of *a*s must equal the number of *b*s, even when all the *a*s must precede the number of *b*s. However, BNF is fully adequate for matching nested beginning and ending tags, such as occur in expressions (parentheses) and statement lists (braces), as we shall see in Section 2.2.

2.2 SYNTACTIC ANALYSIS

The complete *syntax* of a programming language uses the output of lexical analysis as a basis for defining the structure of all the different parts of a program that occur above the lexical level, such as arithmetic expressions (e.g., x+2*y), assignments (e.g., z=2*x+y;), loops (e.g., for (i=0; i<n; i++) a[i]=a[i] + 1;), function definitions, declarations of variables (e.g., int n;), and even complete programs themselves. A language's syntax uses BNF as the primary tool to provide a precise definition and strict guidance for the syntactic analysis phase to detect syntax errors and develop a parse from a stream of tokens (Figure 2.4).

Consider the syntactic categories *Assignment* and *Expression,* which describe all sequences of *Tokens* that describe arithmetic calculations and assignment of the result to a variable. A simple BNF syntax for these categories is shown in Figure 2.7. Notice that this syntax uses the well-defined lexical classes *Identifier* and *Literal,* as well as some members of the *Operator* (+, −, *, and /) and *Separator* lexical classes (left and right parentheses).

Assignment → *Identifier* = *Expression* ;
Expression → *Term* | *Expression* + *Term* | *Expression* − *Term*
    Term → *Factor* | *Term* * *Factor* | *Term* / *Factor*
    Factor → *Identifier* | *Literal* | (*Expression*)

| **Figure 2.7** **A Concrete Syntax for Assignments and Expressions**

Derivations and parse trees for integer-valued expressions can be easily constructed from this grammar, using the same techniques we used for parsing tokens at the lexical level. For instance, Figure 2.8 illustrates a derivation for the *Expression* x+2*y.

In this example, the tree is developed with *Expression* at its root, since that is the grammatical class of interest, and the string being parsed as its leaves, reading from left to right. Dotted arrows in the parse tree indicate abbreviations for grammatical classes

Figure 2.8 Parse Tree for the *Expression* x+2*y

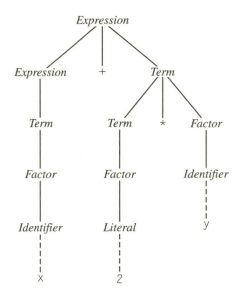

that would be parsed at the lexical level, rather than this level—specifically, *Identifier* and *Literal*. Omitting the subtrees for these specific items simplifies the overall presentation (this is common practice).

Syntactic grammars reveal important information to the compiling process about the structure of the computation described by the program, as well as the particular sequence of tokens that participate in that computation. If we traverse the nodes of this particular parse tree in an *in-order* sequence—that is, from the bottom up and from left to right at each level—we see that the product 2*y is computed first, and that result becomes the second operand in the computation of a sum with x. Other expressions, like 2*x+4*y, have parse trees that describe different sequences of events when traversed in an in-order sequence.

Also, the use of parentheses in expressions is accommodated in this grammar. A parenthesized expression may appear as a *Factor* in a larger expression, in which case it appears at a lower level in the parse tree, and hence will be scanned first (before the larger expression that contains it). Examples that illustrate these ideas are found in the exercises at the end of the chapter.

It is also important to notice that the BNF syntax for a language has limitations. For instance, the syntax for *Expression* does not guarantee that every *Identifier* that appears in that *Expression* has been declared, or that it has been declared to have an int type, as is required by many programming languages. Moreover, the syntax doesn't guarantee that the *Identifiers* used in an expression have been assigned values by the time the expression is executed at run time. For statically typed[5] languages, the first of

---

5. A statically typed language is one in which the types of all identifiers defined in the program can be discovered at compile time, and those types remain unchanged throughout program execution. Languages like C++ and Java are statically typed languages, while languages like Lisp are not. These issues are discussed more fully in Chapter 3.

these limitations can be addressed by using a formal approach called a *type system*. The second of these limitations cannot be addressed until run time.

A complete syntax for the simple imperative language Jay is shown in Appendix B. That syntax defines the structure of various other program elements beyond expressions, such as loops, declarations, and conditional statements. A complete parse tree for a program has as its root the syntactic category *Program* and as its leaves the stream of individual tokens that are the output of lexical analysis. A parse tree for the following very simple program is sketched in Figure 2.9.

```
void main ( ) { int x; x = 1; }
```

Using the rules of the complete grammar for Jay in Appendix B, we see that this program has two major elements, a *Declaration* (int x;) and a *Statement* which is an *Assignment* (x = 1;). The *Assignment* contains a simple *Expression,* which parses to the literal value 1. Details at the lower level of the parse tree are abbreviated using dotted lines to clarify the presentation.

The concrete syntax of the grammatical category *Program* guarantees that these elements are parsed correctly. The parsing process for *Program* is the same as we have illustrated for the BNF syntax of *Expressions* in the foregoing discussion. The shape of the resultant parse tree suggests that the *Declarations* be processed first, followed by the *Statements.* This shape enables type checking to take place, since by the time the *Statements* are reached, the names and types of all the declared variables are known. We will treat this process more carefully when we discuss type checking in Chapter 3.

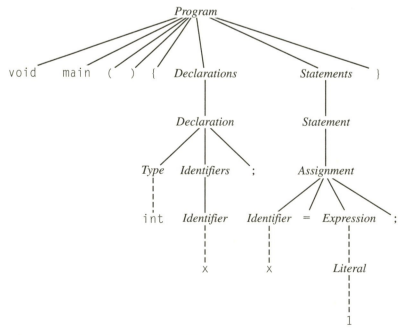

| **Figure 2.9 Sketch of a Parse Tree for a Complete Program**

2.2.1 Ambiguity

A grammar is *ambiguous* if it permits a string to be parsed into two or more different parse trees. Below is an ambiguous grammar *AmbExp* for expressions with integers and subtraction.

$$AmbExp \rightarrow Integer \mid AmbExp - AmbExp$$

This grammar allows an expression to have two different interpretations at run time. Consider, for example, the program fragment $2 - 3 - 4$. When parsed as an *Expression* using the grammar in Figure 2.7, this fragment has one and only one parse tree. When parsed as an *AmbExp*, however, this fragment has two distinct parse trees, as shown in Figure 2.10.

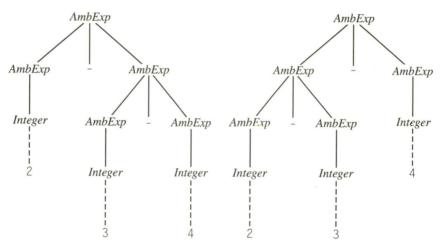

| **Figure 2.10** **Two Different Parse Trees for the *AmbExp* 2 − 3 − 4**

Here, an inorder reading of the left-hand parse tree for $2 - 3 - 4$ suggests a right-associative relationship between the two subtractions, which would give the result $2 - (3 - 4)$, or 3. However, the right-hand parse tree suggests left-association, giving the result $(2 - 3) - 4$, or -5. As readers should suspect, ambiguous syntactic grammars should be avoided in programming language design.

A classical example of ambiguity in language design is known as the "dangling else" problem. It occurs when two adjacent `if` statements are followed by an `else` statement, such as in this simple example:

```
if (x<0)
    if (y<0) y = y-1;
    else y = 0;
```

The issue here is that if the parse attaches the `else` clause to the second `if` statement, y will become 0 whenever x<0 and y>=0. However, if the parse attaches the else clause to the first `if` statement, y will become 0 whenever x>=0. Consider the following pair of grammatical rules for *Conditional* and *Statement* (Figure 2.11).

**Figure 2.11
An Ambiguous
If Statement**

IfStatement → if (*Expression*) *Statement* |

if (*Expression*) *Statement* else *Statement*

Statement → *Assignment* | *IfStatement*

It is not difficult to see that these particular rules produce the dangling else, since they allow two different attachments of the else clause. Consider the above example, whose alternative parse trees are sketched in Figure 2.12.

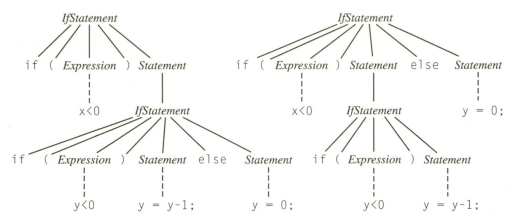

| **Figure 2.12 The "Dangling Else" Grammatical Ambiguity**

Some programming languages, like SR [Andrews 1993] and Ada [Cohen 1996], solve the dangling else problem by providing a special keyword, like fi, to explicitly close every if statement. Others, like C and C++ [Stroustrup 1991], solve it by defining how the attachment should be made, using an explicit, though informal, specification outside the BNF syntax.

That is, the language designer can stipulate the extra-grammatical rule that every else clause will be associated with the textually closest preceding if statement (e.g., delivering the parse on the left in Figure 2.12). If a different attachment is desired, the programmer can always insert braces {} to override this stipulation. That is, to force attach the else clause to the first if statement in the above example (obtaining the parse on the right in Figure 2.12), the programmer could insert braces as shown here:

```
if (x<0)
    { if (y<0) y = y-1; }
else y = 0;
```

Now the second line identifies a *Block,* which is a different kind of *Statement* from a *Conditional* in the BNF grammar, and a *Block* cannot have an optional else clause attached to it. For the details of this distinction, see the BNF syntax for Jay *Statement* and *Block* categories in Appendix B.

Interestingly, Java solves the dangling else problem by expanding the BNF grammar for if statements in a rather bizarre way. That is, Java separates the definition into two different syntactic categories, *IfThenStatement* and *IfThenElseStatement,* each of which is a subcategory of the general category *Statement.* Here is the Java BNF syntax for these [Gosling 1996]:

IfThenStatement → if (*Expression*) *Statement*

IfThenElseStatement → if (*Expression*) *StatementNoShortIf* else *Statement*

Notice that the second of these rules requires a *StatementNoShortIf* before its `else` part. The category *StatementNoShortIf* designates all statements that are not *IfThen-Statements,* and thus it may include other *IfThenElseStatements.* So this stipulation rules out an *IfThenStatement* in the first position position when an else clause follows. This essentially eliminates any ambiguity about how to associate the `else` clause when it occurs in a program. If there is another if statement nested inside this *IfThenElse-Statement,* it must itself have an explicit `else` clause.

2.2.2 Variations on BNF for Syntactic Analysis

Since Algol 60, BNF has been used to describe the syntax of many languages. Several minor variations have been used, but the basic expressive power of BNF has not been affected. These variations have been introduced mainly to improve the clarity of syntax description and the efficiency of syntactic analysis.

Extended BNF (EBNF for short) was introduced to simplify the specification of recursion in grammar rules, and to introduce the idea of an optional part in a rule's right-hand side. Consider the BNF rules from Figure 2.7, for instance:

Expression → *Term* | *Expression* + *Term* | *Expression* − *Term*

Term → *Factor* | *Term* * *Factor* | *Term* / *Factor*

Recall that the first of these rules defines an *Expression* as a series of one or more *Terms* separated individually by + or − signs. EBNF would eliminate the left recursion in these rules and allow them to be equivalently written in the following way:

Expression → *Term*{ [+ | -] *Term*} *

Term → *Factor*{ ['*' | /] *Factor* } *

Here, the star (*) operator denotes "zero or more occurrences of the symbols that are enclosed in braces { } immediately before it." The brackets [and] enclose a series of alternatives from which one must be chosen. Finally, the asterisk (*) indicating multiplication is enclosed in quotes (') to distinguish it from the metalinguistic use of the asterisk as an EBNF operator. To illustrate these ideas more fully, Figure 2.13 shows a derivation for the *Expression* x+2*y that uses the EBNF rule above instead of the BNF-based parse shown in Figure 2.8.

We will prefer the EBNF notation for describing and illustrating the syntax of imperative languages later in this chapter and Chapter 4. This preference is guided by the fact that definitions of language syntax in EBNF tend to be slightly clearer and briefer than BNF definitions. Moreover, EBNF does not force the use of recursive definitions

Figure 2.13 EBNF-Based Parse Tree for the *Expression* x+2*y

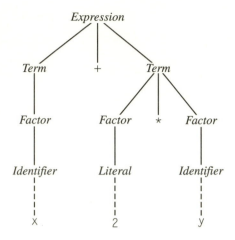

on the reader in every instance. For example, the star (*) notation in EBNF, meaning zero or more occurrences, suggests a loop in the implementation of the structure, rather than a recursive method.

Another common extension to BNF is the affixing of the subscript $_{opt}$ to a symbol on the right-hand side of a grammar rule. This designates that the symbol is optional and can be omitted during the use of that rule in parsing. For example, consider the BNF syntax for *Conditional* given in the foregoing section. Those two rules essentially say that a *Conditional* is formed by writing if, (, an *Expression,*), and a *Statement,* which can be followed optionally by else and another *Statement.* Using the *opt* convention, we can rewrite those rules and achieve the same result:

$$Conditional \rightarrow \text{if} (Expression) Statement \{ \text{else} \ Statement \}_{opt}$$

Other variations on BNF include *syntax diagrams,*[6] made popular by the syntactic definition of the Pascal language. Syntax diagrams are thought to clarify the meaning of various language constructs when they are being taught to beginning programmers. Figure 2.14 gives an example syntax diagram for the idea of *Expression* defined above.

Figure 2.14 Syntax Diagram for *Expressions* with Addition

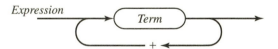

The meaning of this syntax diagram should be self-explanatory: one reads the diagram from left to right, and all the paths that lead to the right-hand arrowhead define legal *Expressions.*

---

6. It should be noted that neither EBNF nor syntax diagrams are any more powerful than BNF for formally describing language syntax. These alternatives are often used because they can provide a clearer or simpler presentation of the syntactic structures they are defining.

2.2.3 Case Study: The Syntax of Java

Java is an immense language. However, the five basic lexical classes introduced in Section 2.2.2 form the basis for Java's lexical syntax. In this section, we give a brief overview of the details of Java's primitive data types and formal syntax. Readers who are interested in pursuing these details more fully are encouraged to read the *Java Language Specification* [Gosling 1996].

Java has *Identifiers, Keywords, Literals, Separators,* and *Operators,* and Java programs are series of these tokens interspersed with *WhiteSpace* and *Comments.*

Java *Identifiers* are made up of *JavaLetters,* which include A–Z, a–z, _, and $. However, the character set from which *JavaLetters,* in fact all Java characters, are taken is the Unicode set rather than the ASCII set. A Unicode character has a 16-bit representation, and the Unicode set allows a much richer collection of individual characters than the ASCII set. However, ASCII is consistently embedded within the Unicode set, so programmers with ASCII keyboards can write Java programs.

The Java *Keywords* are many—47 in all—and none of these keywords can be used as an identifier. They include all the keywords shown in Figure 2.3, along with various others that are necessary to define and write correct Java programs.

Java *Literals* fall into several classes: *Integer, Boolean, FloatingPoint, Character, String,* and *Null.* Although the first three of these are defined in our discussion, the Java definitions of these are necessarily more elaborate. For instance, a Java *Integer* can be expressed in decimal, hexadecimal, or octal notation, and the largest integer literal cannot exceed 2^{63} in magnitude. Java *FloatingPoint* literals may be written in a variety of alternative ways, as shown in the following EBNF description:

$$FloatingPointLiteral \rightarrow Digits \;.\; Digits_{opt}Exponent_{opt}Suffix_{opt} \mid$$
$$.\; Digits\; Exponent_{opt}Suffix_{opt} \mid$$
$$Digits\; Exponent\; Suffix_{opt} \mid$$
$$Digits\; Exponent_{opt}Suffix$$

This definition allows floating point numbers to be written with or without exponents, as in 2.345e−2 or 0.02345. The *Suffix* part can be F or D to specify single or double precision numbers. The IEEE 754 binary floating point standard is cited as a reference for representation of Java floating point numbers. Generally, the range and precision of single precision floating point numbers under this standard is $10^{\pm38}$ and about 8 significant decimal digits. For double precision, these limits extend to $10^{\pm308}$ and 18 significant decimal digits.

Character literals are single Unicode characters enclosed in single quotes ('), while *String* literals are sequences of these enclosed in double quotes ("). The Java *Null* literal is the word `null`, which is widely useful to determine whether an object has been allocated or not.

The complete Java syntax is immense in its number of grammar rules. It is written using a simple variant of EBNF, as suggested by the examples given above. The large number of grammar rules is due in part to the large number of operators in Java, with many different levels of precedence. In our small concrete syntax illustration in Figure 2.7, we had four operators and two levels of precedence. By contrast, Java has about 30 different operators and about 20 different levels of precedence (hence 20 different grammatical classes for various types of *Expression*) to distinguish among them.

A modest flavor of this complexity is revealed in the grammar for the language Jay, shown in Appendix B. There, we have a concrete syntax with 14 operators and 7 levels of precedence, and hence several different grammatical subcategories of *Expression*.

The rest of the Java grammar accounts for the variety of syntactic options available to the programmer for defining classes, declarations, arrays, methods, and so forth. Again, a modest peek at this complexity is provided by the language Jay, whose concrete syntax is given in Appendix B. Readers will become more facile with managing this grammar as we cover the syntactic and semantic aspects of imperative language design in Chapters 3 and 4.

2.3 LINKING SYNTAX AND SEMANTICS

Parsing a program is important at several levels. First, the programmer may use informal parsing to discover the source of errors in a program. The compiler uses parsing to determine whether a program is syntactically correct, according to the grammar rules that define the syntax. Moreover, if the compiler is eventually going to generate executable code it must be able to generate a representation of the program's semantic interpretation that is closer to the code than that which is given by the parse tree. For this reason and many others, it is valuable to define the structure of a programming language on a more functional level than that which is offered by its BNF or EBNF syntax alone.

2.3.1 Abstract Syntax

The abstract syntax of a language is a formal device for identifying the essential syntactic elements in a program without describing how they are concretely constructed. Consider, for example, the following Pascal and C/C++ looping statements:

Pascal	C/C++
`while i<n do begin`	`while (i<n) {`
`    i := i + 1`	`    i = i + 1;`
`end`	`}`

Clearly, the two loops are designed to accomplish the same result; their syntactic differences are nonessential to the fundamental looping process that they represent.

When thinking about a loop abstractly, we discover that the only essential elements are a *test* expression (`i<n` in this case) for continuing the loop and a statement which is the *body* of the loop to be repeated (the assignment statement that increments the variable `i` in this case). All the other elements that appear in these two looping statements constitute nonessential "syntactic sugar." *Abstract syntax* provides a mechanism for the parser to strip away this syntactic sugar and leave a parse tree that contains only the essential elements of the computation that the loop represents.

The abstract syntax of a programming language can be defined using a set of rules of the following form:

$Lhs = Rhs$

where *Lhs* is the name of an abstract syntactic class and *Rhs* is a list of essential components that define a member of that class. Each such component has the form of an ordinary declaration, identifying the member and its name. The individual components are separated by semicolons (;). For example, consider the abstract syntax of a *Loop*.

> *Loop* = *Expression* test; *Statement* body

This definition defines the abstract class *Loop* as having two components, a `test` which is a member of the abstract class *Expression,* and a `body` which is a member of the abstract class *Statement.*

A complete abstract syntax for a language must have these types of rules for all its classes—*Expression, Statement, Loop,* and many others. One immediate by-product of an abstract syntax is that it provides a basis for defining the abstract structure of a language as a set of Java classes. Below, for instance, is a Java class definition for the abstract syntax of *Loop* given above.

```
class Loop extends Statement {
    Expression test;
    Statement body;
}
```

That is, a `Loop` is a kind of `Statement` and has a `test` and a `body`, which are members of the classes `Expression` and `Statement`, respectively. The class hierarchy that is built into object-oriented languages like Java makes this particular specification straightforward to implement; we shall exploit this and other features of Java as we discuss the syntax and semantics of languages in later chapters.

As is the case for BNF, recursion naturally occurs among the definitions in the abstract syntax of a language. Consider, for example, a language in which there are two kinds of statements: *Assignment*s and *Loop*s. An abstract syntax rule for the classes *Statement, Assignment,* and *Loop* can be written as shown in Figure 2.15.

Figure 2.15 Abstract Syntax for *Expression*, *Assignment*, and *Loop*

> *Statement* = *Assignment* | *Loop*
> *Assignment* = *Variable* target; *Expression* source
> *Loop* = *Expression* test; *Statement* body
> *Expression* = *Variable* | *Value* | *Binary*
> *Binary* = *Operator* op ; *Expression* term1, term2

Taken together, these rules are mutually recursive. Surely, we need to provide additional rules to complete the abstract definition of a language's syntax. A *complete* abstract syntax for the language Jay is given in Appendix B, and we shall be referring to it throughout the next several chapters.

At this stage, we might be tempted to ask why we need both abstract and concrete syntax. Aren't they somewhat redundant? In a sense they are, since both forms carry some of the same information about a program. However, in another sense they are not. That is, the concrete syntax tells the programmer concretely what to write in order to have a valid program in language X. However, the abstract syntax allows valid programs in language X and language Y to share common abstract representations. Ideally, an interpreter or run-time system for a program worries less about how certain ideas, like loops, are expressed concretely and more about what specific computational requirements are to be conveyed out of the expression and into the run-time environment for the program.

That is the role of the abstract syntax: to provide a link between syntax and semantics, between form and function. We explore how that link is established in Sections 2.3.2 and 2.3.3.

2.3.2 Abstract Syntax Trees

Consider the following two rules in Figure 2.15 that define the abstract syntax of an *Expression* and *Binary*.

Expression = *Variable* | *Value* | *Binary*
　　Binary = *Operator* op ; *Expression* term1, term2

These two rules name the essential elements of an *Expression* without regard to how it is formed concretely by the programmer. That is, the concrete syntax provides the definition of the form of an expression, while the abstract syntax provides the definition of its essential elements.

An abstract syntax tree provides a concise vehicle for describing the individual elements of an *Expression,* throwing away the intermediate nodes and subtrees that don't contain essential information. To build an abstract syntax tree, each abstract syntactic category—like *Expression* or *Binary*—has an associated node with as many fields as there are distinct elements on the right-hand side of its rule. For instance, the node associated with *Binary* has three fields, and looks like Figure 2.16a. An abstract syntax tree for the expression x+2*y is given in Figure 2.16b.

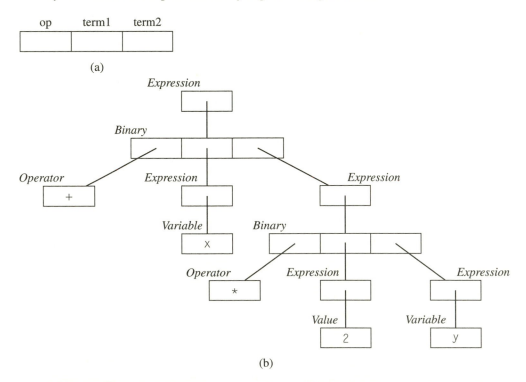

(a)

(b)

Figure 2.16　(a) Structure of a Binary Node. (b) Abstract Syntax Tree for the *Expression* x+2*y

It is helpful to contrast this tree with the tree in Figure 2.8, which was the result of parsing the expression x+2*y from the concrete syntax for *Expression.* The abstract syntax tree contains fewer intermediate nodes and subtrees. However, the abstract tree retains the same essential structure, mirroring the order of execution among the operators + and * in this expression.

It is also useful to begin viewing abstract parse trees as instances of objects in specific syntactic classes, as defined in Java. Section 2.3.3 formalizes the connection between the three levels of syntax—lexical, concrete, and abstract—that we have presented in the foregoing sections.

2.3.3 Recursive Descent Parsing

So far, we have developed formal notations for defining the concrete and abstract syntax of a language, including concrete and abstract parse tree representations for specific program constructs in the language. Now we need to tie these three levels together. This is done by developing an algorithm that analyzes the text of a program and develops an abstract syntax tree for it. Such an algorithm formalizes the lexical and syntactic analysis parts of a programming language processor by defining an effective syntactic analysis or *parsing* algorithm for the language. This algorithm essentially translates the input stream of tokens, which is the program, into an abstract syntax tree, which is the *parse* (recall Figure 2.4).[7]

There are several different algorithms for parsing, and each has various advantages and disadvantages.[8] The particular parsing algorithm we use here is called a *recursive descent parser.* A sketch of the overall structure of the parser is shown in Figure 2.17 for the concrete syntactic class *Assignment* (as defined in Figure 2.7) and its corresponding abstract syntactic class (as defined in Figure 2.15).

The goal of this parser is to build an abstract syntax tree from the stream of characters which is the input text of an assignment statement. The parser has a global variable, `token`, holding the currently scanned tokens. It also has one method for each syntactic category defined by the concrete syntax. In this example, there are methods for the categories *Assignment, Expression, Term,* and *Factor* (following the grammar in Figure 2.7).

Each such method returns a member of the abstract class which it represents. These methods also create links among the abstract class members to form an abstract syntax tree. These links are generated by each method as the syntax and the tokens that appear call for new subtrees to be generated. The entire process pictured in Figure 2.17 represents a left-right pass on the input token stream and a top-down generation of the

---

7. Syntactic analysis is an essential part of all programming language compilers and interpreters. It must determine whether the program is a syntactically valid member of the defined language and report syntax errors to the programmer if any are found. It must also translate the text of a syntactically error-free program into an abstract form. Sometimes that abstract form is the machine code of the target computer. In our case, that abstract form is a member of the class *Program,* as defined by the abstract syntax for Jay (Appendix B).

8. In a compiler design course, these different algorithms would be studied and compared. All of these algorithms are fairly complex, since they need to search the grammatical rules, test to see which ones apply to the particular program in hand, and backtrack whenever one of the rules leads to a dead end.

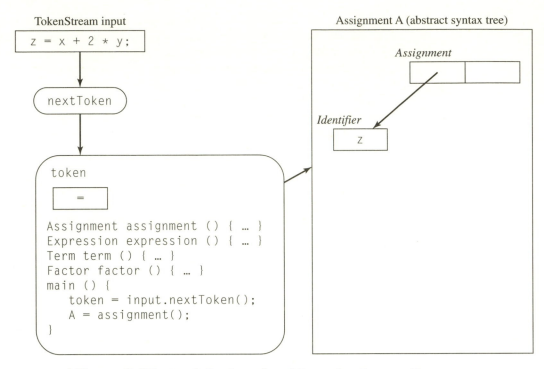

TokenStream input

```
z = x + 2 * y;
```

nextToken

```
token

    =

Assignment assignment () { … }
Expression expression () { … }
Term term () { … }
Factor factor () { … }
main () {
    token = input.nextToken();
    A = assignment();
}
```

Assignment A (abstract syntax tree)

Assignment

Identifier

z

Figure 2.17 Partially Completed Recursive Descent Parse for *Assignments*

corresponding abstract syntax tree. At any point in the process, only the current token in the input stream is needed to determine the next step.[9]

Each method of the recursive descent parser is constructed directly from the structure of the concrete EBNF grammatical rules for the syntactic categories that it represents. Whenever one of these methods needs to retrieve the next token from the input stream, it calls the nextToken method from the TokenStream class, as defined in a previous section. Figure 2.18 shows an algorithm to construct the methods for a recursive descent parser, given an EBNF grammar and a lexical analyzer.[10]

Because of rule 4, the algorithm assumes that in recognizing a nonterminal A, method A is called looking at the first token that is derivable from A and leaves looking at the first token that does not match a string derivable from A. The method A matches the longest string derivable from the nonterminal A.

For example, suppose we want to design a Java method that parses members of the class *Assignment,* which has the following EBNF grammar rule (see Figure 2.7).

Assignment → *Identifier* = *Expression* ;

---

9. Formally, recursive descent parsing is an example of LL(1) parsing process, since it moves from left to right in the input stream and it needs to look ahead only one token in the input stream to make any parsing decision. This feature is guaranteed by the particular grammar under consideration. Most modern languages, such as Java, have grammars that permit efficient parsing.

10. This algorithm is only effective if the rules of the BNF grammar are not left-recursive. If a rule is left-recursive, the method thus constructed will have an infinite loop!

For each nonterminal symbol *A* and set of rules of the form $A \rightarrow \omega$:

1. Add a new method definition with *A* as its return type.
2. Create a new object of class *A*, say *x*.
3. For each member *y* of the sentential form ω,
   a. if *y* is a nonterminal, call the method associated with *y* and assign the result to an appropriate field within *x*.
   b. if *y* is a terminal, check that the value of that token is identical with *y* and, if so, call the `nextToken` method. Otherwise the token is in error.
4. If ω contains a series of symbols that is repeated (indicated by *), insert an appropriate while loop that accommodates any number of repetitions of that series.
5. If there is more than one rule of the form $A \rightarrow \omega$, insert appropriate `if...else` statements that distinguishes the alternatives.
6. Return *x*.

| Figure 2.18 Algorithm for Writing a Recursive Descent Parser from EBNF

For this grammar rule, steps 1 and 2 of the algorithm add to the parser a method that has the following skeleton:

```
Assignment assignment () {
    Assignment a = new Assignment();
    . . .
}
```

Guided by the right-hand side of this rule and step 3 of the algorithm, this new method must contain code that finds an *Identifier,* an *Operator* $(=)$, an *Expression,* and a *Separator* (;), and in that particular order. When these four parts are successfully retrieved, the values of the `source` and `target` fields of the *Assignment* a are assigned the appropriate values, and this method completes its task by returning a (step 6 of the algorithm).

Two auxiliary methods are generally helpful in this process. These are named `match` and `SyntaxError`. The call `match(s)` either retrieves the next token or displays a syntax error, depending on whether or not the current token matches string s. The call `SyntaxError(s)` displays an error message s on the screen and terminates the entire parsing process. Below is the code:

```
private void match (String s) {
  if (token.value.equals(s))
    token = input.nextToken();
  else
    SyntaxError(s);
}

private void SyntaxError(String tok) {
  System.out.println("Syntax error: expecting: " + tok
      + "; saw: " + token.type + " = " + token.value);
  System.exit(0);
}
```

Following these conventions, the completed method for *Assignment* is

```
private Assignment assignment () {
  // Assignment --> Identifier = Expression ;
  Assignment a = new Assignment();
  if (token.type.equals("Identifier")) {
    a.target = new Variable();
    a.target.id = token.value;
    token = input.nextToken();
    match("=");
    a.source = expression();
    match(";");
  }
  else SyntaxError("Identifier");
  return a;
}
```

When it is called, this method assumes that `token` already has the value of the current token, and upon exit `token` will be left with the value of the next token following the fully-parsed assignment statement. This convention is followed for every method that creates an abstract subtree for a particular concrete syntax category.

Critically, this method relies on a method `expression`, which takes the current token (the one that follows the *Operator* =) and parses the ensuing stream of tokens to derive an abstract syntax tree for that *Expression*. Relying on the EBNF grammar for *Expression*, we can construct this method following the guidelines in Figure 2.18 as follows:

```
private Expression expression () {
  // Expression --> Term { [ + | - ] Term }*
  Binary b; Expression e;
  e = term();
  while (token.value.equals("+") || token.value.equals("-")) {
    b = new Binary();
    b.term1 = e;
    b.op = new Operator(token.value);
    token = input.nextToken();
    b.term2 = term();
    e = b;
  }
  return e;
}
```

That is, an *Expression* has at least one *Term,* and if the next token is an *Operator* (+ or −) then it must be followed by another *Term.* Since there can be any number of occurrences of an *Operator* and a *Term,* it is important to embed this process inside a loop that creates a new *Binary* upon each repetition (i.e., each repeated occurrence of an *Operator*). In the end, this method returns the root of the subtree that this process generates.

This method also relies on the existence of a method `term` that returns a *Term* and leaves the `current` token either at the next + or − *Operator* within the *Expression,* or else beyond the last token in the *Expression* altogether. Writing the methods for the remaining syntactic categories *Term* and *Factor* for this grammar is left as an exercise.

2.4 EXAMPLE: JAY—A FAMILIAR MINILANGUAGE

The ideas discussed in this chapter form a basis for describing the lexical, concrete, and abstract syntax, as well as the static type checking requirements of a realistic programming language. In the next few chapters, a language that we call *Jay* will be used as a vehicle for discussing many of the design features and issues for imperative programming languages. This language should be familiar and easy to assimilate for readers who have written some Pascal, C, C++, Ada, Eiffel, or Java programs. While Jay may appear at first to be a subset of C or C++, there are some subtle differences, as we shall discover later.[11] This section informally introduces the basic features of Jay.

Figure 2.19 An Example Jay Program to Compute the *n*th Fibonacci Number

```
// compute result = the nth Fibonacci number
void main () {
   int n, fib0, fib1, temp, result;
   n = 8;
   fib0 = 0;
   fib1 = 1;
   while (n > 0) {
     temp = fib0;
     fib0 = fib1;
     fib1 = fib0 + temp;
     n = n - 1;
   }
    result = fib0;
}
```

Jay has two data types (integer and boolean), variables, assignment statements, conditional statements, and while loops. It has no reals, character strings, function definitions, arrays, I/O, objects, or other embellishments that are usually found in a modern programming language—at least not yet. Later in this study, we will add features to Jay that bring it closer to a modern language. Figure 2.19 shows an example Jay program that computes the *n*th Fibonacci number,[12] given n (not too large) as its "input."

---

11. The design of language Jay is motivated in part by the syntax and semantics of the language Graal, designed by Bertrand Meyer [1990, p. 49]. The name *Graal,* according to Meyer, stands for "*G*reat *r*elief *a*fter *A*da *l*essons!" We have no such clever acronym for Jay; readers are invited to invent one.

12. The Fibonacci numbers are a familiar mathematical sequence, in which the first two numbers are 1 and each successive number is the sum of the two preceding ones. That is, the sequence begins with 1, 1, 2, 3, 5, 8, 13, 21, 34, ... Thus, the *n*th Fibonacci number fib(n) = 1 if n = 0 or 1, and fib(n) = fib(n − 1) + fib(n − 2) otherwise.

2.4.1 Concrete Syntax of Jay

A Jay program is represented as an ASCII text file, which can be viewed as a stream of *InputElements.* Each *InputElement* is either *WhiteSpace,* a *Comment,* or a *Token.* The five token classes discussed in Figure 2.3 are the basic building blocks for writing Jay programs.

In the lexical analysis of a Jay program, all instances of *WhiteSpace* and *Comment* are skipped, so that the meaning of the program text is based on the syntactic and semantic analysis of its *Token* sequence.

The concrete syntax of Jay has expressions that deliver *Integer* results and expressions that deliver *Boolean* results. Arithmetic expressions can use the operators +, −, *, and / in the usual way, but all arguments in an expression must have type int. *Boolean* expressions are formed by using relational operators (<, <=, ==, !=, >, and >=) between arithmetic expressions and logical operators (&&, ||, and !) with other *Boolean* expressions. Various arithmetic (e.g., fib0+temp) and Boolean (e.g., n>0) expressions appear in the example program in Figure 2.19.

Arithmetic expressions are assigned to arithmetic variables, but no implicit type conversion (coercion) takes place, as would be found in most languages. This issue is discussed further in Chapter 4, where you will be asked to extend the Jay language definition so that implicit type conversion occurs during the execution of an arithmetic expression or an assignment. Boolean expressions can be assigned to *Boolean* variables, and they are also used in conditional statements and loops. Several examples of *Assignment* statements (e.g., n=n-1;) appear in the program in Figure 2.19.

Jay also has *Blocks* (series of statements enclosed in braces { }), conditional statements, and while loops. Examples of *Blocks* and while loops appear in the program in Figure 2.19. The concrete and abstract syntax of these forms, together with their static type checking and dynamic semantics, are explained formally in Chapters 3 and 4. Readers will be asked to develop, exercise, and extend an interpreter for Jay programs, to gain a full appreciation of the role of formal methods in the language design process. Many trade-offs in language design can be explored using this approach, such as the definition and implementation of different parameter-passing mechanisms—*call by reference* and *call by value.*

The complete concrete syntax of Jay is given in Appendix B, in both its BNF and its EBNF representation.

2.4.2 Abstract Syntax of Jay

The abstract syntax of Jay extends the basic ideas about *Expression*s and *Statement*s presented in this chapter. In Jay, abstract syntactic definitions are given for the following Jay classes:

- *Program;* having *Declarations* and a *Block.*
- *Declarations;* a sequence of individual variables and their types (illustrated in this chapter).
- *Declaration;* an individual variable and its type.
- *Type;* a member of the set {int, boolean}.

- *Statement;* having subclasses *Block, Skip, Assignment, Conditional,* and *Loop.*
- *Expression;* having subclasses *Variable, Value, Binary,* and *Unary* (illustrated in this chapter).
- *Binary;* having an *Operator* and two *Expressions.*
- *Unary,* having an *Operator* and a single *Expression.*
- *Operator;* &&, ||, !, <, <=, ==, !=, >, >=, +, −, *, and /, representing booleans and, or, and not; relationals less than, less or equal, equal, not equal, greater than, greater, or equal; and arithmetics plus, minus, times, and divide.
- *Block;* a series of individual *Statement*s that are executed in the order they appear. Each one appears at the same level in an abstract syntax tree.

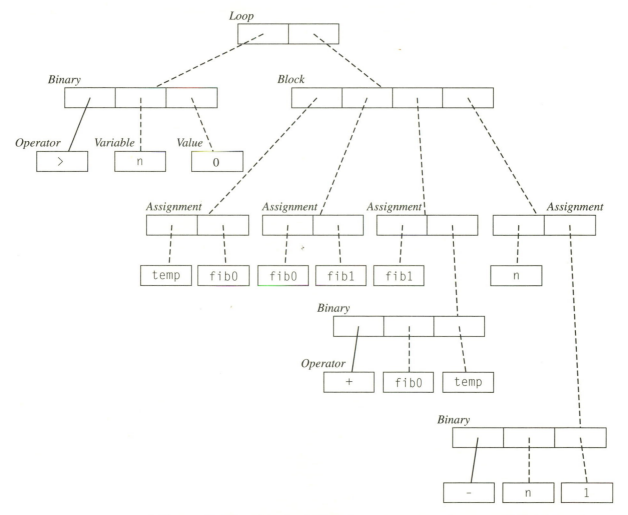

| **Figure 2.20** **Sketch of the Abstract Syntax of a Jay *WhileStatement***

- *Skip;* the empty statement.
- *Assignment;* a statement that assigns the value of an *Expression* to a variable.
- *Conditional;* having an *Expression* (the test) and two *Statement*s (the thenpart and the elsepart), one of which is executed and the other is skipped.
- *Loop;* having an *Expression* (the test) and a *Statement* (the body of the loop) that is repeated as long as the test remains *true*.

Many of these abstract syntax ideas appear in the example Jay program in Figure 2.19. For instance, we see an instance of a *Loop* whose abstract *Expression* is derived from the concrete syntax n>0 and whose abstract *Statement* is a *Block* derived from the syntax:

```
{    temp = fib0;
     fib0 = fib1;
     fib1 = fib0 + temp;
     n = n - 1;
}
```

The essential structure and content of the abstract syntax representation for this entire *Loop* is sketched in Figure 2.20. (For brevity, some intermediate nodes are omitted, as indicated by the dashed lines.)

In Figure 2.20, note that each *Assignment* is a pair, having a target (which is a *Variable*) and a source (which is an *Expression*). Note that the loop itself has a test (which is a *Binary;* a particular kind of *Expression*) and a body (which is a *Block;* a particular kind of *Statement*).

The complete abstract syntax of Jay, formalized in Appendix B, will be used frequently to illustrate our discussions of type systems, semantics, and imperative programming languages in Chapters 3, 4, and 5.

EXERCISES

2.1 Using the grammar rules for *Integer* given in this chapter, develop a leftmost derivation for the integer 4520. How many steps are required for this derivation? In general, how many steps are required to derive an integer with an arbitrary number, say *d*, of *Digits?*

2.2 Develop a parse tree for the *Identifier* value x11, using the BNF syntax given in Figure 2.3.

2.3 Complete the skeleton method nextToken that appears in Figure 2.5, along with the auxiliary methods that it calls. Test this completed tokenStream class using the example Jay program that appears in Figure 2.19 to certify that it finds each token in the input stream and correctly classifies each token type.

2.4 Complete the coding of the lexical syntax of Jay (given in Figure 2.3) as a collection of regular expressions.

2.5 Try to define the language $\{a^n b^n\}$ using regular expressions. Discuss why this might not be possible.

2.6 Develop a derivation for the parse tree shown in Figure 2.8 for the *Expression* x+2*y.

2.7 Develop parse trees for each of the following *Expressions,* as defined by the BNF grammar in Figure 2.7:

(a) (x+2)*y

(b) 2*x+3/y-4

(c) 1

2.8 Repeat the previous exercise using the EBNF definition of *Expression.*

2.9 Argue convincingly that the program fragment 2 − 3 − 4, when parsed as an *Expression* using the grammar in Figure 2.7, has one and only one parse tree.

2.10 Consider the grammar rules for *IfStatement* and *Statement* given in Figure 2.11. Show how they can be altered to eliminate their ambiguity illustrated in the text. That is, show how the grammar can be changed so that the programmer can explicitly distinguish the two alternative attachments of the "dangling else," as shown below:

```
if (x<0) if (x==0) y = y-1; else y = 0; fi fi
if (x<0) if (x==0) y = y - 1; fi else y = 0; fi
```

Here, the new keyword fi is used to end any statement that begins with the keyword if. (It functions like a right brace } that ends a series of statements that begins with a left brace {.) Thus the first of these two statements explicitly attaches the else clause to the second if, while the second statement attaches the else clause to the first if.

2.11 Show how the Java syntax for *IfThenStatement* eliminates any ambiguity in the statement of the previous exercise. That is, sketch the parse tree using the Java BNF rules, and then argue that no other parse trees can be found using these rules.

2.12 Define an abstract syntax tree for each of the parse trees that you defined for question 2.7, using the abstract syntax for *Expression* given in this chapter.

2.13 Complete the recursive descent parser by writing the methods that parse a *Term* and a *Factor,* guided by their EBNF syntax definitions and the algorithm for constructing them given in Figure 2.18. Use the example methods for *Assignment* and *Expression* as models.

2.14 Using the example Jay program in Figure 2.19, identify examples of as many instances of Jay abstract syntactic categories as you can in that program. You may answer this question by just drawing the complete abstract syntax tree that is suggested by the sketch of the abstract syntax tree given in Figure 2.20.

2.15 For the abstract syntax of the Jay *Loop* shown in Figure 2.20, sketch that statement's concrete syntax tree, using the appropriate concrete syntax grammar rules for Jay in Appendix B. Do not sketch all the details; show only the highest level of structure that reveals the concrete syntax of the expression n>0 and the four assignments that appear inside the *Block* which follows that expression.

2.16 Write a complete Jay program to compute the factorial of an integer *n*, given the informal description of Jay in Section 2.4, the formal syntax description in Appendix B, and the Jay program in Figure 2.19 as a guide.

2.17   Add a `display` method to each of the Jay abstract syntax classes so that an abstract syntax tree for *Assignment* can be displayed in an indented notation. For instance, the abstract syntax tree for the *Assignment* z = x + 2*y ; should be displayed as follows when it is passed to your `display` method for assignments:

```
=
    z
    +
        x
        *
            2
            y
```

Type Systems and Semantics

"Ishmael: Surely all this is not without meaning."
Herman Melville, Moby Dick

CHAPTER OUTLINE

Type systems have become enormously important in language design because they can be used to formalize the definition of a language's data types and their proper usage in programs. Type systems are often associated with syntax, especially for languages whose programs are type checked at compile time. For these languages, a type system is a definitional extension that imposes specific syntactic constraints (such as the requirement that all variables referenced in a program be declared) that cannot be expressed in BNF or EBNF. For languages whose programs are type checked at run time, a type system can be viewed as part of the language's semantics. Thus, a language's type system stands at the bridge between syntax and semantics, and can be properly viewed in either realm.

The definition of a programming language is complete only when its semantics, as well as its syntax and type system, is fully defined. The *semantics* of a programming language is a definition of the *meaning* of any program that is syntactically valid from both the concrete syntax and the static type checking points of view.[1]

Program meaning can be defined in several different ways. A straightforward intuitive idea of program meaning is "whatever happens in a (real or model) computer when the program is executed." A precise characterization of this idea is called *operational semantics*.[2] Another way to view program meaning is to start with a formal specification of what the program is supposed to do, and then rigorously prove that the program does that by using a systematic series of logical steps. This approach evokes the idea of *axiomatic semantics*. A third way to view the semantics of a programming language is to define the meaning of each type of statement that occurs in the (abstract) syntax as a state-transforming mathematical function. Thus, the meaning of a program can be expressed as a collection of functions operating on the program state. This approach is called *denotational semantics*.

All three semantic definition methods have advantages and disadvantages. Operational semantics has the advantage of representing program meaning directly in the code of a real (or simulated) machine. But this is also a potential weakness, since defining the semantics of a programming language on the basis of any particular architecture, whether it be real or abstract, confines the utility of that definition for compiler-writers and programmers working with different architectures. Moreover, the virtual machine on which instructions execute also needs a semantic description, which adds complexity and can lead to circular definitions.

Axiomatic semantics is particularly useful in the exploration of formal properties of programs. Programmers who must write provably correct programs from a precise set of specifications are particularly well-served by this semantic style. Denotational semantics is valuable because its functional style brings the semantic definition of a language to a high level of mathematical precision. Through it, language designers obtain a functional definition of the meaning of each language construct that is independent of any particular machine architecture.

In this chapter, we introduce a formal approach to the definition of a language's type system. We also introduce the three models of semantic definition, paying special attention to the denotational model. Denotational semantics is used in later chapters for discussing various concepts in language design and for clarifying various semantic issues. This model is particularly valuable because it also allows us to actively explore these language design concepts in a laboratory setting.

---

1. Not too long ago, it was possible to write a syntactically correct program in a particular language that would behave differently when run on different platforms (with the same input). This situation arose because the definition of the language's semantics was not precise enough to require that all of its compilers translate a program to logically equivalent machine language versions. Language designers have realized in recent years that a formal treatment of semantics is as important as the formal treatment of syntax in ensuring that a particular program "means" the same thing regardless of the platform on which it runs. Modern languages are much better in this regard than older languages.

2. Technically, there are two kinds of operational semantics, called "traditional" and "structured" operational semantics (sometimes called "natural semantics"). In this chapter, we discuss the latter.

3.1 **TYPE SYSTEMS**

A *type* is a well-defined set of values and operations on those values. For example, the familiar type `int` has values $\{\ldots, -2, -1, 0, 1, 2, \ldots\}$ and operations $\{+, -, *, /, \ldots\}$ on those values. The type `boolean` has values {true, false} and operations $\{\&\&, \|, \text{ and } !\}$ on those values.

A *type system* is a well-defined system of associating types with variables and other objects defined in a program. Some languages, like C and Java, associate a single type with a variable throughout the life of that variable at run time, and the types of all variables can be determined at compile time. Other languages, like Lisp and Scheme, allow the type of a variable, as well as its value, to change as the program runs. Languages that are in the former class are often called *statically typed* languages, while languages in the latter are *dynamically typed*.

A statically typed language allows its type rules to be fully defined on the basis of its abstract syntax alone. This definition is often called *static semantics* and it provides a means of adding context-sensitive information to a parser that the BNF grammar cannot provide. This process is identified as *semantic analysis* in Chapter 2, and we will treat it more carefully below.

A *type error* is a run-time error that occurs when an operation is attempted on a value for which it is not well-defined. For example, consider the C expression `x+u.p`, where `u` is defined as the union `{int a; double p;}` and initialized by the assignment:

```
u.a = 1;
```

This expression can raise a type error, since the alternative `int` and `double` values of `u` share the same memory address, and `u` is initialized with an `int` value. If `x` is a `double`, the expression `x+u.p` raises an error that cannot be checked at either compile time or run time.

A programming language is *strongly typed* if its type system allows all type errors in programs to be detected, either at compile time or at run time, before the statement in which they can occur is actually executed. (Whether a language is statically or dynamically typed does not prevent it from being strongly typed.) For example, Java is a strongly typed language, while C is not. That is, in C we can write and execute the expression `x+1` regardless of whether the value of `x` is a number or not. Strong typing generally promotes more reliable programs and is viewed as a virtue in programming language design.

A program is *type safe* if it is known to be free of type errors. All the programs in a strongly typed language are, by definition, type safe. Moreover, a language is type safe if all its programs are. Dynamically typed languages like Lisp must necessarily be type safe. Since all their type checking occurs at run time, variables' types can change dynamically. This places a certain overhead on the runtime performance of a program, since executable type-checking code must be intermingled with the code written by the programmer.

How can we define a type system for a language so that type errors can be detected? This question is addressed in the next section.

3.1.1 Formalizing the Type System

One way to define a language's type system is to write a set of function specifications that define what it means for a program to be type safe.[3] These rules can be written as boolean-valued functions, and can express ideas like "all declared variables have unique names" or "all variables used in the program must be declared."

Since the rules for writing type-safe programs can be expressed functionally, they can be implemented in Java as a set of boolean-valued methods. The basis for this functional definition is a *type map,* which is a set of pairs representing the declared variables and their types. We can write the type map, *tm,* of a program as follows:

$$tm = \{\langle v_1, t_1 \rangle, \langle v_2, t_2 \rangle, \ldots, \langle v_n, t_n \rangle\}$$

where each v_i denotes a *Variable* and each t_i denotes its declared *Type.* For the language Jay, the *Variables* in a type map are mutually unique and every type is taken from a set of available types that are fixed at compile time. For Jay, that set is fixed permanently (it is {int, boolean}). For most languages, like C and Java, that set can be expanded by the programmer by defining new types (typedef's in C, and classes in Java).[4] In any case, here is an example type map for a program that has three variables declared; i and j with type int and p with type boolean:

$$tm = \{\langle i, int \rangle, \langle j, int \rangle, \langle p, boolean \rangle\}$$

A formal treatment of static type checking for a program relies on the existence of a type map that has been extracted out of the *Declarations* that appear at the top of the program. We define the function *typing* for Jay as follows:

typing: *Declarations* → *TypeMap*

$$typing(\text{Declarations d}) = \bigcup_{i \in \{1, \ldots, n\}} \langle d_i . v, d_i . t \rangle$$

This function is easily implemented in Java as follows:

```
TypeMap typing (Declarations d) {
    TypeMap map = new TypeMap();
    for (int i=0; i<d.size(); i++) {
        map.put (((Declaration)(d.elementAt(i))).v,
                 ((Declaration)(d.elementAt(i))).t);
    }
    return map;
}
```

---

3. It is important to note that the BNF-defined concrete syntax of a language is not adequate for defining its type checking requirements. That is, BNF is not a powerful enough device to express ideas like "all declared variables must have unique names." This important limitation of BNF grammars is usually exposed in a study of formal (Chomsky-type) languages, and would occur in a course on the theory of computation or compilers.

4. Moreover, the rules for naming variables in C and Java are more flexible and complex, taking into account the syntactic *environment* in which the variable is declared. We revisit this topic in Chapter 5.

Thus, given a `Vector` of *Declarations* d_i, the method `typing` returns a Java `TypeMap` whose keys are the declared variables $d_i . v$ and whose values are their respective types $d_i . t$; in actuality, a `TypeMap` is an extension of a Java `Hashtable`. Here, we are assuming that the abstract syntax for *Declaration* is defined in Java as follows (see Appendix B):

```
class Declaration {
    Variable v;
    Type t;
}
```

Static type checking for a language can be expressed in functional notation, in which each rule that helps define the type system is a boolean-valued function *V* (meaning "valid"). *V* returns **true** or **false** depending on whether or not a particular member of an abstract syntactic class is valid, in relation to these rules. That is,

V: *Class* → **B**

For example, suppose we want to define the idea that "a list of declarations is valid if all its variables have mutually unique identifiers." This idea can be expressed precisely as follows:

V: *Declarations* → **B**
$V(\textit{Declarations } \mathrm{d}) = \forall i,j \in \{1, \ldots, n\}: (i \neq j \supset d_i . v \neq d_j . v)$

That is, every distinct pair of variables in a declaration list has mutually different identifiers. Recall that the *i*th variable in a declaration list has two parts, a *Variable v* and a *Type t*. This particular validity rule addresses only the mutual uniqueness requirement for variables. In a real language, it is important that this function definition also specify that the type of each variable be taken from the set of available types (such as {`int`, `boolean`} for Jay). This refinement is left as an exercise.

Given this function, the implementation of type checking in Java is not a difficult exercise. As a basis, we can use the abstract syntax which is defined as a set of classes. Assuming that `Declarations` is implemented as a Java `Vector` (see Appendix B), the method `V` for `Declarations` can be viewed as one of a collection of methods `V` which together define the entire static type checking requirements of a language. Here is the Java method `V` for declarations:

```
public boolean V (Declarations d) {
  for (int i=0; i<d.size() - 1; i++)
    for (int j=i+1; j<d.size(); j++)
      if ((((Declaration)(d.elementAt(i))).v).equals
          (((Declaration)(d.elementAt(j))).v))
      return false;
  return true;
}
```

In the interest of efficiency, this method does not exactly mirror the definition given in function *V* for uniqueness among declared variable names. That is, the inner loop controlled by j does not cover the entire range $\{1, \ldots, n\}$ as suggested by the formal definition of this function. Readers should recognize, however, that this implementation is an effective one. Note also that, if we were developing a type checker for a compiler, we would include a device for reporting useful error messages.

Another common feature of a language's typing rules is that every variable referenced from within a statement in a program must be declared. Moreover, every variable used in an arithmetic expression must have a proper arithmetic type in its declaration. These requirements can be defined using the classes *Statement* and *Expression,* contexts in which the variables actually occur. These requirements also use the information in the program's type map as a basis for checking the existence and type conformance for each variable referenced.

For a complete language, a set of functions V will be defined over all of its abstract syntactic classes, including the most general class *Program* itself. A complete program from the abstract syntax point of view has two parts; a series of *Declarations* and a body which is a *Block.* That is,

```
class Program {
   Declarations decpart;
   Block body;
}
```

A complete type check, therefore, can be defined functionally at this most general level by the function V, defined as follows:

V: *Program* $\rightarrow$ **B**
$V(Program\ \mathrm{p}) = V(\mathrm{p.decpart}) \wedge V(\mathrm{p.body}, typing(\mathrm{p.decpart}))$

That is, if the *Declarations* have mutually unique variable names and every statement in the body of the program is valid with respect to the type map generated from the declarations, then the entire program is valid from a type checking point of view.

Our definition of the abstract syntax as a collection of Java classes makes this particular specification simple to implement.

```
public boolean V (Program p) {
    return V(p.decpart) && V(p.body, typing (p.decpart));
}
```

That is, a program has two parts, a decpart, which is a *Declarations,* and a body, which is a *Block.* The type validity of the program's *Block* can be checked only in relation to the particular type map that represents its declarations.

Following is a summary of the all the type-checking requirements of Jay. The details of type validity functions for the individual expression and statement classes in a Jay program are covered in Chapter 4, where we discuss the design of imperative languages in greater generality.

3.1.2 Type Checking in Jay

Jay is a statically and strongly typed language. Thus, all type errors can be checked at compile time, before the program is executed. Here is an informal summary of the type checking requirements of Jay.

- Each declared *Variable* must have a unique *Identifier.*
- Each *Variable*'s type must be either int or boolean.
- Each *Variable* referenced within any *Expression* in the program must have been declared.
- Every *Expression*'s result type is determined as follows:

    If the *Expression* is a simple *Variable* or *Value,* then its result type is the type of that *Variable* or *Value.*

    If the *Expression*'s *Operator* is arithmetic (+, −, *, or /) then its terms must all be type int and its result type is correspondingly int. For example, the *Expression* x+1 requires x to be int (since 1 is int), and its result type is int.

    If the *Operator* is relational (<, <=, >, >=, ==, !=) then its terms must be type int and its result type is boolean.

    If the *Operator* is boolean (&&, ||, or !) its term(s) must be type boolean and its result type is boolean.

- For every *Assignment* statement, the type (int or boolean) of its target variable must agree with the type of its source expression.
- For every *Conditional* and *Loop,* the type of its expression must be boolean.

    To illustrate these requirements, consider the simple Jay program given below:

```
// compute result = the factorial of integer n
void main () {
  int n, i, result;
  n = 8;
  i = 1;
  result = 1;
  while (i < n) {
    i = i + 1;
    result = result * i;
  }
}
```

In this program, the variables n, i, and result used in the program must be declared. Moreover, the *Expressions* result*i and i+1 have both of their operands of type int. Further, the *Expression* i<=n has type boolean, since the operator <= takes operands of type int and returns a boolean result. Finally, each of the *Assignments* in this program has an int type *Variable* as its target and an int type *Expression* as its source. Overall, these features make the simple Jay program above valid with respect to the type rules given above. These ideas will be more formally presented and carefully discussed in Chapter 4.

3.2 SEMANTIC DOMAINS AND STATE TRANSFORMATION

The natural numbers, integers, real numbers, and booleans and their mathematical properties provide a foundational context for programming language design. For instance, the language Jay relies on our mathematical intuition about the existence and behavior of **N** (the natural numbers), **I** (the integers), **B** (the set {*true, false*} of boolean values), and **S** (the set of character strings).

These sets are instances of *semantic domains* for programming languages. A semantic domain is any set whose properties and operations are independently well-understood and upon which the functions that define the semantics of a language are ultimately based.

Three useful semantic domains for programming languages are the environment, the memory, and the locations. The *environment* γ is a set of pairs that unite specific variables with memory locations. The *memory* μ is a set of pairs that unite specific locations with values. The *locations* in each case are the natural numbers **N**.

For example, suppose we have variables i and j with values 13 and -1 at some time during the execution of a program. Suppose that the memory locations are serially numbered beginning at 0, and the variables i and j are associated with the memory locations 154 and 155 at that time. Then the environment and memory represented by this configuration can be expressed as follows:[5]

$$\gamma = \{\langle i, 154\rangle, \langle j, 155\rangle\}$$
$$\mu = \{\langle 0, undef\rangle, \ldots, \langle 154, 13\rangle, \langle 155, -1\rangle, \ldots\}$$

The *state* σ of a program is the product of its environment and its memory. However, for our introductory discussions in this chapter, it is convenient to represent the state of a program in a more simplified form. This representation takes the memory locations out of play and simply defines the *state* σ of a program as a set of pairs $\langle v, val\rangle$ that represents all the active variables and their currently assigned values at some stage during the program's execution.[6] This is expressed as follows:

$$\sigma = \{\langle v_1, val_1\rangle, \langle v_2, val_2\rangle, \ldots, \langle v_m, val_m\rangle\}$$

Here, each v_i denotes a variable and each val_i denotes its currently assigned value. Before the program begins execution, $\sigma = \{\langle v_1, undef\rangle, \langle v_2, undef\rangle, \ldots, \langle v_m, undef\rangle\}$. We also use the expression $\sigma(v)$ to denote the function that retrieves the value of the variable v from the current state.

---

5. The special value *undef* is used to denote the value of a memory location (variable) that is currently undefined (not yet assigned).

6. We shall expand this definition of state in Chapter 5, when it will be important to formally represent the environment in a more dynamic fashion. There, a dynamic environment allows us to precisely characterize the ideas of run-time stack and heap, and thus deal effectively with procedure call, object creation, parameter passing, recursion, and so on. For the elementary language Jay, the environment is static, so the state can be simply represented as a set of variable name-value pairs.

For example, the expression below describes the state of a program that has computed and assigned values to three variables, x, y, and z, after several statements have been executed:

$$\sigma = \{\langle x, 1\rangle, \langle y, 2\rangle, \langle z, 3\rangle\}$$

For this particular state, we can retrieve the value of a variable, say y, by writing the expression $\sigma(y)$, which gives the value 2. The next step in the program might be an assignment statement, such as

```
y = 2*z + 3;
```

whose effect would be to change the state as follows:

$$\sigma = \{\langle x, 1\rangle, \langle y, 9\rangle, \langle z, 3\rangle\}$$

The next step in the computation might assign a value to a fourth variable, as in the assignment

```
w = 4;
```

resulting in the following state transformation:

$$\sigma = \{\langle x, 1\rangle, \langle y, 9\rangle, \langle z, 3\rangle, \langle w, 4\rangle\}$$

State transformations that represent these types of assignments can be represented mathematically by a special function called the *overriding union,* represented by the symbol $\overline{U}$. This function is similar to the ordinary set union, but differs exactly in the way that can represent transformations like the ones illustrated above.

Specifically, $\overline{U}$ is defined for two sets of pairs X and Y as follows:

$X \overline{U} Y = $ replace in X all pairs $\langle x, v\rangle$ whose first member matches a pair $\langle x, w\rangle$
from Y by $\langle x, w\rangle$ and then add to X any remaining pairs in Y

For example, suppose $\sigma_1 = \{\langle x, 1\rangle, \langle y, 2\rangle, \langle z, 3\rangle\}$ and $\sigma_2 = \{\langle y, 9\rangle, \langle w, 4\rangle\}$. Then

$$\sigma_1 \overline{U} \sigma_2 = \{\langle x, 1\rangle, \langle y, 9\rangle, \langle z, 3\rangle, \langle w, 4\rangle\}$$

Another way to visualize the overriding union is through the natural join of these two sets. The *natural join* $\sigma_1 \otimes \sigma_2$ is the set of all pairs in σ_1 and σ_2 that have the same first member. For example,

$$\{\langle x, 1\rangle, \langle y, 2\rangle, \langle z, 3\rangle\} \otimes \{\langle y, 9\rangle, \langle w, 4\rangle\} = \{\langle y, 2\rangle, \langle y, 9\rangle\}$$

Furthermore, the set difference between σ_1 and $\sigma_1 \otimes \sigma_2$, expressed as $\sigma_1 - (\sigma_1 \otimes \sigma_2)$, effectively removes every pair from σ_1 whose first member is identical with the first member of some pair in σ_2. Thus, the expression

$$(\sigma_1 - (\sigma_1 \otimes \sigma_2)) \cup \sigma_2$$

is equivalent to $\sigma_1 \overline{U} \sigma_2$.

Readers may have observed that the operator $\overline{U}$ is a formal and generalized model of the familiar assignment operation in imperative programming. It thus plays a pivotal role in the formal semantics of imperative programming languages like C/C++, Ada, Java, and many more.

3.3 **OPERATIONAL SEMANTICS**

The *operational semantics* of a program provides a definition of program meaning by simulating the program's behavior on a machine model that has a very simple (though not necessarily realistic) instruction set and memory organization. An early operational semantics model was the "SECD machine" [Landin 1966], which provided a basis for formally defining the semantics of Lisp.

Structured operational semantics models use a rule-based approach and a few simple assumptions about the arithmetic and logical capabilities of the underlying machine. Below we develop this kind of operational semantics for Jay, using its abstract syntax as a starting point.

Our operational semantics model uses the notation $\sigma(e) \Rightarrow v$ to represent the computation of a value v from the expression e in state σ. If e is a constant, $\sigma(e)$ is just the value of that constant in the underlying semantic domain. If e is a variable, $\sigma(e)$ is the value of that variable in the current state σ. The two semantic domains for Jay are **I** and **B**, so the function $\sigma(e)$ will deliver either an integer or a boolean value for any Jay expression e.[7]

The second notational convention for operational semantics is that of an *execution rule*. An execution rule has the form $\dfrac{premise}{conclusion}$, which is to be read, "if the *premise* is true, then the *conclusion* is true." Consider the execution rule for addition in Jay, given below:

$$\frac{\sigma(e_1) \Rightarrow v_1 \qquad \sigma(e_2) \Rightarrow v_2}{\sigma(e_1 + e_2) \Rightarrow v_1 + v_2}$$

This defines addition on the basis of the sums of the current values of expressions e_1 and e_2, using the properties of the domain of integers in which the values v_1 and v_2 reside. The operational semantics of the other Jay arithmetic, relational, and boolean operators is defined in a similar way.

For statements, the operational semantics is defined by a separate execution rule for each statement type in the abstract syntax of Jay. Here is the operational semantics for an assignment statement s of the form `s.target = s.source;`

$$\frac{\sigma(s.\text{source}) \Rightarrow v}{\sigma(s.\text{target} = s.\text{source};) \Rightarrow \sigma \, \overline{\cup} \, \{\langle s.\text{target}, v \rangle\}}$$

For example, suppose we have the assignment x = x + 1; and a current state in which the value of x is 5. That is, $\sigma = \{\ldots, \langle x, 5 \rangle, \ldots\}$. The operational semantics of constants, variables, expressions, and assignment, therefore, computes a new state in the following series of execution rule applications (reading from top to bottom):

$$\frac{\dfrac{\sigma(x) \Rightarrow 5 \qquad \sigma(1) \Rightarrow 1}{\sigma(x + 1) \Rightarrow 6}}{\sigma(\text{x = x + 1;}) \Rightarrow \{\ldots, \langle x, 5 \rangle, \ldots\} \, \overline{\cup} \, \{\langle x, 6 \rangle\}}$$

This leaves the state transformed to $\sigma = \{\ldots, \langle x, 6 \rangle, \ldots\}$.

---

7. Note the distinction between the two uses of σ here: when used alone, it denotes a *state,* or a set of name-value pairs; when written as $\sigma(e)$, it denotes a *function* that maps expressions to values.

The execution rule for statement sequences s_1s_2 is also intuitively defined:

$$\frac{\sigma(s_1) \Rightarrow \sigma_1 \qquad \sigma_1(s_2) \Rightarrow \sigma_2}{\sigma(s_1s_2) \Rightarrow \sigma_2}$$

That is to say, if execution of s_1 in state σ yields state σ_1, and execution of s_2 in state σ_1 yields state σ_2, then the compound effect of executing the sequence s_1s_2 in state σ is state σ_2.

For Jay conditionals, which are of the form `s = if (s.test) s.thenpart else s.elsepart`, the execution rule has two versions, one to be applied when the evaluation of `s.test` is *true* and the other to be applied when `s.test` is *false*.

$$\frac{\sigma(s.\text{test}) \Rightarrow true \qquad \sigma(s.\text{thenpart}) \Rightarrow \sigma_1}{\sigma(\text{if } (s.\text{test})s.\text{thenpart else } s.\text{elsepart}) \Rightarrow \sigma_1}$$

$$\frac{\sigma(s.\text{test}) \Rightarrow false \qquad \sigma(s.\text{elsepart}) \Rightarrow \sigma_1}{\sigma(\text{if } (s.\text{test})s.\text{thenpart else } s.\text{elsepart}) \Rightarrow \sigma_1}$$

The interpretation is straightforward. If we have state $\sigma = \{\ldots, \langle x, 6 \rangle, \ldots\}$ and the following Jay statement:

```
if (x<0)
    x = x - 1;
else
    x = x + 1;
```

then the second rule is the only one whose premise $\sigma(x < 0) \Rightarrow false$ is satisfied by the current value of x. This rule concludes that the result of executing the conditional is the same as the result of executing the assignment `x = x + 1;` in state $\sigma = \{\ldots, \langle x, 6 \rangle, \ldots\}$, leaving as a final result the state $\sigma_1 = \{\ldots, \langle x, 7 \rangle, \ldots\}$.

Loops are statements with the general form `s = while (s.test) s.body`. Their execution rules have two different forms, one of which is chosen when the condition `s.test` is *true* and the other when `s.test` is *false*.

$$\frac{\sigma(s.\text{test}) \Rightarrow true \qquad \sigma(s.\text{body}) \Rightarrow \sigma_1 \qquad \sigma_1(\text{while } (s.\text{test}) s.\text{body}) \Rightarrow \sigma_2}{\sigma(\text{while } (s.\text{test}) s.\text{body}) \Rightarrow \sigma_2}$$

$$\frac{\sigma(s.\text{test}) \Rightarrow false}{\sigma(\text{while } (s.\text{test}) s.\text{body}) \Rightarrow \sigma}$$

The first rule says, in effect, that when `s.test` is *true* we execute `s.body` one time and achieve the state σ_1, and then recursively execute the loop starting in this new state. The second rule provides an exit from the loop; if `s.test` is *false,* we complete the loop without changing the state σ.

For example, suppose we have the following loop in Jay, which doubles the value of x until x < 100 is no longer *true:*

```
while (x<100)
    x = 2*x;
```

Beginning with initial state $\sigma = \{\ldots, \langle x, 7 \rangle\}$, the first rule recursively applies, giving the following conclusion:

$$\frac{\sigma(x < 100) \Rightarrow true \quad \sigma(x = 2*x;) \Rightarrow \sigma_1 = \{\ldots, \langle x, 14 \rangle\} \quad \sigma_1(\text{while } (x < 100)\ x = 2*x;) \Rightarrow \sigma_2}{\sigma(\text{while } (x < 100)\ x = 2*x;) \Rightarrow \sigma_2}$$

Now, to compute the final state σ_2, we need to reapply this rule starting from the new state $\sigma_1 = \{\ldots, \langle x, 14 \rangle\}$. A series of applications for this rule eventually leaves the state $\sigma_1 = \{\ldots, \langle x, 112 \rangle\}$, in which case the premise $\sigma(x < 100) \Rightarrow false$ is satisfied and the final state for executing the loop becomes $\sigma_2 = \{\ldots, \langle x, 112 \rangle\}$.

3.4 AXIOMATIC SEMANTICS

While it is important to programmers and compiler-writers to understand what a program does in all circumstances, it is also important for programmers to be able to confirm, or *prove,* that it does what it is supposed to do under all circumstances. That is, if someone presents the programmer with a specification for what a program is supposed to do, the programmer may need to be able to prove, beyond a reasonable doubt, that the program and this specification are absolutely in agreement with each other. That is, the program is "correct" in some convincing way. *Axiomatic semantics* provides a vehicle for developing such proofs.

For instance, suppose we want to prove mathematically that the C/C++ function *Max* in Figure 3.1 actually computes as its result the maximum of its two parameters: *a* and *b*.

| Figure 3.1   A C/C++ Max Function

```
int Max (int a, int b) {
    int m;
    if (a >= b)
        m = a;
    else
        m = b;
    return m;
}
```

Calling this function one time will obtain an answer for a particular *a* and *b*, such as 8 and 13. But the parameters *a* and *b* define a wide range of integers, so calling it several times with all the different values to prove its correctness would be an infeasible task.

Axiomatic semantics provides a vehicle for reasoning about programs and their computations. This allows programmers to predict a program's behavior in a more circumspect and convincing way than running the program several times using as test cases different random choices of input values.

3.4.1 Fundamental Concepts

Axiomatic semantics is based on the notion of an *assertion,* which is a predicate that describes the *state* of a program at any point during its execution. An assertion can define the meaning of a computation, like "*the maximum of a and b,*" without concern for how that computation is accomplished. For instance, the code in Figure 3.1 is just one way of algorithmically expressing the maximum computation; even for a function this simple, there are many minor variations. In any case, the following assertion Q describes the function *Max* declaratively, without regard for the underlying computational process:

$$Q \equiv m = max(a, b)$$

This predicate defines the meaning of the function $Max(a, b)$ for any integer values of a and b. To prove that the program in Figure 3.1 actually computes $Max(a, b)$, we need to show that the logical expression Q is somehow equivalent in meaning to that program. Q is called a *postcondition* for the program *Max*.

Axiomatic semantics allows us to logically derive a series of predicates by reasoning about the behavior of each individual statement in the program, beginning with the postcondition Q and the last statement and working backwards. The last predicate, say P, that is derived in this series of steps is called the program's *precondition*. The precondition thus expresses what must be *true* before program execution begins in order for the postcondition to be satisfied.

In the case of *Max*, the postcondition Q is well-defined for all integer values of a and b. This suggests the following precondition:

$$P \equiv true$$

That is, for the program to be considered for correctness at all, no assumption or precondition is needed.

One final consideration must be taken into account before we look at the details of correctness proofs themselves. That is, for *some* initial values of the variables that satisfy the program's precondition P, executing the program may *never* reach its last statement. This may occur either because the program enters an infinite loop or because it may try to do a calculation that exceeds the capabilities of the machine on which it is running. For example, if we try to compute $n!$ for a large enough value of n,[8] the program will raise an arithmetic overflow condition and halt, thus never reaching its final goal. In general, we must be content to prove correctness of programs only partially—that is, only for those selections of initial values of variables that allow the execution of all its statements to be completed. This notion is called *partial correctness*.

These concerns notwithstanding, we can prove the (partial) correctness of a program by placing its precondition in front of its first statement and its postcondition after its last statement, and then systematically deriving a series of valid predicates as we simulate the execution of each instruction in its turn. For any statement or series of statements s, the following expression

$$\{P\}s\{Q\}$$

represents the predicate that the statement s is partially correct with respect to the precondition P and the postcondition Q. The expression $\{P\}s\{Q\}$ is called a *Hoare triple*[9] and reads "execution of statements s, beginning in a state that satisfies P, results in a state that satisfies Q, provided that s halts."

---

8. 30! exceeds the size of a 32-bit integer.

9. These forms are called *Hoare triples* since they were first characterized by C.A.R. Hoare in the original proposal for axiomatizing the semantics of programming languages [Hoare 1969].

For our example program, we first write the following Hoare triple:

```
{true}
  if (a >= b)
    m = a;
  else
    m = b;
{m = max(a, b)}
```

To prove the validity of this Hoare triple, we derive intermediate Hoare triples $\{P\}s\{Q\}$ that are valid for individual statements s, beginning with the postcondition. This process continues until we have successfully shown that the above Hoare triple is *true* for all initial values of a and b for which the program halts. That is, if we can derive Hoare triples that logically connect the individual lines in a program with each other, we will effectively connect the program's postcondition with its precondition.

How are these intermediate triples derived? That is done by formalizing what we know about the behavior of each type of statement in the language. Programs in Jay-like languages have four basic types of statements: assignments, conditionals, loops, and blocks (sequences). Each statement type has a *proof rule* which defines the meaning of that statement type in terms of the pre- and postconditions that it satisfies. The proof rules for Jay-like languages are shown in Table 3.1.

Table 3.1

Proof Rules for Different Types of Jay Statements

Statement Type	Proof Rule
1. *Assignment* $s = s.target = s.source;$	$\dfrac{true}{\{Q[s.target\backslash s.source]\}s\{Q\}}$
2. Sequence (*Block*) $s = s_1\ s_2$	$\dfrac{\{P\}s_1\{R\} \qquad \{R\}s_2\{Q\}}{\{P\}s_1\ s_2\{Q\}}$
3. *Conditional* $s = if\ (s.test)\ s.thenpart$ $\qquad else\ s.elsepart$	$\dfrac{\{s.test \wedge P\}s.thenpart\{Q\} \qquad \{\neg s.test \wedge P\}s.elsepart\{Q\}}{\{P\}s\{Q\}}$
4. *Loop* $s = while\ (s.test)\ s.body$	$\dfrac{\{s.test \wedge P\}s.body\{P\}}{\{P\}s\{\neg s.test \wedge P\}}$
5. Rule of consequence	$\dfrac{P \supset P' \qquad \{P'\}s\{Q'\} \qquad Q' \supset Q}{\{P\}s\{Q\}}$

These proof rules are all of the form $\dfrac{premise}{conclusion}$, which is similar to the execution rules used in operational semantics. However, proof rules are to be read, "if the *premise* is valid then the *conclusion* is valid."

The *Assignment* proof rule has *true* as its premise, guaranteeing that we can always derive the conclusion; such a rule is called an *axiom*. The notation $Q[a\backslash b]$ means "the state that results from replacing the value of b in Q by a." For instance, if

$\{Q\} \equiv \{x = 1 \wedge y = 4\}$ then $\{Q[1\backslash x]\} \equiv \{1 = 1 \wedge y = 4\}$. Applied to an assignment, rule 1 suggests that the following Hoare triple is valid:

$\{a = max(a, b)\}$
```
  m = a;
```
$(m = max(a, b))$

That is, the replacement of m in the postcondition by a results in precondition of $\{a = max(a, b)\}$. So the assignment rule allows us to reason backwards through a program, deriving preconditions from postconditions in individual statements.

Proof rule 5 allows us to perform arithmetic and logical simplification in a predicate during the proof process. In the above example, for instance, the assertion $\{a \geq b \wedge a = max(a, b)\}$ is implied by $\{a \geq b\}$, so that we can substitute it and form an equivalent Hoare triple using rule 5 as follows:

$$\frac{a \geq b \supset a = max(a, b) \qquad \{a \geq b \wedge a = max(a, b)\}m = a;\{m = max(a, b)\}}{\{a \geq b\}m = a;\{m = max(a, b)\}}$$

This example also suggests that there may be several alternative preconditions that can be derived from a given statement and postcondition, using the proof rules. That precondition which is the least restrictive on the variables in play is called the *weakest precondition*. For instance, the precondition $\{a \geq b\}$ is the weakest precondition for the statement $m - a$; and its postcondition $\{m = max(a, b)\}$. Finding weakest preconditions is important because it enables simplification of the proof at various stages.

A strategy for proving the partial correctness of the rest of the program in Figure 3.1 works systematically from the postcondition backwards through the if, and then through the assignment statements in the then and else parts toward the given precondition.

Next, using the rule 1 for assignments and our postcondition on the else part of the if statement, we obtain:

$\{b = max(a, b)\}$
```
  m = b;
```
$\{m = max(a, b)\}$

As before, we use $a < b$ and rule 5 to show:

$$\frac{a < b \supset b = max(a, b) \qquad \{a < b \wedge b = max(a, b)\}m = b;\{m = max(a, b)\}}{\{a < b\}m = b;\{m = max(a, b)\}}$$

Having proved both premises of rule 3 for a conditional, we can conclude:

$\{true\}$
```
   if (a >= b)
      m = a;
   else
      m = b;
```
$\{m = max(a, b)\}$

In Subsection 3.4.2, we prove the correctness of a program involving a loop.

3.4.2 Correctness of Factorial

Suppose we want to prove mathematically that the C/C++ function *Factorial* in Figure 3.2 actually computes as its result $n!$, for any integer n where $n \geq 1$. By $n!$ we mean the product $1 \times \cdots \times n$.

| **Figure 3.2   A C/C++ Factorial Function**

```
int Factorial (int n) {
    int f = 1;
    int i = 1;
    while (i < n) {
        i = i + 1;
        f = f * i;
    }
    return f;
}
```

So the precondition or input assertion Q for *Factorial* is $1 \leq n$, while the postcondition or output assertion is $f = n!$. In general in a program involving a loop, rule 4 of Table 3.1 is used to break the code into three parts, as follows:

```
{Q}
initialization
{P}
while (test ) {
    loopBody
}
{¬test ∧ P}
finalization
{R}
```

where Q is our input assertion, R is our final or output assertion, and P is the loop *invariant*. An invariant is an assertion that remains *true* for every iteration of the loop. In general, there is no algorithmic way to derive a loop invariant from the input-output assertions for the program.[10] Thus, it is important for proving program correctness that the loop invariant be supplied for each loop.

For the *Factorial* function given in Figure 3.2, the loop invariant P is $\{1 \leq i \wedge i \leq n \wedge (f = i!)\}$. Thus, the *Factorial* program with its input-output assertions and loop invariant can be rewritten as:

$$\{1 \leq n\}$$
```
    f = 1;
    i = 1;
```
$$\{1 \leq i \wedge i \leq n \wedge (f = i!)\}$$

---

10. Finding a loop invariant is often tricky, as is the whole correctness proof process itself. Interested readers are encouraged to find additional sources (e.g., [Gries 1981]) that cover this very interesting topic in more detail.

```
while (i < n) {
    i = i + 1;
    f = f * i;
}
```
$\{i \geq n \wedge 1 \leq i \wedge i \leq n \wedge (f = i!)\}$
$\{f = n!\}$
```
    return f;
```

This effectively reduces the original problem of proving the correctness of the original program to the three problems: (1) proving the initialization part; (2) proving the premise of rule 4; and (3) proving the finalization part. These subproblems may be proved in any convenient order.

The third part seems easiest, since it involves the empty statement (or the skip statement in Jay). The proof can be achieved by repeated applications of rule 5:

$$i \geq n \wedge 1 \leq i \wedge i \leq n \wedge (f = i!) \supset (i = n) \wedge (f = i!) \supset (f = n!)$$

Since $i \geq n$ and $i \leq n$, it follows that $i = n$. The second step involves a substitution of one variable for another.

A strategy for proving the initialization part is to use rule 2 to break a *Block,* or sequence of statements, into its individual components:

$\{1 \leq n\}$
```
    f = 1;
```
$\{R'\}$
```
    i = 1;
```
$\{1 \leq i \wedge i \leq n \wedge (f = i!)\}$

The intermediate assertion R′ can be found from the application of rule 1 by back substitution: $\{1 \leq 1 \wedge 1 \leq n \wedge (f = 1!)\}$. Again, applying rule 1 to R′ on the program fragment:

$\{1 \leq n\}$
```
    f = 1;
```
$\{1 \leq 1 \wedge 1 \leq n \wedge (f = 1!)\}$

we obtain: $\{1 \leq 1 \wedge 1 \leq n \wedge (1 = 1!)\}$, which simplifies to $1 \leq n$. Thus, we have shown:

$$\frac{\{1 \leq n\}f = 1;\{1 \leq 1 \wedge 1 \leq n \wedge f = 1!\} \quad \{1 \leq 1 \wedge 1 \leq n \wedge f = 1!\}i = 1;\{1 \leq i \wedge i \leq n \wedge f = i!\}}{\{1 \leq n\}\ f = 1;\ i = 1;\ \{1 \leq i \wedge i \leq n \wedge f = i!\}}$$

Thus, it only remains to show that P is a loop invariant; this means that we must show the premise of rule 4, namely, that the loop body preserves the truth of the loop invariant:

$$\frac{\{s.\text{test} \wedge P\}s.\text{body}\{P\}}{\{P\}s\{\neg s.\text{test} \wedge P\}}, \text{ where } s \text{ is a loop statement.}$$

Specifically, we must show it for the given loop test, invariant P, and loop body:

$\{i < n \land 1 \le i \land i \le n \land (f = i!)\}$
```
i = i + 1;
f = f * i;
```
$\{1 \le i \land i \le n \land (f = i!)\}$

Again we employ the strategy of using rule 2 for sequences to obtain:

$\{i < n \land 1 \le i \land i \le n \land (f = i!)\}$
```
i = i + 1;
```
$\{R'\}$
```
f = f * i;
```
$\{1 \le i \land i \le n \land (f = i!)\}$

and then applying rule 1 on the assignment to f to find R' by back substitution: $1 \le i \land i \le n \land (f \times i = i!)$. We repeat this strategy using R' and rule 1 on the assignment to i to find: $1 \le i \land i \le n \land (f \times (i + 1) = (i + 1)!)$. If we can show that

$$i < n \land 1 \le i \land i \le n \land (f = i!) \supset 1 \le i + 1 \land i + 1 \le n \land (f \times (i + 1) = (i + 1)!),$$

then our proof is complete by rule 5. Using the following rule from logic:

$$\frac{p \supset q \qquad p \supset r}{p \supset q \land r}$$

and rule 5, we shall prove each term of the consequent separately. First, we must show:

$$i < n \land 1 \le i \land i \le n \land (f = i!) \supset 1 \le i + 1,$$

This follows since $1 \le i$ is a term in the antecedent. Next we must show:

$$i < n \land 1 \le i \land i \le n \land (f = i!) \supset i + 1 \le n,$$

Again, since $i < n$ is in the antecedent and since we are dealing with integers, it follows that $i + 1 \le n$. Finally, we must show:

$$i < n \land 1 \le i \land i \le n \land (f = i!) \supset (f \times (i + 1) = (i + 1)!),$$

Since $1 \le i$, we can safely divide both sides of $f \times (i + 1) = (i + 1)!$ by $i + 1$, resulting in:

$$i < n \land 1 \le i \land i \le n \land (f = i!) \supset (f = i!),$$

which follows since the consequent appears as a term in the antecedent.

This concludes our proof of the (partial) correctness of the *Factorial* function given in Figure 3.2.

3.4.3 Correctness of Fibonacci

Suppose we want to prove mathematically that the C/C++ function *Fib* in Figure 3.3 actually computes as its result the nth Fibonacci number in the series 0, 1, 1, 2, 3, 5, 8, 13, 21, . . . , for any particular nonnegative value of n.

A strategy for proving the partial correctness of the rest of the program in Figure 3.3 works systematically from the postcondition backwards through the if, and then through the assignment statements in the then and else parts toward the given precondition.

| Figure 3.3 A C/C++ Fibonacci Function

```
int Fib (int n) {
    int fib0 = 0;
    int fib1 = 1;
    int k = n;
    while (k > 0) {
        int temp = fib0;
        fib0 = fib1;
        fib1 = fib0 + temp;
        k = k - 1;
    }
    return fib0;
}
```

Rule 2 allows us to break a *Block,* or sequence of statements, into its individual constituents, and rules 3 and 4 allow us to reason through *Conditional* and *Loop* statements to derive their preconditions from their postconditions. As noted above, rule 5 allows us to cast off extraneous information along the way. Rule 5 is also useful when we want to introduce additional information in a predicate to anticipate what may be needed later in the process.

Now we can apply rule 1 two more times to derive a Hoare triple for each of the first three statements in the program:

$\{n \geq 0\}$
```
    fib0 = 0;
```
$\{n \geq 0 \land \text{fib0} = 0\}$

$\{n \geq 0 \land \text{fib0} = 0\}$
```
    fib1 = 1;
```
$\{n \geq 0 \land \text{fib0} = 0 \land \text{fib1} = 1\}$

$\{n \geq 0 \land \text{fib0} = 0 \land \text{fib1} = 1\}$
```
    k = n;
```
$\{n \geq 0 \land \text{fib0} = 0 \land \text{fib1} = 1 \land 0 \leq k = n\}$

Now rule 2 gives us the ability to simplify this. For instance, if s_1 and s_2 are the first two statements in the above fragment, then:

$$\frac{\{n \geq 0\}s_1\{n \geq 0 \land \text{fib0} = 0\} \qquad \{n \geq 0 \land \text{fib0} = 0\}s_2\{n \geq 0 \land \text{fib0} = 0 \land \text{fib1} = 1\}}{\{n \geq 0\}s_1\,s_2\{n \geq 0 \land \text{fib0} = 0 \land \text{fib1} = 1\}}$$

allows us to rewrite the first two of these three Hoare triples as follows:

$\{n \geq 0\}$
```
    fib0 = 0;
    fib1 = 1;
```
$\{n \geq 0 \land \text{fib0} = 0 \land \text{fib1} = 1\}$

Using rule 2 again allows us to establish the validity of the following Hoare triple:

$\{n \geq 0\}$
```
    fib0 = 0;
```

```
fib1 = 1;
k = n;
```
$\{n \geq 0 \land \text{fib0} = 0 \land \text{fib1} = 1 \land 0 \leq k = n\}$

Next we consider the while loop. To deal with it, we need to discover an assertion that is true just before every repetition of the loop, including the first. That is, we need to find the loop's *invariant*. Finding the loop's invariant requires anticipation of what should be true when the loop finally terminates. Here is an invariant for our while loop:

$$INV = \left\{ \begin{array}{c} 0 \leq k \leq n \land Fib(0) = 0 \land Fib(1) = 1 \land \\ \forall j \in \{2, \ldots, n - k + 1\}: Fib(j) = Fib(j - 1) + Fib(j - 2) \land \\ \text{fib0} = Fib(n - k) \land \text{fib1} = Fib(n - k + 1) \end{array} \right\}$$

This says that for every value of k in which the loop has already run, we will have computed the Fibonacci numbers $Fib(0), Fib(1), \ldots, Fib(n - k + 1)$, and the variables `fib0` and `fib1` are identical to the Fibonacci numbers $Fib(n - k)$ and $Fib(n - k + 1)$ respectively. In particular, just before the loop begins we have $k = n$ (i.e., the loop will have computed no numbers), the value of `fib0` is $Fib(0)$, or 0, and the value of `fib1` is $Fib(1)$, or 1.

Note that this invariant is implied by the postcondition we carefully derived for the first three statements in the program. Thus, proof rule 5 allows the invariant to be valid before the first iteration of the loop begins. Looking ahead, we anticipate that when $k = n - 1$ the loop will have just computed $Fib(2)$ and the value of `fib0` will become $Fib(1) = 1$. When $k = n - 2$, the loop will have computed $Fib(2)$ and $Fib(3)$, leaving `fib0` = $Fib(2)$, and so forth.

This process continues until $k > 0$ is no longer true (i.e., $k = 0$), and the invariant asserts that the loop will have computed $Fib(2), Fib(3), \ldots,$ and $Fib(n + 1)$, leaving the value of `fib0` = $Fib(n)$. Using the proof rule $\dfrac{\{s.\text{test} \land P\}s.\text{body}\{P\}}{\{P\}s\{\neg s.\text{test} \land P\}}$ in Table 3.1 for loop s, we relate the loop invariant with the precondition $s.\text{test} \land P$. Thus, when the loop terminates the test condition $k > 0$ is no longer *true*, which forces the following Hoare triple to be valid:

$$\left\{ \begin{array}{c} Fib(0) = 0 \land Fib(1) = 1 \land k = 0 \land \\ \forall j \in \{2, \ldots, n - 0 + 1\}: Fib(j) = Fib(j - 1) + Fib(j - 2) \land \\ \text{fib0} = Fib(n - 0) \land \text{fib1} = Fib(n - 0 + 1) \end{array} \right\}$$

This logically implies the program's postcondition, using proof rule 5 (the rule of consequence) along with some fairly obvious simplifications:

$\{Fib(0) = 0 \land Fib(1) = 1 \land \forall j \in \{2, \ldots, n\}: Fib(j) = Fib(j - 1)$
$\qquad\qquad\qquad\qquad\qquad + Fib(j - 2) \land \text{fib0} = Fib(n)\}$

A final task is to show that the invariant *INV* does remain valid for each repetition of the statements inside the body of the loop. That is, we need to show that the following (ugly!) Hoare triple is valid for every value of $k > 0$:

$$INV = \left\{ \begin{array}{c} 0 \leq k - 1 < n \wedge Fib(0) = 0 \wedge Fib(1) = 1 \wedge \\ \forall j \in \{2, \ldots, n - (k - 1)\}: Fib(j) = Fib(j - 1) + Fib(j - 2) \wedge \\ \text{fib0} = Fib(n - k) \wedge \text{fib1} = Fib(n - (k - 1)) \end{array} \right\}$$

```
int temp = fib0;
fib0 = fib1;
fib1 = fib0 + temp;
k = k - 1;
```

$$INV' = \left\{ \begin{array}{c} 0 \leq k < n \wedge Fib(0) = 0 \wedge Fib(1) = 1 \wedge \\ \forall j \in \{2, \ldots, n - k\}: Fib(j) = Fib(j - 1) + Fib(j - 2) \wedge \\ \text{fib0} = Fib(n - k) \wedge \text{fib1} = Fib(n - (k - 1)) \end{array} \right\}$$

To accomplish this, we use proof rule 5 to simplify intermediate expressions, and substitute equivalent expressions using our knowledge of algebra. For instance, we use the facts that the expression $n - k + 1$ in the above invariant INV is equivalent to $n - (k - 1)$, and $k > 0$ in the invariant is equivalent to $k - 1 \geq 0$.

Looking at the intermediate statements inside a single iteration of the loop, we see that they maintain the validity of the invariant and make progress toward the final computation of $\text{fib0} = Fib(n)$.

$$INV = \left\{ \begin{array}{c} 0 \leq k - 1 < n \wedge Fib(0) = 0 \wedge Fib(1) = 1 \wedge \\ \forall j \in \{2, \ldots, n - (k - 1)\}: Fib(j) = Fib(j - 1) + Fib(j - 2) \wedge \\ \text{fib0} = Fib(n - k) \wedge \text{fib1} = Fib(n - (k - 1)) \end{array} \right\}$$

```
int temp = fib0;
```

$$\left\{ \begin{array}{l} 0 \leq k - 1 < n \wedge Fib(0) = 0 \wedge Fib(1) = 1 \wedge \\ \forall j \in \{2, \ldots, n - (k - 1)\}: Fib(j) = Fib(j - 1) + Fib(j - 2) \wedge \\ \text{fib0} = Fib(n - k) \wedge \text{fib1} = Fib(n - (k - 1)) \wedge \text{temp} = Fib(n - k) \end{array} \right\}$$

```
fib0 = fib1;
```

$$\left\{ \begin{array}{l} 0 \leq k - 1 < n \wedge Fib(0) = 0 \wedge Fib(1) = 1 \wedge \\ \forall j \in \{2, \ldots, n - (k - 1)\}: Fib(j) = Fib(j - 1) + Fib(j - 2) \wedge \\ \text{fib0} = Fib(n - (k - 1)) \wedge \text{fib1} = Fib(n - (k - 1)) \wedge \text{temp} = Fib(n - k) \end{array} \right\}$$

```
fib1 = fib0 + temp;
```

$$\left\{ \begin{array}{l} 0 \leq k - 1 < n \wedge Fib(0) = 0 \wedge Fib(1) = 1 \wedge \\ \forall j \in \{2, \ldots, n - (k - 1)\}: Fib(j) = Fib(j - 1) + Fib(j - 2) \wedge \\ \text{fib0} = Fib(n - (k - 1)) \wedge \text{fib1} = Fib(n - (k - 1)) + Fib(n - k) \wedge \text{temp} = Fib(n - k) \end{array} \right\}$$

```
k = k - 1;
```

$$\left\{\begin{array}{c} 0 \le \underline{k} < n \wedge Fib(0) = 0 \wedge Fib(1) = 1 \wedge \\ \forall j \in \{2, \ldots, n - k\}: Fib(j) = Fib(j - 1) + Fib(j - 2) \wedge \\ \text{fib0} = Fib(n - k) \wedge \text{fib1} = Fib(n - (k - 1)) \wedge \text{temp} = Fib(n - k) \end{array}\right\}$$

To clarify the above, we have underlined that part of the invariant that changes after each of these four statements is taken into account. The last line implies the transformation of the invariant to the following form; since `temp` is a variable to be reassigned at the beginning of the next loop iteration, it can be dropped from the final assertion. Thus, the invariant INV' at the end of a single iteration is transformed as follows:

$$INV' = \left\{\begin{array}{c} 0 \le k < n \wedge Fib(0) = 0 \wedge Fib(1) = 1 \wedge \\ \forall j \in \{2, \ldots, n - k\}: Fib(j) = Fib(j - 1) + Fib(j - 2) \wedge \\ \text{fib0} = Fib(n - k) \wedge \text{fib1} = Fib(n - (k - 1)) \end{array}\right\}$$

The key here is to notice that the values of `fib0` and `fib1` are transformed so that they represent the next adjacent pair of Fibonacci numbers following the pair that they represented at the beginning of this sequence.

The indexing is a bit tricky, but readers should see that the three Fibonacci numbers that influence a single iteration are $Fib(n - k)$, $Fib(n - (k - 1))$, and $Fib(n - (k - 2))$, in ascending order. For instance, when $k = n$, this group of statements begins with `fib0` $= Fib(0)$ and `fib1` $= Fib(1)$. This group of statements ends with $k = n - 1$, `fib0` $= Fib(n - (n - 1)) = Fib(1)$, and `fib1` $= Fib(n - ((n - 1) - 1)) = Fib(2)$.

3.4.4 Perspective

Axiomatic semantics and the corresponding techniques for proving the correctness of imperative programs were developed in the late 1960s and early 1970s. At that time it was the expectation that by now most programs would routinely be proven correct. Clearly that has not happened.

Actually, the importance of correctness proofs in software design has been a subject of heated debate, especially in the early 1990s. Many software engineers reject the notion of formal proof [DeMillo 1979], arguing that it is too complex and time-consuming a process for most programmers to master. Instead they use elaborate testing methods to convince themselves that the software runs correctly most of the time.

The counter argument was made by Dijkstra [1972] who stated that testing could only prove the presence of bugs, never their absence. Consider a simple program that inputs two 32-bit integers, computes some function, and outputs a 32-bit integer. There are 2^{64} possible inputs (approximately 10^{20}), so that even if one could test and verify (!) 100 million test cases per second, complete testing would take approximately 10^5 years. And this is for one of the simplest programs one can imagine!

Is there a middle ground between complex and time-consuming proofs and totally inadequate testing? We believe so.

First, properties of programs other than correctness can be routinely proved. These include safety of programs where safety is a critical issue. Absence of deadlock in concurrent programs is also often formally proved.

Second, the methods in object-oriented programs (as we shall see in Chapter 7) are often quite small in size. Informal proofs of such methods are routinely possible, although not often practiced. One reason for this is that many programmers, largely ignorant of formal program correctness, are not able to precisely state the input-output assertions for the methods they write.

Third, programmers trained in program correctness can and do state input-output assertions for the methods they write using formal English (or other natural language); this leads to vastly improved documentation.

As an example where such formalism could (and should) have been used, consider Sun's `javadoc` documentation for the various `String` methods in JDK 1.1. The comment for the method:

```
public String substring(int beginIndex, int endIndex);
```

states: "Returns a new string that is a substring of this string." How imprecise! How would an implementor carry out an informal proof given such a vague specification? What are the range of valid values for `beginIndex` and `endIndex`? Is the minimum valid value for `beginIndex` 0 or 1? A programmer interested in producing an informal proof of an implementation of `substring` would at least require a more formal description of this method; such a description is left as an exercise.

3.5 DENOTATIONAL SEMANTICS

The *denotational semantics* of a language defines the meanings of abstract language elements as a collection of environment- and state-transforming functions. The *environment* of a program is the set of objects and types that are active at each step during its execution. The *state* of a program is the set of all active objects and their current values. These state-transforming functions depend on the assumption of some primitive types and transformations.

While axiomatic semantics is valuable for clarifying the meaning of a program as an abstract text, operational (or denotational) semantics addresses the meaning of a program as an active object within a computational (or functional) environment. The use of denotational semantics for defining meaning has both advantages and disadvantages. An advantage is that we can use the functional denotations of program meaning as the basis for specifying an interpreter for the language. However, this advantage raises an additional issue. That is, strictly speaking, the use of Java to implement the functional definition of, say, a *Loop* requires that we define the semantics of Java *itself* before using it to implement the semantics of Jay. That is, there is some circularity in using the denotational model as a basis for defining the meaning of a language.

Nevertheless, denotational semantics is widely used, and it allows us to define the meaning of an abstract Jay program as a series of state transformations resulting from the application of a series of functions M. These functions individually define the meaning of every class of element that can occur in the program's abstract syntax tree—*Program, Block, Conditional, Loop, Assignment,* and so forth.

Let Σ represent the set of all program states σ. Then a meaning function M is a mapping from a particular member of a given abstract class and current state in Σ to a new state in Σ. That is:[11]

M: $Class \times \Sigma \rightarrow \Sigma$

For instance, the meaning of an abstract *Statement* can be expressed as a state-transforming function of the form.

M: $Statement \times \Sigma \rightarrow \Sigma$

These functions are necessarily *partial* functions, which means that they are not well-defined for all members of their domain $Class \times \Sigma$. That is, the abstract representations of certain program constructs in certain states do not have finite meaning representations, even though those constructs are syntactically valid. For instance, consider the following insidious, yet syntactically valid, C/C++ statements (assuming i is an int variable).

```
for (i=1; i>-1; i++)
    i--;
```

In this case, there is no reasonable definition for a final state, since the value of i alternates between 1 and 0 as the loop repeats itself endlessly.

Since the abstract syntax of a Jay program is a tree structure whose root is the abstract element *Program*, the meaning of a Jay program can be defined by a series of functions, the first of which defines the meaning of *Program*.

M: $Program \rightarrow \Sigma$
$M(Program\ p) = M(\text{p.body}, \{\langle v_1, undef \rangle, \langle v_2, undef \rangle, \ldots, \langle v_m, undef \rangle \})$

The first line of this definition gives a prototype function M for the program element being defined (in this case, *Program*), while the second defines the meaning of a program, using the abstract syntax definitions of the direct constituents of *Program*. Recall (see Appendix B) that the abstract definition of *Program* has two parts; a decpart (a series of abstract *Declarations*) and a body, which is a *Block*. So this functional definition says that the meaning of a program is the meaning of the program's body with the initial state $\{\langle v_1, undef \rangle, \langle v_2, undef \rangle, \ldots, \langle v_m, undef \rangle \}$. We can predict that, as these meaning functions unfold and are applied to the elements of a specific program, this initial state will change as variables are assigned and reassigned values.

This functional style for defining the meaning of a program is particularly straightforward to implement in Java. The following Java method implements the above definition of function M, assuming the abstract syntax for language Jay that is defined in Appendix B.

```
State M (Program p) {
    return M (p.body, initialState(p.decpart));
}
```

---

11. Some treatments of formal semantics define the meaning of a program as a series of functions in which the name (e.g., $M_{Statement}$) distinguishes it from the rest. In those treatments, $M_{Statement}$: $\Sigma \rightarrow \Sigma$ would be equivalent to our M: $Statement \times \Sigma \rightarrow \Sigma$. This variation is used in the Scheme implementation of Jay semantics in Chapter 8.

```
State initialState (Declarations d) {
  State sigma = new State();
  Value undef = new Value();
  for (int i = 0; i < d.size(); i++)
    sigma.put(((Declaration)(d.elementAt(i))).v, undef);
  return sigma;
}
```

Chapter 4 introduces and discusses the semantics of the remaining abstract program elements. In Section 3.6, we preview that discussion by illustrating the formal semantics of Jay assignment statements and expressions.

3.6 EXAMPLE: SEMANTICS OF JAY ASSIGNMENTS AND EXPRESSIONS

Expressions and assignments abound in imperative programs. Their semantics can be expressed functionally by using the notions of state and state-changing functions that were introduced in Section 3.5. To illustrate, suppose we have the following concrete Jay assignment statement.

```
z = x + 2*y;
```

This statement translates to an abstract *Assignment* whose representation is shown in Figure 3.4, using the methods described in Chapter 2 and the Jay abstract syntax in Appendix B. An abstract *Assignment,* therefore, has two fundamental parts: a source *Expression* and a target *Variable*.

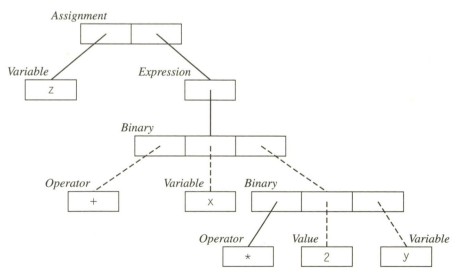

Figure 3.4 Abstract Syntax Sketch for the Jay Assignment
z = x + 2*y;

3.6.1 Meaning of Assignments

The meaning of an *Assignment* can be defined by a state-transforming function of the following kind:

$$M: Assignment \times \Sigma \rightarrow \Sigma$$
$$M(Assignment \text{ a}, State \text{ } \sigma) = \sigma \overline{U} \{\langle a.target, M(a.source, \sigma)\rangle\}$$

What does this say? It is simply a formal way of describing the state that results from transforming the current state σ into a new state that differs from σ only by the pair whose first member is the *Variable* on the left of the *Assignment*. The new pair is constructed by combining that *Variable* with the meaning of the *Expression* on the right of the *Assignment*. The meaning of that *Expression* is (you guessed it!) defined by another function *M*, which will be explained in detail in Subsection 3.6.2.

All we need to know here is that the meaning of an expression is defined by a function *M* that returns a *Value*, since the second member of each pair in the state must be a *Value*. Let's return to our example in Figure 3.4, and let's assume that the current state σ is as follows:

$$\sigma = \{\langle x, 2\rangle, \langle y, -3\rangle, \langle z, 75\rangle\}$$

Intuitively, we expect that the meaning of the source expression in this state, or

$$M(a.source, \sigma) = M(\text{x} + 2\text{*y}, \{\langle x, 2\rangle, \langle y, -3\rangle, \langle z, 75\rangle\})$$

will deliver the *Value* -4, since we are assuming that *M* is fully defined for *Expressions*. Thus,

$$M(\text{z} = \text{x} + 2\text{*y}, \{\langle x, 2\rangle, \langle y, -3\rangle, \langle z, 75\rangle\}) = \{\langle x, 2\rangle, \langle y, -3\rangle, \langle z, 75\rangle\} \overline{U} \{\langle z, -4\rangle\}$$
$$= \{\langle x, 2\rangle, \langle y, -3\rangle, \langle z, -4\rangle\}$$

which completes the state transformation for this assignment.

3.6.2 Meaning of Arithmetic Expressions

In real programming languages, the meaning of an *arithmetic expression* must be carefully and elaborately defined, since expressions have several features that are not readily apparent when they are first read. For example, the innocuous expression x + y/2 may, in the context where x and y are declared as integers, describe a simple integer division followed by an addition. However, if either x or y is declared with type float, this expression conveys somewhat different meaning possibilities, since division may yield a float product, rather than an integer. Moreover, in some languages, x and y may denote vectors or matrices, which would attach an entirely different meaning to this expression. Chapter 4 considers these kinds of issues more carefully, and identifies the elements that must be added to the meaning function for expressions so that situations like these are well-defined.

In this section, we only consider the meaning of a Jay abstract *Expression,* so that we can make some fairly simple assumptions about the types of its arguments and result. That is, we assume that an *Expression* has only int arguments and only the four arithmetic operators (+, −, *, and /) that are defined in the concrete syntax for *Expression* discussed in Chapter 2. Thus, all individual arithmetic operations and results are of type `int`. This discussion uses the following notational conventions:

- $v \in \sigma$ tests whether there is a pair whose *Identifier* is v in the current state σ.
- $\sigma(v)$ is a function that extracts from σ the value in the pair whose *Identifier* is v.

To facilitate the definition of meaning for *Expression,* the auxiliary function *Apply-Binary* is first defined. This function just takes two integer values and calculates an integer result. Here is its definition for the arithmetic operators; note the definition of the operator / is a complicated, mathematical way of specifying the integer quotient of $v1$ divided by $v2$:

$ApplyBinary$: Operator $\times$ *Value* $\times$ *Value* $\rightarrow$ *Value*
$ApplyBinary(Operator\ op,\ Value\ v1,\ Value\ v2)$

$$
\begin{aligned}
&= v1 + v2 && \text{if } op = + \\
&= v1 - v2 && \text{if } op = - \\
&= v1 \times v2 && \text{if } op = * \\
&= floor\left(\left|\frac{v1}{v2}\right|\right) \times sign(v1 \times v2) && \text{if } op = /
\end{aligned}
$$

Using the abstract syntax for *Expression* given in Appendix B, but only insofar as it applies to expressions that have *Integer* operands, we can define the meaning of an *Expression* as follows:

M : *Expression* $\times$ *State* $\rightarrow$ *Value*
$M(Expression\ e,\ State\ \sigma)$

$$
\begin{aligned}
&= e && \text{if } e \text{ is a } Value \\
&= \sigma(e) && \text{if } e \text{ is a } Variable \\
&= ApplyBinary(e.\text{op},\ M(e.\text{term1},\ \sigma),\ M(e.\text{term2},\ \sigma)) && \text{if } e \text{ is a } Binary
\end{aligned}
$$

This function defines the meaning of an expression in a particular state by cases. The first case extracts the value if the expression itself is a *Value.* The second case extracts the value of a variable from the state if the expression is a *Variable.* The third case computes a value by applying the appropriate binary operator to the values of the two terms that accompany the operator, in the case that the expression itself is a binary.

To illustrate, let's return to our familiar example, the expression x+2*y, and assume that it is being evaluated in state $\sigma = \{\langle x, 2\rangle, \langle y, -3\rangle, \langle z, 75\rangle\}$. That is, we want to use these functional definitions to show that $M(x+2*y,\ \{\langle x, 2\rangle, \langle y, -3\rangle, \langle z, 75\rangle\}) = -4$. Recall the abstract representation of the expression x+2*y in Figure 3.4. Since this expression is a *Binary,* we have:

$M(x+2*y,\ \{\langle x, 2\rangle, \langle y, -3\rangle, \langle z, 75\rangle\}) = ApplyBinary(+, A, B)$

$$
\begin{aligned}
\text{where } A &= M(x,\ \{\langle x, 2\rangle, \langle y, -3\rangle, \langle z, 75\rangle\}) \\
\text{and } B &= M(2*y,\ \{\langle x, 2\rangle, \langle y, -3\rangle, \langle z, 75\rangle\})
\end{aligned}
$$

Now the meaning of A is the value of x in state $\sigma = \{\langle x, 2\rangle, \langle y, -3\rangle, \langle z, 75\rangle\}$, or 2, since x is a *Variable.* The meaning of the *Binary B*, however, comes from another application of the function M, which is:

$M(2*y,\ \{\langle x, 2\rangle, \langle y, -3\rangle, \langle z, 75\rangle\}) = ApplyBinary(*, C, D)$

$$
\begin{aligned}
\text{where } C &= M(2,\ \{\langle x, 2\rangle, \langle y, -3\rangle, \langle z, 75\rangle\}) \\
\text{and } D &= M(y,\ \{\langle x, 2\rangle, \langle y, -3\rangle, \langle z, 75\rangle\})
\end{aligned}
$$

The meaning of *C* is 2, since 2 is a *Value*. The meaning of *D* is −3, since y is a *Variable* in state $\sigma = \{\langle x, 2 \rangle, \langle y, -3 \rangle, \langle z, 75 \rangle\}$. With this information, the definition of *ApplyBinary* gives us the meaning of 2*y:

$$M(2{*}y, \{\langle x, 2 \rangle, \langle y, -3 \rangle, \langle z, 75 \rangle\}) = ApplyBinary(*, 2, -3)$$
$$= -6$$

Thus, the meaning of our original expression unravels as follows:

$$M(x{+}2{*}y, \{\langle x, 2 \rangle, \langle y, -3 \rangle, \langle z, 75 \rangle\}) = ApplyBinary(+, 2, -6)$$
$$= -4$$

Note that this example used only the definitions of the functions *ApplyBinary* and *M* defined above, along with the mathematical properties of integer arithmetic to derive this result. It should be clear to readers that the meanings of more complex abstract *Expressions* with binary operations and integer operands are fully defined by these functions.

Several more examples of meaning definition for other Jay abstract program elements will be discussed and illustrated in Chapter 4.

3.6.3 Implementing the Semantic Functions

Implementing the denotational semantics of a programming language provides a ready test bed for experimentation with different semantic models. Implementing the semantics of Jay in Java requires defining a Java class `Semantics` which contains a method for each of the various functions *M* and auxiliary functions (like *ApplyBinary*) that together define the meaning of a program. The methods in this class refer to objects that are defined by the abstract syntax. The abstract syntax thus serves as a bridge between the concrete syntax of a program and its meaning. A complete definition of the Java class `Semantics` is given at the book's website given in the Preface.

A complete collection of semantic methods (that is, one that defines the semantics of *all* the constructs in the abstract syntax) defines, in effect, an interpreter for the language. Such an interpreter can be exercised to test the validity of the semantic definitions, as well as the trade-offs that occur among alternative semantic definitions. In defining a Java interpreter, we recall the limitations of the denotational approach mentioned at the beginning of this chapter. That is, a Java interpreter for Jay, to be complete, relies on the assumption that Java itself has been formally defined. In fact, that is nearly the case—a formal definition of Java has been carefully considered in recent research papers. Interested readers are referred to [Alves-Foss 1999] for more information.

With this strong assumption, we overview the definition of the `Semantics` class by considering the implementations of semantic functions *M* for *Assignment* and *Expression* that were introduced in Subsections 3.6.1–3.6.2. Chapter 4 will continue this development so that a complete interpreter for the small language Jay can be fully constructed.

Since it is a set of unique key-value pairs, the state of a computation is naturally implemented as a Java `Hashtable`, as shown in Figure 3.5. This means that the variable `sigma`, representing σ, can be defined and initialized as follows:

```
State sigma = new State();
```

```
class State extends Hashtable {
// State is implemented as a Java Hashtable

public State( ) { }

public State(Variable key, Value val) { put(key, val); }

public State onion (State t) {
    for (Enumeration e = t.keys(); e.hasMoreElements(); ) {
      Variable key = (Variable)e.nextElement();
      put(key, t.get(key));
    }
    return this;
  }
}
```

| **Figure 3.5   Java Implementation of the State Class**

The functional expression $\sigma(v)$, which extracts from σ the value of variable v, can be implemented in Java as:

```
sigma.get(v)
```

Finally, the overriding union operation, $\sigma \overline{U} \{(v, val)\}$, which either replaces or adds a new variable v and its value *val* to the state, is implemented as the method `onion`, which contains code to insert every pair in the new state `t` into the `Hashtable`, either replacing a pair with a matching key or adding a pair with a new key.

This function provides a straightforward way of implementing the meaning *M* of an *Assignment* statement from its definition:

$M(Assignment$ a, $State$ $\sigma) = \sigma \overline{U} \{\langle a.target, M(a.source, \sigma)\rangle\}$

That is, the Java method in the `Semantics` class is implemented as follows:

```
State M (Assignment a, State sigma) {
    return sigma.onion(new State(a.target, M (a.source, sigma)));
  }
```

The meaning *M* of an arithmetic *Expression* with operators $+$, $-$, $*$, and $/$ follows directly from its definition as well. Since no state transformations occur here, all we are asking is that the Java method return a *Value* (rather than a *State*). Recalling that the meaning of an arithmetic expression is defined as:

$M(Expression$ e, $State$ $\sigma)$
$\quad = e.$val   if e is a *Value*
$\quad = \sigma(e)$ if e is a *Variable*
$\quad = ApplyBinary(e.$op, $M(e.$term1, $\sigma), M(e.$term2, $\sigma))$ if e is a *Binary*

the following Java implementation is suggested:

```
Value M (Expression e, State sigma) {
    if (e instanceof Value)
        return (Value)e;
    if (e instanceof Variable)
        return (Value)(sigma.get((Variable)e));
    if (e instanceof Binary)
        return applyBinary (((Binary)e).op,
                            M(((Binary)e).term1, sigma),
                            M(((Binary)e).term2, sigma));
    return null;
}
```

Considering the function *ApplyBinary*, which is defined for *Expression* as:

$ApplyBinary(Operator\ op,\ Value\ v1,\ Value\ v2)$

$$
\begin{aligned}
&= v1 + v2 && \text{if } op = +\\
&= v1 - v2 && \text{if } op = -\\
&= v1 \times v2 && \text{if } op = *\\
&= floor\left(\left|\frac{v1}{v2}\right|\right) \times sign(v1 \times v2) && \text{if } op = /
\end{aligned}
$$

we have the following direct Java encoding (note that the Java code for integer division is simpler than the mathematical definition).

```
Value applyBinary (Operator op, Value v1, Value v2) {
    if (v1.type.isUndefined() || v2.type.isUndefined())
        return new Value();
    if (op.ArithmeticOp( )) {
        if (op.val.equals(Operator.PLUS))
            return new Value(v1.intValue + v2.intValue);
        if (op.val.equals(Operator.MINUS))
            return new Value(v1.intValue - v2.intValue);
        if (op.val.equals(Operator.TIMES))
            return new Value(v1.intValue * v2.intValue);
        if (op.val.equals(Operator.DIV))
            return new Value(v1.intValue / v2.intValue);
    }
    return null;
}
```

The message in these illustrations is clear. Implementation of these meaning functions *M* in Java is relatively painless and straightforward, once we have settled on a representation scheme for the notion of *State*. The Java `Hashtable` provides that representation directly.

EXERCISES

3.1 Expand the static type checking function *V* for *Declarations* so that it defines the requirement that the type of each variable be taken from a small set of available types, say {int, boolean}. Use the same functional style and abstract syntax for *Declarations* that are discussed in this chapter.

3.2 Expand the Java method that implements the function *V* for *Declarations* so that it implements the additional requirement stated in Question 3.1.

3.3 Argue that the Java method that implements the function *V* for *Declarations* is correct, in the sense that it covers all the cases that the function itself covers.

3.4 Suppose $\sigma_1 = \{\langle x, 1\rangle, \langle y, 2\rangle, \langle z, 3\rangle\}$, $\sigma_2 = \{\langle y, 5\rangle\}$, and $\sigma_3 = \{\langle w, 1\rangle\}$. What are the results of the following operations?

(a) $\sigma_1 \,\overline{U}\, \sigma_2$

(b) $\sigma_1 \,\overline{U}\, \sigma_3$

(c) $\sigma_2 \,\overline{U}\, \sigma_3$

(d) $\varnothing \,\overline{U}\, \sigma_2$

(e) $\sigma_1 \otimes \sigma_3$

(f) $\sigma_2 \otimes \sigma_3$

(g) $(\sigma_1 - (\sigma_1 \otimes \sigma_3)) \cup \sigma_3$

3.5 Complete the operational semantics for the arithmetic, boolean, and logical operators of Jay by writing an execution rule for each operator.

3.6 Derive the complete operational semantics for the following program segment, showing all execution rule applications and deriving the final state that includes the result $\langle \text{fib0}, 3\rangle$. Assume that the initial state $\sigma = \varnothing$.

```
int fib0 = 0;
int fib1 = 1;
int k = 4;
while (k > 0) {
    int temp = fib0;
    fib0 = fib1;
    fib1 = fib0 + temp;
    k = k - 1;
}
```

3.7 Below is a Hoare triple that includes a Jay program segment to compute the product *z* of two integers *x* and *y*.

```
{y ≥ 0}
z = 0;
n = y;
while (n>0) {
    z = z + x;
    n = n - 1;
}
{z = xy}
```

(a) What proof rules in Table 3.1 and additional knowledge about algebra can be used to infer that the precondition in this Hoare triple is equivalent to the assertion $\{y \geq 0 \wedge 0 = x(y - y)\}$?

(b) Using the assignment proof rule, complete the following Hoare triple for the first two statements in this program:

$$\{y \geq 0 \wedge 0 = x(y - y)\}$$
```
z = 0;
n = y;
```
$$\{y \geq 0 \wedge \qquad\qquad\qquad \}$$

(c) Explain how the following can be an invariant for the while loop in this program.

$$\{y \geq 0 \wedge n \geq 0 \wedge z = x(y - n)\}$$

That is, why is this assertion *true* before execution of the first statement in the loop, and why must it be *true* before execution of every successive repetition of the loop?

(d) Show that this invariant holds for a single pass through the loop's statements.

(e) Using the proof rule for loops, show how the invariant is resolved to an assertion that implies the validity of the postcondition for the entire program.

3.8 Write a Jay program segment that computes the sum of a series of integers $a_0, \ldots, a_{n-1}$, given that $n \geq 0$. Write pre- and postconditions for this program, and then develop a proof of its correctness using the proof rules in Table 3.1.

3.9 Write appropriate pre- and postconditions for the method `substring(int,int)` in the class `java.lang.String`.

3.10 Write appropriate pre- and postconditions for the method `indexOf(String)` in the class `java.lang.String`.

3.11 Give a recursive C/C++ implementation of the function *Fib* in Figure 3.3. Prove the partial correctness of your recursive implementation for all values of $n \geq 0$.

3.12 A program has *total correctness* if it (completes its execution and) satisfies its postcondition for *all* input values specified in its precondition.

(a) Experimentally determine the largest value of n for which the function *Fib* in Figure 3.3 delivers a result. What happens when it does not?

(b) Redefine the precondition for *Fib* so that its correctness proof becomes a proof of total correctness.

(c) Revise its correctness proof so that it reflects this new precondition.

3.13 Consider the following sequence of C/C++ statements, which are syntactically valid but have no reasonable semantic interpretation (assuming that i and j have been declared as `int` variables):

```
j = 0;
i = 3/j;
for (i=1; i>-1; i++)
    i--;
```

How are these situations handled when executed by your C/C++ system?

3.14 Give other kinds (beyond those kinds illustrated in the previous question) of C/C++ statements that are syntactically valid but whose meaning cannot be reasonably defined in the semantics of a programming language.

3.15 (a) How does Java define the numerical idea of infinity? (You should look at the *Java Language Specification* [Gosling 1996] for the details.)

(b) Looking at the specifications in the *Java Language Definition,* can you explain in plain English the meaning of the statement i = 3 / j; for all possible values of j, including 0?

(c) (Optional) Can you write a functional definition for the meaning of division in Java using these ideas? Start with the prototype function $M : Division \times \Sigma \rightarrow \Sigma$.

3.16 Consider the expression x + y / 2 in the language C. How many different interpretations does this expression have, depending on the types of x and y. Can you find a language in which this expression can denote vector or matrix arithmetic, when x and y themselves denote vectors or matrices?

3.17 Show how the meaning of each of the following expressions and given states are derived from the functions *M* and *ApplyBinary* given in this chapter. (You developed the abstract syntax for each of these expression as an exercise in Chapter 2.)

(a) $M(z+2)*y, \{\langle x, 2\rangle, \langle y, -3\rangle, \langle z, 75\rangle\})$

(b) $M(2*x+3/y-4, \{\langle x, 2\rangle, \langle y, -3\rangle, \langle z, 75\rangle\})$

(c) $M(1, \{\langle x, 2\rangle, \langle y, -3\rangle, \langle z, 75\rangle\})$

3.18 Show all steps in the derivation of the meaning of the following assignment statement when executed in the given state, using this chapter's definitions of the functions *M* and *ApplyBinary.*

$M(z=2*x+3/y-4, \{\langle x, 6\rangle, \langle y, -12\rangle, \langle z, 75\rangle\})$

Imperative Programming

"I really hate this darn machine;
I wish that they would sell it.
It won't do what I want it to,
but only what I tell it."
Programmer's lament (anonymous)

CHAPTER OUTLINE

Imperative programming is the most widely used and well-developed programming paradigm. It is a paradigm that emerged alongside the first computers and computer programs in the 1940s, and its elements directly mirror the architectural characteristics of most modern computers. This chapter discusses the key programming language features that support the imperative paradigm.

We first complete the treatment of the syntax, type checking, and semantics of the simple imperative language Jay that was begun in Chapters 2 and 3. We then discuss a number of key features of imperative languages that are not in Jay, such as case statements, procedures and parameters, arrays, structures, scope, visibility, and additional data types. While Jay is an approximate syntactic subset of the language C, the type system and semantic features of Jay are representative of other imperative languages as well, including C++, Ada, and Pascal.

The purpose of this discussion is two-fold. First, we continue to use a formal approach to syntax and semantics, which shows how a complete definition of a language can clarify the meaning of its constructs and their variations. Second, we introduce a number of concepts and constructs that are essential for a complete coverage of an imperative language.

4.1 VON NEUMANN MACHINES AND IMPERATIVE PROGRAMMING

In the late 1930s, Alan Turing, John von Neumann, and others recognized that both a program and its data could reside in the main memory of a computer [Turing 1937]. In the 1940s, early computers stored their programs external to the computer's memory, typically using a wire plug-board. The idea of storing a program in the computer's memory led to an enormous increase in the potential power of computers.

The architecture of the so-called von Neumann machine is the basis for imperative programming and imperative languages. The machine has a memory, which contains both program instructions (the *program store*) and data values (the *data store*). Imperative languages have variable declarations, expressions, and commands. Declarations assign names to memory locations and associate types with the stored values. Expressions are interpreted in terms of the current values in the data store; given a name like x, the store returns the current value in the data store that is associated with *x*. Commands are normally executed in the order they appear in the program store, although conditional or unconditional jumps can change the flow of execution. Because of the extensive use of jumps, early programs were often designed using a special kind of graph known as a *flowchart*.

Originally, commands in an imperative language were simple abstractions of the instructions in standard von Neumann machines; these included assignment statements, conditional statements, and branching statements. Assignment statements provided the ability to dynamically update the data store, while conditional and branching statements allowed a set of statements to be either skipped or repeatedly executed. These constructs alone provided an effective basis for writing any program that could be designed.

A programming language is said to be *Turing complete* if it contains integer variables, values, and operations and has assignment statements and the control constructs of statement sequencing, conditionals, and branching statements. All other statement forms (while and for loops, case selections, procedure declarations and calls, etc.) and data types (strings, floating point values, etc.) are provided in modern languages only to enhance the ease of programming various complex applications. The imperative language Jay is thus Turing complete. Our implementation of the semantic model for Jay in other languages in later chapters should convincingly demonstrate that other paradigms have the same computational power as imperative programming.

An *imperative programming language* is one which is Turing complete and also supports a number of fundamental features that have emerged with the evolution of the imperative programming paradigm since the 1940s. These additional features include:

- Data types for real numbers, characters, strings, booleans and their operators;
- Control structures, for and while loops, case (switch) statements;
- Arrays and element assignment;
- Record structures and element assignment;
- Input and output commands;
- Pointers; and
- Procedures and functions.

This chapter addresses most of these features, using those which appear in Jay as a starting point. This discussion utilizes the approach to concrete and abstract syntax, type systems, and denotational semantics given in the previous chapters. The complete Jay syntax, type system, and semantics are summarized in Appendix B, to facilitate cross-referencing.

4.2 NAMING AND VARIABLES

Names, or *identifiers,* in Jay are used to denote locations in the data store and are a subset of the naming conventions in Java. Jay names are composed of letters and digits; the first character of a name must be a letter. There is no restriction on the number of characters in a name, except that a name must fit on a single line. Unlike Java and C, names in Jay are case-insensitive; the names `fib`, `Fib`, and `FIB` are all the same. Other languages, like Ada and Lisp, are also case-insensitive.

Some names in Jay are *reserved,* which means that they may not be used for variable names. These names include the type names `int` and `boolean` as well as the statement words: `while`, `if`, and `else`. Many modern languages choose to limit the number of reserved words to important words that delimit statements or commands.

In some languages (e.g., Pascal and Scheme), some names are merely *predefined;* the programmer is free to redefine them. Library function names generally fit into this category. Such a feature can be either a blessing or a curse. On the one hand, it helps to minimize the number of reserved words in a language. On the other hand, it can lead to confusing programs. For example, consider the following (legal) Pascal program fragment, which redefines the meaning of the predefined identifier `true`, and in effect reverses its usual boolean interpretation:

```
program yecch;
var true : boolean;
begin
    true := false;
    ...
end.
```

In Jay, each location in the data store is declared with a unique name and an associated type. Associated with each name in the data store is a value of the associated type. The unique name requirement is guaranteed via a static (compile-time) type validity check:

$$V(\textit{Declarations d}) = \forall i,j \in \{1, \ldots, n\}: (i \neq j \supset d_i \cdot v \neq d_j \cdot v)$$

Thus, a Jay program cannot declare two different variables with the same name without violating this rule.

Most imperative languages use a more elaborate and generous naming convention that takes into account the *scope* of a declaration. That is, these languages allow multiple uses of the same name as long as their scopes do not overlap. Unlike Jay, these languages support functions and a more elaborate block structure that allows a name to be redeclared and reused. We shall return to this issue later in this chapter and in Chapter 5.

4.3 ELEMENTARY TYPES, VALUES, AND EXPRESSIONS

A Jay *type* is defined as a set of values and a set of operations on those values. The basic data types in Jay are `int` and `boolean`. The type `int` has values $\{\ldots, -2, -1, 0, 1, 2, \ldots\}$ and the operations of addition $(+)$, subtraction $(-)$, multiplication $(*)$, integer division $(/)$, and the relationals $(==, !=, <, <=, >, >=)$. The type `boolean` has values {true, false} and the logical operations (&&, ||, and !).

A Jay *Expression* is either a *Value,* a *Variable,* a *Binary,* or a *Unary.* The type of an expression is defined on the basis of the types of its constituents:

1 The type of an *Expression* consisting of a value is just the type of that value.
2 The type of an *Expression* which is a *Variable* is the type of that *Variable.*
3 The type of a *Binary* is either `int` or `boolean`. If the *Operator* is arithmetic, then the type of the *Expression* is `int`; if relational or boolean, then the type is `boolean`.
4 The type of a *Unary* is `boolean`.

These rules can be expressed formally as a function on *Expressions.* The *type map* of a *Program* is a set of pairs, each of which contains a *Variable* and a *Type,* which are defined by the program's declarations.

$$tm = \{\langle v_1, t_1 \rangle, \langle v_2, t_2 \rangle, \ldots, \langle v_n, t_n \rangle\}$$

Given a type map, the auxiliary function *typeOf* defines the type of an *Expression,* which was given informally above.

typeOf(*Expression e, TypeMap* tm)

$=$ e. type	if e is a *Value*
$= e \in \text{tm} \supset \text{tm}(e)$	if e is a *Variable*
$= e. \textit{op} \in \{\textit{ArithmeticOp}\} \supset \text{int}$	if e is a *Binary*
$= e. \textit{op} \in \{\textit{BooleanOp, RelationalOp}\} \supset \text{boolean}$	
$= e. \textit{op} \in \{\textit{UnaryOp}\} \supset \text{boolean}$	if e is a *Unary*

For example suppose we have the following declarations and three expressions:

```
int x, y;

x+2*y
x<2*y
x<2*y && x>0
```

These declarations give the type map $tm = \{\langle x, int\rangle, \langle y, int\rangle\}$. So the type of these expressions are defined by the *typeOf* function as follows:

typeOf(x+2*y, *tm*) = int	since + ∈ *ArithmeticOp*
typeOf(x<2*y, *tm*) = boolean	since < ∈ *RelationalOp*
typeOf(x<2*y && x>0, *tm*) = boolean	since && ∈ *BooleanOp*

The types of the various subexpressions can be similarly defined using the function *typeOf*.

However, defining the type of an expression doesn't make it valid. An *Expression* is valid if it is either:

1 An int or boolean *Value,*
2 A *Variable* in the program's type map, or
3 A *Binary* or *Unary* whose operands satisfy the following additional constraints.
   (a) A *Binary* whose operator is either an *ArithmeticOp* or *RelationalOp* must have two valid operands of type int/.
   (b) A *Binary* whose operator is a *BooleanOp* must have two valid operands of type boolean.
   (c) A *Unary* must have a *UnaryOp* as its operator and a valid boolean operand.

All other combinations of operand types and operators are invalid *Expressions.* These constraints are defined functionally (and recursively) as follows:

V(Expression e, TypeMap tm)

= true	if *e* is a *Value*
= *e* ∈ tm	if *e* is a *Variable*

= *V(e*.term1, *tm*) ∧ *V(e*.term2, *tm*)
   ∧ *typeOf(e*.term1, tm) = int ∧ *typeOf(e*.term2, tm) = int
                     if *e* is a *Binary* ∧ *e. op* ∈ {*ArithmeticOp, RelationalOp*}
= *V(e*.term1, *tm*) ∧ *V(e*.term2, *tm*)
   ∧ *typeOf(e*.term1, *tm*) = boolean ∧ *typeOf(e*.term2, *tm*) = boolean
                     if *e* is a *Binary* ∧ *e. op* ∈ {*BooleanOp*}
= *V(e*.term, *tm*) ∧ *typeOf(e*.term, *tm*) = boolean ∧ *e.op* = !
                     if *e* is a Unary

Considering again the three expressions above, these rules guarantee that each one is valid. Let's apply these rules to the first expression to assure its type validity.

$$V(x+2*y, tm) = V(x, tm) \wedge V(2*y, tm) \wedge typeOf(x, tm) = int \wedge typeOf(2*y, tm) = int$$
$$\text{since } + \in ArithmeticOp$$

To complete this, we must now apply the appropriate functions *V* and *typeOf* to establish each of the following:

V(x, *tm*)	since x ∈ *tm*
V(2*y, *tm*) = *V*(2, *tm*) ∧ *V*(y, *tm*)	
∧ *typeOf*(2, *tm*) = int ∧ *typeOf*(y, *tm*) = int	since * ∈ *ArithmeticOp*
typeOf(x, *tm*) = *tm*(x) = int	since x is a *Variable*
typeOf(2*y, *tm*) = int	since * ∈ *ArithmeticOp*

The first, third, and fourth of these are direct consequences of the *V* and *typeOf* function definitions. The second of these requires an additional justification of the four conjuncts on its right-hand side. But the functions *V* and *typeOf* allows us to establish them as well:

$V(2, tm)$	since 2 is a *Value*
$V(y, tm)$	since y $\in$ *tm*
$typeOf(2, tm) = \text{int}$	since 2 is a value
$typeOf(y, tm) = tm(y) = \text{int}$	since *y* is a *Variable*

Thus, the type validity of the expression x+2*y for the given type map is confirmed.

Jay is *strongly typed,* so that every variable is bound to a single type and all instances of an operation on a variable can be type-checked. Thus, a type error, in which an operation that is illegal for the type of its operands, cannot occur at run time.

4.3.1 Semantics

An implementation of Jay in Java will hide the actual size (in bits or bytes) for its types. That is, the formal semantic domain for Jay integers and booleans assumes the properties of integers **I** and booleans **B** as they occur in mathematics, while our implementation of Jay semantics relies on Java's own "native" implementation for integers and booleans as a realization for Jay semantics. While this is mathematically unsatisfying (for instance, the mathematical set **I** is infinite in size, while the Java integers are finite), it simplifies our discussion and our ability to implement the formal semantic model.

Nevertheless, the meaning of a Jay *Expression* can be defined functionally, using the semantic domains **I** and **B** as a basis. The meaning of an *Expression* is either a *Value,* the value of a *Variable* in the current state, or the result of applying a binary or unary operator to the meanings of its operands.

$M(Expression\ e,\ State\ \sigma)$

$= e.\text{val}$	if *e* is a *Value*
$= \sigma(e)$	if *e* is a *Variable*
$= ApplyBinary(e.\text{op}, M(e.\text{term1}, \sigma), M(e.\text{term2}, \sigma))$	if *e* is a *Binary*
$= ApplyUnary(e.\text{op}, M(e(.\text{term}, \sigma)))$	if *e* is a *Unary*

The functions *ApplyBinary* (*ApplyUnary*) compute a *Value* when given a binary (unary) *Operator* and two (one) *Value*s as operands. It assumes that the functions $+$, $-$, $*$, $/$ carry their usual mathematical meaning in their appropriate semantic domains. Here is the definition:

$ApplyBinary(Operator\ op,\ Value\ v1,\ Value\ v2)$

$= v1 + v2$	if $op = +$
$= v1 - v2$	if $op = -$
$= v1 \times v2$	if $op = *$
$= floor\left(\left\lvert\dfrac{v1}{v2}\right\rvert\right) \times sign(v1 \times v2)$	if $op = /$
$= v1 < v2$	if $op = <$
$= v1 \le v2$	if $op = <=$
$= v1 = v2$	if $op = ==$
$= v1 \ne v2$	if $op = !=$
$= v1 \ge v2$	if $op = >=$
$= v1 > v2$	if $op = >$
$= v1 \wedge v2$	if $op = \&\&$
$= v1 \vee v2$	if $op = \lVert$

Note the definition of the operator $/$ is a complicated, mathematical way of specifying the integer division of $v1$ divided by $v2$, although the Java implementation is straightforward (actually simpler to express). For example, recall from Chapter 3 how we use these functional definitions to compute the meaning of expressions like x+2*y, assuming a current state like $\sigma = \{\langle x, 4\rangle, \langle y, -7\rangle\}$.

$$
\begin{aligned}
M(x+2*y, \sigma) &= ApplyBinary(+, M(x, \sigma), M(2*y, \sigma)) && \text{since } x+2*y \text{ is a } Binary \\
&= ApplyBinary(+, 4, ApplyBinary(*, M(2, \sigma), M(y, \sigma))) && \\
&&& \text{since } \sigma(x) = 4 \text{ and } 2*y \text{ is a } Binary \\
&= ApplyBinary(+, 4, ApplyBinary(*, 2, -7)) && \text{since } \sigma(y) = -7 \\
&= ApplyBinary(+, 4, -14) && \text{since } 2 \times -7 = -14 \text{ in domain } \mathbf{I} \\
&= -10 && \text{since } 4 - 14 = -10 \text{ in domain } \mathbf{I}
\end{aligned}
$$

While our definitions of the operators for *ApplyBinary* rely on their meanings in the domains **I** and **B**, that is not always necessary or desirable. Consider the meanings of the boolean operators $\wedge$ and $\vee$ which are given in Table 9.1, and which correspond to the Jay operators && and ||. An alternative definition for the meaning of these two operators can be given by:

$ApplyBinary(Operator\ op,\ Value\ v1,\ Value\ v2)$
  $= if\ v1\ then\ v2\ else\ false$ if $op = \&\&$
  $= if\ v1\ then\ true\ else\ v2$ if $op = ||$

In this alternative definition, the boolean operators only evaluate their right operand if needed to determine the truth or falsity of the entire expression. Otherwise the left operand alone is used. Readers should see that this alternative definition is logically equivalent to the traditional one. This evaluation method is called *short-circuit evaluation*. In practice, this definition is preferred because of its obvious efficiency advantage over the traditional definition.

For example, consider the following C-style code for searching an array A containing n values for a given value x. Assume that we are given an index i and the value x to be found. Without short-circuit evaluation, we would need to employ an if statement within the loop to check for the key and break out of the loop when a match is found:

```
int i = 0;
while (i<n) {
    if (A[i] == x) break;
    i = i + 1;
}
```

This code guarantees that the reference A[i] is not evaluated if i<n is not true, so the loop safely avoids exceeding the bounds of the array A.

With short-circuit evaluation, this same code can be written more succinctly as:

```
int i = 0;
while (i<n && A[i] != x)
    i = i + 1;
```

In the while loop test, the second condition is not evaluated in case i<n is *false*, so that an array bounds error cannot occur. Many languages, such as C, C++, and Ada, provide short-circuit evaluation.

4.3.2 Elementary Types in Real Languages

Data types in programming languages can be partitioned into two classes: elementary types and structured types. Elementary types denote data values that can be stored in a fixed memory space, while structured types require a variable memory space to store their values. Table 4.1 summarizes the elementary types that are available in C++, Ada, and Java.

Table 4.1

Elementary Types in Some Programming Languages

Type	C/C++	Ada	Java
Byte			byte
Integer	short, int, long	integer	short, int, long
Real number	float, double, long	float, decimal	float, double
Character	char	character	char
Boolean		boolean	boolean
Pointer	*	access	

Memory requirements for these different types are usually based on the following delineations of memory units:

- *Nibble:* four contiguous bits of memory; a half-byte
- *Byte:* 8 contiguous bits of memory
- *Half-word:* 16 contiguous bits = 2 bytes
- *Word:* 32 contiguous bits of memory = 4 bytes
- *Double word:* 64 contiguous bits = 8 bytes
- *Quad word:* 128 contiguous bits = 16 bytes

In Java, the notion of "byte" is defined as an explicit type, and a Java byte accommodates $2^8 = 256$ distinct binary values. A Java short value occupies a half-word, an int value occupies a word, and a long value occupies a double word.

A Java decimal or real number can be either float or double, depending on the precision and range of values that the programmer needs. A float value requires a 32-bit memory word, while a double value requires a 64-bit word. This is the same in C++, Ada, and most other programming languages.

Real values are represented using scientific notation, which expresses each number as a product of a decimal number with a single nonzero digit to the left of the decimal point and an appropriate power of 10. For example, the number 123.45 written in scientific notation is 1.2345×10^2. While computers use the binary number system rather than the decimal number system, the principle is the same. A real value is written as a product of a binary real value with a single 1 to the left of the binary point and an appropriate power of 2.

Consider representing the decimal real number 3.375 in binary scientific notation. Conversion to binary is done by splitting the number into its integer and fractional parts and converting each part separately to binary. The integer part of 3.375 is 3, which in binary is 11_2. The fraction part 0.375 happens to have a convenient form in binary, since $0.375 = 0.25 + 0.125 = 2^{-2} + 2^{-3} = 0.011_2$. Thus,

$$3.375_{10} = 11.011_2 = 1.1011_2 \times 2^1$$

Modern computers use the IEEE 754 standard for floating point values [Goldberg 1991]. This standard is summarized in Figure 4.1.

Single precision:

Double precision:

| **Figure 4.1** **IEEE 754 Floating Point Number Representation**

A single precision normalized floating point number has a sign bit s (0 denotes nonnegative and 1 denotes negative), an exponent e denoting a power of 2 between -126 and 127 (called "excess 127 notation"), and a mantissa m denoting a binary fraction in the range 0 through 2^{23}. Altogether, this represents the number $\pm 1.m \times 2^{127-e}$. The double precision version allows more bits for the exponent and binary fraction, thus adding to the range of values that can be represented, as well as their number of significant digits.

Single precision allows a range of approximately $\pm 10^{38}$ to 10^{-38}, while double precision allows a range of $\pm 10^{308}$ to 10^{-308}. Single precision numbers have about 7 significant decimal digits in the mantissa, while double precision number precision have 16 significant decimal digits. The IEEE 754 standard also provides unique representations for unusual numbers, like infinity (all 1s in the exponent and all 0s in the mantissa) and "not a number" (NaN) (all 1s in the exponent and not all 0s in the mantissa). Denormalized floating point numbers are also defined to provide a representation for numbers that are smaller than the smallest normalized value (all 0s in the exponent and any nonzero mantissa).

To continue our example, consider the decimal number 3.375. It has a sign bit of 0, since the number is positive. The exponent is 128 in decimal or 1000 0000 in binary, since the exponent is stored in excess 127 notation. Finally, the mantissa is the value after the binary point: 101 1000 0000 0000 0000 0000 in single precision binary. Putting together the sign, exponent, and mantissa, we get:

1 1000 0000 101 1000 0000 0000 0000 0000

Many exact decimal numbers like 0.2 do not have exact representations in binary floating point; in particular $5 \times 0.2 \neq 1.0$. These and other problems associated with floating point arithmetic are discussed in some detail in [Hennessy 1998, Chapter 4] and in [Goldberg 1991].

Some languages, like Cobol and PL/I, provide an additional decimal data type, called *fixed point,* which is stored in binary coded decimal (BCD). A fixed point decimal number has a fixed number of digits to the right of the decimal point; it uses a *nibble,* or half-byte, for every digit in the number and the rightmost nibble for the sign (for a signed decimal number). For example, the number 213.1 has a three-byte fixed point representation shown in Figure 4.2. The compiler keeps track of the number of decimal places and uses shifting to align the decimal point as needed.

Figure 4.2 Fixed Point Representation for 213.1

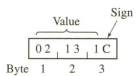

Fixed point decimal is preferred in banking and other accounting applications where 2-digit decimal accuracy is required to precisely represent a currency value (like $0.20). IBM mainframe and some RS/6000 computers provide hardware support for fixed point arithmetic.

A Java `char` value uses the Unicode [Unicode 2000] character set, which is a 16-bit standard for character encoding. Traditionally, programming languages have used the more conventional ASCII[1] 7-bit standard. The Unicode set provides a rich assortment of characters that allow Java programs to embody a more international vocabulary than its predecessors. A sampling of the Unicode character set's coverage of the world's languages and other character sets is given in Table 4.2.

As the table suggests, the Unicode standard includes codes for character sets that span the world's major written languages. It also includes punctuation marks, diacritics, mathematical symbols, and a wide array of other technical symbols. It provides codes for modifying characters, such as the tilde ($\sim$), and codes that are used to encode accented letters (ñ). The current version of Unicode defines codes for 49,194 characters from the world's alphabets and other symbol sets.

The language C does not recognize character strings as a distinct data type. Instead strings are encoded as arrays of ASCII characters, one character per byte, terminated by a *nul* character (all bits zero). Thus, the string "hello" would be encoded in hexadecimal as:

```
68 65 6c 6c 6f 00 ...
```

Depending on the declared length of the character string array, the characters following the ASCII character *nul* would have unknown or undefined values. Thus, in the

---

1. ASCII is the "American Standard Code for Information Interchange," which is a subset of the ISO standard 8859-1 8-bit code known as the "Latin-1" character set. Latin-1 is properly embedded within the Unicode set, as shown in Table 4.2.

Table 4.2

Sampling of the
Unicode Character
Set

Unicode Value (hex)	Characters	Unicode Value (hex)	Characters
\u0000-\u007F	ASCII set	\u0F00-\u0FBF	Tibetan
\u0100-\u024F	Latin extended	\u10A0-\u10FF	Georgian
\u0300-\u036F	diacritics	\u2000-\u206FF	punctuation
\u0370-\u03FF	Greek	\u20A0-\u20CF	currency
\u0400-\u04FF	Cyrillic	\u2190-\u21FF	arrows
\u0530-\u058F	Armenian	\u2200-\u22FF	mathematics
\u0590-\u05FF	Hebrew	\u2300-\u23FF	technical
\u0600-\u06FF	Arabic	\u2440-\u245F	OCR
\u0B80-\u0BFF	Tamil	\u25A0-\u25FF	geometrics
\u0C00-\u0C7F	Telugu	\u2700-\u27BF	Dingbats
\u0C80-\u0CFF	Kannada	\u30A0-\u30FF	Katakana
\u0E00-\u0E7F	Thai	\u3200-\u32FF	CJK letters
\u0E80-\u0EFF	Lao	\uAC00-\uD7A3	Hangul

language C the string "hello" requires 6 storage bytes, one for each character plus one for the *nul* character.

In contrast, in the language Java each character in a string is stored in Unicode using 2 bytes per character. Furthermore, a string is a language-defined object type, so its exact representation is hidden from the programmer. A string has an exact size needed to store all the characters in the string. Thus, the hexadecimal representation of the Java string "hello" would be:

```
00 68 00 65 00 6c 00 6c 00 6f
```

The left-hand byte of every ASCII character in Unicode is zero (hex 00).

4.3.3 Expressions in Real Languages

In actual programming languages, a richer variety of operators, and hence a richer variety of expressions, is available. Moreover, languages like C, C++, Ada, and Java perform various tasks automatically during the evaluation of an expression. Consider the summary of C, C++, and Java operators shown in Table 4.3.

This table reveals a lot about the evolution of C-like languages over the last three decades. First, these languages provide many more operators than Jay, although Jay's operator set is an approximate subset of these. Second, note that the C operators are a proper subset of the C++ operators. This reflects the fact that C++ was designed as a true extension of C, so that C++ must provide all of C's operators. Third, Java provides several fewer operators than C++, reflecting a design goal of simplification rather than extension.

Looking at the details of Table 4.3, we note that the operators are listed in decreasing order of precedence. This ordering reflects the structure BNF grammars that formally define the syntax of C/C++/Java expressions. We also note that the smaller set

Table 4.3

Summary of Operations and Operators in C, C++, and Java

Operation (decreasing precedence)	C Operators	C++ Operators	Java Operators
Scope resolution		::	
Member selection (2), subscripting, function call, size of object or type	. -> [] () n/a	. -> [] () sizeof	n/a n/a [] () n/a
Unary negation, complement, bitwise complement, increment, decrement, address-of, dereference, allocate, deallocate, cast	- ! ~ ++ -- & * n/a n/a () sizeof	- ! ~ ++ -- & * new delete () n/a	- ! ~ ++ -- n/a n/a n/a n/a () n/a
Member selection (2)	,	.* ->*	,
Multiply, divide, modulo	* / %	* / %	* / %
Add, subtract	+ -	+ -	+ -
Left shift, right shift	<< >>	<< >>	<< >>
Less than, less or equal, greater than, greater or equal	< <= > >=	< <= > >=	< <= > >=
Equal, not equal	== !=	== !=	== !=
Bitwise ∧	&	&	&
Bitwise exclusive ∨	^	^	^
Bitwise inclusive ∨	|	|	|
Logical ∧	&&	&&	&&
Logical inclusive ∨	||	||	||
Conditional expression	? :	? :	? :
Assignment	= *= /= %= += -= <<= >>= &= |= ^=	= *= /= %= += -= <<= >>= &= |= ^=	= *= /= %= += -= <<= >>= &= |= ^=
Exception		throw	
Sequencing	,	,	,

of operators that appear in Jay expressions (the arithmetic, relational, and boolean operators) is consistent in its precedence ordering with that of the larger set shown in this table. That is, multiplication and division have higher precedence than addition and subtraction, which in turn have higher precedence than the relational and boolean operators.

It may seem that several C operators, like bitwise inclusive ∨ and all 11 variations of the assignment operator, appear to be obscure and have questionable value in practice. On the contrary, one of C's design goals is to facilitate programming at the operating system level, where strategic use of bitwise operations that save a few nanoseconds of running time is a valuable exercise.

We also note that some of these operators, like sizeof, address-of, and dereference, are not carried by Java. Java designers strived to remove the system-level details from the programmers' vernacular. Unlike its predecessors, this language does not let the programmer use and manipulate pointers (references) or explicitly manage the details of the run-time heap. A more thorough discussion of garbage collection and run-time storage management is the subject of Chapter 5.

Also, note that assignment is an operator in these languages, so that a C/C++/Java assignment may occur in any context where any other expression may occur. This is a strict departure from Jay, Pascal, and Ada, where assignment is a kind of statement and nothing more. The implication of treating assignment as an operator is that intermediate assignments may be embedded within an expression while it is being evaluated. Consider the following C/C++/Java loop which contains an array referencing expression:

```
Sum = 0;
while (i<n)
    Sum = Sum + A[i++];
```

Here, the index i is post-incremented, after the selection of A[i] is taken from the array A and added to Sum, which saves an additional line in the program for separately incrementing i.

We also point out that the operators || and && in these languages use short-circuit evaluation, with the payoff in reliability discussed above. The conditional operator ?: is an unusual one, and is a device for embedding a complete "if...then...else" statement inside a larger expression. Its general form is:

```
<exp1> ? <exp2> : <exp3>
```

Which reads "if <exp1> then <exp2> else <exp3>." Consider the following statement which computes c as the maximum of a and b:

```
c = (a > b) ? a : b ;
```

This single statement is thus equivalent to the conventional form:

```
if (a>b)
    c = a;
else
    c = b;
```

4.3.4 Operator Overloading, Conversion, and Casting

C, C++, and Java all offer extensive support for overloading their operators and converting intermediate results to compatible types along the way. An operator is *overloaded* if it can be used in different contexts with different types of operands and compute a different result. For example, consider the following assignment:

```
k = i / j
```

In the language Jay, this expression always carries the same meaning, since the only data type available is int. When executed, this statement computes the integer quotient of two integer values and assigns that result as the new value of k.

In languages like C, C++, and Java, the situation is more complex. For instance in Java, the outcome of this assignment depends on the arithmetic types of i, j, and k and admits the possibility of an intermediate conversion along the way.[2] A *conversion* (sometimes called a *cast*) is just the translation of a data value from one type to an equivalent value in another type. For instance, in Java the int value 1 is equivalent to the float value 1.0, which is equivalent to the double value 1.0d.

The rules for conversion in Java are long and tedious.[3] Here is a summary of the ones that apply to expressions with arithmetic operators and values.

- If either operand is of type double, convert the other one to double, and compute a double result.

- Otherwise, if either operand is float, convert the other to float and compute a float result.

- Otherwise, if either operand is long, convert the other to long and compute a long result.

- Otherwise, convert both operands to type int and compute an int result.

Similar rules are effective for C, C++, and other languages, thus saving the programmer the tedium of explicitly converting intermediate values in most arithmetic calculations. Returning to our example, we see that the types of i and j will determine the type and value of the result of division that is specified. For example, if i is int and j is double, the value of i will be converted to an equivalent double value, and a double quotient will be computed. If, on the other hand, both operands happen to be int, then no conversion will be done and an int quotient will be computed.

Assignment conversion in Java, as might be expected, follows a somewhat more restrictive set of rules.

- If the expression on the right has type byte, short, char, int, long, or float, its value may be "widened" to an equivalent double value.

- If it is byte, short, char, int, or long, it may be widened to a float value.

- If it is byte, short, char, or int, it may be widened to a long value.

- If it is byte, short, or char, it may be widened to int.

- If it is byte or short, it may be widened to char.

- If it is byte, it may be widened to short.

The process of widening is the graceful conversion of a narrower type (set of values) to a type that is a superset of those values. For instance, all bytes are int's, but not all int's are bytes. Thus, in our example, if the type of k is double and the type of the result

---

2. In C++, the situation is more complex, since it permits operators like / to be redefined for new combinations of operands. For instance, if i, j, and k are character strings, the assignment k = i/j might leave k with the string that contains all characters of i that are not in j (sort of a specialized string reduction operator). This can be accomplished in C++ by redefining the meaning of / for the special case in which its two operands are character strings.

3. For a more detailed treatment, see the *Java Language Specification,* Chapter 5.

of i/j is int, a widening will automatically be performed which converts that result to double before it is assigned to k.

Suppose the reverse is true; that is, suppose k is int and the result of i/j is double. In this case, a "narrowing" conversion takes place, in which information may be lost. For instance, there's no way to convert the double value 1.5d to an int without losing the fraction. So there are additional rules in Java that govern assignment conversion and take this into account. That is, a narrowing conversion may be used in an assignment if all of the following are true:

- The expression on the right is a constant expression.
- The type of the variable on the left is byte, short, or char.
- The value of the expression is representable in the type of the variable on the left.

Other conversions are not possible and, because of Java's commitment to strong static typing, all errors of this sort can be detected at compile time. In our example, for instance, if k is an int and the result of i/j is double, a compile time (type) error will result. This is not the case for C, C++, and other languages, whose type systems are less secure.

Explicit conversion from one type to another can be specified using the *cast* operator. Thus, in our well-worn example, we may cast the double quotient i/j to int before assigning it to the int variable k:

```
k = (int)(i/j);
```

Now a different dynamic is at work. Here, we are overriding the warning that information may be lost (casting our fate to the wind, so to speak!), and we are saying it's okay to go ahead and truncate that double quotient—the program can live with the resulting loss of information. What Java does that other languages typically don't do is force the programmer to explicitly override a negative consequence rather than allow it to slip through until run time where the consequence might be much more difficult to detect.

In Subsection 4.3.5, we explore the language design implications of just one of these features, namely to overload the arithmetic operators with floating point, as well as integer arithmetic.

4.3.5 Jay Extension: Floating Point Numbers and Operators

Suppose we want to add a floating point type to Jay, much as it appears in C or in Java. A number of steps are needed.

First, in the concrete syntax all of the arithmetic and relational operators would be *overloaded,* which means that, for example, an addition denoted by + could represent either an integer addition or a floating point addition. At the machine level, these are fundamentally different operations because of the way in which integer values are stored versus floating point values. Even more importantly, an integer division always results in an integer value, with truncation toward zero. Thus, 1/3 as an integer divide results in the value 0, while a floating point divide of 1.0/3.0 results in an approximately accurate value of 0.333333. . . .

Second, in the abstract syntax, each overloaded operator has different operators for the floating point semantic domain than for the integer domain. For instance, integer addition might be denoted by + and floating point addition by another operator, say +*f*.

Furthermore, some concrete expressions have operators of both types, integer and floating point. These are often called *mixed-mode* expressions. In this case, the integer value is automatically *coerced* (or "promoted") to an equivalent value in floating point before the operator is applied, and this activity would be made explicit at the abstract syntax level. For instance, the sum of the floating point variable x and the integer variable i would be given in the abstract syntax as shown in Figure 4.3.

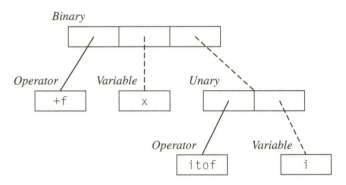

Figure 4.3   Abstract Syntax for the Mixed-Mode Expression x+i

Assume here that the itof Unary operator has been added to the semantic domain of Jay and the abstract definition of Unary operations now includes this operator. This, therefore, is the abstract representation of the following concrete expression that describes the sum of a float and an integer.

```
x + i
```

Note that the implicit conversion of i to floating point is made explicit in the abstract syntax by the type-checker, after discovering the difference between x and i in the type map. This mimics what compilers do when compiling programs in languages such as Java.

Further, the Jay semantic definition of the meaning of *ApplyBinary* needs to be extended to accommodate both integer and floating point arithmetic and comparison operations. For example, here are the extensions for floating point arithmetic:

$$
\begin{aligned}
ApplyBinary(Operator\ op,\ Value\ v1,\ Value\ v2) &= v1 + v2 &&\text{if } op = +\text{f} \\
&= v1 - v2 &&\text{if } op = -\text{f} \\
&= v1 \times v2 &&\text{if } op = *\text{f} \\
&= v1\ /\ v2 &&\text{if } op = /\text{f}
\end{aligned}
$$

Completion of this sketch as a full extension of Jay with floating point arithmetic is left as an exercise.

4.4   **SYNTAX AND SEMANTICS OF JAY STATEMENTS**

This section discusses the formal syntax, type checking validity rules, and semantics of statements in Jay, which are characteristic of the basic statements found in all imperative languages. There are five kinds of statements in Jay. The concrete syntax identifies these as follows:

Statement → ; | *Block* | *Assignment* | *IfStatement* | *WhileStatement*

The abstract syntax defines the following five corresponding statement categories:

Statement = *Skip* | *Block* | *Assignment* | *Conditional* | *Loop*

While using some different names at the abstract level might seem to be unnecessarily pedantic, we shall see later that these abstract syntax categories are more general than their corresponding categories in the concrete syntax. For instance, there are several concrete realizations of the abstract notion of *Loop,* only one of which is a *WhileStatement.*

4.4.1 *Syntax and Type Checking*

The type checking rules for statements are intuitive; a *Statement* is valid for a collection of declared variables (defined as the program's *type map*) if all the elements of the particular statement category that it represents are valid. This is summarized in Figure 4.4 for the five different statement types in Jay.

$$
\begin{aligned}
V(\textit{Statement } s, \textit{TypeMap } \text{tm}) &= \text{true} && \text{if } s \text{ is a } \textit{Skip} \\
&= s.\text{target} \in \text{tm} \wedge V(s.\text{source, tm}) \wedge tm(s.\text{target}) = typeOf(s.\text{source, } tm) \\
&&& \text{if } s \text{ is an } \textit{Assignment} \\
&= V(s.\text{test, tm}) \wedge typeOf(s.\text{test, tm}) = \text{boolean} \wedge V(s.\text{thenbranch, tm}) \wedge V(s.\text{elsebranch, tm}) \\
&&& \text{if } s \text{ is a } \textit{Conditional} \\
&= V(s.\text{test, tm}) \wedge typeOf(s.\text{test, tm}) = \text{boolean} \wedge V(s.\text{body, tm}) \\
&&& \text{if } s \text{ is a } \textit{Loop} \\
&= V(b_1, \text{tm}) \wedge V(b_2, \text{tm}) \wedge \cdots \wedge V(b_n, \text{tm}) && \text{if } s \text{ is a } \textit{Block} = b_1 b_2 \ldots b_n \wedge n \geq 0
\end{aligned}
$$

| Figure 4.4   Type Checking Validity Function for Jay Statement Categories

A Jay *Skip* statement is written as a standalone semicolon in the concrete syntax and translated into an abstract (and empty) *Skip* statement. A *Skip* statement is always valid for type checking.

The Jay concrete and abstract syntax and type checking functions for an *Assignment* and an *Expression* were discussed in Chapters 2 and 3. Readers are referred to those earlier discussions to review these features.

The concrete syntax of a Jay *IfStatement* is recursive, and the syntactic ambiguity of the definition below was also discussed in Chapter 2.

IfStatement → if (*Expression*) *Statement* |
          if (*Expression*) *Statement* else *Statement*

In the concrete syntax, recall that the else part is optional, which translates into a *Skip* statement in the following abstract syntax for *Conditional* when it is missing.

Conditional = Expression test; *Statement* thenbranch, elsebranch

An abstract *Conditional* statement has type validity, according to Figure 4.4, when the following requirements are met:

- Its test must be a valid expression and have type boolean, and
- Its thenpart and elsepart must be valid statements.

This is a stricter type-checking requirement than that found in many programming languages. For example, C has no boolean type. Instead, it interprets the integer values 0 and nonzero as *false* and *true,* respectively. Requiring only that an if statement's test be an expression, C compilers convert the result of that expression to an integer value with this particular "pseudoboolean" interpretation. Java, on the other hand, has the boolean type and type-checking requirements for if statements that mirror those of Jay.

The concrete syntax of a Jay *WhileStatement* is much like an *IfStatement,* except that it is introduced by the keyword `while`.

WhileStatement → while (*Expression*) *Statement*

The Jay *WhileStatement* translates into an abstract *Loop,* which has a test and a body:

Loop = Expression test; *Statement* body

For the *Loop* to be type valid, the function *V* in Figure 4.4 requires that:

- The test must be a valid expression of type boolean, and
- The body must be a valid statement.

Finally, the concrete syntax of a Jay *Block* provides a syntactic device for the programmer to logically group a sequence of statements into a single statement, often as part of an *IfStatement* or a *WhileStatement:*

Block → {*Statements*}

Abstractly, a *Block* is just a sequence of statements:

*Block = Statement**

For type checking, a *Block* is valid if each of its statements is valid, which is formally defined in Figure 4.4.

For example, the following simple Jay program fragment can be used to convince ourselves that these rules together guarantee strong type checking for any concrete Jay program.

```
while (i>0) {
    if (i%2==1) odds = odds+1;
    i = i-1;
}
```

Let's assume that all the variables in this segment are declared: i and odds, giving the following type map *tm*:

$tm = \{\langle i, int \rangle, \langle odds, int \rangle\}$

Clearly, the abstract statement types that come into play in this program are *Loop, Block, Conditional,* and *Assignment.* We want to establish the truth of the following function:[4]

V(while (i>0) { if (i%2==1) odds = odds+1; i = i−1;}, *tm*)

Since this is an abstract *Loop,* we need to show that both of the following are *true*:

(a) *V*(i>0, *tm*) ∧ *typeOf*(i>0, *tm*) = boolean
(b) *V*({ if (i%2==1) odds = odds+1; i = i−1;}, *tm*)

Now (a) can be shown to be true because i>0 is valid in the given type map and its type is boolean (using the *V* and *typeOf* functions for Jay *Expressions,* as discussed in an earlier section).

Part (b) requires an application of the validity rule for *Block*s. Thus, we must show that both of the following are true:

(b_1) *V*(if (i%2==1) odds = odds + 1;, *tm*)
(b_2) *V*(i = i−1;, *tm*)

Here, (b_1) requires a validity check on an abstract *Conditional,* while (b_2) requires a validity check on an *Assignment.* Thus, Figure 4.4 suggests that we establish the following to be *true*:

(b_{11}) *V*(i%2==1, *tm*) ∧ *typeOf*(i%2==1, *tm*) = boolean
(b_{12}) *V*(odds = odds+1;, *tm*)
(b_{21}) i ∈ tm
(b_{22}) *V*(i−1, *tm*)
(b_{23}) *tm*(i) = *typeOf*(i−1, *tm*)

Piece by piece, the type validity of this program fragment is thus established, with a final few steps required to establish the type and validity of the *Expression*s in (b_{11}), the validity of the *Assignment* in (b_{12}) and the *Expression* in (b_{22}), and the equality of the type of i and the type of the *Expression* i−1 in (b_{23}). These steps are left as an exercise.

4.4.2 Semantics

The meaning of a Jay *Statement* is defined on the basis of the particular type of statement that it represents, alongside the current state, σ, of the computation as discussed in earlier sections. Since there are only five different types of Jay statements, we consider each of them in turn, beginning with the trivial one.

That is, the meaning of a *Skip* statement is an identity function on the state; since it is an empty statement it cannot change the current state of the computation.

M(*Skip* s, *State* σ) = σ

---

4. For brevity and clarity, we use concrete, rather than abstract tree representations in this illustration.

The meaning of an abstract *Assignment* and its expression was discussed extensively in Chapter 3. Here is a brief example, which will help refresh those ideas:

```
x = a + b;
```

Suppose the current state has both a and b, as follows:

$$\sigma = \{\langle a, 3\rangle, \langle b, 1\rangle, \langle x, 88\rangle\}$$

Since Jay is strongly typed, this *Assignment* is valid by the time the following meaning function is applied. Thus, run-time type errors (such as assigning a boolean value to x in the current state) cannot occur.

$$M(x=a+b;, \sigma) = \sigma \, \overline{U} \, \{\langle x, M(a+b, \sigma)\rangle\}$$

Readers should see that the meaning of this *Assignment* requires taking the values 3 and 1 from the current state, summing them, and producing a new state that replaces the value of x with the sum 4. Note also that this function is well-defined only if a and b have been assigned values before this statement is interpreted. If either a or b do not appear in the type map, the function M for this assignment is not defined. This is another instance in which the meaning functions of denotational semantics are necessarily partial functions.

The meaning of an abstract *Conditional* depends on the truth or falsity of the test in the current state. If the test is true, then the meaning of the *Conditional* is the meaning of the `thenbranch`; otherwise, it is the meaning of the `elsebranch`:

$$\begin{aligned} M(\textit{Conditional } c, \textit{State } \sigma) &= M(c.\text{thenbranch}, \sigma) && \text{if } M(c.\text{test}, \sigma) \text{ is } \textit{true} \\ &= M(c.\text{elsebranch}, \sigma) && \text{otherwise} \end{aligned}$$

Consider the following code to compute the maximum of 2 numbers a and b:

```
if (a > b)
    max = a;
else
    max = b;
```

Given the state $\sigma = \{\langle a, 3\rangle, \langle b, 1\rangle\}$, the meaning of this conditional gives the following interpretation:

$$\begin{aligned} M(\text{if } (a>b) \text{ max=a; else max=b;}, \sigma) &= M(\text{max=a;}, \sigma) && \text{if } M(a>b, \sigma) \text{ is } \textit{true} \\ &= M(\text{max=b;}, \sigma) && \text{otherwise} \end{aligned}$$

Using the definition of $M(\textit{Expression}, \sigma)$, we see that $M(a>b, \sigma)$ is *true* in this particular state, so that the meaning of this Conditional is the same as that of the first *Assignment*, or $M(\text{max=a;}, \sigma)$. Knowing what we do about the meaning of *Assignment*s, we see that the final state becomes:

$$\sigma = \{\langle a, 3\rangle, \langle b, 1\rangle, \langle max, 3\rangle\}$$

The meaning of a *Block* is just that of its statements applied to the current state in the order they appear. That is, if a *Block* has no statements the state is not changed.

Otherwise, the state resulting from the meaning of the first *Statement* in the *Block* becomes the basis for defining the meaning of the rest of the block. This is a recursive definition.

$$M(Block\ b,\ State\ \sigma) = \sigma \qquad\qquad\qquad\qquad\qquad \text{if } b = \varnothing$$
$$= M((Block)b_{2...n},\ M((Statement)b_1,\ \sigma)) \quad \text{if } b = b_1 b_2 \ldots b_n$$

Consider the following *Block* with the initial state $\sigma = \{\langle i, 3\rangle, \langle fact, 1\rangle\}$.

```
{fact = fact * i; i = i - 1;}
```

The meaning of this is defined as follows:

$$M(\{fact=fact*i; i=i-1;\}, \sigma) = M(\{i=i-1;\}, M(fact=fact*i;, \sigma))$$
$$= M(\{\}, M(i=i-1;, M(fact=fact*i;, \sigma)))$$
$$= M(\{\}, M(i=i-1;, M(fact=fact*i;, \{\langle i, 3\rangle, \langle fact, 1\rangle\})))$$
$$= M(\{\}, M(i=i-1;, \{\langle i, 3\rangle, \langle fact, 3\rangle\}))$$
$$= M(\{\}, \{\langle i, 2\rangle, \langle fact, 3\rangle\})$$
$$= \{\langle i, 2\rangle, \langle fact, 3\rangle\}$$

The first two lines and the last line in this interpretation unravel the meaning of a block, while the remaining lines apply the two assignments to the original state in the order that they appear in the *Block*. This illustrates that we can formally explain what happens when any sequence of statements is executed.

Semantically, a *Loop* specifies the repeated execution of its body until its test becomes *false*. This means that the meaning function *M* for a *Loop* is either an identity (if the test is not *true*) or the meaning of the same loop when applied to the state resulting from executing its body one time. This is a recursive definition.

$$M(Loop\ l,\ State\ \sigma) = M(l,\ M(l.body,\ \sigma)) \qquad \text{if } M(l.test,\ \sigma) \text{ is } true$$
$$= \sigma \qquad\qquad\qquad\qquad\quad \text{otherwise}$$

Consider the following example that computes the factorial of N, given an initial state $\sigma = \{\langle N, 3\rangle\}$.

```
fact = 1;
i = N;
while (i > 1) {
    fact = fact * i;
    i = i - 1;
}
```

It should be clear that the meaning of the first two statements in this example leaves the state $\sigma = \{\langle i, 3\rangle, \langle fact, 1\rangle, \langle N, 3\rangle\}$. Now, recalling what we know about the meaning of the block {fact = fact * i; i = i − 1;} from the previous paragraph, we can begin to analyze the meaning of this particular *Loop* as follows:

$$M(while(i>1)\{fact=fact*i; i=i-1;\}, \sigma)$$
$$= M(while(i>1)\{fact=fact*i; i=i-1;\}, M(\{fact=fact*i; i=i-1;\}, \{\langle i, 3\rangle, \langle fact, 1\rangle\}))$$

That is, we interpret the body once in the given state, and then pass the resulting state back to the function *M* for the *Loop* itself. This gives the following series of state transformations:

$(M(\text{while}(i>1)\{\text{fact}=\text{fact}*i; \ i=i-1;\}, \sigma))$
$\quad = M(\text{while}(i>1)\{\text{fact}=\text{fact}*i; \ i=i-1;\}, M(\{\text{fact}=\text{fact}*i; \ i=i-1;\}, \{\langle i, 3\rangle, \langle \text{fact}, 1\rangle, \langle N, 3\rangle\}))$
$\quad = M(\text{while}(i>1)\{\text{fact}=\text{fact}*i; \ i=i-1;\}, M(\{\text{fact}=\text{fact}*i; \ i=i-1;\}, \{\langle i, 2\rangle, \langle \text{fact}, 3\rangle, \langle N, 3\rangle\}))$
$\quad = M(\text{while}(i>1)\{\text{fact}=\text{fact}*i; \ i=i-1;\}, M(\{\text{fact}=\text{fact}*i; \ i=i-1;\}, \{\langle i, 1\rangle, \langle \text{fact}, 6\rangle, \langle N, 3\rangle\}))$
$\quad = \{\langle i, 1\rangle, \langle \text{fact}, 6\rangle\}$

Of course, for each of the middle three lines, the function *M* for *Block, Assignment,* and *Expression* is used to transform the state that is shown on the line below it. The last line results from the test i>1 becoming *false*, in which case the state is unchanged. This function is, of course, a partial function too, since a *Loop* can be written that never halts. In that case, it should be clear that the last line in interpretations like the one above will never be reached.

This completes our treatment of semantics for the language Jay. An implementation of Jay's type checking and semantic functions in Java is suggested in Appendix B. A complete Java implementation of Jay syntax, type system, and semantics, as well as animations of several Jay programs, can be found at the book's website given in the Preface. These tools can be used to exercise the functions discussed in this chapter with various sample Jay programs.

4.5 SYNTAX AND SEMANTICS OF STATEMENTS IN REAL LANGUAGES

Most imperative languages are not as simple as Jay in the variety of statement types that they offer. In this section, we discuss the syntax and semantics of several other statements that are commonly found in imperative languages. These include other forms of the loop and conditional statements as well as the continue and break statements. In this exercise, we shall see that the Jay abstract syntax provides a robust target for representing most of these statement types. That is, the general abstract class *Loop* accommodates several types of loops beyond the Jay *WhileStatement,* and the abstract class *Conditional* accommodates other kinds of conditionals beyond the Jay *IfStatement.*

4.5.1 For Loops

Most imperative languages have a counting loop statement, which captures the following recurring pattern:

```
i = initial;
while (i<=final) {
    Statement
    i = i + increment;
}
```

As this example shows, a counting loop statement is logically unnecessary in an imperative language, since it can be easily simulated with a while loop. However, most languages provide a counting loop statement because of its economy and utility in many programming situations.

A simple C/C++/Java-like counting loop, called a *for loop,* has the following concrete syntax:

ForStatement → for *(Assignment1$_{opt}$; Expression$_{opt}$; Assignment2$_{opt}$) Statement*

The control of a *ForStatement* has three parts, which serve to count how many times the *Statement* is executed. The first part uses an *Assignment* to initialize a counting variable, the second part supplies in *Expression* the condition for repeating the loop, and the third part specifies how the counting variable is to be incremented after each repetition of *Statement.* (If the first and third parts are not given, the *ForStatement* degenerates to a *WhileStatement.*) Thus, the above example can be rewritten as a *ForStatement* as follows:

```
for (i=initial; i<=final; i=i+1)
    Statement
```

This compression of four lines into two illustrates why the for statement is so widely used in programming. The initialization, test, and increment parts of a loop can be embedded conveniently inside the first line of the statement, making it more compact and perhaps less prone to error than the comparable while structure.

This particular relationship between for and while statements at the concrete syntax level can inform a strategy for mapping a *ForStatement* into an abstract *Loop.* Such a mapping adds two additional *Blocks* to accommodate the initialization and increment steps. That is, a concrete *ForStatement* is mapped to the following abstract structure by a recursive descent parser in the following way.

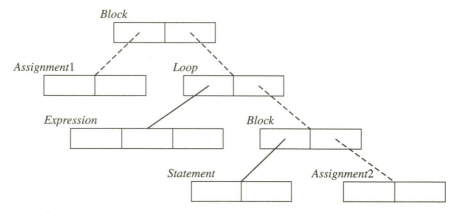

Our example *For* statement maps into this abstract structure when we make the following associations:

```
Assignment1      i=initial
Expression       i<=final
Assignment2      i=i+increment
```

A useful byproduct of this association is that the functional type checking and semantic rules for *Loop* are already established in Jay, so now they apply equally well to

*ForStatement*s. For instance, the type of the *Expression* in the *ForStatement* is still guaranteed to be boolean, and the type validity of the two assignments in the *ForStatement* are still guaranteed. Moreover, the semantic functions for *Block*, *Loop*, and *Assignment* are equally useful for this new *ForStatement* construct, since we have defined it in a way that utilizes abstract concepts that are already defined.

This *ForStatement* extension to Jay is very much in the spirit of C/C++/Java, in that the *Assignment* and the test are reevaluated in the current state each time the loop is executed; this is clearly specified by the abstract model. In contrast, Pascal-like languages limit counting loops to either counting up by one, or counting down by one, with the number of times the loop is executed determined at loop entry time; the initial and final values of the counted loop variable are determined when the loop is encountered and changes to these values do not affect the trip count. C-like languages allow any test and incrementation statement, even empty ones and ones not involving the counting loop variable itself.

An example of a *For* loop to compute N factorial is:

```
fact = 1;
for (i = N; i > 1; i = i - 1)
    fact = fact * i;
```

4.5.2 Do Statements

Another type of looping construct is the *repeat loop,* which performs its test for exit after each iteration of the *Statement* rather than before. The while and for statements both test for continuing the loop before each iteration of the *Statement.* Thus, it is possible that the loop body will not be executed at all.

Sometimes it is useful for the body of a loop to be guaranteed at least one execution. One reason for such an occurrence is that the execution of the loop defines the initial value of the variable used in the loop test. Following C/C++/Java conventions,[5] the concrete syntax of a repeat loop can be defined as a *DoStatement:*

DoStatement → do *Statement* while (*Expression*)

In this case, physical placement of the test after the loop body implies that the loop body is executed before the test is evaluated. As with the *WhileStatement* and *ForStatement,* a body of more than one statement can easily be achieved by using a *Block.*

The abstract syntax for the *DoStatement* can be represented as a mapping to an abstract *Block* containing a *Statement* and a *Loop.* This forces execution of the *Statement* one time just before the *Loop* is entered and the test is made. Details of that mapping and a discussion of its type checking and semantic functional definitions are left as an exercise.

4.5.3 Switch (Case) Statements

In addition to the simple *IfStatement* already defined in Jay, many imperative languages provide a multiway conditional statement as well. One early implementation scheme for such a construct was effectively an indexed jump. The value being tested was used as

---

5. Pascal and Ada call this statement a *repeat statement,* which calls for the repeated execution of a *Statement* until a condition becomes *true*; that is, while the logical negation of that condition remains *false*. The two are equivalent in practice, and we will not dwell on these minor differences here.

index into an array that gave the effective address of the case to be executed. Thus, in many languages the variable being tested is effectively limited to an integer value.

Following C-like languages the syntax of our *SwitchStatement* is as follows:

SwitchStatement → switch (*Expression*) {*Cases*}
Cases → *Case Cases* | *Default*
Case → *CaseHead Cases* | *CaseHead Statement*
CaseHead → case *Literal* :
Default → default : *Statements*

The grammar states that a *SwitchStatement* begins with the keyword `switch`, followed by an *Expression* in parentheses, followed by a series of *Cases* in braces. The *Cases* are ended by a default case (a slight deviation from C-style languages, in which the default is optional). Each *Case* (including the default case) has a *CaseHead* followed by a list of statements (note that the statements are not required to be enclosed within braces). The *CaseHead* for the *default* case consists of the keyword `default` followed by a colon; for the others, the keyword `case` is followed by a *Literal* and a colon. Thus, except for the default case, each case can have list one or more literal values. Unlike C-like languages, our version of the *SwitchStatement* does not require a `break` statement to terminate a case and end execution of the case statement (we return to this question below).

Within these constraints, we can model the *SwitchStatement:*

```
switch ( e ) {
    case v₁: s₁
    case v₂: s₂
    . . .
    case vₙ: sₙ
    default: sₙ₊₁
}
```

as a series of *IfStatement*s in the following form:

```
if (e==v₁) s₁
else if (e==v₂) s₂
    . . .
else if (e==vₙ) sₙ
else sₙ₊₁
```

This model is not fully general for the given syntax, since it ignores the possibility that each *CaseHead* may have more than one literal value associated with it. Nevertheless, mapping the *SwitchStatement* to a series of *IfStatement*s in this way provides a convenient way to clarify its type checking rules and semantics. However, in doing so, we must consider the subtle differences between these two forms. For instance, the *Expression* in an *IfStatement* can be any boolean-valued expression, while in a *Switch-Statement* it must be an equality comparison whose second term is a *Literal*. That requirement can be guaranteed by the parser as it generates the abstract syntax.

Given a proper model in the form of a series of abstract *Conditional*s inside a *Block,* the remaining type checking requirements for *SwitchStatement* are subsumed by those of the Jay *Conditional* and *Block.* The semantics of *SwitchStatement* are also subsumed by the existing semantics of Jay *Conditional*s and *Block*s, so no further work needs to be done beyond the lexical and syntactic stages to add this new statement type to Jay.

An example of a switch is the following code to compute the maximum of two numbers x and y;

```
switch (x > y) {
    case true: z = x;
    default: z = y;
}
```

We leave it as an exercise how to deal with other variations, such as dropping the requirement to have a default case.

4.5.4 Break and Continue Statements

Two other statements that are frequently found in imperative languages are called *break* and *continue*. These allow a program to interrupt the normal flow of control inside a *WhileStatement, ForStatement,* or *SwitchStatement;* they are not found in other contexts.

The syntax of these statements is simple:

Break → break ;
Continue → continue ;

Such a constraint should be enforced by the concrete syntax, but often is not since it makes the grammar too confusing. This validity check can be done as follows.

The break is used in either of two ways. As part of a switch statement, it is used to terminate the execution of the current case. In fact, normally the statement list of each case must be terminated by a break statement to prevent the flow of control from continuing into the next case. As already noted, we do not require a break statement to terminate a case in our Jay extension presented above. Semantically, the break statement in Jay has only a single use: namely, to terminate execution of the loop or the switch. A continue statement is similar, in that the current iteration of the loop body is terminated with control proceeding directly to the loop test and beginning the next iteration. If the loop test is true, then the loop body is again executed. If the loop test is false, then the entire loop is terminated.

The type checking requirements of break and continue are nil. Specification of the semantics of break and continue are left as an exercise.

4.6 SCOPE, VISIBILITY, AND LIFETIME

In this section, we switch gears and consider the overall structure of programs in imperative languages. That is, we consider extensions of Jay that would add the possibility of declaring and using global variables, as well as nested and unnested procedures and functions. The next section proposes specific Jay syntactic extensions that would add global declarations, functions and parameters to its repertoire.

Consider the following C/C++-like program shown in Figure 4.5. It has two global variables and three functions, including a main function. (Enclosing the program in a

Figure 4.5 Example Program with Functions and Parameters

```
package K {
    int h, i;
    void A(int x, int y) {
        boolean i, j;
        B(h);
        ...
    }
    void B(int w) {
        int j, k;
        i = 2*w;
            w = w+1;
        ...
    }
    void main() {
        int a, b;
        h = 5; a = 3; b = 2;
        A(a, b);
        ...
    }
}
```

`package` wrapper makes this a Java-like program, so this discussion applies to all three languages.)

To clarify reusing the same *Identifier* within a program and resolving references to *Identifiers* with their declarations requires the introduction of the concepts of *scope, hiding,* and *visibility.* The *scope* of a variable declaration is that collection of statements which can access that variable. C-like languages, including Java and Jay, and Pascal-like languages, including Ada, all use *static scoping,* in which variable references can be resolved by an inspection of the source text of the program without regard to its execution history. The static scope of a global variable includes all statements in the program. The static scope of a local variable includes only those statements inside the function where it is declared. Thus, scopes are either disjoint or nested.

Thus, the same *Identifier* can be reused inside different functions to name different variables. Also, a global *Identifier* can be redeclared inside a function. If a name declared in an outer scope is redefined in an inner scope, the new declaration is said to *hide* the outer declaration. A name is *visible* in a statement if its scope includes that statement and the name is not hidden. Some languages provide a mechanism for referencing a hidden name; for example, in Java a hidden class variable, say x, can be referenced as `this.x`, where `this` refers to the current object. A name is *local* if it is declared in the current scope, and it is *global* if it is declared in an outer scope.

Consider the function A in our example program. The scope of local variables i and j, as well as parameters x and y, declared in function A includes only those statements within the body of A. The scope of the functions B and `main` in the program are disjoint from function A, so that the local variables declared in B and `main` are not visible in A. The scope of the global *Identifier*s i and h includes the function A; hence, h is visible within A, but the global i is within scope but hidden (not visible) within A.

The definition of what constitutes a scope varies among languages. Some programming languages allow scopes to be nested and variables to be declared at any level of nesting, so that the static scope of a variable has a more complex definition than it does in Jay.

Pascal basically follows the rules outlined above as to what constitutes a scope; however, Pascal allows function declarations to be nested. The language C, following the Algol tradition, allows any compound statement to contain new declarations, and hence, introduce a new scope. In the Algol family of languages, any compound statement which declared new variables was termed a *block;* C-like languages do not follow this terminology. C, however, does not allow function declarations to be nested. Java follows the C rules with respect to compound statements and the nesting of function declarations.

A typical example from a C-like language occurs in sorting, in which we wish to exchange two array elements:

```
...
if (a[i] > a[j]) {
    int t = a[i];
    a[i] = a[j];
    a[j] = t;
}
```

The scope of the variable t is precisely the body of the if statement; this is useful in that it allows a variable to have the minimum scope it needs.

Pascal, Modula, and Ada all permit the nesting of functions or procedures. Consider the following skeletal Pascal program:

```
program main;
    var x : integer;
    procedure p1;
        var x : real;
        procedure p2;
        begin { p2 }
            ... x ...
        end; { p2 }
    begin { p1 }
        ... x ...
    end; { p1 }
    procedure p3;
    begin { p3 }
        ... x ...
    end; { p3 }
begin { main }
    ... x ...
end.
```

The reference to x in p3 and main refer to the integer x declared in main, while the references to x in p1 and p2 refer to the real (float) x declared in p1. In these languages procedures and functions can be arbitrarily nested. Note that although Java does not allow the nesting of methods, it does permit the nesting of classes, which are referred to as *inner classes*.

In a for loop, Java allows the initializer statement to declare a new variable. In this case, the scope of the variable is limited to the for statement itself:

```
for (int i = 0; i < 10; i++) {
    System.out.println(i);
    ...
}
... i ... // illegal reference to i
```

The reference to i following the for loop is illegal, since the scope of the variable declared in the for initializer is limited to the for statement. Ada also limits the scope of the for loop variable to the for statement; however, in Ada the for loop variable is implicitly and automatically declared.

The purpose of these examples is to indicate that the definition of what constitutes a scope varies from one language to another, even within the same basic family of languages. For example, is the formal parameter list in a function header in the same scope or an outer scope from the function body itself? This can vary from one language to another. It can also vary from one compiler to another in that some compilers do not implement precisely and exactly the definition of a scope in the language being compiled.

Early languages such as Fortran, C, and Pascal insisted that a locally defined identifier be unique in its scope; in other words, an identifier could not be declared twice within the same scope. Later languages, starting with Ada, permitted *overloading* of names, allowing multiple definitions of the same identifier within the same scope, so long as context could be used to distinguish which declaration was being referenced. For example, Java allows within a class both instance variables and methods to have the same name, since a use of method name is always followed syntactically by parentheses:

```
class Overloading {
    int name;     // an instance variable
    int name ( ) { ... }     // a method
    ...
    name = name( ); //  instance variable = method call
    ...
}
```

Java also allows method names within the same class to be overloaded, as long as the actual method invoked can be determined by either the number or types of the parameters. An example occurs in the PrintStream class in which the methods print and `println` are heavily overloaded:

```
public class PrintStream extends FilterOutputStream {
    ...
    public void print(boolean b);
    public void print(char c);
    public void print(int i);
    public void print(long l);
    public void print(float f);
    public void print(double d);
    public void print(char[] s);
    public void print(String s);
    public void print(Object obj);
    ...
}
```

In contrast, Modula has uniquely named output routines for writing the various primitive data types, since Modula does not support overloading of names.

4.7 SYNTAX AND TYPE SYSTEM FOR METHODS AND PARAMETERS

Suppose we want to extend Jay so that a program consists of a collection of functions (methods), static global declarations, and a main method.[6] The program in Figure 4.5 would be an example of such an extension. This section discusses the formal definition of this extension by considering its impact on the concrete syntax, abstract syntax, type checking rules, and semantics of Jay.

4.7.1 Concrete Syntax

The concrete syntax of this extension requires a new definition of the notion of *Program* as a collection of functions that includes a "main" method. Below are BNF rules which, when added to those in Appendix B, will accomplish this extension.

$$
\begin{aligned}
Program &\rightarrow \text{package } Identifier \ \{ \ Declarations \ Methods \ MainMethod \ \} \\
Methods &\rightarrow \varepsilon \mid Methods \ Method \\
Method &\rightarrow Type \ Identifier \ \ (\ Parameters_{opt} \ ) \ \{ \ Declarations \ Statements \ \} \\
Type &\rightarrow \text{int} \mid \text{boolean} \mid \text{void} \\
Parameters &\rightarrow Parameter \mid Parameters, \ Parameter \\
Parameter &\rightarrow Type \ \ Identifier \\
MainMethod &\rightarrow \text{void main } () \ \{ \ Declarations \ Statements \ \}
\end{aligned}
$$

For example, the program discussed in Figure 4.5 is an example of this augmented Jay syntax; its package *Identifier* is K, it has two global variables h and i, and its methods

---

6. Here, and in later discussions, we use the term *method* to mean "procedure," "function," "subprogram," or "subroutine." This term actually originated with the emergence of object-oriented languages, but we find it to be a useful umbrella term for all these others, since it conveys the same basic idea.

are identified as A, B, and main. Methods A and B have *Type* void, since they return no result and are called by standalone statements. A has two `int` parameters and B has one.

The syntax of Jay must also be augmented to allow a method call to appear either as a separate statement or as a factor within an expression. Thus, the following BNF rule changes are needed for Appendix B.

$$Statement \rightarrow ; \mid Block \mid Assignment \mid IfStatement$$
$$WhileStatement \mid CallStatement \mid ReturnStatement$$
$$CallStatement \rightarrow Identifier \ (\ Arguments_{opt}\ )\ ;$$
$$ReturnStatement \rightarrow return \ Expression \ ;$$
$$Arguments \rightarrow Expression \mid Arguments , Expression$$
$$Factor \rightarrow Identifier \mid Literal \mid Call \mid (\ Expression\ )$$
$$Call \rightarrow Identifier \ (\ Arguments_{opt}\ )$$

For example, the program above has two *CallStatements,* one from main to A and one from A to B. The call to A has two arguments, a and b, and the call to B has one argument, h. This program has no *Calls,* since neither A nor B returns a result. A *ReturnStatement* is used only within a method that does not have *Type* void.

4.7.2 Abstract Syntax

Refinements to the abstract syntax of Jay for methods and calls are summarized in Figure 4.6. Readers should refer to Appendix B to recall the abstract definitions of concepts not redefined here. Underlined sections of these rules indicate changes to existing rules in Appendix B.

$$Program = Declarations \ \underline{globals;\ Methods}\ body$$
$$Methods = Method*$$
$$Method = Type \ t; \ String \ id; \ Declarations \ params; \ Declarations \ locals; \ Block \ body$$
$$Type = int \mid boolean \mid \underline{void}$$
$$Block = Statement*$$
$$Statement = Skip \mid Block \mid Assignment \mid Conditional \mid Loop \mid \underline{Call} \mid \underline{Return}$$
$$Call = String \ name; \ Expressions \ args$$
$$Expressions = Expression*$$
$$Return = Expression \ result$$
$$Expression = Variable \mid Value \mid Binary \mid Unary \mid \underline{Call}$$

Figure 4.6   New Abstract Syntax Rules for Jay with Methods and Globals

A sketch of the abstract syntax for the example program K is shown in Figure 4.7.

4.7.3 Static Type Checking

With this new framework, the Jay type system can be refined to provide appropriate constraints for these syntactic additions. New validity rules are needed to assure that Jay remains type safe in the following ways:

- Every method and global variable in the program has a unique id.

- All the local variables and parameters declared within a method have mutually unique id's and valid types.

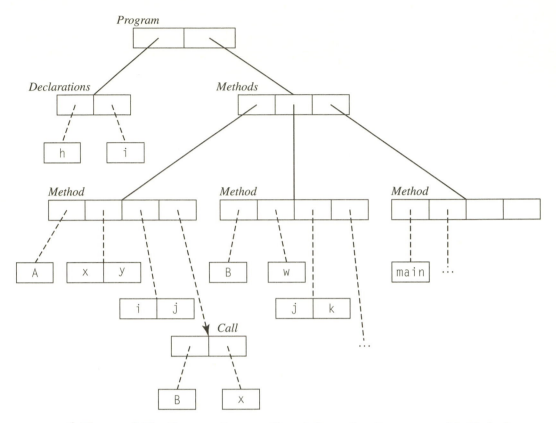

Figure 4.7   Abstract Syntax Sketch for a Jay Program with Globals and Methods

- All the statements and expressions within the body of each method are valid with respect to the variables and parameters that are accessible to them.

- A *Return* appears in every method that has a nonvoid *Type,* and the type of the *Expression* in that statement must be identical with that *Type.*

- Every *Call* has a name identical with the name of a *method* in the program, and has the same number of arguments as that *method* has parameters.

- Every argument in a *Call* has the same type as the *Type* given for the corresponding parameter in the *method* with the same name.

The notion of "type map" for these programs is defined differently than the type map for Jay. That is, these programs allow multiple definitions of the same *Identifier,* one of which is accessible by a particular statement in the program. For instance, in the example Jay program the *Identifier* i names both a global variable and a local variable inside the method A.

The informal definition of *static scope* given in the previous chapter can be made more precise using the familiar ideas of type map and overriding union. Suppose we let tm_g denote the type map for the global variables declared at the beginning of the program—that is, the set of all pairs of these variables and their types. For the example program K, this would be $tm_g = \{(h, int), (i, int)\}$. We can define the type map for any method m, tm_m, as the overriding union of tm_g and the set of all pairs of m's local variables and parameters and their respective types. For example, in our program K, we have:

$$tm_A = tm_g \overline{U} \{\langle x, int\rangle, \langle y, int\rangle, \langle i, boolean\rangle, \langle j, boolean\rangle\}$$
$$= \{\langle h, int\rangle, \langle x, int\rangle, \langle y, int\rangle, \langle i, boolean\rangle, \langle j, boolean\rangle\}$$
$$tm_B = tm_g \overline{U} \{\langle w, int\rangle, \langle j, int\rangle, \langle k, int\rangle\}$$
$$= \{\langle h, int\rangle, \langle i, int\rangle, \langle w, int\rangle, \langle j, int\rangle, \langle k, int\rangle\}$$
$$tm_{main} = tm_g \overline{U} \{\langle a, int\rangle, \langle b, int\rangle\}$$
$$= \{\langle h, int\rangle, \langle i, int\rangle, \langle a, int\rangle, \langle b, int\rangle\}$$

This idea can be incorporated into a new definition of the Jay method *typing* for any set of global declarations g and method m with parameters p and local declarations d, as follows:

$$typing_m: Declarations \times Declarations \times Declarations \rightarrow TypeMap$$
$$typing_m(g, p, d) = tm_g \overline{U} (tm_p \cup tm_d),$$

where

$$tm_g = \bigcup_{i \in 1,...,ng} \langle g_i \cdot v, g_i \cdot t\rangle$$

$$tm_p = \bigcup_{i \in 1,...,np} \langle p_i \cdot v, p_i \cdot t\rangle$$

$$tm_d = \bigcup_{i \in 1,...,nd} \langle d_i \cdot v, d_i \cdot t\rangle$$

With this definition, the type validity rules for Jay with globals and methods can be formalized, beginning with the validity rule for *Program:*

$$V: Program \rightarrow \mathbf{B}$$
$$V(Program\ p) = V(p.globals) \wedge \forall m \in p.body:$$
$$V(m, typing_m(p.globals, m.params, m.locals))$$

That is, a program is valid if its global variable declarations are valid and each of its methods (including the main) is valid with respect to its own type map, as defined above. This means that our program K is valid if the following conditions are simultaneously true:

$$V(\{\langle h, int\rangle, \langle i, int\rangle\})$$
$$V(A, typing_A (\{\langle h, int\rangle, \langle i, int\rangle\}, A.params, A.locals))$$
$$V(B, typing_B (\{\langle h, int\rangle, \langle i, int\rangle\}, B.params, B.locals))$$
$$V(main, typing_{main} (\{\langle h, int\rangle, \langle i, int\rangle\}, main.params, main.locals))$$

The validity of a method is defined in an intuitive way:

$$V: Method \times TypeMap \rightarrow \mathbf{B}$$
$$V(Method\ m, TypeMap\ tm) = V(m.params) \wedge V(m.locals) \wedge V(m.body, tm)$$
$$\wedge \forall s \in m.body: s\ is\ a\ Return \supset typeOf(s.result) = m.t$$
$$\wedge m.t \neq void \equiv \exists s \in m.body: s\ is\ a\ Return$$

That is, a method is valid if its parameters and locals have mutually unique names and valid types, the method's body is valid with respect to its type map, and the method contains an appropriate *Return* statement (whenever its type is nonvoid). For example, in the above program we require that $V(A, tm_A)$, $V(B, tm_B)$ and $V(main, tm_{main})$.

To complete the type specification for Jay with globals and methods, we need to add validity rules for the newly-defined statements *Call* and *Return* in the abstract syntax (see Figure 4.6). This is left as an exercise.

EXERCISES

4.1   Discuss the advantages and disadvantages of having case-sensitive identifiers in a programming language, with respect to program reliability, type checking, and compile-time complexity.

4.2   In the current implementation, Jay identifiers are not case-sensitive. Can they be made case-sensitive? What changes need to be made to the Jay implementation to make this happen? (see Appendix B, and recall that Java has two different String comparison operators, `equals` and `equalsIgnoreCase`.)

4.3   Can a language have no reserved words? That is, suppose every reserved word (such as `if` and `for`) were merely a predefined identifier, which the programmer is free to redefine. Can such a language exist? Explain.

4.4   Using the strategy and example type map *tm* illustrated in Section 4.3, show that each of the following expressions is valid.
(a) $V(x{<}2{*}y, tm)$
(b) $V(x{<}2{*}y \text{ \&\& } x{>}0, tm)$

4.5   Complete the definition of a Jay extension that will allow floating point variables, arithmetic expressions, and assignments to occur, as suggested in Section 4.3. Consider all changes that would need to be made to the concrete and abstract syntax, type system (functions V), and semantics (functions M) to make this happen. Besides **I** and **B**, what additional semantic domain needs to be added?

4.6   Complete the demonstration of type validity for the program fragment in Section 4.4, by showing the type and validity of the *Expressions* in (b_{11}), the validity of the *Assignment* in (b_{12}) and the *Expression* in (b_{22}), and the equality of the type of i and the type of the *Expression* i$-$1 in (b_{23}).

4.7   The meaning function M given in Appendix B for the Jay abstract class *Loop* is implemented recursively. Give an alternative nonrecursive implementation for $M(Loop, \sigma)$.

4.8   The meaning function M given in Appendix B for the Jay abstract class *Block* is implemented using a loop. Give an alternative recursive implementation for $M(Block, \sigma)$.

4.9   Show how any *ForStatement* can be mapped by a recursive descent parser to the abstract structure suggested in Subsection 4.5.1, by writing the method `forStatement` that generates the correct abstract syntax.

4.10   Implement the *DoStatement* extension in Jay, using the guidelines suggested in Subsection 4.5.2.
(a) What additions, if any, need to be added to the lexical syntax of Jay to make this extension possible?
(b) Discuss the type checking and semantic functional definitions that are required to fully implement this extension to Jay.

4.11 Explore the complete syntax of *SwitchStatement* as found in C, C++, or Java. Develop an effective extension of the Jay concrete syntax that more effectively models reality and properly integrates the use of *Break* and *Continue* statements inside of *SwitchStatement*s. Discuss the development of an appropriate semantic function *M* that would fully explain this statement.

4.12 (Team project) Complete the Jay interpreter outlined in the software suite by:
(a) Writing all the remaining functions of the recursive descent parser,
(b) Implementing all the remaining type checking functions (*V*), and
(c) Implementing the remaining semantic functions (*M*).

Test your interpreter using the sample Jay program given in Chapter 2, as well as several others that are given in the software suite at the book website given in the Preface.

4.13 (Team project) Following the ideas discussed in this chapter and using the basic Jay interpreter that you designed in the previous question, add floating point numbers and operator overloading to Jay. To simplify this task, complete the following steps in the order shown:
(a) Show all additions to the Jay Concrete Syntax (see Appendix B).
(b) Show all additions to the Jay Abstract Syntax.
(c) Show all changes to the Jay Static Type Checking rules (*V* functions).
(d) Show all changes to the Jay Semantics (*M* functions).

4.14 Define type checking validity rules for the statement types Call and Return. Hint: consider augmenting the definition of *V*(*Statement* s, *TypeMap* tm) in Appendix B by adding two more cases:
(a) s is a *Call*, and
(b) s is a *Return*.

Memory Management

5

"To understand a program you must become both the machine and the program."
Attributed to Alan Perlis

CHAPTER OUTLINE

Chapters 3 and 4 discussed types and type systems for imperative programming languages. This chapter revisits that discussion by considering how memory is managed for different values with those various types. *Memory management* is the process of binding values to memory, taking into account both the static and the dynamic characteristics of these values.

Values in programming languages can be assigned to any of three different categories of memory: static memory, the run-time stack, and the heap. *Static memory* is allocated to values whose storage requirements are known before run time and remain constant throughout the life of the running program. The *run-time stack* is the center of control for dispatching active methods (procedures and functions), their local variables, and their parameter-argument linkages, as they gain and relinquish control to the caller. The *heap* is the least structured of the three memory categories, and contains all other values that are dynamically allocated during the run-time life of the program.

The structure of the run-time stack is predictable and regular. A "stack frame" is pushed onto the top of the stack whenever a method is called, and popped from the stack at the time the method returns control to the caller. The structure of the heap, however, is far less predictable and regular. The heap becomes fragmented as it is used for the dynamic allocation and deallocation of storage blocks. At any point in time, the active memory blocks in the heap are not contiguous. For that reason, programming languages use "garbage collection" algorithms to manage the heap as blocks of memory become unusable during the run of a program.

5.1 THE OVERALL STRUCTURE OF RUN-TIME MEMORY

Memory at run time divides into three parts, the *static area,* the *run-time stack,* and the *heap.* This structure is pictured in Figure 5.1.

Figure 5.1 The Structure of Run-Time Memory

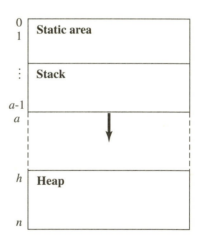

As this figure suggests, the stack is a contiguous region of storage that grows and shrinks at one end during run time. The heap, on the other hand, is a region of storage whose active blocks are spread out from each other in an unpredictable pattern during run time. Heap blocks are accessed indirectly using references called *pointers,* which appear either in the stack or elsewhere in the heap.

Initial space for the run-time stack and the heap is allocated in a way that reflects the dynamic features of the program and remains inside the limits of that fixed block of addresses $\{0, \ldots, n\}$ called the program's *address space.* The size of the static area is fixed before run time, the top of the stack is marked by address $a - 1$, and the beginning of the heap is marked by the address h. The following invariant relation must hold throughout the program run, to avoid raising the stack overflow condition:

$$0 \leq a \leq h < n$$

The parameters h and n are initially defined at the beginning of run time; some programs require very little predefined heap space, while others require a lot. Similarly, the maximum stack size can vary among different programs, depending upon the maximum depth of nested method calls that occur during the program run.

To accommodate the dynamic behavior of the stack and the heap, a more detailed concept of state is needed than that which we used in Chapter 3. That is, the memory address space must be managed explicitly when defining stack frames and blocks of space in the heap. We can do this by identifying the *environment* γ_m of an active method[1] m as a set of pairs that unite those variables which are accessible to m with specific memory addresses. The *memory* μ is a set of pairs that relate locations with values. The *locations* are the finite subset $\{0, \ldots, n\}$ of the natural numbers $\mathbf{N}$ which identifies the program's *address space*. Those locations to which no variable has yet been allocated at some point during execution are marked *unused,* while those locations to which a variable has been allocated but has no value yet assigned are marked *undefined.*

For example, suppose that the variables i and j have values 13 and -1 at some time during the execution of a method m, that k has no value yet assigned, and that these variables are associated with memory locations 154, 155, and 156 at the time they are allocated. Then the environment and memory represented by this configuration can be expressed as follows:

$\gamma_m = \{\langle i, 154\rangle, \langle j, 155\rangle, \langle k, 156\rangle\}$
$\mu = \{\ldots \langle 154, 13\rangle, \langle 155, -1\rangle, \langle 156, undef\rangle \ldots \langle a - 1, undef\rangle,$
$\qquad \langle a, unused\rangle \ldots \langle n, unused\rangle\}$

The *state* σ_m of an active method m in a program is the product of m's environment and the memory; that is, $\sigma_m = \gamma_m \times \mu$. The *address* of a variable v under this redefinition is given by $\gamma_m(v)$, and the *value* of that variable is given by $\mu(\gamma_m(v))$, which is also denoted by $\sigma_m(v)$. For this example, we have

$\gamma_m(i) = 154, \quad$ and
$\sigma_m(i) = \mu(\gamma_m(i)) = 13$

Now the *assignment* of a new value to a variable can be defined using the overriding union operator that was introduced in Chapter 3. For example, suppose we want to assign the value 20 to the variable i in the example above. That assignment can be given by:

$\mu \,\overline{\mathrm{U}}\, \{\langle \gamma_m(i), 20\rangle\}$
$\quad = \mu \,\overline{\mathrm{U}}\, \langle 154, 20\rangle$
$\quad = \{\ldots \langle 154, 20\rangle, \langle 155, -1\rangle, \langle 156, undef\rangle \ldots \langle a - 1, undef\rangle \ldots \langle n, unused\rangle\}$

Allocation of variables to addresses in the static area and the run-time stack is serial, beginning at address 0. At any time during the run of a program, the range of active addresses in these two areas is $\{0, \ldots, a - 1\}$, where a is the number of active variables. In this model, we make the strong assumption that every variable's value takes exactly one addressable unit of memory. (In Chapter 4, we saw that this is not the case in real systems. However, we shall make this assumption throughout this chapter in order to

---

1. Throughout this chapter, we use the term *method* to signify any procedure, function, or subroutine that is called in an imperative program. In Chapter 7, we shall see how methods are generalized so that they take part in the definition of classes within the object-oriented paradigm.

keep the discussion simple.) Thus, the addressing function $\gamma_m(v)$ must deliver a value in the range $\{0, \ldots, a - 1\}$, for any active variable v in the stack during execution of method m.

Within this model, the allocation of memory for a group of new *Declaration*s d_1, $d_2, \ldots, d_k$ in the static area or the run-time stack can be given by the function *allocate,* defined as follows:

$$allocate(d_1, d_2, \ldots, d_k, \sigma) = \gamma' \times \mu'$$

where $\gamma' = \gamma \cup \{\langle v_1, a\rangle, \langle v_2, a + 1\rangle, \ldots, \langle v_k, a + k - 1\rangle\}$
$\mu' = \mu \,\overline{U}\, \{\langle a, undef\rangle, \langle a + 1, undef\rangle, \ldots, \langle a + k - 1, undef\rangle\}$
$a' = a + k$

giving the new state $\sigma' = \gamma' \times \mu'$. Notice that the creation of γ' is an ordinary set union rather than an overriding union. This anticipates that some variables in γ' will share the same name but will have different memory addresses. Also, *allocate* is well-defined as long as $a + k < h$; that is, there is sufficient memory space available for allocating the new variables.

Removing a group of k variables from the top of the run-time stack is given by *deallocate* as follows:

$$deallocate(d_1, d_2, \ldots, d_k, \sigma) = \gamma' \times \mu'$$

where $\gamma' = \gamma - \{\langle d_k, a\rangle, \langle d_{k-1}, a - 1\rangle, \ldots, \langle d_1, a - k + 1\rangle\}$
$\mu' = \mu \,\overline{U}\, \{\langle a, unused\rangle, \langle a - 1, unused\rangle, \ldots, \langle a - k + 1, unused\rangle\}$
$a' = a - k$

Notice here that the creation of γ' is an ordinary set difference, and that the function *deallocate* is well-defined as long as $a - k \geq 0$.

Recall that the value of an individual memory location is marked *undef*ined at the time it is allocated, indicating that no value is yet stored there. That memory location is marked *unused* when the variable assigned to it is deallocated. We use this memory model and these functions later in Subsection 5.2.1 when we discuss memory management for method calls, arrays, and other structures.

5.2 METHODS, LOCALS, PARAMETERS, AND THE RUN-TIME STACK

Whenever a method is called, including the main method, a new set of "local" declarations is allocated space on the run-time stack. This space is part of a block called a *stack frame,* which remains active throughout the life of the call and then is relinquished to the system when control returns to the caller. Since an active method can (and usually does) call another method, this causes another stack frame to be pushed onto the stack. The stack frame contains spaces for the called method's argument values, local variables, a *static link* to the static area, and a *dynamic link* to the stack frame for the method that called this method. This basic structure of a stack frame is shown in Figure 5.2.

At any time during program execution, the run-time stack contains a frame for every method whose call is still active at that time, with the most recently called method's

Figure 5.2 Structure of a Called Method's Stack Frame

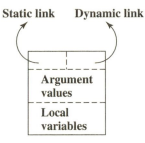

Figure 5.3 Example Program with Methods and Parameters

```
package K {
    int h, i;
    void A(int x, int y) {
        boolean i, j;
        B(h);
        ...
    }

    void B(int w) {
        int j, k;
        i = 2*w;
            w = w+1;
        ...
    }
    void main() {
        int a, b;
        h = 5; a = 3; b = 2;
        A(a, b);
        ...
    }
}
```

frame at the top of the stack. This situation can be illustrated using the simple Java-like program introduced in Chapter 4 and shown again in Figure 5.3.

When main is initially called, the static memory contains variables h and i, and a new stack frame is pushed onto the stack with the variables a and b, as shown in the left-hand part of Figure 5.4.

When A is called by main, another frame is created with A's local variables (i and j) together with the values of the arguments corresponding to parameters x and y (3 and 2). Finally, when B is called from A, a third frame is placed on the stack with an argument value 5 for parameter w. The first assignment within B therefore assigns the value 2*w = 10 to the static global variable i, which is reached through the static link in the stack frame for B.

This convention for stack management can support either static or dynamic scoping for declarations. *Static scoping* means that the scope of each variable is determined by the program's static structure; that is, all references to nonlocal variables are references to static global variables, like h and i in the example above. For example, the assign-

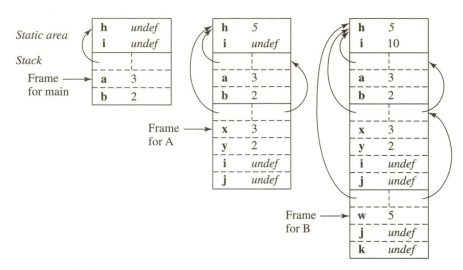

Static area

Stack

Frame for main

Frame for A

Frame for B

| **Figure 5.4** **Run-Time Stack with Stack Frames for Method Invocations**

ment i=2*w inside B would change the value of the global variable i (rather than any other variable i), since that one is within the static scope of B. Static scoping reaches variables via the static links in the stack frames. Languages like C and C++ allow no method nesting and thus have a strictly static scoping strategy.[2]

Dynamic scoping means that the scope of a variable is determined by the sequence of method calls that occurs at run time. It requires that all references to nonlocal variables be resolved at run time, which is done by searching through the chain of dynamic links to find the first instance of a variable with that name. In the above example, the use of dynamic scoping would mean that the assignment i=2*w inside B would change the value of the variable i declared locally within the calling method A, rather than the globally declared variable i.

Dynamic scoping was used in languages like APL and early versions of Lisp. However, for a variety of reasons, it is not a common feature of modern languages. For instance, dynamic scoping compromises the ability to statically type check references to nonlocal variables, since not all the nonlocals for a statement inside a called method can be statically identified. Moreover, all variables in a method that calls other methods are visible to those called methods (and hence can be altered); this visibility tends to reduce the reliability of a program in general. Finally, as suggested by the example above, access to a nonlocal variable by following a chain of dynamic links tends to be more time-consuming than access to a nonlocal in a statically scoped environment. For these reasons, dynamic scoping tends not to be a feature of modern programming languages.

5.2.1 Program State I: Stack Allocation

Turning to the semantics of Jay with methods, we first formalize the notions of static memory, stack, and stack frame that were introduced earlier in this section. The store is a series of address-value pairs, in the address range from 0 to *n*.

---

2. While Java allows no method nesting inside a class, it does allow complete classes to be nested inside each other; these nested classes are called *inner classes*.

In Jay, the value associated with an address can be either *unused, undef*ined, an integer, a boolean, or an *address. Unused* and *undef*ined values were introduced in Section 5.1. *Addresses* are values that reference other memory locations, and are denoted by $@r$, where r is an integer in the program's address space $\{0, \ldots, n\}$.

The initial state for a program starts with the assumption that all locations in the address space are *unused:* $\sigma_0 = \varnothing \times \mu(0) = \{\langle 0, unused \rangle, \langle 1, unused \rangle, \ldots, \langle n, unused \rangle\}$. The initial state of a program p, σ_g, is the result of allocating memory to the program's global variables, given σ_0. That is, $\sigma_g = allocate(p.\text{globals}, \sigma_0)$.

For example, the program K given in Figure 5.3 has the following initial state:

$$\sigma_g = allocate(K.\text{globals}, \sigma_0)$$
$$= \gamma_g \times \mu$$
$$= \{\langle h, 0 \rangle, \langle i, 1 \rangle\} \times \{\langle 0, undef \rangle, \langle 1, undef \rangle, \langle 2, unused \rangle, \ldots, \langle n, unused \rangle\}$$

The state achieved when method main begins execution simulates the addition of that method's stack frame to the current state. That is achieved by allocating space on the stack for the static link, the dynamic link, and each of main's locals, and then initializing the static and dynamic links to address 0 for the program K.

$$\sigma_{main} = allocate(slink, dlink, main.\text{locals}, \sigma_g)$$
$$= \gamma_{main} \times \mu$$

where $\gamma_{main} = \gamma_g \; \overline{U} \; \{\langle slink, 2 \rangle, \langle dlink, 3 \rangle, \langle a, 4 \rangle, \langle b, 5 \rangle\}$
$$= \{\langle h, 0 \rangle, \langle i, 1 \rangle, \langle slink, 2 \rangle, \langle dlink, 3 \rangle, \langle a, 4 \rangle, \langle b, 5 \rangle\}$$

and $\mu = \left\{ \begin{array}{c} \langle 0, undef \rangle, \langle 1, undef \rangle, \\ \langle 2, @0 \rangle, \langle 3, @0 \rangle, \langle 4, undef \rangle, \langle 5, undef \rangle, \\ \langle 6, unused \rangle, \ldots, \langle n, unused \rangle \end{array} \right\}$

This corresponds to the initial state of memory shown on the left in Figure 5.4.

The state reached by a call to any other method m (having np parameters and nd locals) from state $\sigma = \gamma \times \mu$ is similar, except that additional space is required for allocating the argument values.

$$\sigma_m = allocate(slink, dlink, m.\text{params}, m.\text{locals}, \sigma)$$
$$= \gamma_m \times \mu$$

The active environment during the life of this call to method m thus becomes

$$\gamma_m = \gamma_g \, \overline{U} \left\{ \begin{array}{c} \langle slink_m, a \rangle, \langle dlink_m, a + 1 \rangle, \\ \langle p_1, a + 2 \rangle, \langle p_2, a + 3 \rangle, \ldots, \langle p_{np}, a + np + 1 \rangle \\ \langle d_1, a + np + 2 \rangle, \langle d_2, a + np + 3 \rangle, \ldots, \langle d_{nd}, a + np + nd + 1 \rangle \end{array} \right\}$$

and the active memory becomes:

$$\sigma(slink_{main}) = @0$$
$$\sigma(dlink_{main}) = @a - 1$$

$$\mu = \mu(a) \, \overline{U} \left\{ \begin{array}{c} \langle a, @0 \rangle, \langle a + 1, @a - 1 \rangle, \\ \langle a + 2, v_1 \rangle, \langle a + 2, v_2 \rangle \ldots, \langle a + np + 1, v_{np} \rangle, \\ \langle a + np + 2, undef \rangle, \ldots, \langle a + np + nd + 1, undef \rangle, \\ \langle a + np + nd + 2, unused \rangle, \ldots, \langle n, unused \rangle \end{array} \right\}$$

The *values* $v_1, v_2, \ldots, v_{np}$ associated with the parameters for the life of the call are determined in different ways, as described in Subsection 5.2.2.

5.2.2 Argument-Parameter Linkage

The arguments need to be "passed" from the call to the called method. There are two principal ways for passing arguments in a call: by value and by reference.

Passing an argument *by value*[3] means that the value of the argument is obtained at the time of the call and placed in a memory location for the corresponding parameter. The example program in Figure 5.3 provides an illustration of this, both in the call A(a,b) from main, and in the call B(x) from A.

For instance, notice that the run-time stack in Figure 5.4 shows values 3 and 2 for A's parameters x and y. Now all references to x and y from within A are using these copies of the values of arguments a and b rather than the originals, so that the original values of a and b are effectively write-protected for the life of the call.

Passing an argument *by reference* means that the address of the argument (given by the name of a simple variable, array, or structure) is associated with the corresponding parameter, so that the parameter becomes an indirect *reference* to the corresponding argument. Thus all assignments to the parameter within the life of the call directly affect the value of that variable which is the argument.

For example, suppose the program in Figure 5.3 had the argument for parameter w inside method B passed by reference rather than by value. Now the assignment

```
w = w+1;
```

inside B will directly increment the value of h rather than a copy of that value inside B's stack frame. To make this effective, the *address* of the variable h is passed by the call, as shown in Figure 5.5.

Figure 5.5   Passing an Argument by Reference Example

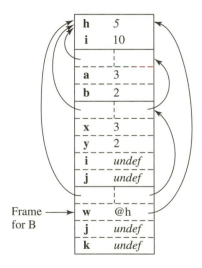

Other argument-parameter linkage conventions are less widely used. These are called *passing by result, passing by value-result,* and *passing by name.* An argument passed by result has no argument value associated with the parameter at the beginning of the call, but the final value computed for the parameter is copied out to the argument at the end of the life of the call. An argument passed by value-result is copied into a local variable at the beginning of a call's activation and then copied out to the corresponding argument at the end of the activation. An argument passed by name has its actual concrete syntax copied into each location in the method that references that parameter. This is an example of "late binding," where the expression in the call is not evaluated until it is needed by the method.[4]

Argument-passing by value and by reference can be incorporated into the formal semantic model by defining the values $v_1, v_2, \ldots, v_{np}$ of the parameters with the arguments $r_1, r_2, \ldots, r_{np}$ in the call from within method m as follows:

$$\forall i \in \{1, \ldots, np\}: v_i = \sigma_m(r_i) \qquad \text{if } r_i \text{ is passed by value}$$
$$= \gamma_m(r_i) \qquad \text{if } r_i \text{ is passed by reference}$$

Passing arguments by value is a widely used convention in programming languages; C, C++, Ada, Java, and many others support it. Passing an argument by reference is used in cases when the actual value of the argument must be changed during the life of the call. Passing by reference is also preferred when the argument passed is not a scalar object—such as an array, a structure, or an object. In these cases, the space and time overhead created by making a complete copy of the object passed by value is avoided by simply passing the object by reference instead. The main disadvantage of passing by reference is that side-effects on the original value of the argument passed may not be desired by the caller. For instance, if the call of B by A with argument h does not want the current value of h to be changed during the life of the call, passing h by reference should be avoided.

In most languages, the distinction between value and reference parameter passing is made within the method declaration. In the C++ programming language, an ampersand (&) is written to signal a reference parameter, and its absence signals a value parameter. For example, if method B in Figure 5.3 were written in C++, its first line would be altered as follows to signal a reference parameter:

```
void B(int& w) {
    int j, k;
    i = 2*w;
    w = w+1;
    ...
}
```

and the call from A would remain:

```
B(h);
```

That is, the declaration of parameter w in B requires that the argument in any call provide an address (the name of a variable, array, or structure, but not an expression

---

4. Late binding is often called *lazy evaluation,* and is revisited in Chapter 8.

with operators). The impact of declaring w by reference in this call is to alter the value of h in the caller's environment when the statement w=w+1; is executed inside method B. Had w not been called by reference, the value of h would not have been altered by this statement.

In Java, *all* arguments are passed by value, but those which are "reference types" (arrays and objects that are members of classes) are passed differently than those which are elementary types (byte, short, int, long, float, double, char, boolean). That is, elementary types are passed by placing a copy of their value in the stack frame, as explained above. However, reference types are passed by associating a copy of their reference (address) with the parameter. Thus, the following swap method will not exchange the arrays associated with parameters A and B:

```
void swap(int[] A, int[] B) {
    int[] temp = A;
    A = B;
    B = temp;
}
```

However, the following Java swap method will exchange the values of the *i*th and *j*th entries in the array associated with parameter A.

```
void swap(int[] A, int i, int j) {
    int temp = A[i];
    A[i] = A[j];
    A[j] = temp;
}
```

5.2.3 Semantics of Call and Return

Extending the function M defined for Jay in Appendix B and the new statement type *Call* for Jay defined in Figure 4.6 (previous chapter), the meaning of a call can be formalized using our memory model:

$M(Call\ s, State\ \sigma) = deactivate(s.\text{name}, M(s.\text{name.body}, activate(s.\text{name}, s.\text{args}, \sigma)))$

That is, to compute the final state resulting from executing the call s, the following three steps are required:

1. Activate the call of s with arguments s.args, by creating a new stack frame and establishing the value/reference associations between arguments and parameters.
2. Determine the meaning of the body of s in the new state created by this activation.
3. Deactivate the call by removing the stack frame created in step 1.

Activation of a call to method m from within method c in state σ can be formally defined in the following way:

$activate(m, c.\text{args}, \sigma)$
$= allocate(slink, dlink, m.\text{params}, m.\text{locals}, \sigma - c.\text{params} - c.\text{locals})$

where $\forall i \in \{1, \ldots, np\}$: $\mu(m.\text{params}_i, \sigma_m) = M(c.\text{args}_i, \sigma)$

That is, all the arguments are passed by value. Note also that an activation removes the calling method's parameters and locals from the active environment for the life of the call. This enforces the idea of static scoping discussed earlier in this section.

Deactivation of a call reverses the effect of the activation by removing the stack frame thus created and restoring the calling method's local variables and parameters to the active environment. That is:

$$deactivate(m, \sigma) = deallocate(slink, dlink, m.params, m.locals, \sigma) \, \overline{U} \, c.params \, \overline{U} \, c.locals$$

To illustrate, consider the call to A from main in our well-worn example program K. There are two arguments x and y in this call, corresponding to the two parameters a and b. The state when the call occurs is:

$$\sigma_{main} = \gamma_{main} \times \mu$$

where $\gamma_{main} = \{\langle h, 0\rangle, \langle i, 1\rangle, \langle a, 2\rangle, \langle b, 3\rangle\}$
and $\mu = \{\langle 0, 5\rangle, \langle 1, undef\rangle, \langle 2, 3\rangle, \langle 3, 2\rangle, \langle 4, unused\rangle, \ldots, \langle n, unused\rangle\}$

(For simplicity, static and dynamic links are omitted from this illustration.) Activation of the call to A from *main* thus creates the following state:

$$\sigma_A = \gamma_A \times \mu$$

where $\gamma_A = \gamma_{main} - \{\langle a, 2\rangle, \langle b, 3\rangle\} \, \overline{U} \, \{\langle x, 4\rangle, \langle y, 5\rangle, \langle i, 6\rangle, \langle j, 7\rangle\}$
        $= \{\langle h, 0\rangle, \langle x, 4\rangle, \langle y, 5\rangle, \langle i, 6\rangle, \langle j, 7\rangle\}$

$$\text{and } \mu = \left\{ \begin{array}{l} \langle 0, 5\rangle, \langle 1, undef\rangle, \langle 2, 3\rangle, \langle 3, 2\rangle \\ \langle 4, 3\rangle, \langle 5, 2\rangle, \langle 6, undef\rangle, \langle 7, undef\rangle \\ \langle 8, unused\rangle, \ldots, \langle n, unused\rangle \end{array} \right\}$$

Note here that the global variable i has become hidden from the active state for this call, since another variable with the same name is declared locally within A. The local variables a and b within main are also removed from the active environment for the life of this call. This state corresponds to the second stack shown in Figure 5.4.

Next, execution of the body of A leads to a call of B, with the global variable h passed by value as an argument. Thus, activation of the call to B leaves:

$$\sigma_B = \gamma_B \times \mu$$

where $\gamma_B = \gamma_A - \{\langle x, 4\rangle, \langle y, 5\rangle, \langle i, 6\rangle, \langle j, 7\rangle\} \, \overline{U} \, \{\langle w, 8\rangle, \langle j, 9\rangle, \langle k, 10\rangle\}$
        $= \{\langle h, 0\rangle, \langle i, 1\rangle, \langle w, 8\rangle, \langle j, 9\rangle, \langle k10\rangle\}$

$$\text{and } \mu = \left\{ \begin{array}{l} \langle 0, 5\rangle, \langle 1, undef\rangle, \langle 2, 3\rangle, \langle 3, 2\rangle \\ \langle 4, 3\rangle, \langle 5, 2\rangle, \langle 6, undef\rangle, \langle 7, undef\rangle \\ \langle 8, 5\rangle, \langle 9, undef\rangle, \langle 10, undef\rangle \\ \langle 11, unused\rangle, \ldots, \langle n, unused\rangle \end{array} \right\}$$

This state corresponds to the third stack shown in Figure 5.4.

Execution of the body of B in this state changes the value of the global variable i, leaving the following state upon return to A. Notice that the stack frame for B returns the state of its memory locations to *unused*.

$$\sigma_A = \gamma_A \times \mu$$

where $\gamma_A = \{\langle h, 0\rangle, \langle x, 4\rangle, \langle y, 5\rangle, \langle i, 6\rangle, \langle j, 7\rangle\}$

$$\text{and } \mu = \left\{ \begin{array}{c} \langle 0, 5\rangle, \langle 1, 10\rangle, \langle 2, 3\rangle, \langle 3, 2\rangle \\ \langle 4, 3\rangle, \langle 5, 2\rangle, \langle 6, \textit{undef}\rangle, \langle 7, \textit{undef}\rangle \\ \langle 8, \textit{unused}\rangle, \ldots, \langle n, \textit{unused}\rangle \end{array} \right\}$$

Finally, when control returns to `main`, its state includes the new value of global variable `i` and reflects the abandonment of the stack frame for A, which has terminated:

$$\sigma_{main} = \gamma_{main} \times \mu$$

where $\gamma_{main} = \{\langle h, 0\rangle, \langle i, 1\rangle, \langle a, 2\rangle, \langle b, 3\rangle\}$
and $\mu = \{\langle 0, 5\rangle, \langle 1, 10\rangle, \langle 2, 3\rangle, \langle 3, 2\rangle, \langle 4, \textit{unused}\rangle, \ldots, \langle n, \textit{unused}\rangle\}$

5.3 POINTERS

Pointers are commonly used in C, C++, and Ada. A pointer is implemented as a memory address, or reference, and provides a level of indirection in referencing a value or collection of values that other data types do not. Pointers are usually depicted by an asterisk (*) in C-style languages, and by an arrow ($\rightarrow$) in a diagram of dynamic (stack and heap) memory. We use arrows throughout this text in our diagrams that illustrate stack and heap memory management.

To illustrate the use of pointers in C-style programming, consider the linked list of integers shown in Figure 5.6, in which a Node is defined as follows:

```
struct Node {
    int key;
    Node* next;
}
Node* head;
```

Here, a Node is a pair of values, an integer `key` and a pointer `next`. The special pointer `head` refers to the first `Node` in the list.

| Figure 5.6   A Simple C-Style Linked List in the Heap

The following code searches this list for a given key, assuming that the pointer named `head` references the front of the list and the value `x` is to be found. Using short-circuit evaluation, the following loop traverses this list to find a `key` that matches `x`.

```
Node* p = head;
while (p != NULL && p->key != x)
        p = p->next;
```

Coming out of this loop, the value of p is either NULL (indicating that x is nowhere in the list) or a reference to the first instance of a Node whose key matches x.

Pointers are often viewed as the bane of reliable software development, since they tend to be error-prone and unsafe when placed in the hands of programmers. Pointers often complicate the proper implementation and management of data structures. Languages that require the program to manage pointers to allocate dynamic heap data structures also expect the program to properly restore heap blocks when they are no longer used. Garbage collection is, as we shall see, a complex process, and most programs do not do it well.

While these languages (notably C and C++) have not yet found a way to remove pointers from their vocabulary, other languages (such as Java) have done so. As we shall see, removing explicit pointers from the language does not diminish the utility of the heap for dynamic allocation of complex structures. Java relies on automatic garbage collection strategies to reclaim heap space that is freed when it is no longer needed by the program.

5.4 ARRAYS

Conventionally, structured types in imperative languages include arrays and record structures. *Arrays* are ordered sequences of values that all share the same type. *Records* are finite collections of values that have different types. Because of this distinction, arrays and structures use different strategies for allocating memory and referencing individual values within them. This section and Sections 5.5–5.6 discuss these distinctions.

An *array* is an ordered finite sequence of values of the same type. Here are some examples of Java array declarations and their interpretations:

```
int[] A = new int[10]; // an array of 10 int values
float[][][] B = new float[3][4][2]; // a 3x4x2 array of 24 floats
char[][] C = new char[4][3]; // a 4x3 array of 12 char values
Object[] D = new Object[8]; // an array of 8 Object references
```

An array may have any number of dimensions; A and D are one-dimensional arrays, while B and C are three- and two-dimensional, respectively.

In general, array memory is dynamically allocated at the time it is declared and its dimensions become known. Array declarations share the same scope rules as simple variables. In Java, arrays are treated like objects, and so their elements are allocated space in the heap. In other languages, arrays may be allocated space in either the static area, the run-time stack or the heap. We shall follow the Java conventions for array storage allocation in the following discussion.

In some languages, all the elements of an array are preinitialized at the time they are declared; in others they are not. For instance, Java follows the convention that arrays of numbers (int, float, short, long, double) have all their elements preinitialized at 0, arrays of char are preinitialized at '\u0000', arrays of references to objects are preinitialized at null, and arrays of booleans are preinitialized at false.

In some languages, the program can initialize an array's elements at the time the array is declared. The following Java declaration initializes all six integers in the array C to 1:

```
int[][] C = {{1, 1, 1},{1, 1, 1}};
```

Regardless of the size or type of object in an array, a convention must be established for storing and referencing an individual element. In languages like C, C++, Ada, and Java, a one-dimensional array reference takes the form

```
name[index]
```

where "name" is the name of the array and "index" is an integer-valued expression that identifies the position of the element within the array, relative to the position of the first element. For instance, the Java reference A[3] is a reference to the element that is at position 3 in the array A, relative to the position 0 for the first element. C, C++, and Java all use this *0-origin indexing,* in which the first element in the array has the index 0 and the remaining elements are indexed $1, \ldots, n - 1$ and n is the size of the array. Ada, like its predecessor Pascal, uses *1-origin indexing* by default (elements are normally indexed with values in the range $1, \ldots, n$), but it also allows the programmer to define a different range of index values as needed.

If we were to add arrays to Jay, we would need to:

1 Modify the concrete syntax to allow for the declaration of arrays and for variable references to be array references.
2 Modify the abstract syntax as well.
3 Modify the type checking so that indices are only used with arrays.
4 Modify the meaning functions to reference specified array elements.

5.4.1 Syntax and Type Checking for Arrays

The concrete syntax for adding one-dimensional arrays to Jay can be described by the following rules:

Declaration → Type Identifiers | *ArrayDeclaration*

ArrayDeclaration → Type [] *Identifier* = new *Type* [*Integer*]

Variable → Identifier | *Identifier* [*Expression*]

Here, the underlined parts indicate the changes required for the Jay syntax to accommodate array declarations and references. For instance, the following is a declaration of the array A with 10 integer entries.

```
int [] A = new int [10];
```

The abstract syntax for adding arrays to Jay has the following modifications:

Declaration = Variable v; *Type* t | *ArrayDeclaration*

ArrayDeclaration = Variable v; *Type* t; *Integer* size

Variable = String id | *ArrayVariable*

ArrayVariable = String id; *Expression* index

The Jay type checking functions *V* must be altered to ensure that every array name within the current environment is unique; the integer value which is the size of the array is greater than zero; every expression that is an index of an *ArrayVariable* has type integer; and every assignment statement whose target is an *ArrayVariable* has an integer-valued expression as its index. These requirements are ensured by first altering the typing function that generates a type map from a series of declarations:

typing: Declarations → TypeMap

$$typing(Declarations \text{ d}) = \bigcup_{i \in \{1...,n\}} \begin{matrix} \langle d_i.v, d_i.t, d_i.size \rangle & \text{if } d_i \text{ is an } ArrayDeclaration \\ \langle d_i.v, d_i.t \rangle & \text{otherwise} \end{matrix}$$

This function thus creates a type map with a series of triples (for array declarations) and pairs (for ordinary declarations).

Using this function, the following alterations to the *V* functions for Jay can be made to accommodate the type checking of arrays.

$$V(Declarations \text{ d}) = \forall i \in \{1, \ldots, n\}: \left(\begin{matrix} d_i \in ArrayDeclaration \supset 0 < d_i.size/ \\ d_i.t \in \{\text{int, boolean}\}/ \\ \forall j \in \{1, \ldots, n\}: i \neq j \supset d_i.v \neq d_j.v \end{matrix} \right)$$

This alteration ensures that the declared size of an array is a positive integer value, disallowing declarations like:

```
int [] A = new int[-5]
```

V(Expression e, TypeMap tm)
= $e \in \text{tm} \land typeOf(e.\text{index}) = \text{int}$ if *e* is an *ArrayVariable*

This function prevents the index of an *ArrayVariable* appearing in an *Expression* from having a noninteger type. For instance, the assignment

```
x = A[y];
```

would require y to have type `int`.

V(Statement s, TypeMap tm) = $typeOf(s.\text{target.index}, tm) = \text{int}$
if *s* is an *Assignment* and s.target is an *ArrayVariable*

Thus function forces the target of an assignment which is an *ArrayVariable* to have an integer-valued index. For instance, in the assignment

```
A[y] = x + 1;
```

the type of y must be `int`.

5.4.2 Array Allocation and Referencing
To provide integrity for the storage and retrieval of individual array elements, a language must define a convention for allocating memory to arrays and associating index values

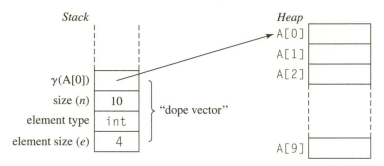

Figure 5.7 **Dynamic Memory Allocation for the One-Dimensional Array A**

with actual memory addresses. A commonly used convention for this purpose is illustrated in Figure 5.7 for the array A declared below.

```
int[] A = new int[10];
```

An array has an associated "dope vector," which contains information that enables effective addressing and type checking of references to individual entries, A[i]. In this example, for instance, every reference A[i] must have a value of i between 0 and 9, and every assignment to A[i] must be a value of type int. A strongly typed language requires that array references like A[i] be checked in this way every time they are executed. Since the value of i cannot be determined before run time, the dope vector is an additional piece of memory that must be created whenever an array is declared and initialized.

With this information, we can define the calculation of the address of A[i] with element size e, for any value of i within the range $0, \ldots, n - 1$ (see Figure 5.7).

$$\gamma(A[i]) = \gamma(A[0]) + e \cdot i$$

For example, the memory address of A[2] is calculated as:

$$\gamma(A[2]) = \gamma(A[0]) + 8$$

These conventions generalize to a two- or higher-dimensional array by extending the dope vector with sufficient information to enable the calculation of the address of an individual element. A memory allocation for the two-dimensional array C declared below is illustrated in Figure 5.8.[5]

```
char[][] C = new char[4][3];
```

Here, we assume that individual elements are stored in contiguous memory locations, one row at a time. This is called *row major order.* Calculation of the address of

---

5. In different languages, array memory allocation can occur either in the heap, in the stack, or in the static area. The illustration here favors the Java implementation of arrays, which are always allocated in the heap.

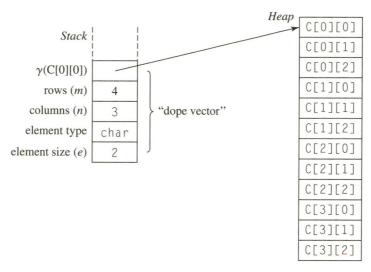

C[i][j], for any valid indexes i and j, can be defined in the following general way, again taking into account the number of addressable units (bytes) an individual element requires.

$$\gamma(C[i][j]) = \gamma(C[0][0]) + e(ni + j)$$

For example, the address of C[2][1] is computed by:

$$\gamma(C[2][1]) = \gamma(C[0][0]) + 2(3 \times 2 + 1)$$
$$= \gamma(C[0][0]) + 14$$

In all languages, range checking for array references cannot occur until run time, since the values of indexes i and j generally vary during program execution. For languages with 0-origin indexing, the following range checking code must be executed at run time:

- For the reference A[i], check that $0 \le i < n$.
- For the reference C[i][j], check that $0 \le i < m \wedge 0 \le j < n$.

In languages like Ada, which allow programmers to diverge from 0-origin indexing, the dope vector must contain additional information that enables effective address calculation and run-time type checking for references like A[i] and C[i][j]. This information includes the (nonzero) lower bound for each array index, in addition to the array size or the upper bound for that index. We leave the details of this problem as an exercise.

5.5 STRUCTURES

A *structure* or *record structure* is a collection of elements that do not all share the same type, and is distinguished from an array in this way. Modern programming languages have structures as central elements, and they all implement structures using similar strategies.

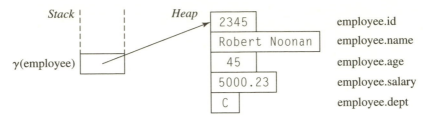

| **Figure 5.9** **Sample Structure Representing an Individual Employee**

A sample C structure representing an individual employee is defined below (a comparable Java class definition is shown on the right), and its memory requirements are described in Figure 5.9.[6]

```
typedef struct {              class employeeType {
    int id;                       int id;
    char[25] name;                String name = new String[25];
    int age;                      int age;
    float salary;                 float salary;
    char dept;                    char dept;
} employeeType;               }
employeeType employee;        employeeType employee;
```

Significantly, every field within a record structure may have a different data type (in this example, int, string, and float) than the others, and the fields have mutually unique names. An individual field of a variable that is a record structure is referenced by a *qualified reference* using "dot" notation. In this example, the notation employee.age for example is a qualified reference that identifies an individual employee's age, 45.

The type validity and semantic implications of structures are several. First, the names of fields within the structure must be mutually unique, and the name of the structure itself must be unique from that of any variable declared within the same scope. Second, the name of a field referenced on the right of a dot must be among the field names defined for the structure whose type is the variable referenced. Third, the type of each component must be compatible with that of any value assigned to it. For instance, the assignment

```
employee.age = y;
```

is valid only if age is a defined field of the record structure employeeType and the type of the variable y matches the type of that field. Fourth, the semantics of expression evaluation and assignment must be defined to allow proper memory addressing for a qualified reference whenever it appears in an expression or as the target of an assignment.

---

6. We note that C structs can be allocated either in the stack or in the heap. This illustration shows the heap allocation only.

5.5.1 Syntax and Type Checking for Structures

Adding structures to Jay requires alterations to its concrete and abstract syntax, type checking functions, and semantic functions. As a working example, consider the following C-like structure type and variable declarations:

```
struct point {
    int x;
    int y;
}
point p = new point();
p.x = 1;
p.y = p.x + 1;
```

Here are the alterations to the concrete syntax of Jay that accommodates structure declarations and references, with changed sections underlined.

Declaration → *Type Identifiers* | *RecordDeclaration*
RecordDeclaration → struct *Identifier* { *Declarations* }
Type → int | boolean | *Identifier*
Assignment → *Variable* = *Expression* ;
Factor → *Variable* | *Literal* | (*Expression*)
Variable → *Identifier* | *Identifier* . *Identifier*

The abstract syntax of Jay can be modified to capture the essential elements of record structures:

Declaration = *Variable* v; *Type* t | *RecordDeclaration*
RecordDeclaration = *String* rt; *Elements* e
Elements = *Element**
Element = *String* ef; *Type* et
Variable = *String* id | *QualifiedVariable*
QualifiedVariable = *String* id; *String* field
Type = int | boolean | *String* rt

To facilitate type checking, the new notion of *record map* parallels the familiar notion of *type map,* and contains a series of record type (*rt*) declarations, and is defined as follows:

$$rm = \{\langle rt_1, e_1\rangle, \langle rt_2, e_2\rangle, \ldots, \langle rt_n, e_n\rangle\}$$

That is, a record map is a set of pairs, each pair naming a record type *r* and a set of elements *e*. The elements *e* of a record type declaration have the form:

$$e = \{\langle ef_1, et_1\rangle, \langle ef_2, et_2\rangle, \ldots, \langle ef_n, et_n\rangle\}$$

where the *ef*'s are the field names and the *et*'s are their types. For example, the single declaration of the record type *rt* = point, would have the following record map:

$$rm = \{\langle point, \{\langle x, int\rangle, \langle y, int\rangle\}\rangle\}$$

This describes a record map with a single user-defined type point.

The function *recordTyping* creates a record map from a series of record definitions, and can be expressed in the following way:

recordTyping: RecordDeclaration → RecordMap

$$recordTyping(\text{String } rt, \text{Elements } e) = \left\langle rt, \bigcup_{i=1,\ldots,n} \langle ef_i, et_i \rangle \right\rangle$$

This requires that the definition of the *typing* function (Appendix B) be modified in the following way:

$$typing(\text{Declarations } d) = \left\{ \begin{array}{l} \displaystyle\bigcup_{d_i \notin RecordDeclaration} \langle d_i.\text{v.id}, d_i.\text{v.t} \rangle, \\[2em] \displaystyle\bigcup_{d_i \in RecordDeclaration} recordTyping(d_i.e) \end{array} \right\}$$

Thus, the declarations of type `point` and `point p` given above would generate the following record map:

$$\{\langle \text{point}, \{\langle \text{x, int}\rangle, \langle \text{y, int}\rangle\}\rangle, \langle \text{p, point}\rangle\}$$

Now the type checking requirements of a record declaration are that its element field names (*ef*) are unique, its element types (*et*) are either int or boolean, and its name (*rt*) is distinct from that of every other variable and record type declared within the same scope. For a nonrecord declaration, either its type is int or boolean or the name (*rt*) of a record declaration. Finally, as with Jay, all type and nontype declarations must mutually unique names. This is ensured formally by the following (messy!) definition of *V*.

$V(\text{Declarations } d) = \forall i \in \{1, \ldots, n\}$:

$$(d_i = \langle rt_i, e_i \rangle \in RecordDeclaration) \supset \left(\begin{array}{l} \forall j, k \in \{1, \ldots, n_i\}: ef_j \neq ef_k \wedge \\ \forall j \in \{1, \ldots, n_i\}: et_j \in \{\text{int, boolean}\} \end{array} \right.$$

$$(d_i = \langle v_i, t_i \rangle \notin RecordDeclaration) \supset \left(\begin{array}{l} t_i \in \{\text{int, boolean}\} \wedge \\ \exists k \in \{1, \ldots, n\}: \\ \qquad d_k = \langle rt_k, e_k \rangle \in RecordDeclaration \wedge \\ \qquad rt_k = t_i \end{array} \right.$$

$$\forall j \in \{1, \ldots, n\}: i \neq j \supset v_i \neq v_j$$

The validity rule for an *Expression* (Appendix B) can now be extended to cover qualified variables as well as simple variables, using the record map as a basis for checking. Here is the formal definition:

$V(\text{Expression } e, \text{TypeMap } tm, \text{RecordMap } rm)$
    $= e \in tm \wedge e.\text{field} \in rm(e.\text{type})$ if *e* is a *QualifiedVariable*
    $= e \in tm$ otherwise

That is, a qualified variable's field name must be among the field names defined in the record map for the variable's type. In our example, the field name x in the expression `p.x` must be among the field names defined by p's type, which is `point`.

To obtain the type of an expression that contains qualified variables, the *typeOf* function defined in Appendix B may be expanded as follows:

typeOf(*Expression* e, *TypeMap* tm, *RecordMap* rm)
    = *e* ∈ tm ⊃ *rm*(*e*.type, *e*.field)   if *e* is a *QualifiedVariable*
    = *e* ∈ tm ⊃ *tm*(*e*)   otherwise

The function *rm* retrieves the type of a field from a given *RecordMap,* in the same way that the function *tm* retrieves the type of a variable from a *TypeMap* (Appendix B). For example,

typeOf(p.x, {⟨p, point⟩}, {⟨point, {⟨x, int⟩, ⟨y, int⟩}⟩}) = *rm*(point, x) = int

since p.x is a *QualifiedVariable*.

Now the type checking function *V* given in Appendix B extends naturally to accommodate the possibility of a qualified variable as the source or target of an *Assignment*.

V(*Statement* s, *TypeMap* tm, *RecordMap* rm)
    = s.target ∈ tm ∧ *V*(s.source, tm, rm)
        ∧ *typeOf*(s.target, tm, rm) = *typeOf*(s.source, tm, rm)

That is, the type of the *Expression* that is the source must match the type of the (qualified) *Variable* that is the target.

5.6 SEMANTICS OF ARRAYS AND STRUCTURES

Here we augment the Jay semantic functions so that they support the one-dimensional arrays and structures whose syntax and type checking functions were defined in Chapter 4. This activity relies on the heap allocation strategies discussed above. Here, we assume that arrays and structures are allocated space in the heap, and they are accessed by a reference in the run-time stack.

5.6.1 Program State II: Heap Allocation

Unlike the stack, memory space in the heap is not always allocated and deallocated at one end. Instead, any block of memory in the heap may be allocated or deallocated at any time. A block of memory in the heap is activated by creating a "pointer" to it, but the size and location of that block depends on the available space in the heap at the time the request is made. Objects that require this distinguished use of heap space can include dynamic arrays and record structures.

The functions *new* and *delete* can be defined to provide a formal basis for describing the meaning of pointers and heap memory management. The function *new* finds a block of *unused* locations in the heap.

new(k, μ) = (b, μ′)

where b = *min m*: h ≤ m ≤ n ∧ ∀i ∈ {m, . . . , m + k − 1}: μ(i) = *unused*
    μ′ = μ $\overline{\cup}$ {⟨a, *undef*⟩, ⟨a + 1, *undef*⟩, . . . , ⟨a + k − 1, *undef*⟩}

That is, *new* finds the smallest address b of a contiguous block of k locations in the heap that are all *unused,* and marks those locations *undef*ined. If no such address b exists

h

7	*undef*	12	0
3	*unused*	*unused*	*unused*
undef	0	*unused*	*unused*
unused	*unused*	*unused*	*unused*

...

n

h

7	*undef*	12	0
3	*unused*	*unused*	*unused*
undef	0	*undef*	*undef*
undef	*undef*	*undef*	*unused*

...

n

│ Figure 5.10 The *New* (5) Heap Allocation Function Call: Before and After

in the heap, a "heap overflow" occurs and the *new* function fails. Otherwise, the value of b thus returned is a pointer, or reference, to the beginning of the heap block thus allocated.

For example, the effect of the function *new*(5) is shown in Figure 5.10, given an arbitrary heap state shown on the left. The shaded blocks on the right indicate the five heap blocks that are identified by *new* and marked *undef*ined. The address $h + 10$ is returned by *new* in this case.

The function *delete* reverses the effect of *new,* in the sense that it returns to *unused* status a block of heap locations. This is defined as follows:

$$delete(b, k, \mu) = \mu'$$

where $\mu' = \mu \ \overline{U} \ \{\langle b, unused \rangle, \langle b + 1, unused \rangle, \ldots, \langle b + k - 1, unused \rangle\}$

Here, the address b is used to mark the beginning of the block, and k gives the number of contiguous locations to be returned to the heap. The effect of *delete*($h + 10$, 5) is shown in Figure 5.10 by reading the right-hand heap as the before state and the left-hand heap as the after state.

5.6.2 Semantics of Arrays

The semantics of arrays can be implemented using the *new* and *delete* functions that manage blocks of heap space, as defined in Subsection 5.6.1. That is, a new array is allocated using the stack and the heap. The stack gains a new location to contain the address of the heap block that holds the array. The heap gains a new block that contains the entries of the array itself, laid out contiguously in the manner discussed in Subsection 5.6.1. This is illustrated in Figure 5.11.

Formally, memory allocation for arrays can be defined by extending the *allocate* function in the following way:

$$allocate(d_1, d_2, \ldots, d_k, \sigma) = \gamma' \times \mu'$$

$$\text{where } \gamma' = \gamma \cup \{\langle v_1, a \rangle, \langle v_2, a + 1 \rangle, \ldots, \langle v_k, a + k - 1 \rangle\}$$

$$\forall i \in \{0, \ldots, k - 1\}: \mu' = \begin{pmatrix} \mu \ \overline{U} \ \{\langle a + i, new(d_i.size) \rangle\} & \text{if } d_i \text{ is an } ArrayDeclaration \\ \mu \ \overline{U} \ \{\langle a + i, undef \rangle\} & \text{otherwise} \end{pmatrix}$$

$$a' = a + k$$

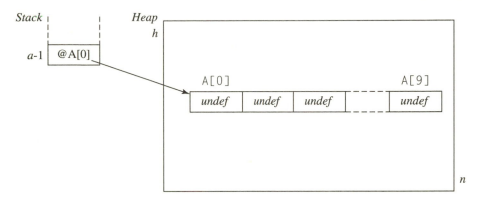

This definition corresponds directly to the picture in Figure 5.11 for allocating stack and heap space for the *ArrayDeclaration* int[] A = new int[10]).

In a similar way, the function *deallocate* can be extended to handle arrays by using the *delete* function in a straightforward way. The definition of this function is given below.

$$deallocate(d_1, d_2, \ldots, d_k, \sigma) = \gamma' \times \mu'(a')$$

$$\text{where } \gamma' = \gamma - \{\langle d_k, a\rangle, \langle d_{k-1}, a - 1\rangle, \ldots, \langle d_1, a - k + 1\rangle\}$$

$$\forall i \in \{0, \ldots, k - 1\}: \mu' = \begin{pmatrix} delete(a + i, d_i.\text{size}) & \text{if } d_i \text{ is an } ArrayDeclaration \\ \mu \,\overline{U}\, \{\langle a + i, unused\rangle\} \end{pmatrix}$$

$$a' = a - k$$

Now the semantics of expression evaluation can be extended to cover array references in the following way.

$$M(Expression \text{ e}, State \text{ } \sigma) = \sigma(e) \quad \text{if } e \text{ is an } ArrayVariable \wedge 0 \leq e.\text{index} < \sigma(e.\text{size})$$

The last part of this definition provides run-time range checking for array references inside arithmetic or boolean expressions. Now the definition of function $\sigma(e)$ from Section 5.1 must be extended so that it can retrieve the value of an array variable. That is:

$$\sigma(v) = \mu(\mu(\gamma(v)) + v.\text{index}) \quad \text{if } v \text{ is an } ArrayVariable$$
$$= \mu(\gamma(v)) \quad \text{otherwise}$$

Suppose we have the array variable A[5]. Then the value of A[5] is retrieved from the heap block allocated for A by retrieving the address of A[0] (denoted by $\mu(\gamma(v))$), adding 5 (denoted by $v.\text{index}$), and retrieving the value stored there (denoted by $\mu(\mu(\gamma(v)) + v.\text{index})$).

Finally, the semantics of array element assignment can be defined by extending the meaning of an *Assignment* (Appendix B) as follows:

$$M(Assignment \text{ s}, State \text{ } \sigma) = \sigma \,\overline{U}\, \{\langle\mu(\gamma(s.\text{target})) + M(s.\text{target.index}, \sigma), M(s.\text{source}, \sigma)\rangle\}$$
$$\text{if } s.\text{target is an } ArrayVariable$$

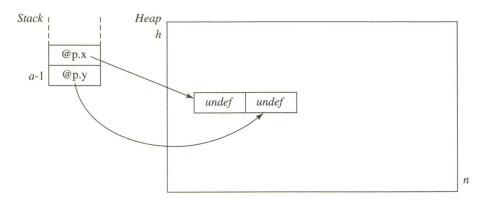

Figure 5.12   Allocation of Stack and Heap Space for the Declaration of Point p

Suppose we have the assignment A[5]=3. Then we want to override the value in that location of the heap block addressed by A[5] (that is, $\mu(\gamma(s.\text{target}))$ + $M(s.\text{target.index}, \sigma)$) by the value of the source expression 3 (denoted by $M(s.\text{source}, \sigma)$).

5.6.3 Semantics of Structures

To define the semantics of record structures, we need to define what happens in the stack and the heap when a new record type variable declaration is encountered. The situation is similar to that which occurs for arrays—the stack gains an entry for the new record variable, and that entry is a pointer to a block of heap space which accommodates all the fields in the record. This is illustrated in Figure 5.12 for our declaration of variable p with record type point.

To support this activity, it is natural to use the *new* and *delete* functions defined for the heap, along with the *allocate* and *deallocate* functions defined for the run-time stack. That is, memory allocation for a variable declaration d whose type is the record type

$$\langle rt, \{\langle ef_1, et_1\rangle, \langle ef_2, et_2\rangle \ldots , \langle ef_k, et_k\rangle\}\rangle$$

can be defined by extending the *allocate* function in the following way:

$$allocate(d, \sigma) = \gamma' \times \mu'$$

$$\text{where } b = @new(k)$$
$$\gamma' = \gamma \cup \{\langle d.ef_1, b\rangle, \langle d.ef_2, b + 1\rangle, \ldots , \langle d.ef_k, b + k - 1\rangle\}$$
$$\forall i \in \{0, \ldots , k - 1\}: \mu' = \mu \,\overline{U}\, \{\langle b + i, undef\rangle\}$$
$$a' = a + k$$

Notice that, like array storage allocation, this function makes the strong assumption that every element of a structure declaration requires one addressable memory location. This assumption is not realistic, but we are making it to avoid muddling the presentation.

With this definition, we can define the meaning of an *Expression* that has a qualified variable in the following way:

$$M(Expression \text{ e}, State \text{ } \sigma) = \text{e.id} \in \sigma \supset \sigma(\text{e.id, e.field}) \quad \text{if e is a } QualifiedVariable$$
$$= \text{e.id} \in \sigma \supset \sigma(\text{e}) \quad \text{otherwise}$$

So, for example, the meaning of the *Expression* p.x is the value stored in the heap location referenced by the pointer @p.x, which is in the run-time stack.

Finally, the meaning of an *Assignment* that has a qualified variable as its target can be formalized as:

M(*Assignment* a, *State* σ)

$= \sigma \ \overline{U} \ \{\langle \text{a.target.id . a.target.field}, M(\text{a.source}, \sigma)\rangle\}$ if a.target is a *QualifiedVariable*

$= \sigma \ \overline{U} \ \{\langle \text{a.target}, M(\text{a.source}, \sigma)\rangle\}$ otherwise

For example, if $\sigma = \{\langle \text{p.x}, \textit{undef}\rangle, \langle \text{p.y}, \textit{undef}\rangle\}$, then the assignment p.x = 1; gives the following new state:

$$\sigma \ \overline{U} \ \{\langle \text{p.x}, M(1, \sigma)\rangle\} = \{\langle \text{p.x}, \textit{undef}\rangle, \langle \text{p.y}, \textit{undef}\rangle\} \ \overline{U} \ \{\langle \text{p.x}, 1\rangle\}$$
$$= \{\langle \text{p.x}, 1\rangle, \langle \text{p.y}, \textit{undef}\rangle\}$$

5.7   MEMORY LEAKS AND GARBAGE COLLECTION

A major shift of attention in language design occurred with the strong commercial emergence of object-oriented languages in the 1990s. Much of this attention was due to the need for efficient and effective heap management, since the heap is the place where all objects are created, referenced, and manipulated. Along with active objects, the heap contains "inactive" objects—that is, blocks that had been allocated during an earlier stage of program execution and then relegated to the status of "no longer needed." These objects are affectionately known as *garbage,* since they have no useful purpose once they are discarded.

Once the heap space becomes full, it is important to have a strategy to reclaim those blocks of memory that contain garbage, so they can be reused by other objects that require heap space. Such a strategy is called *garbage collection,* and several garbage collection algorithms have been used more-or-less successfully over the last 25 years or more. The first languages that had a need for garbage collection were the functional languages, notably Lisp, since their memory requirements were dominated by the need to dynamically create, destroy, and change the structure of linked lists. The main garbage collection algorithms in use today are mainly derived from implementation strategies for functional languages.

5.7.1 Widows and Orphans

Garbage occurs in the heap. It is any block of memory that cannot be accessed by the program; that is, there is no pointer whose value references that block. Garbage can be easily created. Consider the following simple Java-like example, which initiates the creation of nodes in a linked list:

```
class node {
     int value;
     node next;
}
...
node p, q;
p = new node();
q = new node();
q = p;
```

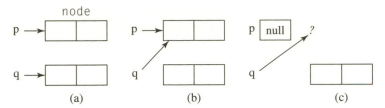

Figure 5.13 Creating Widows and Orphans: A Simple Example

The last statement creates a "memory leak" as shown in Figure 5.13b. In this situation, the node that had been referenced by q in Figure 5.13a has now becomes an *orphan*. Moreover, adding the following statement at the end of this program fragment

```
delete(p);
```

creates a dangling reference, or *widow*, out of q, as illustrated in Figure 5.13c.

C and C++ default the garbage collection responsibility to the programmer. That is, they provide explicit tools (like the `delete` function above) to explicitly return heap blocks to the system for reuse.[7] Java, Lisp, and other languages provide automatic garbage collection and take the responsibility for heap memory management out of the hands of programmers.

Three major strategies have served as a foundation for modern garbage collection algorithms. These are called *reference counting, mark-sweep,* and *copy collection.* We summarize these three strategies in Subsections 5.7.2–5.7.4.

5.7.2 Reference Counting

Reference counting assumes that the initial heap is a continuous chain of nodes called the *free_list*, each node having an additional integer field that contains a count of the number of pointers referencing that node (initially 0). As the program runs, nodes are taken from the free list and connected to each other via pointers, thus forming chains. Figure 5.14 is an example heap in which each node's reference count (RC) is shown as an integer inside a dotted line.

At this moment, there are four nodes and three are active, and the *free_list* contains all other nodes in the heap that are available for future use. Thus, three nodes are directly or indirectly accessible from p or q (which are assumed to be static global variables or local variables allocated within a stack frame).

The reference counting algorithm is applied dynamically; that is, whenever a `new` or `delete` operation occurs on a pointer, the algorithm is activated and as many orphans as possible are returned to the *free_list*. In this scheme, an orphan is simply a node whose reference count becomes zero, or any of its descendents (in the chain) whose reference count becomes zero as a result of a `delete` operation. With a `new` operation, the algorithm removes a node from the *free_list* and initializes its reference count to 1. With a pointer

---

7. Recent implementations of C and C++ have begun to provide garbage collection options, thereby relieving the programmer from this responsibility.

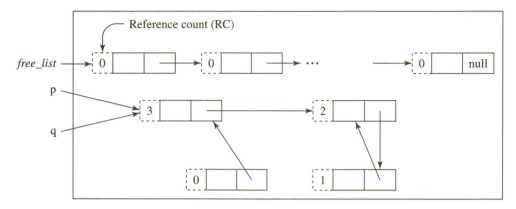

| Figure 5.14 **Node Structure and Example Heap for Reference Counting**

assignment, such as

```
q = p;
```

the reference count for the node currently referenced by q is decreased by 1 (and, if that count becomes 0, the reference count for its descendent is decreased by 1, and so on), the reference count for the node newly referenced by q is increased by 1, and q is finally assigned the reference value of p.

A careful examination of the reference counting algorithm reveals its fundamental weakness as a garbage collector. That is, it fails to return to the *free_list* any garbage that occurs in the form of an isolated circular chain. For instance, look at the effect of applying the algorithm to the heap shown in Figure 5.14 when the following statement is executed:

```
p->next = null;
```

This statement leaves the active heap from Figure 5.14 in the following condition:

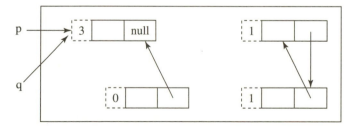

Here, two nodes are in an isolated chain pointing to each other (their reference counts are each 1). However, the algorithm cannot return either of these to the *free_list*, since such an action can be made only if a node's reference count is 0. A more detailed treatment of this algorithm is given as an exercise.

Overall, reference counting has two major disadvantages and one major advantage as a garbage collection algorithm. Its advantage is that it occurs dynamically, whenever a pointer assignment or other heap action is triggered by the program. Thus, the overhead associated with garbage collection is naturally distributed over the run-time life of the program. Its two disadvantages are (1) its failure to detect inaccessible circular chains, as illustrated above, and (2) the storage overhead created by the need to append an integer reference count to every node in the heap.

5.7.3 Mark-Sweep

Unlike reference counting, the *mark-sweep* algorithm is called into action only when the heap is full; that is, the *free_list* has become empty. Thus, several thousand pointer assignments and heap block allocations and deallocations may take place with no garbage-collection overhead occurring. But once mark-sweep is invoked, a more elaborate and time-consuming process interrupts the program than was the case for reference counting. Yet the main advantage of mark-sweep over reference counting is that it reclaims *all* garbage in the heap, whether or not the nodes form an isolated chain. Another advantage of mark-sweep is that it avoids the memory overhead required by adding an integer reference count to every node in the heap.

The mark-sweep algorithm makes two passes on the heap whenever it is invoked. During Pass I, all chains of references into the heap that originate from active variables in the run-time stack are followed, and every heap block that can be reached in this process is "marked" as accessible. All blocks that remain unmarked in Pass I are thus identified as orphans. Pass II traverses *every* block in the heap, returning all unmarked blocks to the *free_list* and unmarking all blocks that had been marked during Pass I. An example initial configuration for the mark-sweep algorithm is shown in Figure 5.15, where the dotted line surrounds a "mark bit" (MB) in each node which is initially 0.

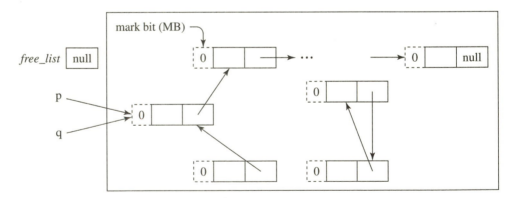

| Figure 5.15 Node Structure and Example for Mark-Sweep Algorithm

Here is a more precise description of the mark-sweep algorithm, which may be called whenever a new node is requested by the program. That is, when the assignment on the left is executed, the meaning on the right is implied:

```
q = new node();      if (free_list == null)
                         mark_sweep();
                     q = free_list;
                     free_list = free_list.next;
```

Pass I of the mark-sweep algorithm traverses the run-time stack and, for every reference R to a heap address, calls the following recursive method:

```
Mark(R):        if (R.MB == 0)
                    R.MB = 1;
                if (R.next != null)
                    Mark(R.next);
```

In our example, suppose that p and q are the only stack variables that reference the heap. Pass I would leave the heap in the configuration shown in Figure 5.16.

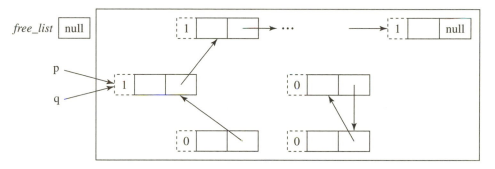

| **Figure 5.16 Heap after Pass I of Mark-Sweep**

Pass II, the "sweep pass," traverses the entire heap and returns all unmarked nodes to the *free_list*. Recall that h and n denote the bottom and top of the heap, as originally defined in Figure 5.1.

```
Sweep():    i=h;
            while (i<=n) {
                if (i.MB == 0)
                    free(i);
                else i.MB = 0;
                i = i + 1;
            }
```

The method `free(N)` restores the node referenced by N to the *free_list*. That is,

```
free(N):   N.next = free_list;
           free_list = N;
```

The result of Pass II on our example heap is shown in Figure 5.17. Here we assume that the top and bottom of the heap (h and n) are in the upper-left and lower-right corners of the figure, so that the bottom-most nodes that appear in the picture are the last nodes to be returned to the *free_list*.

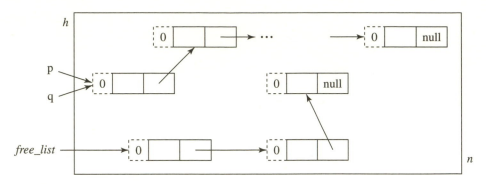

| **Figure 5.17** **Heap after Pass II of Mark-Sweep**

Now that the *free_list* is nonempty, the original assignment q = new node() can be completed in an obvious way.

5.7.4 Copy Collection

Copy collection represents a kind of time-space compromise when it is compared with mark-sweep. Like mark-sweep, copy collection is called only when the heap is full; i.e., the *free_list* is null. And it is significantly faster than mark-sweep because it makes only one pass on the heap. However, copy collection requires significantly more memory because at any one time only half the entire heap space is actively available for allocating new blocks.

For copy collection, the heap is divided into two identical blocks, called the *from_space* and the *to_space,* as shown in Figure 5.18. Here, no extra field is required in each node for a reference count or mark bit. Instead, all the active nodes are initially resident in the *from_space,* the *to_space* is unused, and *free_list* points to the next available block in the *from_space* that can be allocated.

This initialization is accomplished by the following algorithm:

```
from_space = h;
top_of_space = h + (n - h)/2;
to_space = top_of_space + 1;
free_list = from_space;
```

Now whenever a new node is allocated, the next available block in the *free_list* is retrieved. If none is available, the allocated blocks are repacked into the *to_space,* and the roles of *from_space* and *to_space* are reversed. This is accomplished in the following way:

```
q = new node():  if (free + 1 > top_of_space)
                     flip();
                 if (free + 1 > top_of_space)
                    abort('heap full')
                 q = free_list;
                 free_list = free_list + 1;
```

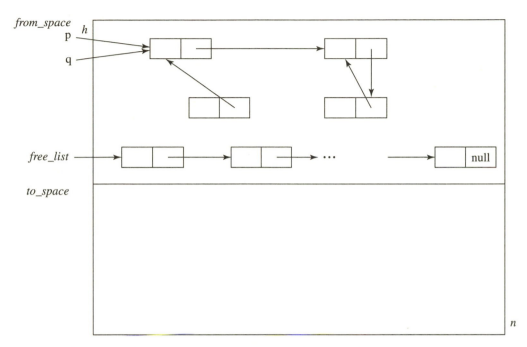

| Figure 5.18 Initial Heap Organization for Copy Collection

The methods *flip* and *copy* accomplish this role reversal, reassigning the *top_of_space* pointer and repacking the active blocks into the beginning of the *to_space*.

```
flip():      from_space, to_space = to_space, from_space;
             top_of_space = to_space + (n - h)/2;
             free_list = to_space;
             for R in roots
                 R = copy(R);


copy(R):     if (atomic(R) || R == null)
                 return R;
             if (!forwarded(R))
                 R' = free_list;
                 free_list = free_list + 2;
                 forwarding_address(R) = R';
                 R' = copy(R.value);
                 R'+1 = copy(R.next);
             return forwarding_address(R);
```

During this process, a referenced node R in the *from_space* can be either "forwarded" (copied to the *to_space*) or not. If it has been forwarded, each successive reference to node R is assigned its new address in the *to_space*. If it has not been forwarded, copy(R) copies it to the *to_space* using the next available node in the *free_list*. This is a recursive process, since node R may have descendants in the *from_space* that need to be forwarded as well.

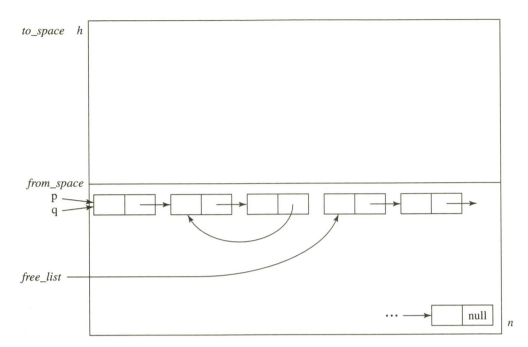

| Figure 5.19   Result of a Copy Collection Activation

The result of this process eliminates all inaccessible nodes in *from_space* and *to_space,* and a tight repacking of the active nodes in *to_space.* This is shown in Figure 5.19 for our example (assuming that the *free_list* had become empty).

The performance trade-off between copy collection and mark-sweep can be summarized in the following way. If R is the number of active heap blocks and the "residency" r is defined as the ratio of R to the heap size $n - h$, then the efficiency e (measured as the amount of memory reclaimed per unit time) is greater for copy collection when r is much less than $(n - h)/2$. However, mark-sweep becomes more efficient than copy collection as r approaches $(n - h)/2$.[8]

5.7.5 *Garbage Collection Strategies in Java*

Dozens of different garbage collection algorithms are in use today, and most of them are more complex than the three simple strategies discussed above. For example, some language implementations use a hybrid strategy, selecting between mark-sweep and copy collection depending on the residency r in the heap at the time garbage collection is invoked.

In Sun's Java system, the garbage collector runs as a low-priority process called a "thread," which executes whenever demand on processing time from other threads is low.[9] This reduces the number of garbage collection calls needed during peak processing times. Also in Java, the program can explicitly call the garbage collector using the call System.gc(). This invokes garbage collection immediately, regardless of the state of the heap at the time of the call.

---

8. For a more general discussion of garbage collection algorithms and their performance, see [Jones 1996].

9. We discuss Java threads in detail in Chapter 11.

EXERCISES

5.1 Consider the following declarations and memory allocation (assume that the structured type employeeType is the one defined in Section 5.5):

```
int * x = new int (-7);
employeeType y = new employeeType();
int [] A = new int [10];
```

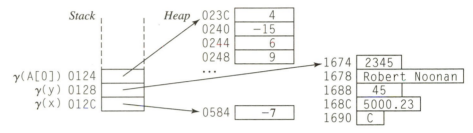

What is the value of each of the following expressions?

(a) $\mu(x)$

(b) $\mu(\mu(x))$

(c) $\gamma(y.\text{age})$

(d) $\sigma(y.\text{name})$

(e) $\gamma(A[3])$

(f) $\mu(A[3])$

5.2 Consider the example program and the stack frames shown in Figure 5.4. Show how these frames' contents would be changed if the language used dynamic scoping rather than static scoping.

5.3 The run-time stack strategy discussed in this chapter is particularly robust for supporting recursive methods. Show how the following recursive method that computes the greatest common divisor will affect the frames in the run-time stack each time it is called and returned, using the initial call gcd(24,10).

```
int gcd(int x, int y) {
    if (y==0) return x;
    else return gcd(y, x % y);
}
```

Assume for this exercise that the structure of the stack frame in Figure 5.2 is augmented to accommodate the called method's return value, as shown below:

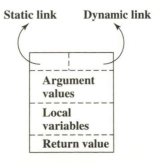

5.4 Consider the linked list shown in Figure 5.6. Using pointers and the declared variables shown there, write a C-style loop that will create this particular list.

5.5 Consider the following Java program.

```java
class myProgram {
    int[] A = {0, 3, 6, 9, 12, 15, 18, 21};
    int arg;
    boolean binsearch(int low, int high) {
        int k;
        if (low > high)
            return false;
        k = (low+high)/2;
        if (arg == A[k])
            return true;
        else if (arg < A[k])
            return search(low, k-1);
        else
            return search(k+1, high);
    }
    void main () {
        int result;
        arg = 5;
        result = binsearch(0, 7);
    }
}
```

(a) Draw a diagram of the complete stack and heap structure when this program initially calls the function `binsearch`. Assume the same stack frame modification that is given for Exercise 5.3.

(b) Show how the stack changes for each of the next two calls of `binsearch`.

(c) Show the final stack and heap contents after control has finally returned to `main` and a value has been assigned to the variable `result`.

5.6 Suggest how the array dope vector can be modified so that non 0-origin array elements can be effectively addressed and range checked for index out of range. Show how this modified dope vector can define each of the following array declarations:

(a) `int[] D = new int[3..6];`

That is, the expressions `D[3]`, `D[4]`, `D[5]`, and `D[6]` denote the four entries in the array `D`.

(b) `float[][] E = new float[3..6][[2..7];`

That is, `E` has $4 \times 6 = 24$ entries.

5.7 Redefine each of the equations given for one- and two-dimensional array indexing, so that the addresses of array elements defined by expressions `D[i]` and `E[i][j]` can be effectively computed. Use the information in the dope vectors you developed in the previous question.

(a) What is the effective address of the expression `D[5]`, using your new equation, relative to the (virtual) address of `D[0]`?

(b) What is the effective address of the expression E[4][4], using your new equation, relative to the address of E[0][0]?

5.8 Some versions of Fortran do not allocate storage for two-dimensional arrays in "row major order." Instead, they use "column-major order," in which the elements in each column occupy a series of contiguous memory locations.

(a) Describe how the addressing function $\gamma(C[i][j]) = \gamma(C[0][0]) + e(ni + j)$ defined in this chapter for array C needs to be changed so that the address of C[i][j] is effectively addressed when C itself is allocated in column-major order.

(b) Draw a picture of the memory layout for the elements of C, assuming C is stored in column-major order.

5.9 Consider the following familiar loop structure for the two-dimensional array C declared in this chapter.

```
for (i=0; i<m; i++)
    for (j=0; j<n; j++)
        C[i][j] = 3;
```

Here, the calculation of the address of C[i][j] requires two multiplications and two additions every time the loop is repeated. Can you think of a way in which this calculation can be made more efficient for this particular common loop structure? That is, can you express the calculation of the address $\gamma(C[i][j])$ as a function of the address $\gamma(C[i-1][j])$?

5.10 The function *deallocate* can be extended to handle heap deallocation for arrays by using the *delete* function, in the following way:

$$deallocate(d_1, d_2, \ldots, d_k, \sigma) = \gamma' \times \mu'(a')$$

$$\text{where } \gamma' = \gamma - \{\langle d_k, a \rangle, \langle d_{k-1}, a - 1 \rangle, \ldots, \langle d_1, a - k + 1 \rangle\}$$

$$\forall i \in \{0, \ldots, k - 1\}: \mu' = \begin{pmatrix} delete(a + i, d_i.\text{size}) & \text{if } d_i \text{ is an } ArrayDeclaration \\ \mu \, \overline{U} \, \{\langle a + i, unused \rangle\} & \end{pmatrix}$$

$$a' = a - k$$

Show the effect of this definition when it is applied to the deallocation of heap space for the array shown in Figure 5.11.

5.11 Show what the record map *rm* looks like for the two record types point and employee given in this chapter.

5.12 Show how the state $\sigma = \{\langle p.x, 1 \rangle, \langle p.y, undef \rangle\}$ changes for the assignment

```
p.y = p.x + 1;
```

using the declarations of p and point given in this chapter. Show all the details of this state transformation.

5.13 Completion of a procedure call (that is, deallocation of a stack frame) can create garbage in the heap. Discuss the specific circumstances under which this can occur.

5.14 Design a complete reference counting garbage collection algorithm, using the discussion and elementary node structure given in this chapter. Hint: assume that the heap has an address space with integer range $\{h, \ldots, n\}$ and that each node requires three addressable units of memory: one for the reference count, one for the value, and one for a pointer to another node in the heap. Consider the following auxiliary methods:

- `free(N)`: restore the node referenced by N to the *free_list*
- `delete(N)`: decrement the reference count for node N; if its reference count becomes 0, then `delete(N.next)` and `free(N)`. (This one's recursive.)
- `N = M`: `delete(N)`, increment the reference count for M, and assign N = M.

5.15 Determine the status of garbage collection in the current development of the C++ language. Is there an interest in adding automatic garbage collection to the C++ standard? Explain.

5.16 (Team project) Extend the implementation of Jay that you completed in Chapter 4 so that it includes methods. This will require that you complete the following three tasks:
   (a) Augment your recursive-descent parser to accommodate the concrete and abstract syntax of methods.
   (b) Augment the implementation of type-checking functions *V* to accommodate the type checking of methods, as defined in this chapter.
   (c) Augment the implementation of semantic functions *M* to accommodate the semantics of methods, as defined in this chapter.

5.17 (Team project) Extend your implementation of Jay so that it includes arrays. Use the concrete and abstract syntax, type-checking functions *V*, and semantic functions *M* for arrays that are defined in this chapter. This will require that you complete the three tasks described in Exercise 5.16.

5.18 (Team project) Extend your implementation of Jay so that it includes record structures. Use the concrete and abstract syntax, type-checking functions *V*, and semantic functions *M* for record structures that are defined in this chapter. This will require that you complete the three tasks described in Exercise 5.16.

Exception Handling

6

". . . exceptions are necessary for managing the complexity of error handling.
A language that lacks such facilities forces its users to laboriously simulate them."

Bjarne Stroustrup, LinuxWorld

CHAPTER OUTLINE

In this chapter we explore the subject of exceptions and exception handling. An *exception* is a condition detected by an operation that cannot be resolved within the context of the operation. A typical example of an exception would be a division by zero, which would cause a hardware interrupt. To *throw an exception* is to signal that an exception has occurred. In the case of a division by zero, the exception is thrown by the computer hardware. To *catch an exception* means that the exception thrown causes control to be transferred to an exception handler. In the case of the division by zero, control is transferred by a hardware interrupt to an interrupt routine, which normally prints an appropriate message and terminates the offending program.

Exceptions can occur at many levels of abstraction. At the hardware level, exceptions include many illegal operations, such as division by zero, integer overflow, floating point underflow or overflow, and so on. At the programming language level, exceptions can be caused by such events as an illegal array index, attempting to read a value of the wrong type, an attempted access to an object through a null pointer, and so on. There can also be a need for exceptions within a program or an application; an example would be attempting to execute a pop operation on an empty stack.

In dealing with an exception facility in a programming language, we must consider how an exception is thrown and how an exception handler is associated with a particular exception. For a long time, no language in widespread use provided a truly general and usable exception mechanism; a few languages such as Cobol and PL/I provided limited exception facilities. Beginning with Ada, newer languages have either included an exception mechanism (as in the case of Java) or later incorporated one (as in the case of C++).

The reason for including exceptions in modern languages is clear: to simplify the programmer's task in developing more robust applications. This has become critically important as computers have been included (or embedded) in other devices such as car engines, aircraft control systems, and so forth. In fact, these latter types of applications are precisely the ones for which Ada was originally designed. A computer that is running a car engine or flying an aircraft cannot be allowed to stop simply because an exceptional condition has occurred. The program running the embedded computer must deal with the situation and continue as best it can. Such applications must be *robust* and continue to operate in many unexpected error situations.

Unlike in the earlier chapters, we are not going to develop a formal semantic model of exceptions based on denotational semantics. Although such models exist [Alves-Foss 1999], the mathematics is even more forbidding than that of Chapter 5. Instead we shall present a more conceptual model of exceptions. This conceptual style will be continued through the remaining chapters.

In the remaining sections of this chapter we consider how exceptions are handled in programming languages that lack a general exception facility. Then we consider a model for exceptions and discuss how the exception mechanism in Java fits this model.

6.1 TRADITIONAL TECHNIQUES

Cobol was the first widely used language to provide a primitive exception handling facility. PL/I, which attempted to combine the best features of Fortran, Cobol, and Algol, greatly extended the ability of a program to handle exceptions. PL/I allowed a program to handle a long list of language-defined exceptions, as well as the ability to define application-specific exceptions. In the early 1980s until the advent of Ada, most programming languages developed in the 1960s and 1970s, including C, Pascal, and Modula, did not provide a general exception handling facility. The designers of Ada took advantage of the experience of PL/I programmers, as well as the experimental languages CLU [Liskov 1979; Liskov 1981] and Mesa [Mitchell 1979].

First, we consider the question of how programmers deal with exceptional situations in languages such as C, Pascal, and Fortran that do not support an exception mechanism. For dealing with application level exceptions, one technique that is widely used is to have a function return an unusual or illegal value in the case of failure. For example, in searching an array for a specific value, if the value is found, typically the index of the value is returned. But if the value is not contained within the array, then (in the case of 0-indexed arrays) the value −1 is returned, to indicate that the value was not found. Java uses this approach when searching a Vector using the `indexOf` method, which returns −1 if the object being searched for is not found.

Similar situations pervade many of the libraries in Java. In retrieving the value associated with a given key in a Hashtable, Java returns a null object if the key is not in the Hashtable. Similarly, in reading lines from a BufferedReader using the `read Line` method, a null object is returned at end of file. This approach is also widely used in the standard C libraries.

Whether such situations are truly exceptions or just part of the normal processing of tables and files is a subject of some debate. In Java the situations above are not considered exceptions, while in Ada, for example, one is expected to continue reading until encountering an end of file that triggers an exception. In contrast, Pascal requires an explicit test for end of file before executing a read; encountering an end of file during a read triggers a fatal exception from which there is no recovery.[1]

One possible explanation for the difference in philosophies between Ada and Java is that in Java exceptions are objects. Thus, creating an exception involves a heap allocation that must eventually be garbage collected after the exception has been handled. In Ada an exception is a primitive type built into the language, so the cost of generating and handling exceptions is less than it is in Java.

An approach taken for functions for which no unusual or illegal value exists is to add an error parameter (or to return an error code for an otherwise `void` function). An example from Turbo Pascal is the `val` function which is used to convert a string representation of a number to binary:

```
val(numberString, int, error);
```

If the variable `numberString` contained the value *'123'* before the call on `val`, then afterward *int* has the value 123 and `error` has the value 0. If instead `numberString` contained the value *'1x3'*, then after the call on `val`, `int` would be undefined and `error` would have the value 2, representing the position in the string where the illegal character occurred.

For the type of applications for which Ada and Java are intended, such mechanisms are a poor substitute for a true exception mechanism. Consider, for example, the following code in Pascal to read a set of numbers from a file and compute their sum:

```
sum := 0.0;
while not eof(file) do begin
   read(file, number);
   sum := sum + number;
end;
```

Several different possible exceptions prevent this from being robust code. First, if there is whitespace after the last number, the end of file test will return *false* after the last number, but the read will skip the whitespace and throw a fatal exception when the end

---

1. Pascal lacks an exception handling mechanism.

of file is detected. Another type of exception can occur if an input value is not a valid number, for example, the value contains a nondigit character. This also results in a fatal exception, since languages like Pascal, C, Fortran, and so forth provide no exception handling mechanism.

So, although Pascal has a numeric input capability, it cannot be used in a robust application because of the possibility that a user might enter an illegal number. Instead numeric values have to be read into a string and then converted to a number by the application. Pascal does not even provide a library routine for this, although some implementations, such as Turbo Pascal, do. A good exception mechanism allows the use of these *unsafe* routines, providing a way to deal with errors when they occur.

In Section 6.2 we deal with the various design issues encountered when adding an exception mechanism to a programming language.

6.2 **MODEL**

When an exception is triggered for any reason, the flow of control is transferred to an exception handling mechanism. Several design issues arise in designing an exception mechanism.

First, how is a handler associated with the particular exception thrown? At the hardware level, each exception corresponds to a hardware interrupt. There is basically only a single interrupt handler for each type of interrupt. In a large application, such an arrangement is less useful than allowing different portions of an application to associate individual exception handlers with a particular exception; this provides a great deal of flexibility at the application level.

As we shall see in more detail in Section 6.3, Ada, C++, and Java all allow an exception handler to be associated with a block of code. Such a block can be an entire method or function, or merely a group of statements embedded in a larger construct, such as a simple statement sequence, an if statement, or a loop.

If there is no exception handler in the method or function of the statement or operation that throws the exception, then the search is propagated up the call stack to the calling routine. If the method or function call is contained in a block with a handler for the given excepetion, then the exception is caught there. Otherwise the search continues up the call stack for an appropriate exception handler.

Another design issue is whether or not the exception handler can resume the code or method that throws the exception; the latter case is termed *termination*. Interrupt handlers in an operating system implement the resumption model; that is, after dealing with the interrupt the handler is free to resume whatever code threw the interrupt. Exception handling mechanisms in Ada, C++, and Java all use the termination model; the code signaling the exception cannot be resumed.

The alternative to the termination model is *resumption*. In this case, after the exception is handled, the flow of control is returned to the operation immediately after the one which throws the exception. PL/I uses the resumption model.

All of this is depicted pictorially in Figure 6.1 using Java syntax for exception handling.

PL/I programmers can achieve the result of the termination model by executing a return or nonlocal goto in the exception handler. Similarly, careful programming in Java, Ada, and C++ allows the programmer to simulate the resumption model.

| Figure 6.1 Exception Handling

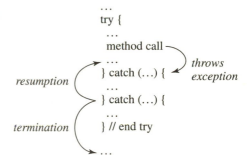

In Section 6.3 we consider the exception mechanism in Java. The mechanisms in Ada and C++ are sufficiently similar to Java to allow this treatment to serve as a general introduction to exception handling.

6.3 EXCEPTIONS IN JAVA

An exception in Java is an object of an exception class; Figure 6.2 shows the hierarchy of exception classes in Java.

Exceptions in Java are subclasses of `Throwable` and are divided into three categories: errors in the virtual machine (`Error` and its subclasses); runtime exceptions (`RuntimeException` and its subclasses) such as access through a null object or an illegal subscript; and all others. Note that the latter two categories are subclasses of the class `Exception` and, by convention, have the word *exception* as part of their name. Similarly, virtual machine errors, by convention, all have the word *error* as part of their name. Exceptions of type `Error` are not normally the concern of the programmer; they include such virtual machine errors as out of memory, runtime stack overflow, and so on.

Exceptions, as opposed to virtual machine errors, are divided into *checked* and *unchecked* exceptions. Formally in Java a checked exception is an instance of the class `Exception` or one of its subclasses that is not an instance of `RuntimeException`. Checked exceptions are application-level exceptions. The Java class libraries contain a wide variety of exceptions, including I/O exceptions, network exceptions, and so on. An unchecked exception is an instance of the class `RuntimeException` or one of its subclasses. The Java language requires that checked exceptions be caught by an exception handler. The programmer is not required to provide an exception handler for an unchecked exception,

Figure 6.2 Java Exception Type Hierarchy

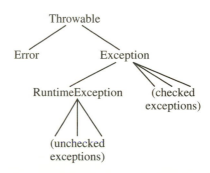

although one may be provided if desired. Examples include substring or array indices out of bounds, access through a null object, arithmetic exceptions such as divide by zero, and so on.

A programmer-defined exception in Java is an object of class `Exception` or one of its subclasses; thus, a programmer-defined exception can be checked or unchecked. An exception may contain an arbitrary string message. Thus, the class `Exception` has two constructors, whose signatures are:

```
public Exception( );
public Exception(String s);
```

Thus, one creates a new exception by subclassing `Exception` or one of its subclasses, as shown in Figure 6.3.

```
class StackUnderflowException extends Exception {
    public StackUnderflowException() { super(); }
    public StackUnderflowException(String s){  super(s);}
}
```

I Figure 6.3 Creating a New Exception Class

A typical use of such an exception would be:

```
if (stack == null)
    throw new StackUnderflowException();
```

Note that exception objects (as opposed to subclasses) are rarely named, since their only purpose is to be thrown. Subclasses of `Exception` may hold additional information or provide specialized behavior. However, in most cases they exist only to provide new exception subtypes. The most common subtype is the `IOException` and its subclasses in the package `java.io`.

A Java method (including constructors) is required to specify via a `throws` clause in the method header any checked exception that it does not catch itself. An example is the `readLine` method of a BufferedReader:

```
public String readLine( ) throws IOException;
```

A Java compiler can then ensure that each checked exception is caught and, hence, dealt with by the application. Exceptions are caught in one of two ways. Either a call to a method that potentially throws an exception must appear in a `try` statement or the method containing the call must declare which exceptions it throws. Consider the following code which given a *filename* attempts to open that file for input:

```
try{
    BufferedReader infile = new BufferedReader(
                                        new FileReader(filename));
    ... // process file
} catch (FileNotFoundException e) {
    System.out.println("File not found: " + filename);
    System.exit(1);
} // try
```

Each `catch` has the general format of a method header, in that it specifies the type (or super type) of the exception that it is catching and a formal argument, which can be used like any object. In this case if the exception is thrown, a message is printed and the application terminated via a nonzero exit (error exit, by convention). If there were no exit, the flow of control would continue with the next statement after the `try`; thus, Java uses the termination model for handling exceptions. The general form of a `try` statement is:

```
try {
    ... // code containing 1 or more method invocations
    ... // that throw exceptions
    ...
} catch (...) { ...
} catch (...) { ...
...
} finally { ... }
```

If an exception is thrown, each `catch` clause is evaluated in order until a match occurs. Then the block associated with that `catch` clause is executed. Each `try` can have as many `catch` clauses as desired. Note that a single `try` can be used to catch multiple exceptions across many separate commands, so long as each possible checked exception is caught. A simple way to simulate an unconditional `catch` for checked exceptions is to use `Exception` as the class in the last `catch` clause.

The `finally` clause, if present, is always executed, whether an exception is thrown or not. It is not possible to avoid executing the code in the `finally` clause; even if the block of code executed ends in a `return` or `exit`, the `finally` clause will still be executed.

The other alternative to using a `try` on calls to methods that throw exceptions is to have the containing method rethrow the exception via a `throws` clause:

```
public void readFile(BufferedReader infile) throws IOException {
    String line;
    while ((line = infile.readLine()) != null) {
        ... // process line
    }
}
```

This routine reads lines via the `readLine` method of class `BufferedReader`, which can throw an `IOException`. Because the call to `readLine` does not appear in a `try` statement, the `readFile` method must declare that it does not handle the exception. Note that at end of file, the `readLine` routine returns a null object, rather than throwing an end of file exception.[2]

---

2. In contrast, Ada throws an exception at end of file. One possible explanation for this difference is that in Ada exceptions are not objects. So there is no need to allocate memory, and later deallocate memory, for an exception.

Java allows an application programmer to throw an exception, either an instance of the class *Exception* or one of its subclasses. Exceptions are thrown with a *throw* statement:

```
throw new Exception( );
```

At this point the normal flow of control is terminated, with control being transferred to the matching `catch` of the nearest surrounding `try`. If one does not exist, the called method rethrows the exception and the process continues up the call stack.

Note that the exception thrown above is anonymous, in that no named reference to it is kept. Since the flow of control does not continue past this point, it usually serves no purpose to keep a reference to the exception.

Normally, the exception thrown would be one of the subclasses of `Exception`, perhaps even with a message attached:

```
throw new StackUnderflowException("pop on an empty stack");
```

Of course, creating a new subtype of exception would have to be done using the normal class mechanism. An example of this is provided in Section 6.6. A full description of classes and inheritance is contained in Chapter 7. The major purpose of creating new exceptions is to provide a name meaningful to the application and to group exceptions by category. An example of the latter is `IOException` which is the parent class of all of the input/output exceptions.

In Sections 6.4–6.7, we give common uses of exception handling, ranging from handling Java class library exceptions to defining our own.

6.4 EXAMPLE: MISSING ARGUMENT

A typical example of an exception causing termination of the current processing of data occurs in many applications that require one or more arguments from the command line. Consider the case where the application requires a single file name as a command line argument. The typical code for handling such a scenario in the main method might appear as:

```
public static void main(String[] arg) {
  BufferedReader rdr = null;
  try {
    rdr = new BufferedReader(new FileReader(arg[0]));
  } catch (IndexOutOfBoundsException e) {
    System.err.println("Missing argument.");
    displayUsage( );
    System.exit(1);
  } catch (FileNotFoundException e) {
    System.err.println("Cannot open file: " + arg[0]);
    System.exit(1);
  }
  process(rdr);
}
```

In the case of normal processing, the application user supplies a valid file name when the application is invoked, which is then successfully opened and processed by the application, producing a result. However, several things can go wrong. The application user could forget to supply an argument or, alternatively, the user could supply an argument which is either not a file name or, a file which cannot be read by the application. Since the application requires a valid input filename for its argument, in the event of one of the errors above, it chooses to issue an appropriate error message and quit.

If no argument is supplied on the command line, then the reference `arg[0]` throws an `ArrayIndexOutOfBoundsException`, since the index exceeds the actual size of the array. Normally, use of indexing need not appear in a `try` statement; doing so in this case allows the application to supply an application-specific error message, rather than the Java language error message. The latter would presumably be unintelligible to the user. The same result could have been achieved in a language without exception handling by an appropriate if statement protecting the `arg[0]` reference. Either style can be used in languages that support exception handling.

Note also that the `catch` catches an `IndexOutOfBoundsException`, which is the parent class of the exception actually thrown. Other than the relative brevity of the parent class name, there seems little reason in this case to prefer one versus the other. One use of this feature is to list all specific exceptions first and then use a parent class (for example, `Exception`) effectively as a catch for all other exceptions.

The other problem that can occur is that the file cannot be opened for reading. This can be caused by any number of situations. The argument supplied may not be a valid filename, the file may not exist (note that the attempt is to open the file for input), or the file may not be accessible (for example, the user does not have read access to the file). In any of these cases, the constructor for the class `FileReader` throws a `FileNotFoundException`. In this case, the Java programmer must either embed the constructor call in a `try`, or specify that the method, in this case `main`, throws the exception. The Java language insists that methods specify via the `throws` clause which exceptions are not caught, so that a Java compiler can ensure that some method in the application eventually catches the exception. In this particular case, the exception is caught in the `main` method and an appropriate error message given.

Note that in this example each `catch` ends with an error exit (nonzero code). It seems as if the exit call could be moved to a `finally` clause. If an exception is thrown, first the appropriate `catch` is executed and then the `finally` clause is executed. However, the `finally` clause would be executed even if no exception were thrown. It cannot be avoided, even if the code for the `try` clause ended in a return or exit itself.

The solution given above has one undesirable aspect to it. The call to the method `process` cannot be included inside the `try` block. If it were, any index bounds exception that is uncaught in the method `process` (since it is an unchecked exception) results in the missing argument message; this is very error prone and, hence, undesirable. Moving the call to `process` outside the `try-catch` block means having to declare a `BufferedReader` variable outside the `try-catch` block and explicitly initializing it to `null`.

An alternative solution in this case is to ensure that the length of the `arg` array is at least one. This solution is given in Figure 6.4. This code is a classic example of the termination model used by Java in implementing exceptions. If the file cannot be opened for any reason, then it is not processed. The code where the exception occurred cannot

```
public static void main(String[] arg) {
  try {
  if (arg.length < 1) {
  System.err.println("Missing argument.");
  displayUsage( );
  System.exit(1);
  }
  process(new BufferedReader(new FileReader(arg[0])));
  } catch (FileNotFoundException e) {
  System.err.println("Cannot open file: " + arg[0]);
  System.exit(1);
  }
}
```

| Figure 6.4 Missing Argument Exception

be resumed. In the next example, we explore how the resumption model of handling exceptions can be simulated in Java using a loop.

6.5 **EXAMPLE: INVALID INPUT**

Another common scenario occurs when an application prompts a user for input and a keying problem occurs. In this case, we assume the simple expedient of notifying the user of the problem and reprompting for another input.

In the case of Java, there is no overloaded *read* method for the different primitive data types that converts from the text representation of, for example, an integer to internal representation (32-bit binary for integers), as there is for print. Instead, a string representation of the number is read and converted to (for example) an int. Assuming that a BufferedReader object in has been created using:

```
BufferedReader in = new BufferedReader(new InputStreamReader(System.in));
```

then the required code is given in Figure 6.5 .

```
while (true) {
  try {
    System.out.print ( "Enter number : " );
    number = Integer.parseInt(in.readLine ( ));
    break;
  } catch (NumberFormatException e) {
    System.out.println ( "Invalid number, please reenter.");
  } catch (IOException e) {
    System.out.println("Input error occurred, please reenter.");
  } // try
} // while
```

| Figure 6.5 Invalid Input Exception

If a valid number is entered, then no exception is thrown and the loop is terminated. However, if an invalid number is keyed, then an exception is thrown, an error message is printed, and the loop is repeated, reprompting the user for a number. Good programming practice requires that the user have some other means of exiting this potentially infinite loop.

Note that the `readLine` method may throw an `IOException`, which must also be handled by the `try` statement. In this example we use the simple expedient of reprompting for another number. Other possibilities exist.

The invalid input example uses an infinite loop to circumvent the termination model of exceptions used in Java. The loop is terminated only if no exception is thrown. Otherwise the loop is used to try again. Thus, use of the loop allows the programmer to effectively achieve a resumption model of exception handling.

In Section 6.6, we show how an exception specific to an application can be created and thrown.

6.6 EXAMPLE: THROWING AN EXCEPTION

In developing a reusable class or method, errors may occur that the class developer would like the programmer to deal with. Most languages that provide exception handling allow the programmer to create application-specific exceptions and throw them under the appropriate conditions. These usually represent conditions that the user of the class or method may wish to recover from.

A typical example would be the development of a stack class. Assume that we have created the `StackUnderflowException` class given in Figure 6.6. If the stack is empty, a `pop` operation is undefined. Thus, the typical code for `pop` on a `Stack` class of `int`'s using an array implementation is given in Figure 6.7.

```
class StackUnderflowException extends Exception {
  public StackUnderflowException( ) { super(); }
  public StackUnderflowException(String s){ super(s);}
}
```

| Figure 6.6 StackUnderflowException Class

```
class Stack {
  int stack[];
  int top = 0;
  ...

  public int pop() throws StackUnderflowException {
    if (top <= 0)
        throw new StackUnderflowException("pop on empty stack");
    return stack[--top];
  }
  ...
}
```

| Figure 6.7 Throwing an Exception

The code declares an array named `stack` to hold up to some maximum number of integer values; the variable `top` keeps track of the current top of the stack. `StackUnder-flowException` is declared as a subclass of the class `Exception`; note that it has no methods of its own, instead relying on its parent class for its methods. This is normal practice for declaring exception classes in Java.

The method `pop` is very simple; first, it decrements `top` and then returns the value of `stack[top]` using the decremented value of `top`. However, this operation is unsafe; if the original value of `top` is less than or equal to zero, an `ArrayIndexOutOfBoundsException` will be thrown. However, the caller of this method need not deal with the exception. Also, the kind of exception thrown will change if the code were modified to use a linked list implementation.

So instead a `StackUnderflowException` is created and thrown, as needed, by the pop method. The header of the method is required to list any exception that it can throw. As seen in our previous examples, any use of the `pop` method requires the programmer to explicitly catch this exception.

As shown in Figure 6.6, creating a new exception is fairly simple, usually requiring the writing of just a class declaration with two constructors.

6.7 AN ASSERTION CLASS

In this section we develop an assertion class that allows us to insert assertions into our code. As you may recall from Section 3.4, these assertions typically represent input assertions, output assertions, or loop invariants. In practice, the assertion class would be used for input assertions. Recall the proof of function *Fib* from Section 3.4. Inserting a check that the input variable *n* is nonnegative is simple. Inserting an assertion that the correct term of the Fibonacci sequence is computed requires having an alternative method for computing the answer; in general, this is unworkable.

We would like the assertion class [Fowler 2000] to be simple and easy to use. The first thing we must do is to create a new exception. To avoid having to add lots of try-catch statements we make our assert exception a subclass of `RuntimeException`. Logically, an assert is like an index out of bounds: we expect it to occur only if the programmer has made an error. So, like using an index, we will be able to make assertions without worrying about the need for try-catch statements. Our required exception class is given in Figure 6.8.

```
class AssertException extends RuntimeException {
    public AssertException( ) { super( ); }

    public AssertException(String s) { super(s); }
}
```

| **Figure 6.8 AssertException Class**

Next we develop the assertion class itself. Since there is no data to be stored within an assertion object, we opt to make the class a simple library of static methods. One method clearly required is to assert that a particular boolean condition is true. The code for this method is straightforward; if the condition is false, the method throws an `AssertException`. Another useful method asserts that execution should not reach this point; the implementation always throws an exception. Finally, we include a boolean constant which, if desired, can be used to optimize assertions out of the client[3] code, if desired. Our assertion class is given in Figure 6.9.

```
class Assert {
    static public final boolean ON = true;
    static public void isTrue(boolean b) {
        if (!b) { throw new AssertException("Assertion failed"); }
    }

    static public void shouldNeverReachHere() {
        throw new AssertException("Should never reach here");
    }
}
```

| Figure 6.9 Assert Class

As an example of the use of this class, consider the revised stack class given in Figure 6.10. In this version of the stack class, it is the client's responsibility to check that a stack is not empty before invoking a pop operation. Therefore, the programmer merely asserts that the stack is not empty as part of the pop operation. In the event that a run-time exception is ever triggered by the assert, this would be considered a bug in the client code.

| Figure 6.10 Using
| Asserts

```
class Stack {
    int stack[];
    int top = 0;
    ...

    public boolean empty() { return top <= 0; }

    public int pop() {
        Assert.isTrue(!empty());
        return stack[--top];
    }
    ...
}
```

Note that since the pop method throws a RuntimeException, a throws clause is not needed in the method header. The philosophy used here is quite different than the one used in Section 6.6. Here the developer of the class imposes certain restrictions on the clients of the class; these restrictions are enforced through the use of assertions.

Should a client of our stack class ever logically execute the following code sequence:

```
Stack stack = new Stack();
stack.pop();
```

---

3. As defined in Subsection 7.2.1, a *client* of a class C is any code that declares a variable of type C.

a run-time exception will be thrown, resulting in a message like the following:

```
AssertException: Assertion failed
        at Assert.isTrue(Assert.java:4)
        at Stack.pop(Stack.java:13)
        at ...
```

Adequate testing should eliminate the possibility of such assertion exceptions ever being triggered. Inserting them into code serves partially to document assumptions made about the state of a method or object. In the past, such assumptions may have been only implicit. Our assertion class allows such assumptions to be explicitly stated. Thus, assertions serve as an aid in detecting subtle semantic code errors.

There may be some concern about how assertions affect the performance of production code. In such cases, an assertion can be stated as:

```
if (Assert.ON) Assert.isTrue( condition );
```

By changing the declaration of ON to false and recompiling, most Java compilers will remove the if statement altogether.

This concludes our treatment of exceptions, although we shall use them freely wherever appropriate in later chapters.

EXERCISES

6.1   How does the C++ model for exceptions differ from the Java model?

6.2   How does the Ada model for exceptions differ from the Java model?

6.3   Explain how a catch clause is similar to a method heading. How do they differ?

6.4   Modify the invalid numeric input example of Section 6.5 so that the user has at most three tries to input a valid integer.

6.5   Incorporate the invalid numeric input example of Section 6.5 into a program that reads a sequence of numbers from the user until a negative number is entered and then computes the sum and average of the sequence of numbers. Verify that the application behaves correctly in the presence of invalid numeric input.

6.6   Extend the stack class of Section 6.6 with an appropriate constructor and a main method to test the stack.

6.7   Extend the stack class of Section 6.6 with a push method that throws a stack overflow exception if a push is made on a full stack.

6.8   Extend the stack class of Section 6.7 with an appropriate constructor and a main method to test the stack.

6.9   Extend the stack class of Section 6.7 with a push method that throws a stack overflow exception if a push is made on a full stack.

6.10 Using the assert class developed in Section 6.7, rewrite the type checking code for Jay given in Appendix Section B.4.

6.11 Using the assert class developed in Section 6.7, rewrite the semantics code for Jay given in Appendix Section B.5.

Object-Oriented Programming

"I am surprised that ancient and modern writers have not attributed greater importance to the laws of inheritance . . ."

Alexis de Tocquevile, *Democracy in America*, 1840

CHAPTER OUTLINE

In this chapter we present the object-oriented paradigm using the language Java. If you are not familiar with Java, a brief Java tutorial is available in Appendix C.

Like C++ and Ada, Java is a mixed imperative and object-oriented language. However, it is harder to write an imperative program in Java than it is in either C++ or Ada95, since the latter are extensions of imperative languages. If we were picking a language purely for its object-oriented features, Smalltalk [Goldberg 1989] or Eiffel [Meyer 1988] would have been better choices. For example, in Smalltalk everything is an object, including the *if* and *loop* control structures.

First we describe the idea of data abstraction and the object-oriented model as an extension of data abstraction. We then cover some of the basic language features of languages that support object-oriented programming, including inheritance and virtual methods. Then, we give some interesting examples of object-oriented programming problems and their Java solutions. We conclude the chapter with a consideration of formal correctness of object-oriented programs.

7.1 DATA ABSTRACTION AND MODULAR PROGRAMMING

In the imperative programming view, a program can be thought of as "algorithms plus data structures" [Wirth 1976]. A systematic way of producing a program [Wirth 1973] is to start with a description of the function computed by a program, together with its input and output, and systematically break such functions down into more primitive functions using sequencing, iteration, and choice. At each stage of the process, both a function to be computed and its data are broken down into less abstract realizations. The process terminates when all of the functions to be computed and their input-output data can be realized as primitive statements and data respectively in the chosen implementation language.

Thus, in imperative languages, the primary abstraction mechanism is the procedure or function. The process which solves the problem specified by the program is repeatedly broken down into simpler, more primitive functions. Very early in the development of imperative languages the value of libraries of reusable functions was recognized. Even in the 1960s, Fortran and Algol included a number of standard mathematical functions, including `sin`, `cos`, `sqrt`, and so on.

The development of functions allows the programmer to use *procedural* or *functional abstraction,* in which the programmer is only concerned with the interface of the function and what it computes. A classic example would be a sort routine, in which the program under development wants to sort an array of numbers, and is otherwise isolated from the details of how the sort is performed. Thus, any given sort routine could always be replaced by a faster one. The interface to such a sort routine might consist of:

```
sort(list, len);
```

where `list` is the array of numbers to be sorted and `len` contains the number of numbers in the list.

One of the developments in imperative programming was an effort in the 1970s and 1980s to extend abstraction to include *data abstraction* or *abstract data types*. Recall from Chapter 3 that a type is a set of data together with the operations on those data. Most primitive types in a language fit this notion well. For example, the type `float` has the standard arithmetic operations of addition, subtraction, and so forth, together with the relational operators. It is abstract because the use of type `float` in programs does not depend on its concrete representation.

Data abstraction is supported by providing some sort of *encapsulation* mechanism to limit both the scope and the visibility of the data values and the functions defined for the values. One such crude mechanism is provided by separate or independent compilation of functions.

Consider, for example, the encapsulation of a stack of integers. An implementation should provide the usual operations: `push`, `pop`, `top`, and `empty`. Other operations, such as the ability to initialize the stack, may also be required by a particular implementation. Consider the implementation code in the language C given in Figure 7.1

```c
#include <stdio.h>

struct Node {
    int  val;
    struct Node* next;
};
typedef struct Node* STACK;

STACK stack = NULL;

int empty( ) {
    return stack == NULL;
}

int pop( ) {
    STACK tmp;
    int rslt = 0;
    if (!empty()) {
        rslt = stack->val;
        tmp = stack;
        stack = stack->next;
        free(tmp);
    }
    return rslt;
}

void push(int newval) {
    STACK tmp = (STACK)malloc(sizeof(struct Node));
    tmp->val = newval;
    tmp->next = stack;
    stack = tmp;
}

int top( ) {
    if (!empty())
        return stack->val;
    return 0;
}
```

I Figure 7.1 A Simple Stack in C

In C a separate header file provides the specification of the *interface* of the stack. An interface contains only the *signature* for each function, which includes its name, its return type, and the types of each of its parameters. Omission of a function or global data variable from the header file effectively hides it from use by other parts of the program.[1]

The use of independent compilation to provide an encapsulation mechanism for a stack does not give us a true abstract data type. The difficulty results from the fact that we cannot declare variables to be of type stack. The code presented in Figure 7.1 defines only a single instance of a stack, not a *type* stack.

In contrast, Figure 7.2 defines a type stack that allows the programmer to declare multiple variables of this type. This header file gives just a specification of the type stack; it would normally be included both in the implementation file (Figure 7.3) and in any client that uses the type stack. In this case the stack is actually a pointer to a record that implements a linked list. The operations on the stack restrict the view of the linked list to be that of a stack. In this implementation, the stack must be explicitly initialized (operation newstack), and the stack being manipulated must be passed as an explicit argument to each function. As with the previous implementation the stack is a collection of elements that all have the same type.

```
struct Node {
    int  val;
    struct Node* next;
};
typedef struct Node* STACK;

int empty(STACK stack);
STACK newstack( );
int pop(STACK stack);
void push(STACK stack, int newval);
int top(STACK stack);
```

| **Figure 7.2   A Stack Type in C**

The use of independent compilation and pointers in C allows for the construction of a type stack, which encapsulates both data and operations (or functions) on that data. However, the language C suffers from the fact that access by stack clients (called *public access*) to the underlying representation of the stack as a linked list is permitted. This can be a particular problem if the client needs to extend the *abstract data type* but does not have access to the source code; in this case the temptation to directly access the underlying representation can be overwhelming.

The key notion of data abstraction is to bundle code and data together in a single package or module so that the functions provide a public interface to a logical data type. Direct support for this concept can be found in "units" (of some versions) in Pascal, in "modules" in Modula, and in "packages" in Ada. The use of modules/packages allows

---

1. Note that C allows both global data and functions to be declared static, which enforces this hiding. However, use of the keyword static for this role can be criticized as misleading. This use of the keyword static to enforce information hiding in C does not appear to be widespread.

```
#include "stack.h"
#include <stdio.h>

int empty(STACK stack){
    return stack == NULL;
}

STACK newstack( ) {
    return (STACK) NULL;
}

int pop(STACK stack) {
    STACK tmp;
    int rslt = 0;
    if (!empty()) {
        rslt = stack->val;
        tmp = stack;
        stack = stack->next;
        free(tmp);
    }
    return rslt;
}

void push(STACK stack, int newval) {
    STACK tmp = (STACK)malloc(sizeof(struct Node));
    tmp->val = newval;
    tmp->next = stack;
    stack = tmp;
}

int top(STACK stack) {
    if (!empty())
        return stack->val;
    return 0;
}
```

| **Figure 7.3 Implementation of Stack Type in C**

for the separation of the logical interface or specification from the physical implementation. In particular, modules/packages allow the programmer to restrict access to the underlying concrete representation of the abstract data type.

The language Pascal was designed by Nicklaus Wirth in the late 1960s as a teaching language, and by the late 1970s and early 1980s Pascal had become widely adopted in colleges and universities for use in their curricula. Following the Algol tradition, a Pascal program was a single compilation unit, which made it unsuitable for writing large, industrial-strength applications, particularly in the systems area. In the late 1970s Wirth developed a series of languages named Modula for developing applications such as operating systems [Wirth 1983]:

> The language Modula-2 is a descendant of its direct ancestors Pascal and Modula. Whereas Pascal has been designed as a general purpose language and after implementation in 1970 has gained wide usage, Modula had emerged from experiments in multiprogramming. . . . Modula-2 emerged from careful design deliberations as a language that includes all aspects of Pascal and extends them with the important module concept and those of multiprogramming. . . . We shall subsequently use *Modula* as synonym for Modula-2.

Modula divides a module into a definition part and an implementation part. Unlike the languages C and C++, the separate compilation facilities of Modula ensure full type checking of modules. When exporting a type to achieve an abstract data type, Modula allows the opaque export only of pointer types. This has the beneficial side effect of reducing the need for recompilations.

A Modula implementation of the type stack that is comparable to the one given in the language C appears in Figure 7.4 and Figure 7.5.

```
DEFINITION MODULE Stack;
    EXPORT QUALIFIED STACK, empty, pop, push, top;

    TYPE STACK;
    PROCEDURE empty(stack: STACK): BOOLEAN;
    PROCEDURE newstack: STACK;
    PROCEDURE pop(VAR stack: STACK): INTEGER;
    PROCEDURE push(VAR stack: STACK; val: INTEGER);
    PROCEDURE top(stack: STACK): INTEGER;
END Stack;
```

Figure 7.4   Abstract Data Types in Modula (1 of 2)

```
IMPLEMENTATION MODULE Stack;
    TYPE STACK = POINTER TO Node;
        Node = RECORD
            val : INTEGER;
            next : STACK;
        END;

    PROCEDURE newstack: STACK;
    BEGIN
        return NIL
    END newstack;

    PROCEDURE pop(VAR stack: STACK): INTEGER;
    VAR  rslt : INTEGER;
        tmp  : STACK;
```

```
BEGIN
    rslt := 0;
    IF (stack <> NIL)
    BEGIN
        rslt := stack^.val;
        tmp := stack;
        stack := stack^.next;
        delete(tmp);
    END;
    RETURN rslt
END pop;

PROCEDURE empty(stack: STACK): BOOLEAN;
BEGIN
    RETURN stack = NIL
END empty;

PROCEDURE push(VAR stack: STACK; val: INTEGER);
VAR tmp : STACK;
BEGIN
    NEW(tmp);
    tmp^.val := newval;
    tmp^.next := stack;
    stack := tmp
END push;

PROCEDURE top(stack: STACK): INTEGER;
BEGIN
    IF (stack <> nil)
        RETURN stack^.val;
    END;
    RETURN 0;
END top;
END Stack;
```

| Figure 7.5   Abstract Data Types in Modula (2 of 2)

7.2   **THE OBJECT-ORIENTED MODEL**

Even with the evolution of modules and packages in the 1980s, problems remained. One such problem was that no mechanism for automatic initialization and finalization of a value of the given type was provided. Initializations that are commonly needed include opening of a file, memory allocation, and initialization of variables local to the module. Finalization might include closing files and deallocating memory. Another problem with modules was that they provided no simple way to extend a data abstraction by adding new operations. Both of these problems were solved by the idea of a "class," the main building block for object-oriented languages, which emerged in the 1980s and 1990s.

7.2.1 Basic Concepts

In an object-oriented language the data type is bound together with the initializations and other operations on that type. The type is referred to as a *class,* local variables are called *instance variables,* their initializations are accomplished by special methods called *constructors,* and other operations are implemented by *methods.* The basic structure of a class declaration in Java is as follows, where C denotes the class name and M denotes a method of the class:

```
public class C {
    public int i,j;                      // instance variables i and j
    public C ( <parameters> ) { <code> }  // a constructor for C
    public <type> M ( <parameters> ) { <code> }
    ...
}
```

An advantage of the object-oriented approach is the provision for a *constructor,* in which memory is allocated for the object and the instance variables of the class can be initialized. In Java, each constructor for a class bears the same name C as the class itself and has no stated return type. If no explicit constructor is provided in Java, a parameterless constructor is supplied automatically. As with all methods, the constructor can be *overloaded;* that is, several constructors can be provided with different signatures.

A *client* of a class C is any program that declares a variable of type C. Such a variable is called an *object.* For instance, a client program may declare a variable x to be an object of class C in the following way:

```
C x;
C x = new C ( <arguments> );
```

The second of these two declarations both declares and initializes x by calling a constructor. In effect, this creates a new object in the heap referenced by x, as shown graphically in Figure 7.6.

Figure 7.6 Initialization of an Object in the Heap

Now the client code can refer to the individual instance variables of x as x.i and x.j, provided that i and j are declared public in the class definition. Moreover, a client of class C may call any of its public methods M to access or change the value of an object, such as x. In object-oriented programming, this is called *message passing.* Dot (.) notation is used to specify the call, and arguments may be passed as well, just as in imperative programming:

```
x.M ( <arguments> )
```

Each method or instance variable in class C can be declared to have a particular level of visibility—*private, protected,* or *public*[2]—with regard to its client classes.

A `public` variable or method is visible to any client of the class; for most classes, the instance variables are not public. The public methods of a class define the interface of the class to the outside world. Most methods of a class are public.

A `private` variable or method is visible only to the current class and not to either of its subclasses[3] or to the outside world. Following the software design principle of *information hiding,* it is common practice to make all instance variables private and allow client access by subclasses only through public or protected methods. This minimizes the changes that would need to be made if the concrete representation of the abstract type were to change.

A `protected` variable or method is visible only to a subclass of the class. This allows subclasses direct access to the instance variable or method. Protected visibility is the least common.

Another form of restricting visibility is to use an *inner class,* that is, to declare a class within a class.

To illustrate these ideas more concretely, an implementation of the foregoing abstract data type stack as a Java class is given in Figure 7.7. In this example, we have arbitrarily restricted the stack to being a stack of `int`'s, although, as we shall see shortly, normally one would not do so in Java.

```
public class Stack {
    private class Node {
        int  val;
        Node next;
        Node(int v, Node n) {
            val = v; next = n;
        }

    }

    private Node stack = null;

    public int pop( ) {
        int rslt = stack.val;
        stack = stack.next;
        return rslt;
    }

    public void push(int v) { stack = new Node(v, stack); }
}
```

I Figure 7.7 A Simple Stack Class in Java

---

2. In Java, if no visibility is specified, the variable or method is `public` to the package (i.e., the file of classes in which it is declared) and `private` elsewhere.

3. Subclasses are discussed in Section 7.3.

Here, the class Stack has an embedded private class Node, which is not accessible to any of Stack's clients. That is, a Node is an idea used by the class Stack's methods to facilitate implementation of the push and pop methods. But the details of a Node are hidden from the Stack's clients, who have access only to the push and pop methods (since they are public).

Class Node has two instance variables (val and next) and a constructor. Notice that class Stack is a client of class Node, since it declares its own local instance variable stack to be a Node. To illustrate the dynamics of this class, consider the following code that might appear in a program that is a client of Stack.

```
Stack s = new Stack();
```

Note that class Stack has no constructor explicitly defined. In this case, any client program that creates a Stack object must use the above form to initialize the object. That is, every class has an implicit parameterless constructor available to its clients.

Following this declaration of Stack s, a client can now specify any number of push and pop operations on this object using dot notation. For example, here is a sequence of statements that leaves s with the values 1 and 5 (with 5 at the top):

```
s.push(1);
s.push(2);
s.pop();
s.push(5);
```

The effect of this declaration and four statements is shown in Figure 7.8. Note here that three nodes now exist in the heap, one of which has become "garbage" as a result of the call s.pop(). The most recently pushed Node is at the top of the stack and is referenced by s.

Figure 7.8   Creation of a Stack with Two Values

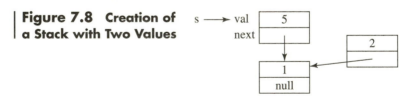

A common way to think of a program in the object-oriented paradigm is as a collection of interacting objects that communicate via message passing. In effect, each object can be viewed as a separate machine having both data and operations on that data. Multiple objects can be instances of the same class; in this case, although the operations are the same, the data is distinct. For instance, in our stack example the program can contain multiple instances of stacks, each with its own collection of data in the heap.

Objects communicate by passing messages among themselves. At most, one machine (object) can be executing at a time. When a machine passes a message to another machine, it invokes a particular method (function) of the receiving machine, passes the parameters (message contents) appropriate to the method, and then waits until the receiving machine returns a response (return value).

This gives us an *object-based language,* which allows us to create any number of instances of an abstract data type. Even this is a new way of thinking about programming, in which data is no longer passive, acted upon by functions, but active. We send data messages, and the data acts on those messages transforming itself as needed.

In Subsections 7.2.3 and 7.2.6, we add inheritance and dynamic dispatch of methods, arriving at *object-oriented languages.* For large programs, the object-oriented paradigm is a fundamentally different way of thinking about programs. For a complete treatment of object-oriented design and programming see [Budd 2000], [Hortsmann 1995], and [Perry 1996].

7.2.2 Initialization of Objects

Classes play two very important and distinct roles. First, they determine the type of an object. As such, they determine what messages (method calls) are legal and precisely which method is being called. In a statically typed language, such as Java, these checks are performed at compile-time, while in a dynamically typed language, such as Smalltalk, the checks are not performed until run-time.

One of the deficiencies of implementing abstract data types in an imperative language is the inability to automatically ensure that the abstract data type is properly initialized. This is commonly done by appropriate documentation. However, since the compiler cannot ensure that the appropriate routine is called, failure to initialize an abstract data type is a common problem.

In the example below[4], two constructors are provided; the *default constructor* is the one with no arguments:

```
public class Concordance {
    public Concordance ( ) { this(false); }
    public Concordance (boolean allowDupl) {
        this.allowDupl = allowDupl;
    }
...
```

The default constructor (the one with no arguments) invokes the second constructor with the value `false` for its argument. Either constructor can be used to create an object of type `Concordance`.

C and C++ use *copy semantics* for arrays and objects; an assignment copies the value from one location to another. In contrast, Java (like Smalltalk) uses *reference semantics* for arrays and objects. For the primitive data types, Java uses copy semantics. In reference semantics, the assignment `a = b` forces `a` and `b` to refer to the same object; any change to `a` changes `b` and vice versa. To derive the effect of copy semantics in Java, you must use an object's `clone()` method.

---

4. A *concordance* is a useful tool for analyzing texts; it consists of an alphabetized list of all the words and their locations in the text.

Effectively, objects in Java are really pointers; however, Java hides pointers from the programmer. It does not provide &, ->, or * operators or pointer arithmetic, as in C. Although Java requires explicit allocation of objects via the `new` operator:

```
Concordance c = new Concordance();
```

there is no explicit deallocation (such as the `delete` operator of C++). Instead, memory is automatically deallocated (and later garbage collected, as discussed in Chapter 5) whenever an object is no longer referenced. The familiar problem of memory leaks in C or C++ thus disappears in Java.

The default value for all objects or variables of reference type in Java is `null` (which is a reserved word). Any attempt to reference an object's fields or methods through a null pointer or reference causes a run-time exception. Thus, a constructor is commonly used to initialize an object's instances variables.

7.2.3 Inheritance

The object-oriented paradigm supports code reuse through *inheritance*. Classes exist in an object-oriented language in a class hierarchy. A class can be declared as a *subclass* of another class, which is called the *parent class* or *superclass*. The subclass inherits the variables and methods of its parent. Inheritance is commonly used as a vehicle for code sharing between a parent class and its subclasses.

In an object-oriented language, classes exist in a hierarchy. In both Smalltalk and Java the class hierarchy forms a tree rooted in the most general class *Object*. In Java, a class D is a subclass of another class C when it extends or specializes the meaning of class C by adding new instance variables or methods, or by modifying the definitions of existing methods in C. A class definition uses the `extends` keyword to indicate its superclass; if this keyword is omitted, the class is implicitly a subclass of the most general class *Object*. Here is a simple subclass extension D of the class C that was sketched in Subsection 7.2.1:

```
public class D extends C {
    public int k;
    public <type> N ( <parameters> ) { <code> }
}
```

By extending C, subclass D is said to *inherit* the instance variables i and j, and the method M, from class C. Thus, a client of class D can declare an object y in the following way:

```
D y = new D ();
```

and create an object y like the one shown in Figure 7.9.

Figure 7.9 Initialization of an Object with Inherited Features

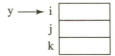

Here, object y has instance variables i, j, and k, as well as access to methods M (declared in the parent class) and N. Thus, the following references and calls are possible for the object y:

```
y.M ( <arguments> )
y.N ( <arguments> )
y.i
y.j
y.k
```

For a more concrete example, consider the following partial class definitions for Vector and Stack:

```
class Vector extends Object {
    public void insertElementAt (Object obj, int index) { ... }
    public Object elementAt (int index) { ... }
    ...
}

class Stack extends Vector {
    public Object pop( ) { ... }
    public void push(Object obj) { ... }
    ...
}
```

Here, the class Stack is declared to be a subclass of the class Vector, which in turn is a subclass of the class Object as shown in Figure 7.10.

Figure 7.10 Sample Class Hierarchy

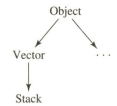

In this case, a client of the Stack class cannot only call the usual push and pop methods, but it can also call the methods insertElementAt and elementAt, defined in the parent class Vector. These latter methods allow insertion and retrieval of objects at an arbitrary point in the stack.[5]

Java, like Smalltalk, allows a class to extend only a single class, thus permitting only single inheritance; in contrast, C++, allows multiple inheritance. Thus, in Java the class hierarchy is strictly a tree with the class Object at the root.

---

5. Arbitrary insertion and deletion of elements is definitely not "stack-like" behavior, and Java's Stack class has been criticized for this particular design decision.

Another major difference between Java and C++ is that in Java all method dispatching is done at run time, usually referred to as *virtual methods.* In general, an object declared to be of type `Vector` can in reality be any subclass of `Vector`, for example, a `Stack`:

```
Vector v;
...
System.out.print(v.toString());
```

In this example, the run-time type of v is unknown; it could be a `Vector`, a `Stack`, or some other subclass of `Vector`. So the actual `toString` method invoked depends on the run-time type of v. This is distinctly different from statically typed imperative languages, in which the actual function being invoked is determined before run time.

Unlike Java, C++ allows *multiple inheritance,* in which a class may inherit instance variables and methods from several distinct classes. This has two distinct advantages: it facilitates code reuse, and it allows a subclass to be substituted for any of its parent classes (using pointers in C++). The disadvantage is that the semantics of inheritance are greatly complicated. As we shall see shortly, interfaces in Java provide an alternative to obtain the second advantage, although interfaces do not allow for code inheritance.

However, before we consider interfaces, we first consider the concept of an abstract class.

7.2.4 Abstract Classes

Java allows a class to be declared *abstract,* in which case one or more of its methods are declared to be `abstract`; that is, code for the method is not provided by the class but must instead be provided by its subclasses. Abstract classes are used to define a public interface to be shared by a set of classes. Abstract classes also differ from concrete classes in that instance variables are often declared to be `protected` (so that the subclasses can reference them) rather than `private`.

The Java class `Dictionary` is an abstract class. Although a variable or formal parameter can be declared to be of type `Dictionary`, it is illegal to create (initialize) an object of an `abstract` class. Another way of stating this is that the run-time type of an object cannot be an abstract class. This restriction ensures that a call cannot be made to an abstract (unimplemented) method.

We saw in Chapter 2 that a Jay expression could be either a binary expression, a variable reference, or a value. Pictorially, this would be represented by the following class diagram:

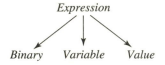

In this case, there never would be a concrete object of actual type `Expression`, only one of its subclasses. Hence, `Expression` could be declared to be an abstract class, meaning that any attempt to create a new instance (i.e., to construct a `new Expression()`

in the heap) would be identified at compile-time as an error. Expression represents only a logical grouping of its subclasses.

```
abstract class Expression { ... }

class Binary extends Expression { ... }
class Variable extends Expression { ... }
class Value extends Expression { ... }
```

This is a typical use of abstract classes, which we shall explore in an example after first considering the concept of an interface.

7.2.5 Interfaces

In addition to ordinary classes, Java also provides for the declaration of interfaces, which provide another form of a reference data type.[6] An *interface* declares a collection of features identified by abstract methods. Syntactically an interface declaration looks like an abstract class definition:

```
public abstract interface Enumeration {
    public abstract boolean hasMoreElements();
    public abstract object nextElement();
}
```

An interface is always abstract whether it is declared abstract or not. Furthermore, all of the methods in an interface must be abstract; only constants (final variables) may be concretely declared in an interface.

Because it is not a class, an interface does not have a constructor. One of the most common usages of an interface is similar to that of a function pointer in C or C++. It ensures that any class that implements the interface class provides concrete definitions of all its methods, independent of the nature of the class which implements the interface. A practical example of the use of an interface class is given in the eight queens program in Section 7.5.

A class implements an interface, rather than extending it. To implement an interface a class must implement all of the methods of an interface, not just some of them. Consider, for example, the definition of StringTokenizer:

```
public class StringTokenizer extends Object
        implements Enumeration {
    public boolean hasMoreElements() { ... }
    public Object nextElement() { ... }
    ...
}
```

---

6. Some like to think of an interface as an alternative to multiple inheritance. However, unlike classes, interfaces do not provide a means of reusing code.

In the case of a `StringTokenizer`, the overall type may not be important, particularly when passed as a parameter. A called method may just want to invoke the methods associated with the `Enumeration` interface.

7.2.6 Polymorphism and Late Binding

According to the dictionary, the term *polymorphic* means "having many forms." In object-oriented languages polymorphism refers to the late binding of a call[7] to a specific method in an object. This can occur with either subclasses or interfaces in Java.

Basically, you have an object of a declared (or apparent) type T whose actual type may vary at run time. Consider the following method call:

```
obj.m();
```

The declared or apparent type T of the object `obj` guarantees that all subtypes of T implement an appropriate method `m`; Java verifies this at compile time. The actual instance of the method `m` that is called depends on the actual or dynamic type of the object `obj` at runtime.

Consider an application that implements a drawing program or an algorithm animation system. In such a program there are many different kinds of graphical objects, such as circles, rectangles, and so forth, all of which must be capable of displaying themselves in a window. Assume each graphical object has a `paint` method (following the Java AWT convention). Somewhere the system keeps a list of these objects and periodically must ask each object to repaint itself, represented by the following pseudocode:

```
foreach8 (GraphicalObj obj in list) {
    obj.paint();
    ...
}
```

Each graphical object paints itself according to its own logic; squares are drawn differently from circles, and both are drawn differently from text. So the actual `paint` method being called varies according to the actual (dynamic) type of the graphical object. Yet, abstractly, each is merely asked to paint itself in turn. This is the heart of polymorphism in object-oriented programming.

To be truly polymorphic, the various instances of the `paint` method must uphold the principle of *substitutability,* which holds that each instance of the paint method performs the same abstract function, with only the code being particularized for the graphical object being painted. Thus, for each instance of a graphical object, the logical behavior of the paint function is indistinguishable from the others. Without the principle of substitutability, the pseudocode given above would not work.

---

7. As we shall see in Chapter 8, the use of the term *polymorphism* in object-oriented programming is distinct from its use in functional programming.

8. Java, unlike some languages, such as Perl, lacks a foreach loop construct; however, this loop can be accomplished in Java using an Enumeration and a while loop.

Note that the declared or apparent type can be either a super type or an interface type. The Java compiler verifies at compile time that a method with the appropriate signature exists for the specified object using the declared or apparent type. However, a compiler cannot insure that the abstract function performed is logically the same, i.e., verify that the methods as implemented uphold the principle of substitutability. This is the responsibility of the programmer.

Additional examples of polymorphism will be given in Sections 7.3 and 7.5 of this chapter. This completes our discussion of classes and objects. In the sections which follow and their associated exercises, we attempt to illustrate many of these points again. Our first example is that of the meaning of a Jay arithmetic expression.

7.3 EXAMPLE: EXPRESSION EVALUATION

The abstract syntax and meaning of an expression in the language Jay was first defined in Chapters 2 and 3. The abstract syntax of a Jay expression is also defined in Figure 7.11. In this example, as previously, we will leave the treatment of unary expressions as an exercise. Our goal here is to use a more object-oriented style to build a set of classes to mimic this structure; this means that the meaning functions should be directly embedded into the classes that implement the abstract syntax:

Expression = Variable | *Value* | *Binary*
  Variable = String id
    Value = int intValue | *boolean* boolValue
    Binary = Operator op; *Expression* term1, term2
  Operator = BooleanOp | *RelationalOp* | *ArithmeticOp*

I **Figure 7.11 Expression Abstract Syntax of Jay**

As previously, the way to achieve this aim is to make *Expression* the parent or superclass, with each of the elements of the abstract syntax a subclass. In this way, we can avoid an instance of *ad hoc polymorphism* in which the meaning method must test its operand to determine what operation is to be performed. Instead we can use true polymorphism by asking an *Expression* for its meaning without regard to whether the *Expression* is a *Variable,* a *Value,* or a *Binary.* Such a class hierarchy is depicted below:

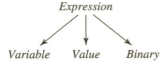

Now the question arises: What methods should each of these classes have? Clearly each class needs a constructor and an *evaluate,* or meaning, method. In redoing these classes, we shall omit, for the sake of brevity, any methods which are used solely as part of type validity checking. We will implement these classes generally in a bottom-up, left-to-right fashion, beginning with the class `Variable`.

The definition of the meaning of an *Expression* in state σ: is given in Figure 7.12.

Such a meaning function is easily added to the class `Variable`, as show in Figure 7.13. The meaning of a *Variable* is simply its value in the current state. In object-oriented programming, the expression *e* is the receiver of the message, unlike the mathematical expression where *e* is an explicit argument to the meaning function.

M: Expression $\times \Sigma \rightarrow$ *Value*
M(Expression e, State σ)

= *e*	if *e* is a *Value*
= $\sigma(e)$	if *e* is a *Variable*
= *ApplyBinary(e.op, M(e.term1, σ), M(e.term2, σ))*	if *e* is a *Binary*
= *ApplyUnary(e.op, M(e(.term, σ)))*	if *e* is a *Unary*

❙ Figure 7.12   Meaning of an Expression

```
class Variable extends Expression {
  String id;

  public Variable(String id) { this.id = id; }
  public boolean equals(Object obj) {
    String s = ((Variable)obj).id;
    return id.equalsIgnoreCase(s);  // case-insensitive identifiers
  }
  public int hashcode() { return id.hashcode(); }

  public Value M(State sigma) {
    return (Value)(sigma.get(this));
  }
}
```

❙ Figure 7.13   The Variable Class

Implementing the `Value` class involves a little more analysis. Although the abstract syntax has only two types of values, the definition of the meaning of an expression introduces a third kind of value. An *undefined* value is used as the initial value of a variable that has not been explicitly assigned a value. Recall from Chapter 3 that the `Value` class had a type field that kept track of whether a value was boolean, integer, or undefined. In object-oriented programming, this is termed *ad hoc polymorphism* and is normally to be avoided.

In our revised version, we extend the `Value` class by having three distinct subclasses: `IntValue`, `BooleanValue`, and `UndefValue`. However, because we wish to effectively hide these three subclasses and use the same constructors as previously for the `Value` class, we do not make the `Value` class an abstract class. Again, in this solution, given in Figure 7.14, we use true polymorphism and late binding to request of a `Value` its meaning without regard to whether the run-time instance of the `Value` object is an integer value, a boolean value, or an undefined value.

```
class Value extends Expression {
  public Value(int i) { return new IntValue(i); }
  public Value(boolean b) { return new BooleanValue(b); }
  public Value( ) { return new UndefValue(); }

  public boolean isUndef( ) { return false; }
  public int intVal( ) { return -1; }
  public boolean boolVal( ) { return false; }
  public Value M(State sigma) { return this; }
}
```

| Figure 7.14   The Value Class

The constructors for the `Value` class are an instance of the *Factory* pattern [Cooper 2000; Gamma 1995], in that they effectively hide the subclasses. A client merely calls one of the constructors for `Value`, but in reality gets back an instance of a subclass.

The boolean function `isUndef` is provided so that a client can determine whether a particular value is actually undefined; the method returns *false*. In this way only the subclass `UndefValue` has to override this particular method.

The methods `intVal` and `boolVal` are provided so that a client can extract the underlying integer or Boolean value. As we shall see, since a Jay program has been verified to be type safe, this can be done without error. The subclass `IntValue` must override the `intVal` method, while the subclass `BooleanValue` must override the `boolVal` method. These functions are used in applying the meaning of an operator to a `Value`.

Note that the meaning function for the `Value` class essentially does nothing; in actuality, it returns the receiver of the meaning message.

We next implement the `IntValue` subclass in Figure 7.15. It provides only a constructor and a meaning method named `intVal`, which returns the underlying integer value when needed for arithmetic operations. The `BooleanValue` subclass is similar and is left as an exercise.

The `UndefValue` class is provided in Figure 7.16. It provides no explicit constructor, and thus uses the default constructor. It overrides the `isUndef` method, returning *true;*

```
class IntValue extends Value {
  int intVal;
  public IntValue(int i) { intValue = i; }
  public intVal( ) { return intVal; }
}
```

| Figure 7.15   The IntValue Subclass of the Value Class

```
class UndefValue extends Value {
  public isUndef() { returns true; }
}
```

| Figure 7.16   The UndefValue Subclass of the Value Class

note that this method is logically unnecessary, since one could use the built-in `instanceof` operator to determine the class.

In the abstract syntax `Binary` serves as a grouping mechanism, in that every binary expression is either an instance of an add, a subtract, and so on. One possible implementation is to make the `Binary` class abstract, with specific subclasses for `AddBinary`, `SubtractBinary`, and so on. An alternative is to make the operator into an abstract class, with specific subclasses for `AddOp`, `SubtractOp`, and so on. In this alternative, the mathematical `applyBinary` function would be a method in which each operator implements its specific semantics or meaning.

In keeping with the underlying mathematics, we choose the latter approach. In Figure 7.17 we show the class `Binary`. In this case, the implementation of the meaning function is straightforward; first each term is asked for its meaning, and then the operator is asked to apply itself to the resulting values.

```
class Binary extends Expression {
  Operator op;
  Expression term1, term2;

  public Binary(Operator o, Expression t1, Expression t2) {
    op = o;  term1 = t1;  term2 = t2;
  }

  public Value M(State sigma) {
    return op.apply(term1.M(sigma), term2.M(sigma));
  }
}
```

| Figure 7.17   The Binary Class

The `Operator` class and the related `ArithmeticOp`, `RelationalOp`, and `BooleanOp` classes are equally straightforward. Because they contain no instance variables and need no explicit constructors, they are declared abstract; the implementation is given in Figure 7.18. The only method needed in class `Operator` is `apply`, which must be

```
abstract class Operator {
  public abstract Value apply(Value v1, Value v2);
}

abstract class ArithmeticOp extends Operator { }
abstract class RelationalOp extends Operator { }
abstract class BooleanOp extends Operator { }
```

| Figure 7.18   The Operator, ArithmeticOp, RelationalOp, and BooleanOp Classes

implemented by the concrete subclasses. The `ArithmeticOp`, `RelationalOp`, and `BooleanOp` subclasses are needed in the type verification methods, but not in implementing the meaning functions.

Each concrete subclass of `Operator` need only implement the `apply` method for the given operator, since each such object knows what class it is a member of. Since each such subclass has no instance variables, the default constructor can be used. The implementation of the `AddOp` class is given in Figure 7.19; the others are left as exercises.

```
class AddOp extends ArithmeticOp {
  public Value apply(Value v1, Value v2) {
    if (v1.isUndef() || v2.isUndef())  return new Value();
    return new Value(v1.intVal() + v2.intVal());
  }
}
```

| Figure 7.19 The AddOp Subclass of the Operator Class

In order to apply itself, an add operator first checks to see if either of its operands is an undefined value; if so, it then returns an undefined value. Otherwise, both operands must be integer values, since this was verified during type checking. Thus the *apply* method can safely access the integer values of each operand to add them arithmetically.

Finally, there remains only to implement the `Expression` class. But from the abstract syntax of Figure 7.11, an expression is really just an instance of a `Variable`, a `Value`, or a `Binary`. So the conclusion is that the class `Expression` should be an abstract class with an abstract meaning method as shown in Figure 7.20.

```
abstract class Expression {
  public abstract Value M(State sigma);
}
```

| Figure 7.20 The Expression Class

The world of the `Expression` class and its subclasses are an illustration of the *Command* design pattern [Gamma 1995; Cooper 2000], in which each of the subclasses of `Expression` is responsible for evaluating itself and returning the appropriate response. The Command pattern is heavily used in graphics applications, in which different graphics objects are asked to draw or paint themselves on the screen; the invoking method does not know or care how the painting is done.

In the `Value` class, implementing the `isUndef` method in the parent class demonstrates the power of inheritance to reuse code, even if some subclasses, for example, `UndefValue`, have to override the default implementation with a more appropriate one.

This reimplementation of the `Expression` class and its subclasses necessitates minor changes to the `Parser` class in Chapter 2 and to the type-checking class in

Chapter 3. An interesting project (left as an exercise) is to redo the type checking for expressions in this more object-oriented style.

To motivate the use of these object-oriented concepts, we next consider the process of designing a concordance generating program—its objects, methods, and interactions.

7.4 **EXAMPLE: CONCORDANCE**

A concordance is an alphabetical index that shows the lines in a document where each word might be found. For example, a concordance for this paragraph might appear as:

Word	Line Number
a	1, 2
alphabetical	1
an	1
appear	2

Concordances are typically used as aids in the study of massive works, such as the Bible or Shakespeare. Variants of a concordance program can be used to produce all nonnoise words in a text, an index in a book, and a cross-reference listing of a computer program's variables and functions or methods.

One could argue that perhaps all this design is overkill for something as simple as a concordance application in Java. But we are using this simple application to illustrate the process of object-oriented design.

We want to develop a system of classes that, given the name of a file containing a document, produces a concordance of the document. We would like the ability to produce either an exhaustive concordance, that is, all words, or just a list of principal words. In the latter case, noise words such as "a," "an," "the" would be ignored. For the sake of simplicity, the program uses line numbers, rather than page numbers.

A simple method of recognizing the major objects in the problem space, plus their role in a program's model of reality, is to identify the nouns used in describing the problem space. The common nouns usually identify the major classes needed in the solution. A more complete treatment of the process of object-oriented design is given in [Booch 1994]; another treatment of this problem appears in [Budd 2000, p. 324].

In the concordance problem description given above, the common nouns are: "concordance," "words," "line numbers," "document," and, implicitly, "report." The word class can be modeled with the Java class `String`, while line numbers can be modeled using `int`'s. That leaves as major classes to be constructed: concordance, document, and report.

In order to maintain the generality of the design of the `Concordance` class, it should be decoupled both from the form of its input and from the form of its output. For the latter, enumerators should be provided that allow an output `Report` class to enumerate over the list of words and their associated line numbers.

The input case is less clear. The constructor of the `Concordance` class could require that an enumerator be provided that allows the `Concordance` class to pull all the words and associated numbers from the enumerator, one per call, but this seems like more work than is necessary. The alternative is to provide an add method which allows a Document class to push all the words into the concordance.

In a very real sense a concordance is just a special kind of dictionary. Thus, the methods of the Concordance class should be roughly those of Java's Dictionary interface class. This is the approach that was adopted.

A hashtable was chosen as the underlying implementation method for the Concordance class, since a Hashtable class is defined in Java. This makes the implementation for all but the add method fairly trivial, as seen in Figure 7.21. Two constructors are provided; the second constructor can be used to allow for duplicate line numbers. The Concordance class also provides two enumeration methods for use by a Report class.

```java
import java.util.*;

public class Concordance {
    private Dictionary dict = new Hashtable();
    private boolean allowDupl = false;

public Concordance (boolean allowDupl) {
    this.allowDupl = allowDupl;
}

public Concordance ( ) { this(false); }

public void add (Object word, Object number) {
    Vector set = (Vector) dict.get(word);
    if (set == null) { // not in Concordance
        set = new Vector( );
        dict.put(word, set);
    }
    if (allowDupl || !set.contains(number))
        set.addElement(number);
}

public Enumeration keys( ) { return dict.keys( ); }

public Enumeration elements (Object word) {
    return ((Vector)dict.get(word)).elements( );
}
}
```

| Figure 7.21　The Concordance Class

The Concordance class has an add method for entering words and line numbers. The word is entered into the hashtable as the key, with the associated value being a set of line numbers (in the case duplicates are not allowed). In Java 1.1 a set of arbitrary objects is not directly implemented as a class, so the decision is made to implement the set as a `Vector` and explicitly test for duplicate line numbers when appropriate. Since `Hashtable`'s get method returns an `Object`, this value must be cast as a `Vector` to use the `addElement` method to add additional line numbers. Also, note that `Vector` can only store objects, not primitive types, so the `add` method requires that the caller convert the line number to an appropriate `Object`, most probably an `Integer` object. We have made the parameters to the `add` method more general than needed; the formal parameter `word` is typed as the more general class `Object`, rather than a `String`, and the parameter `number` is also typed as an `Object` rather than an `Integer`.

A separate `Document` class (see Figure 7.22) reads lines from a file and enumerates all the words in the line, adding them to the concordance. The constructor reads the given input file a line at a time, and then converts the text to lowercase if the file is to be processed in a case-insensitive manner. The constructor then uses a `StreamTokenizer` to pull words one at a time from the line and add them to the concordance. Note the use of an `Enumeration` to enumerate the words in the line.

```
import java.util.*;
import java.io.*;

public class Document {

public Document (BufferedReader input, boolean sensitive,
        Concordance dict) throws IOExecption {
    final String delims = "\t\n.,!?;:()[]{}";
    String line;
    for (int count = 1; (line = input.readLine())!=null; count++){
        if (!sensitive) line = line.toLowerCase( );
        Enumeration e = new StringTokenizer(line, delims);
        while (e.hasMoreElements( ))
            dict.add(e.nextElement( ), new Integer(count));
    }
}
}
```

I Figure 7.22 The Document Class

It is a simple matter to create a second constructor that deletes noise words. However, to do a program cross-reference, a different `Document` class has to be provided, since the `Document` class is coupled to the structure of the document being read.

Finally, for testing purposes a simple `Report` class (see Figure 7.23) outputs the list of words and their line numbers to the console. It is a simple matter to construct a different `Report` class which handles wrapping long lines, HTML output, or XML output.

Enumerations are used twice in the `Report` constructor. First, an `Enumeration` is used to process all the words in the concordance. For each word an `Enumeration` is used to enumerate the set of line numbers.

```
import java.util.Enumeration;
import java.io.*;
public class Report {

public Report (Concordance dict, PrintWriter out) {
    Enumeration e = dict.keys( );
    while (e.hasMoreElements( )) {
        Object word = e.nextElement( );
        out.print(word + ":");
        Enumeration f = dict.elements(word);
        while (f.hasMoreElements( ))
            out.print(" " + f.nextElement( ));
        out.println( );
    }
}
}
```

| Figure 7.23 **The Report Class**

Note that when a word is returned, it is not cast back to the class String. Instead, it is left ostensibly as an Object, although Java's run-time system knows it is a String. Thus, when the word is concatenated with a space prior to being printed, the toString method is called. In reality, the method invoked is String's toString method, not Object's. Similar comments apply to the printing of the line numbers (which are Integer's). This demonstrates the power of using virtual methods.

The concordance example is interesting because it demonstrates the power of having a good library of classes to use when implementing an application. It particularly shows off the power of enumerators in Java, which are an instance of the *Iterator* design pattern [Gamma 1995]. Iterators allow the programmer to traverse a data structure or container class while keeping the code independent of the data structure being traversed.

7.5 **EXAMPLE: BACKTRACKING**

In this example we develop an object-oriented version [Noonan 2000] of Wirth's *backtracking algorithm* [Wirth 1976, p. 137]:

> A particularly intriguing programming endeavor is the subject of "general problem solving." The task is to determine algorithms for finding solutions to specific problems not by following a fixed rule of computation, but by trial and error. The common pattern is to decompose the trial-and-error process into partial tasks. Often these tasks are most naturally expressed in recursive terms and consist of the exploration of a finite number of subtasks.

As we shall see in Chapter 9, backtracking is the basis for logic programming.

The general solution that Wirth presents is a recursive procedure that iterates through a series of trial moves. Each move is tested to see if it satisfies an appropriate *validity* criterion. If it does, the move is recorded, and if the problem is not yet solved, the procedure calls itself recursively to try the next level; if the recursive call fails, then the current move is undone and the next move is tried. The process of trying moves continues until either a completely successful solution is found or all the moves at the current level are unsuccessfully tried.

An object-oriented version of this algorithm is presented in Figure 7.24. Abstractly, the method `attempt` implements the general algorithm. The formal parameter `level` is used to keep track of the recursive level. The local variable `successful` is used to keep track of whether a solution to the entire problem has been solved; thus, at each recursive level `successful` is initially set to false. Within a level, moves are successively generated, tested, and, if valid, recorded; only then is the next level tried recursively. Moves that do not result in a solution to the general problem are undone. The process terminates when either a solution is found or the set of moves at the current level is exhausted.

```java
import java.util.Enumeration;

public class Backtrack {

    Backtracker b;

public Backtrack (Backtracker b) { this.b = b; }

public boolean attempt (int level) {
    boolean successful = false;
    Enumeration e = b.moves(level);
    while (!successful && e.hasMoreElements()) {
        Object move = e.nextElement();
        if (b.valid(level, move)) {
            b.record(level, move);
            if (b.done(level))
                successful= true;
            else {
                successful = attempt(level+1);
                if (!successful)
                    b.undo(level, move);
            } // if done
        } // if valid
    } // while
    return successful;
} // attempt
}
```

I Figure 7.24   Object-Oriented Backtracking Algorithm

```
import java.util.Enumeration;

public abstract interface Backtracker {
    public abstract Enumeration moves(int level);
    public abstract boolean valid(int level, Object move);
    public abstract void record(int level, Object move);
    public abstract boolean done(int level);
    public abstract void undo(int level, Object move);
}
```

I Figure 7.25   Backtracker Interface

The constructor takes a single parameter which encapsulates the specifics of the problem to be solved. As defined by the Backtracker interface in Figure 7.25, these methods are:

1   An Enumeration moves, which is the set of all possible trial solutions on a given level.
2   A Boolean function valid, which determines whether the current move satisfies the validity criteria.
3   A method record, which records the current move on the current recursive level; a method undo is provided for undoing this recording.
4   A boolean method done, which determines whether the solution as recorded solves the problem.

Consider the *eight queens* problem where eight mutually antagonistic queens (from the game of chess) must be placed on a board so that no queen is capable of capturing any other queen in a single move.[9] For the sake of generality, we let the number 8 be a parameter that can be set to any integer value greater than zero. Consider the position for a 4 × 4 chess board shown below:

	0	1	2	3
0	Q			
1				
2		Q		
3				

The level represents the column number, which would currently be set at 2.[10] The set of possible moves represents the set of valid row numbers, namely, {0 . . . 3}. It is easy to determine visually that no queen can be validly placed in column 2. Hence, the

---

9. A queen can move any number of squares either horizontally, vertically, or on either diagonal provided it does not pass or cross over another chess piece. A chess piece that lands on a square occupied by another chess piece is said to *capture* that piece.

10. Note that an equivalent solution proceeds row by row rather than column by column.

search for a solution has to back up to column 1 and move that queen from row 2 to row 3, before proceeding forward again.

In designing our Queens class, we need to decide on a representation for the chess board. One possibility is an $n \times n$ square matrix. However, a little investigation reveals that such a representation is fairly cumbersome in checking the validity or "safeness" of a new position. Instead, we use a set of four one-dimensional arrays.

The first array named rowPos takes a column number as an index and indicates for that column the row number, or position, of a queen, if it contains one. For the sample board shown above:

```
rowPos[0] = 0
rowPos[1] = 2
```

This array is used in printing a successful board configuration. A row is defined to be safe if no queen occupies that row. This information can be represented by a Boolean array named row which takes a row number as an index and indicates whether there is a queen in that row. For the sample board above:

```
row[0] = true        row[2] = true
row[1] = false       row[3] = false
```

indicating that rows 0 and 2 have queens and the other rows do not. We next note that in a southwest-diagonal[11] the sum of the row and column numbers is constant:

	0	1	2	3
0	0	1	2	3
1	1	2	3	4
2	2	3	4	5
3	3	4	5	6

This information can be captured by a Boolean array named swDiag which takes the sum of the row and column numbers as an index and indicates whether a queen occupies that southwest-diagonal. For an $n \times n$ board the set of indices ranges from 0 to $2n - 2$. For our sample board above:

```
swDiag[0] = true
swDiag[3] = true
```

and the remainder are *false*, indicating that the southwest-diagonals 0 and 3 have queens and the other southwest-diagonals do not.

---

11. That is, a diagonal that extends from upper right to lower left on the board.

Finally we note that in a southeast-diagonal[12] the difference of the row and column numbers is constant:

	0	**1**	**2**	**3**
0	0	-1	-2	-3
1	1	0	-1	-2
2	2	1	0	-1
3	3	2	1	0

This information can be captured by a Boolean array named `seDiag` which takes the difference of the row and column numbers as an index and indicates whether a queen occupies that southeast-diagonal. For an $n \times n$ board the set of indices ranges from $-n + 1 \ldots n - 1$; since all Java arrays are 0-based, we add $n - 1$ to the difference, giving a range of $0 \ldots 2n - 2$. For our sample board above:

```
seDiag[3] = true      southeast-diagonal 0 + n − 1
seDiag[4] = true      southeast-diagonal 1 + n − 1
```

and the remainder are *false*. This completes our representation of the chess board.

Having completed the data representation, the methods of the `Queens` class can be implemented. The constructor is passed the value n, the size of the chess board; this value is stored as the variable `MAXROW` and is used to allocate the arrays cited above. However, the actual row and column numbers used are 0-based to simplify their use as array indices.

Implementing the `Backtracker` interface methods to solve the eight queens problem is straightforward:

- A *move* varies from 0 to $n - 1$ to accommodate Java's 0-based arrays; a trial *move* corresponds to a potential row position within a column. So the enumerator `moves` must simply iterate over the values $0 \ldots n - 1$.
- The method `done` merely checks to see if column number (its parameter) plus one is at least `MAXROW`.
- The method `valid` checks to see if the row, southwest-diagonal, and southeast-diagonal are all empty (false).
- Recording a move (the method `record`) corresponds to marking the row, southwest-diagonal, and southeast-diagonal as occupied (true); undoing a move corresponds to making them unoccupied. The variable `rowPos` is used to record for each column the row position of the queen within the column, which is later used for display purposes. A private method `setPosition` is used for both recording and undoing moves.

The `Queens` class, which is shown in Figure 7.26, also includes a `display` method for printing the solution and a simple `main` method for testing the application.

---

12. That is, a diagonal that extends from upper left to lower right.

| **Figure 7.26**

```java
import java.io.*;
import java.util.Enumeration;

public class Queen extends Object implements Backtracker {

    int MAXROW = 8;        // board size
    boolean swDiag[];
    boolean seDiag[];
    boolean row[];
    int rowPos[];

    public Queen(int n) {
        MAXROW = n;
        swDiag = new boolean[2*MAXROW-1];
        seDiag = new boolean[2*MAXROW-1];
        row = new boolean[MAXROW];
        rowPos = new int[MAXROW];
    }

    private void setPosition(int rowNo, int colNo,
            boolean occupied) {
        row[rowNo] = occupied;
        swDiag[rowNo+colNo] = occupied;
        seDiag[rowNo-colNo+MAXROW-1] = occupied;
    }

    public boolean valid(int colNo, Object move) {
        int rowNo = ((Integer)move).intValue();
        System.out.println("Try: " + rowNo + ", " + colNo);
        return (!row[rowNo])
            && (!swDiag[rowNo+colNo])
            && (!seDiag[rowNo-colNo+MAXROW-1]);
    }

    public boolean done(int colNo) {
        return colNo + 1 >= MAXROW;
    }

    public void record(int colNo, Object move) {
        int rowNo = ((Integer)move).intValue();
        System.out.println("Record: " + rowNo + ", " + colNo);
        rowPos[colNo] = rowNo;
        setPosition(rowNo, colNo, true);
    }

    public void undo(int colNo, Object move) {
        int rowNo = ((Integer)move).intValue();
        System.out.println("Undo: " + rowNo + ", " + colNo);
```

```
        rowPos[colNo] = 0;
        setPosition(rowNo, colNo, false);
    }

    public void display( ) {
        for (int i = 0; i < MAXROW; i++) {
            for (int j = 0; j < MAXROW; j++)
                if (rowPos[j] == i)
                    System.out.print("Q");
                else
                    System.out.print(" ");
            System.out.println( );
        }
    } // display

    public Enumeration moves(int level) {
        return new QueenEnumeration( );
    }

    private class QueenEnumeration
            implements Enumeration {
        int  rowNo = 0;

        public boolean hasMoreElements( ) {
            return rowNo < MAXROW;
        }

        public Object nextElement( ) {
            return new Integer(rowNo++);
        }
    } // QueenEnumeration

    public static void main(String args[]) {
        Queen q = new Queen(4);
        Backtrack b = new Backtrack(q);
        if (b.attempt(0))  q.display( );
    } //main

} //class Queen
```

| Figure 7.26 Object-Oriented Eight Queens Program

Solutions to other backtracking problems, such as *knight's tour,* graph reachability, the maze problem, and so forth, can be produced by implementing the methods defined by the Backtracker interface. This process of implementing a particular algorithm is simply a matter of filling in the details of the five methods in the Backtracker interface. These are left as exercises.

7.6 **CORRECTNESS**

In this section we discuss formal correctness of object-oriented programs, following the approach of Liskov and Guttag [2000]. We illustrate this approach with the development of the `Stack` class presented in Figure 7.7.

As we saw in an earlier chapter, correctness proofs require that each method be augmented with pre- and postconditions. Consider, for example, the method pop:

```
public int pop( ) {
    int rslt = stack.val;
    stack = stack.next;
    return rslt;
}
```

What is the precondition of this method? The references `stack.val` and `stack.next` are valid only if the stack is not a null object, or equivalently, the stack is not empty. But what is the postcondition? Informally, we know that the top element of the stack has been removed and its value is the value returned by the pop operation. We would like to use a technique that isolates the client from having to reference the internal state of a class.

One specification method defines the *internal state* of a class in terms of a set of axioms on the visible operations [Guttag 1977; Guttag 1978]. First, we formally define the syntax of our operations:

new: $\rightarrow Stack$
pop: $Stack \rightarrow Stack$
push: $Stack \times int \rightarrow Stack$
top: $Stack \rightarrow int$
empty: $Stack \rightarrow boolean$

This syntactic specification says that there is a constructor (*new*) which takes no arguments and produces an object of type *Stack*. Similarly, there is a *pop* operation which takes an object of type *Stack* and produces an object of type *Stack*. Unlike the Java code, each operation is restricted to producing a single result.

Having specified the syntax of our operations, next we specify the meaning of these basic operations as axioms:

$S \in$ Stack $\land E \in int \supset$
A1: $pop(new(\ )) = error$
A2: $pop(push(S, E)) = S$
A3: $top(new(\ )) = error$
A4: $top(push(S, E)) = E$

The preconditions state that applying either the *top* or *pop* operation to an empty stack is not allowed; doing so results in an error. Then, the *top* and *pop* operations are defined in terms of the most recent *push* operation.

Having constructed a specification as a set of axioms, one must address the question of whether the axiom set correctly defines our intuition about the abstract data type being defined. Other questions that must be addressed include whether the axiomatization is consistent and complete. An axiomatization is inconsistent if the same theorem can be proved both *true* and *false.* An axiomatization is incomplete if some theorem cannot be shown either *true* or *false.* Despite these difficulties, this approach is advocated by Meyers [1997].

A simpler approach, particularly for informal proofs, is to use a *representation specification,* in which a specific mathematical or abstract representation is chosen for the data type and then each operation is mapped onto that representation. One possibility for our Stack class is to use a list $\{x_1, \ldots, x_n\}$ representation, with the push and pop operations operating on the left (low-order) end of the list. Then the precondition of the pop operation would be:

$$\{this \neq \{\ \}\}$$

i.e., the current object, *this,* is not the empty list. Then the postcondition would be:

$$\{if(this = \{x_1, \ldots, x_n\})\ this' = \{x_2, \ldots, x_n\} \wedge \text{return } x_1\}$$

which states that the pop operation returns the first element of the sequence and that the output or final value of *this* (marked with a prime) has its first element removed. To understand whether or not this is correct, we would also have to understand that the representation specification states that insert and delete operations are at the left (or low-order) end of the list. If, for example, the push operation were to insert new elements onto the right end of the sequence, then, in actuality, what we have defined is a queue rather than a stack.

Given this insight, the Stack class which appears in Figure 7.7 (without the Node inner class) would be:

```
class Stack {
   // REP: this = {x1, ... xN},
   //      and all insert/delete operations are at the left
   //      (low order) end of the list
   private Node stack = null;
   ...
}
```

Next, we give the empty operation and its specification:

```
public boolean empty() {
   // PRE: none
   return  stack == null;
   // POST: return this == { }
}
```

Informally, an empty mathematical list corresponds to an empty linked list; thus the stack (*this*) is empty if and only if the variable stack is null.

Next we give the push operation and its specification:

```
public void push(int v) {
   // PRE: none
   stack = new Node(v, stack);
   // POST: if (this == {x1, ..., xN}) this' == {v, x1, ..., xN)
}
```

Again, informally, access to the linked list occurs only at one end, so all inserts and deletes occur at the same end. Whether this end is denoted as the left (low-order) end or the right end of the list representation is an arbitrary choice. Note also that we are assuming the correctness of the Node class, although this could be proved, if desired.

Finally, we return to the problem which started all this, namely, what are the pre- and postconditions of the pop operation?

```
public int pop( ) {
    // PRE: not empty(this)
    Assert.isTrue(!empty(stack));
    int rslt = stack.val;
    stack = stack.next;
    return rslt;
    // POST: if this = {x1, x2, ..., xN} then
    //        return x1 and this' = {x2, ..., xN}
}
```

The precondition states that the stack cannot be empty or the pop method will be undefined; in this case, we ensure the precondition at runtime using the Assert class of Chapter 6. Failure of the Assert terminates the program. The Java code removes the first element from the list and returns the value of the list element removed.

The postcondition specifies the effect in terms of the abstract list representation, where *this'* is the output (abstract) value of the object. The first postcondition states that the method returns the top of the stack (as defined by the list representation). The second postcondition says that the output stack (marked by the prime) is defined as the input stack with the first element removed.

This concludes our examination of object-oriented programming.

EXERCISES

7.1 Given an example of a feature from each of Java and C/C++, which promote or violate the following language design principles: automation, simplicity, security, regularity, portability. Do not cite an example given in the text.

7.2 Complete the implementation of the Expression class and its subclasses: BooleanValue, SubtractOp, and so on. Construct a test driver that directly builds abstract syntax trees, displays them to the console, and then evaluates and prints the value of the Expression.

7.3 Using the recursive-descent parsing methods of Chapter 2, write a test driver for the above Expression evaluator that takes a properly spaced Polish prefix expression as a single command line argument and uses a recursive descent parser to construct the abstract syntax tree.

7.4 Add the unary not operator to the Expression evaluator above. Discuss the alternatives of adding a new superclass (as is done in Chapter 2) for both binary and unary operators versus just adding a unary minus as a concrete subclass to the existing Expression class.

7.5 Using Appendix B as a reference and the meaning functions of the Expression class as a guide, redo the type checking of expressions in this more object-oriented style.

7.6 Using the Concordance program from Figure 7.21, carry out the following experiments. For each experiment carry out the specified task and answer the associated questions as needed. For any experiment that fails (gets a compilation error), undo the change before proceeding with the next experiment.

(a) First, construct an appropriate test driver that takes the name of the file from the command line and then processes that file. Test your concordance program on an appropriate input file.

(b) In the class `Concordance` change the class of `dict` from the class `Dictionary` to `Hashtable`. Then recompile and rerun `Concordance`. Has anything changed? Why or why not? Explain.

(c) In the call to `add` in the `Document` class add a cast to `String`, and on the header for function `add` change the type of `word` from `Object` to `String`. Then recompile and rerun `Concordance`. Has anything changed? Why or why not? Explain.

(d) On the call to `add` eliminate the conversion of the value of `line` to `Integer` (via the newInteger(line)), and on the header for function `add` change the type of `line` from `Integer` to `int`. Then recompile and rerun `Concordance`. Has anything changed? Why or why not? Explain.

(e) In the `Report` class, change the type of `word` to `String` and add a cast to `String`. Then recompile and rerun `Concordance`. Has anything changed? Why or why not? Explain.

(f) In the `Report` class, change `f.nextElement()` to `f.nextElement.toString()`, then recompile and rerun `Concordance`. Has anything changed? Why or why not? Explain.

7.7 Implement knight's tour [Wirth 1976, p. 137] using the `Backtrack` class and its associated `Backtracker` interface. Note that the smallest chess board (greater than 1) for which a solution exists is 5 × 5; verify this.

Given is a $n \times n$ board with $4n^2$ fields. A knight—allowed to move according to the rules of chess—is placed on the field with initial coordinates (x_0, y_0). The problem is to find a covering of the entire board, if there exists one, i.e., to compute a tour of $n^2 - 1$ moves such that every field of the board is visited exactly once.

7.8 Modify the `Backtrack` class's `attempt` method so that it generates all solutions. Test your solution on eight queens.

7.9 Consider all the classes that define the abstract syntax of Jay (Appendix B).

(a) Find a class that is a client of another class.

(b) Find a class that is a subclass of another class.

7.10 (Team Project) Add display methods to the Jay abstract syntax so that the call `p.display()`, where `p` is a Jay abstract program, displays all the elements of the program.

7.11 Classes in Java are not *generic* as they are in C++; that is, C++ allows us to specify `Vector<int>` `v` to define a vector of `int`'s. This allows us to extract the *i*th element from `v` and add one to it without an explicit cast. Discuss the advantages and disadvantages of generics in programming languages. Research recent proposals to add generics to Java.

7.12 (Team Project) Consider the possibility of designing a complete object-oriented implementation of Jay, incorporating all of its type checking (*V*) and meaning (*M*) functions inside the classes of its abstract syntax.

(a) Outline the structure of the methods that would appear in each class.

(b) What simplifications of the functions *V* and *M* are achieved by this change?

(c) Complete the implementation.

Note: This task is partially completed as the file `Program.java`, which is available at the website given in the Preface. There, Jay's meaning functions *M* are incorporated directly inside its abstract classes.

7.13 Using the `Stack` class in Section 7.6 as a guide, add a `top` method and give its pre- and postconditions. Also rewrite the code and postcondition of the `pop` method to use `top`.

7.14 Using the `Stack` class in Section 7.6 as a guide, implement a `Queue` class with operations enqueue, dequeue, and front. Give a representation specification for a queue. For each method give pre- and postconditions and an informal proof of correctness.

7.15 Give a representation specification for the `String` class using Section 7.6 as a guide (`java.util. String`). Give pre- and postconditions for the method `indexOf(String)`.

7.16 Implement an IntSet class with operations `insert`, `delete`, `isIn`. Using the `Stack` class in Section 7.6 as a guide, produce a representation specification and pre- and postconditions for each method.

Functional Programming

> *"It is better to have 100 functions operate on one data structure than 10 functions on 10 data structures."*
> **Attributed to Alan Perlis**

CHAPTER OUTLINE

Functional programming emerged as a distinct paradigm in the early 1960s. Its creation was motivated by the needs of researchers in artificial intelligence and its subfields—symbolic computation, theorem proving, rule-based systems, and natural language processing. These needs were not particularly well-met by the imperative languages of the time.

The original functional language was Lisp, developed by John McCarthy [1960] and described in the *LISP 1.5 Programmer's Manual* [McCarthy 1965]. The description is notable both for its clarity and its brevity; the manual has only 106 pages! It contains not only a description of the Lisp system but also a formal definition of Lisp itself. To quote the authors [McCarthy 1965, p. 1]:

> The Lisp language is primarily for symbolic data processing. It has been used for symbolic calculations in differential and integral calculus, electrical circuit design, mathematical logic, game playing, and other fields of artificial intelligence.

The essential feature of functional programming is that a computation is viewed as a mathematical function mapping inputs to outputs. Unlike imperative programming, there is no implicit notation of state and therefore no need for an assignment statement. Thus, the effect of a loop is modeled via recursion, since there is no way to increment or decrement the value of a variable in the state. As a practical matter, however, most functional languages do support the notions of variable, assignment, and looping. The point here is that these elements are not part of the "pure" functional programming model, and so we will not emphasize them in this chapter.

Since any deterministic imperative program can be viewed as a mathematical function mapping inputs to outputs, a theory of program correctness has been developed using this view of programs as functions as a basis [Mills 1975]. We shall see in this chapter that a pure functional programming language provides convincingly better support for program correctness proofs than an imperative language. That is, absent the notion of state and loop, and requiring all computations to be defined by functions on linear data structures (lists), we can avoid the complex proof machinery of the Hoare triple (introduced in Chapter 3) to prove that a program is correct. Thus, the function viewed in this way is a copy of the problem specification, rather than a translation of the specification into another paradigm.

Because of its relative purity, functional programming is viewed by some as a more reliable paradigm for software design than imperative programming. This view is difficult to document, however, since the vast majority of (artificial intelligence) applications for which functional programming is used are not readily amenable to solutions in the imperative paradigm, and conversely. For a more careful discussion of the merits of functional programming versus imperative programming, see [Hughes 1989].

8.1 FUNCTIONS AND THE LAMBDA CALCULUS

A typical mathematical function such as the square of a number is easily specified:

```
Square(n) = n * n
```

This definition gives the name of the function, followed by its arguments in parentheses, followed by an expression that defines the meaning of the function. Square is understood to be a function that maps from the set of real numbers $\mathbf{R}$ (its *domain*) to the set of real numbers $\mathbf{R}$ (its *range*), or more formally:

Square: $\mathbf{R} \rightarrow \mathbf{R}$

A function is said to be *total* if it is defined for all elements in its domain, and *partial* otherwise. The Square function is total over the set of real numbers.

In imperative programming languages, a variable such as x denotes a location in memory. So the statement:

```
x = x + 1
```

literally means "update the program state by adding 1 to the value stored in the memory cell named x and then storing that sum back into that memory cell." Thus, the name x is used to denote both a value (as in x + 1), often called an *r-value,* and a memory address, called an *l-value.*[1]

In mathematics, variables are somewhat different in their semantics: they always stand for actual expressions and are immutable. In mathematics there is no concept of "memory cell" or updating the value of a memory cell. So-called *pure* functional programming languages eliminate the memory cell notion of a variable in favor of the mathematical notion; that is, a variable names an immutable value, which also eliminates the assignment operator. However, most functional programming languages retain some form of assignment operator and are, thus, called *impure.*

One consequence of the lack of memory-based variables and assignment is that functional programming has no notion of state, as was used in defining the meaning of the imperative language Jay. The value of a function such as *Square* depends only on the values of its parameters and not on any previous computation or even the order of the evaluation of its parameters. This property of a functional language is known as *referential transparency.*

The foundation of functional programming is the *lambda calculus,* developed by Church [1941]. A lambda expression specifies the parameters and definition of a function, but not its name. For instance, here is a lambda expression that defines the function square discussed above.

$$(\lambda x \cdot x^*x)$$

The identifier x is a parameter for the (unnamed) function body x*x. Application of a lambda expression to a value is denoted by:

$$((\lambda x \cdot x^*x)2)$$

which evaluates to 4.

This example is an illustration of an applied lambda calculus. What Church actually defined was a *pure* or *uninterpreted* lambda calculus, in the following way:

1 Any identifier is a lambda expression.
2 If *M* and *N* are lambda expressions, then the *application* of *M* to *N*, written (MN), is a lambda expression.
3 An *abstraction,* written $(\lambda x \cdot M)$, where x is an identifier and M is a lambda expression, is also a lambda expression.

---

1. The terms *r-value* and *l-value* were originally coined because they referred to the values returned by the right- and the left-hand sides of an assignment, respectively.

A simple set of BNF grammar rules for the syntax of this pure lambda calculus can be written as:

$$LambdaExpression \rightarrow ident \mid (M\ N) \mid (\lambda\ ident \cdot M)$$
$$M \rightarrow LambdaExpression$$
$$N \rightarrow LambdaExpression$$

Examples of lambda expressions are:

x
$(\lambda x \cdot x)$
$((\lambda x \cdot x)(\lambda y \cdot y))$

In the lambda expression $(\lambda x \cdot M)$, the identifier x is said to be *bound* in the subexpression M. Any identifier not bound in M is said to be *free*. Bound variables are simply placeholders. Any such identifier can be renamed consistently with any identifier free in M without changing the meaning of the lambda expression. Formally, the free variables in a lambda expression can be defined as:

$free(x) = x$
$free(MN) = free(M) \cup free(N)$
$free(\lambda x \cdot M) = free(M) - \{x\}$

A substitution of an expression N for a variable x in M, written $M[N/x]$, is defined as follows:

1 If the free variables of N have no bound occurrences in M, then the term $M[N/x]$ is formed by replacing all free occurrences of x in M by N.
2 Otherwise, assume that the variable y is free in N and bound in M. Then consistently replace the binding and corresponding bound occurrences of y in M by a new variable, say u. Repeat this renaming of bound variables in M until the condition in Step 1 applies, then proceed as in Step 1.

The following examples illustrate the substitution process:

$x[y/x] = y$
$(xx)[y/x] = (yy)$
$(zw)[y/x] = (zw)$
$(zx)[y/x] = (zy)$
$[\lambda x \cdot (zx))[y/x] = (\lambda u \cdot (zu))[y/x] = (\lambda u \cdot (zu))$
$(\lambda x \cdot (zx))[x/y] = (\lambda u \cdot (zu))[y/x] = (\lambda u \cdot (zu))$

The meaning of a lambda expression is defined by the following reduction rule:

$$((\lambda x \cdot M)N) \Rightarrow M[N/x]$$

This is called a *beta-reduction,* and can be read "whenever we have a lambda expression of the form $((\lambda x \cdot M)N)$, we may simplify it by the substitution $M[N/x]$." A beta-reduction therefore represents a single function application.

An *evaluation* of a lambda expression is a sequence $P \Rightarrow Q \Rightarrow R \Rightarrow \cdots$ in which each expression in the sequence is obtained by the application of a beta-reduction to the previous expression. If P is a lambda expression, then a *redux* of P is any subexpression obtained by a beta-reduction. A lambda expression that does not contain a function application is called a *normal form.*

An example of an evaluation is:

$$((\lambda y \cdot ((\lambda x \cdot xyz)a))b) \Rightarrow ((\lambda y \cdot ayz)b) \Rightarrow (abz)$$

In this example, we evaluated the innermost λ expression first; we could have just as easily done the outermost reduction first:

$$(\lambda y \cdot ((\lambda x \cdot xyz)a))b = (\lambda x \cdot xbz)a = abz$$

The equality of lambda expressions is termed *beta-equality* both for historical reasons and because the term suggests beta-reducibility from one expression to the other. Informally if two lambda expressions M and N are equal, written $M = N$, then M and N can be reduced to the same expression (up to renaming their variables). Beta-equality deals with applying an abstraction $(\lambda x \cdot M)$ to an argument N, and so it provides a fundamental model for the notions of function call and parameter passing in programming languages.

A functional programming language is essentially an applied lambda calculus with constant values and functions built in. The pure lambda expression (xyx) can just as easily be written $(x \text{ times } x)$ or $(x * x)$. Note also that this last form can be written in prefix style like $(* x x)$. When we add constants such as numbers with their usual interpretation and definitions for functions, such as $*$, we obtain an applied lambda calculus. For instance, $(* 2 x)$ is an expression in an applied lambda calculus. As we shall see, pure Lisp/Scheme and Haskell are examples of applied lambda calculi.

An important distinction in functional languages is usually made in the way they define function evaluation. In languages such as Scheme, all arguments to a function are normally evaluated at the time of the call. This is usually referred to as *eager evaluation,* or *call by value* (as discussed in Chapter 5). With eager evaluation, functions such as `if` and `and` cannot be defined without potential run-time errors, as in the Scheme function:

```
(if (= x 0) 1 (/ 1 x))
```

which defines the value of the function to be 1 when `x` is zero and `1/x` otherwise. If all arguments to the `if` function are evaluated at the time of the call, division by zero cannot be prevented.

An alternative to the eager evaluation strategy is termed *lazy evaluation,* in which an argument to a function is not evaluated (it is deferred) until it is needed. As an argument passing mechanism lazy evaluation is equivalent to *call by name*. Lazy evaluation is the default mechanism in the language Haskell. Although we will not explore them here, Scheme also has mechanisms which permit the use of lazy evaluation when desired by the programmer.

An advantage of eager evaluation is efficiency in that each argument passed to a function is only evaluated once, while in lazy evaluation an argument to a function is reevaluated each time it is used, which can be more than once. An advantage of lazy evaluation is that it permits certain interesting functions to be defined that cannot be implemented in eager languages. (This will be illustrated in Subsection 8.6.2.) Even the above definition of the function `if` becomes error-free with a lazy evaluation strategy, since the division (/ 1 x) will only occur when $x \neq 0$.

In the pure lambda calculus, the function application:

$$((\lambda x \cdot * \ x \ x)5) = (* \ 5 \ 5)$$

does not give any interpretation to either the symbol 5 or the symbol *. Only in an applied lambda calculus would we achieve a further reduction to the number 25.

A key aspect of functional programming is that functions are treated as first-class values themselves. A function name may be passed as a parameter, and a function may return a function as a value. Such a function is sometimes termed a *functional form.* An example of a functional form would be a function g that takes as parameters both a function and a list (or sequence of values) and applies the given function to each element in the list returning a list. Using Square as an example then:

```
g(f, [x1, x2, ...]) = [f(x1), f(x2), ...]
```

or

```
g(Square, [2, 3, 5]) = [4, 9, 25]
```

There are many other useful functional forms.

8.2 SCHEME: AN OVERVIEW

As the original functional programming language, Lisp has many features that are carried over into later languages, and so Lisp provides a good basis for studying other functional languages. Over the years a number of variants of Lisp were developed; today only two major variants remain in widespread use: Common Lisp [Steele 1990] and Scheme [Kelsey 1998; Dybvig 1996]. As languages which attempt to unify a number of variants, both Scheme and Common Lisp contain a number of equivalent functions. This chapter presents a purely functional subset of Scheme.

When viewed as a "pure" functional language, our Scheme subset[2] has no assignment statement. Instead programs are written as (recursive) functions on input values which produce output values; the input values themselves are not changed. In this sense Scheme notation is much closer to mathematics than are the imperative and object-oriented programming languages like C and Java.

Without an assignment statement, our Scheme subset makes heavy use of recursive functions for looping, in preference to the *while* statement that we find in Jay, for example. Despite this, it can be proved that such a subset is *Turing complete,* in that any computable function can be implemented in that subset. That is, a functional language is Turing complete when it has integer values and operations, a way of defining new functions using existing functions, conditionals (if statements), and recursion.

A proof that this idea of Turing completeness is equivalent to the one in Chapter 4 for imperative languages is beyond the scope of this text. However, the use of Scheme

---

2. The full language Scheme has an assignment statement called set!, which we shall avoid using in this discussion.

to implement the denotational semantics of Jay given in this chapter should provide convincing, although informal, evidence that a purely functional language is at least as powerful as an imperative language. The converse is also true, since Scheme and Lisp interpreters are implemented on von Neumann machines which basically implement the imperative paradigm (see Chapter 4).

8.2.1 Expressions

Expressions in Scheme are constructed in Cambridge-prefix notation, in which the expression is surrounded by parentheses and the operator or function precedes its operands, as in the example:

```
(+  2  2)
```

If this expression is presented to a Scheme interpreter, it evaluates to the value 4. An advantage of this notation is that it allows arithmetic operators like + and * to take an arbitrary number of operands:

```
(+)                        ; evaluates to 0
(+ 5)                      ; evaluates to 5
(+ 5 4 3 2 1)              ; evaluates to 15
(*)                        ; evaluates to 1
(* 5)                      ; evaluates to 5
(*  1  2  3  4  5)         ; evaluates to 120
```

Note that a semicolon starts a comment, which continues until the end of the line.

These arithmetic expressions are examples of Scheme lists; both data and programs (functions) are represented by lists. When a Scheme list is interpreted as a function, the operator or function name follows the left parenthesis and the remaining numbers are its operands. More complicated expressions can be built using nesting:

```
(+  (*  5  4)  (-  6  2))
```

which is equivalent to 5*4 + (6 − 2) in infix notation, and evaluates to 24.

Global variables are defined in Scheme using the function define. To define a variable f equal to 120 we would enter the expression:

```
(define  f  120)
```

The function define is the only one that we will examine that changes its environment, rather than merely returning a value. However, we will not treat define as an assignment statement in our Scheme subset;[3] we only use it to introduce a global name for a value, as in mathematics.

---

3. The function set! is a true assignment in Scheme in that it may be used to change the value of an existing variable. Many Scheme texts use the set! function at a global level as equivalent to define.

8.2.2 Expression Evaluation

To understand how Scheme evaluates expressions, three major rules apply.

First, names or symbols are replaced by their current bindings. Assuming the definition of the variable f from the previous section:

```
f                       ; evaluates to 120
(+  f  5)               ; evaluates to 125
                        ; using the bindings for +, f
```

This use of f is an example of the first rule.

The second rule is that lists are evaluated as function calls written in Cambridge prefix notation:

```
(+)                     ; calls + with no arguments
(+ 5)                   ; calls + with 1 argument
(+ 5 4 3 2 1)           ; calls + with 5 arguments
(+ (5 4 3 2 1))         ; error, tries to evaluate 5 as
                        ; a function
(f)                     ; error; f evaluates to 120, not
                        ; a function
```

The third rule is that constants evaluate to themselves:

```
5                       ; evaluates to 5
nil                     ; evaluates to nil, predefined
#t                      ; is true, predefined
```

One can prevent a symbol or list from being evaluated by quoting it using the quote function or the apostrophe ('), as in:

```
(define  colors  (quote  (red  yellow  green)))
(define  colors  '(red  yellow  green))
```

Note that there is no closing apostrophe; the apostrophe quotes the symbol or list immediately following it. You can also quote symbols:

```
(define  x  f)      ; defines x to be 120 (value of f)
(define  x  'f)     ; defines x to be the symbol f
(define  acolor 'red) ; defines acolor to be red
(define  acolor red)  ; an error, symbol red not defined
```

8.2.3 Lists

As we have seen, the fundamental data structure of Scheme is the list; it is used for both commands and data. We have seen a number of examples of constant lists, that is, lists that represent themselves. In this section we shall see how to put things into lists and how to get them out.

First, let us define some lists of numbers:

```
(define evens '(0 2 4 6 8))
(define odds '(1 3 5 7 9))
```

Pictorially, the list evens would be represented as shown in Figure 8.1a.

Note that the symbol nil marks the end of the list; by convention Scheme lists should always end with a nil.[4] In imperative linked list terms, the nil can be thought of as a nil or null pointer. If the nil had been missing from the end of the list, Scheme would display it as:

```
(0 2 4 6 . 8)
```

which is an abnormal structure. However, this sort of structure can sometimes be (mistakenly) generated by some of the Scheme functions discussed below, which would eliminate the last node in Figure 8.1a, giving the memory map of Figure 8.1b instead:

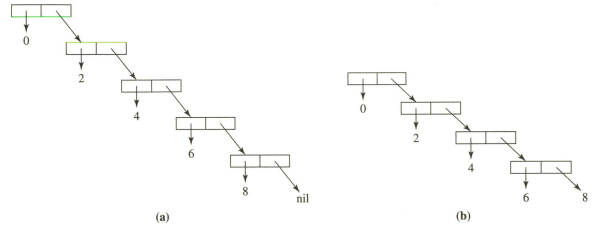

(a)　　　　　　　　　　　　　　　　　　　**(b)**

| **Figure 8.1**　**Structure of a List in Scheme**

These sorts of "dotted" lists in Scheme are to be avoided; standard Scheme programming practice dictates that all lists end in nil.

The basic function for constructing a list is cons, which takes two arguments—the second argument in a cons should be a list:

```
(cons 8 nil)                 ; gives (8)
(cons 6 (cons 8 nil))        ; gives (6 8)
(cons 4 (cons 6 (cons 8 nil))) ; gives (4 6 8)
```

---

4. The value nil is implemented by the null reference, as discussed earlier in Chapter 5. Sometimes nil is written as ( ).

A node in a Scheme list has two parts, the first element or the "head" of the list, and the list of remaining elements or its "tail." The function `car` returns the head of the list, while the function `cdr` returns the tail. Referring again to the list `evens` pictured in Figure 8.1, the following examples illustrate these functions:

```
(car evens)           ; gives 0
(cdr evens)           ; gives (2 4 6 8)
(car (cdr evens))     ; gives 2
(cadr evens)          ; gives 2
(cdr (cdr evens))     ; gives (4 6 8)
(cddr evens)          ; gives (4 6 8)
(car '(6 8))          ; gives 6
(car (cons 6 8))      ; gives 6
(cdr '(6 8))          ; gives (8)
(cdr (cons 6 8))      ; gives 8, not (8)
(car '(8))            ; gives 8
(cdr '(8))            ; gives ()
```

Note that Scheme allows sequences of `car`'s and `cdr`'s (up to five) to be abbreviated by including only the middle letter; thus, `cadr` is a `car` of a `cdr`, `cddr` is a `cdr` of a `cdr`, and so on.

Higher level functions for putting lists together include the `list` and `append` functions. The `list` function takes a variable number of arguments and constructs a list consisting of those arguments:

```
(list 1 2 3 4)         ; gives (1 2 3 4)
(list '(1 2) '(3 4) 5) ; gives ((1 2) (3 4) 5)
(list evens odds)      ; gives ((0 2 4 6 8) (1 3 5 7 9))
(list 'evens 'odds)    ; gives (evens odds)
```

In contrast, the `append` function takes two arguments both of which should be lists and concatenates the second list onto the end of the first list:

```
(append '(1 2) '(3 4))  ; gives (1 2 3 4)
(append evens odds)     ; gives (0 2 4 6 8 1 3 5 7 9)
(append '(1 2) '())     ; gives (1 2)
(append '(1 2) (list 3)) ; gives (1 2 3)
```

To add a single number to the front of the list of even numbers, we would use the `cons` function:

```
(cons 10 evens)         ; gives (10 0 2 4 6 8)
```

The empty list (`nil` value) at the end of the list is important; as we shall see, in recursively traversing a list, we always check for the empty list at the end.

Since Scheme was designed to process lists, it contains a number of special list processing functions. Because the need frequently arises, there is a special function named `null?` to test for an empty list:

```
(null?  '())            ; returns #t or true
(null?  evens)          ; returns #f or false
(null?  '(1 2 3))       ; returns #f
(null?  5)              ; returns #f
```

Scheme contains a number of functions for testing if one object is equal or equivalent to another. Rather than enumerating these and their differences, we will rely on the `equal?` function, which is fairly general. This function returns *true* (#t) if the two objects have the same structure and contents; otherwise it returns *false*:

```
(equal? 5 5)                ; returns #t
(equal? 5 1)                ; returns #f
(equal? '(1 2) '(1 2))      ; returns #t
(equal? 5 '(5))             ; returns #f
(equal? '(1 2 3) '(1 (2 3)) ; returns #f
(equal? '(1 2) '(2 1))      ; returns #f
(equal? () ())              ; returns #t
```

8.2.4 Elementary Values

So far, all the values we have seen in Scheme are either numbers or symbols (names). There are actually quite a few different types of numbers, including integers, rationals, and floating point numbers. Other types of Scheme elementary values include characters, functions, symbols, strings, and lists. Each of these can be tested for using the appropriate predicate; for example, all of the following return #t:

```
(pair?  evens)
(list?  evens)
(symbol?  'evens)
(number?  3)
```

In addition to the types of values listed above, there are also Boolean values: #t which stands for *true* and #f which stands for *false*. So all the predicate tests above return the value #t. All values except #f and the empty list ( ) are interpreted as #t when used as a predicate.

8.2.5 Control Flow

The two control-flow constructs we will use are the `if` and the `case`. The `if` function comes in the usual two flavors: the if-then and the if-then-else. Abstractly these appear as:

```
(if   test   then-part)
(if   test   then-part   else-part)
```

An example of each is:

```
(if (< x  0) (- 0 x))
(if (< x  y) x y)
```

The first if function returns the negative of x if x is less than zero, and nil otherwise. The second function returns the smaller of the two values of x and y.

The case function is much like the case in Ada and the switch in Java; the case function has an optional else which, if present, must be the last case. A simple case to compute the number of days in a month (ignoring leap years) is:

```
(case  month
    ((sep apr jun nov)      30)
    ((feb)     28)
    (else  31)
)
```

Note that each specific case takes an unquoted list of constants, except the else.

8.2.6 Defining Functions

Functions are defined using the define function, which has the following general form:

```
(define name  (lambda (arguments) function-body))
```

Thus, our minimum function can be defined:

```
(define min (lambda (x y) (if (< x y) x y)))
```

Recall that Scheme, like Lisp, is an applied lambda calculus with the ability to give names to specific lambda definitions.

Since programmers quickly tire of entering the word lambda and the extra set of parentheses, Scheme provides an alternative way of writing the define function:

```
(define (name arguments) function-body)
```

Using this alternative, the minimum function can be rewritten as:

```
(define (min  x  y) (if (< x y) x y))
```

An example of a function to compute the absolute value of a number would be:

```
(define (abs x) (if (< x 0) (- 0 x) x))
```

More interesting functions occur when we use recursion to define a function in terms of itself. One example from mathematics is the venerable factorial function, which can be defined in Scheme as:

```
(define (factorial n)
   (if (< n 1) 1 (* n (factorial (- n 1)))
))
```

For example, the function application `(factorial 4)` evaluates to 24 using the above definition in the following way:

```
(factorial 4) = (* 4 (factorial 3))
              = (* 4 (* 3 (factorial 2)))
              = (* 4 (* 3 (* 2 (factorial 1))))
              = (* 4 (* 3 (* 2 (* 1 (factorial 0)))))
              = (* 4 (* 3 (* 2 (* 1 1))))
              = (* 4 (* 3 (* 2 1)))
              = (* 4 (* 3 2))
              = (* 4 6)
              = 24
```

Even simple iterative tasks such as adding a list of numbers are accomplished recursively in Scheme. Here, we assume that the numbers form a list `(a1 a2...an)` whose elements are to be summed:

```
(define (sum alist)
   (if (null? alist)  0
       (+ (car alist) (sum (cdr alist)))
))
```

Note that this sum function is identical to Scheme's built-in addition function (+).

The `sum` function exhibits a pattern common to a wide variety of Scheme functions. The function recurses through the list after first testing for an empty list. This test is often called the *base case* in recursive definitions. The *recursive step* proceeds by adding the first element of the list to the sum of the remainder of the list (the recursive application of the function). The function is guaranteed to terminate because at each recursive step of the computation, the list argument becomes shorter by taking the `cdr` of the list.

Other interesting Scheme functions manipulate lists of symbols, rather than just numbers. All the following functions presented here are already defined in Scheme; we present them as examples of recurring patterns in Scheme programming.

The first example computes the length of a list; that is, its number of elements, counting sublists as single elements. Examples of the use of the `length` function include:

```
(length '(1 2 3 4))          ; returns 4
(length '((1 2) 3 (4 5 6)))  ; returns 3
(length ())                  ; returns 0
(length 5)                   ; error
```

The definition of the `length` function closely follows the pattern set by the `sum` function with only minor differences:

```
(define (length alist)
   (if (null? alist) 0 (+ 1 (length (cdr alist))))
))
```

The function application `(length '((1 2) 3 (4 5)))` yields:

```
(length '((1 2) 3 (4 5)))
    = (+ 1 (length '(3 (4 5))))
    = (+ 1 (+ 1 (length '((4 5)))))
    = (+ 1 (+ 1 (+ 1 (length ()))))
    = (+ 1 (+ 1 (+ 1 0)))
    = (+ 1 (+ 1 1))
    = (+ 1 2)
    = 3
```

Another simple function is the `member` function which tests to see whether an element `elt` (which can be a list) occurs as a member of a given list. If not, the function returns the empty list. Otherwise it returns the remainder of the list starting at the element found, which is interpreted as *true*, since it is not `null`. Examples of the use of the `member` function include:

```
(member 4 evens)              ; returns (4 6 8)
(member 1 evens)              ; returns ()
(member 2 '((1 2) 3 (4 5)))   ; returns ()
(member '(3 4) '(1 2 (3 4) 5)) ; returns ((3 4) 5)
```

The `member` function is most commonly used as a predicate. Again, the definition starts with the base case, namely an empty list, in which case `member` returns the empty list. Otherwise, it tests to see if the head of the list is equal to the element sought; if yes, it returns the list and otherwise recurses on the tail of the list.

```
(define (member elt alist)
   (if (null? alist) ()
       (if (equal? elt (car alist)) alist
           (member elt (cdr alist))
)))
```

Our last simple function is `subst`, which is used to substitute its first argument for all occurrences of its second argument in a list (its third argument). Like the member function, the checking for equal objects is only done at the top level of the list:

```
(subst 'x 2 '(1 2 3 2 1))      ; returns (1 x 3 x 1)
(subst 'x 2 '(1 (2 3) 2 1))    ; returns (1 (2 3) x 1)
(subst 'x 2 '(1 (2 3) (2)))    ; returns (1 (2 3) (2))
(subst 'x '(2 3) '(1 (2 3) 2 3)) ; returns (1 x 2 3)
(subst '(2 3) 'x '(x o x o))   ; returns ((2 3) o (2 3) o)
```

This function is interesting since it must build the output list as the result of the function, rather than simply returning one of its arguments as the `member` function does.

With this caveat, it is similar in structure to the member function:

```
(define (subst x y alist)
   (if (null? alist) ()
       (if (equal? x (car alist))
           (cons y (subst x y (cdr alist)))
           (cons (car alist) (subst x y (cdr alist)))
)))
```

8.2.7 Let Expressions

Commonly, in defining a function a subexpression may occur several times. Scheme follows the convention in mathematics of allowing the introduction of a name for a subexpression. This is accomplished via the let function which has the following general form:

```
(let ((var1 expr1) (var2 expr2) ...) body)
```

Judicious use of a let function can improve comprehension of a function definition. A side effect of using a let is that Scheme only evaluates the expression once, instead of each time it occurs. An example of the use of a let function follows:

```
(let ((x 2) (y 3)) (+ x y))        ; returns 5
(let ((plus +) (x 2)) (plus x 3))  ; returns 5
```

A more interesting use of a let function is its use inside the definition of a function:

```
(define (subst x y alist)
   (if (null? alist) ()
       (let ((head (car alist)) (tail (cdr alist))
           (if (equal? x head)
               (cons y (subst x y tail))
               (cons head (subst x y tail))
))))
```

As in mathematics, a let function merely introduces a set of names for common expressions. The names are bound to their values only in the body of the let function. A more extensive example of the let function occurs in Subsection 8.4.2.

In Scheme the order of evaluation of the values *expr1*, *expr2*, and so on is not implied. Another way of stating this is that each value is evaluated independently of the bindings of the names *var1*, *var2*, and so on. If it is necessary to refer to an earlier name in a later expression, the let* function should be used.

In all the above examples, the arguments to a function have been either atoms or lists. Scheme also allows a function to be a formal parameter to another function being defined:

```
(define (mapcar fun alist)
   (if (null? alist) ()
       (cons (fun (car alist)) (mapcar fun (cdr alist)))
) )
```

The `mapcar` function has two parameters, a function `fun` and a list `alist`; it applies the function `fun` to each element of a list, building a list from the results. As an example, consider a function of one argument which squares the argument:

```
(define (square x) (* x x))
```

This function can be used with `mapcar` to square all the elements of a list:

```
(mapcar square '(2 3 5 7 9))  ; yields (4 9 25 49 81)
(mapcar (lambda (x) (* x x)) '(2 3 5 7 9)) ; an alternative
```

In the first example, the first parameter is a defined function. In the second example, a nameless function is passed using lambda notation for defining it.

This ease of defining functional forms gives Scheme (and Common Lisp) an ease of extensibility. With such a facility users can easily add many apply-to-all functional forms. Many simple Scheme functions are defined this way. We will see an example of the use of a function as an argument in the eight queens example discussed below.

8.3 DEBUGGING

Many (but not all) Scheme interpreters provide a function named `trace` to aid in understanding why a function is returning the wrong answers. Unfortunately, the `trace` function is not a part of Standard Scheme, so even when it is included, its output may vary slightly from one implementation to another. Below we give an example of the use of the `trace` function to trace the `factorial` function discussed above:

```
> (trace factorial)
> (factorial 4)
Trace: (factorial 4)
Trace: (factorial 3)
Trace: (factorial 2)
Trace: (factorial 1)
Trace: (factorial 0)
Trace: Value = 1
Trace: Value = 1
Trace: Value = 2
Trace: Value = 6
Trace: Value = 24
24
> (untrace factorial)
> (factorial 4)
24
```

Tracing can be turned off via the `untrace` function.

For those Scheme implementations that lack a trace function, the same effect can be achieved via the standard imperative technique of embedding debugging print commands. In Scheme the most convenient function to use is `printf`, which is similar to the function of the same name in C. The `printf` function takes as its first argument a string which specifies how the output is to be displayed; in Scheme the code ~a is used to display a value, while ~n is used to represent an end of line code. Using this, we can rewrite the factorial function to get output similar to that above using:

```scheme
(define (factorial n)
    (printf "(factorial ~a ~n)" n)
    (if (<= n 0)  1
        ; else
        (let ((x (* n (factorial (- n 1)))))
            (printf "(factorial ~a) = ~a ~n" n x)
            x
        )
))
```

Below we give an example of the use of this "modified" factorial function:

```scheme
> (factorial 3)
(factorial 3)
(factorial 2)
(factorial 1)
(factorial 0)
(factorial 1) = 1
(factorial 2) = 2
(factorial 3) = 6
6
```

This works easily because both the define and let functions allow a sequence of functions as a body and return the value of the last function computed.

8.4 **EXAMPLE: SCHEME APPLICATIONS**

This section develops a selection of more interesting examples that combine to illustrate the unique value of functional programming in Scheme. The first example revisits the semantics of Jay, which were originally discussed and implemented in Java. The second example, symbolic differentiation, is a rather classic one, while the third example reconsiders the eight queens problem presented in Chapter 7.

8.4.1 Formal Semantics of Jay

In this section we implement much of the formal semantics of Jay using Scheme. Recall that a key notion in the semantics of imperative languages is that of a state, which consists of a set of variables bound to their current values. Mathematically, these bindings are represented as pairs.

$$\sigma = \{\langle id_1, val_1 \rangle, \langle id_2, val_2 \rangle, \ldots, \langle id_m, val_m \rangle\}$$

In our Java implementation, this particular set was implemented as a hashtable in which the variable identifier was the key and the associated value was the current value of the variable (see Appendix B).

A fundamental idea in the Scheme implementation is that a state is naturally represented as a list, with each element of the list being a pair representing the binding of a variable to its value. So the Jay state:

$\{\langle x, 1 \rangle, \langle y, 5 \rangle\}$

can be represented as the Scheme list:

```
((x  1) (y  5))
```

Next we implement the state access functions named `get` and `onion` (overriding union) from the Java implementation (see Appendix B).

Recall that the `get` function is used to obtain the value of a variable from the current state. In Scheme the code needed is similar to the `member` function:

```
(define (get id sigma)
   (if (equal? id (caar sigma))) (cadar sigma)
      (get  id  (cdr sigma))
))
```

Since the Jay type system requires that all variables used in a program be declared, there cannot be a reference to a variable that is not in the state. Thus, the function `get` is simpler than the `member` function in this regard, since it does not need to check for a null list.

An application of the `get` function is:

```
(get 'y '((x 5) (y 3) (z 1)))
    = (get 'y '((y 3) (z 1)))     ; since not (equal 'y 'x)
    = 3                           ; since (equal 'y 'y)
```

A good model for the `onion` (overriding union) function is the previously defined `subst` function, with one difference being the structure of the lists and the other being that there must be exactly one occurrence of each variable in the state:

```
(define (onion id val sigma)
   (if (equal? id (caar sigma))
      (cons (list id val) (cdr sigma))
      (cons  (car  sigma) (onion id val (cdr sigma)))
))
```

Again the `onion` function is able to make the simplifying assumption that the variable for which we are searching occurs within the state; hence, there is no need to check for a null list as the base case. The other simplifying assumption is that there is only a single occurrence of the variable within the state; hence, the `onion` function need not continue to recurse in the then portion of the `if` function.

An application of the `onion` function is:

```
(onion 'y 4 '((x 5) (y 3) (z 1)))
  = (cons '(x 5) (onion 'y '((y 3) (z 1))) ; since not (equal 'y 'x)
  = (cons '(x 5) (cons '(y 4) '((z 1))))   ; since (equal 'y 'y)
  = '((x 5) (y 4) (z 1))
```

In the following discussion of semantic functions for Jay, we assume that statements in Jay abstract syntax (see Appendix B) are represented as Scheme lists:

```
(skip)
(assignment target source)
(block s1 ... sn)
(loop test body)
(conditional test thenbranch elsebranch)
```

In Scheme the data to each type of abstract syntax is not named as it was in Java but rather is a positional parameter in the list. Thus, in a loop statement the test is the second element of the list, while the body is the third element.

The meaning function for a Jay statement can be written as a simple Scheme case statement:

```
(define (m-statement statement sigma)
  (case (car statement)
      ((skip)        (m-skip (cdr statement) sigma))
      ((assignment)  (m-assign (cdr statement) sigma))
      ((block)       (m-block (cdr statement) sigma))
      ((loop)        (m-loop (cdr statement) sigma))
      ((conditional) (m-conditional (cdr statement) sigma))
))
```

The implementation of these meaning functions is equally straightforward and follows from the mathematical definitions in Appendix B. For example, a skip instruction leaves the state unchanged, so the output state is a copy of the input state.

```
(define (m-skip statement sigma) sigma)
```

For a block, recall its mathematical definition from Appendix B:

$$M(Block\ b,\ State\ \sigma) = \sigma \qquad\qquad\qquad\qquad\qquad\qquad\quad \text{if } b = \varnothing$$
$$= M((Block)b_{2...n},\ M((Statement)b_1,\ \sigma)) \quad \text{if } b = b_1 b_2 ... b_n$$

This is implemented in Scheme by first interpreting the meaning of the first statement in the list, and then recursively applying this function to the remainder of the list. We have already stripped the block tag from the head of the list in the m-statement function.

```
(define (m-block alist sigma)
  (if (null? alist) sigma
      (m-block (cdr alist) (m-statement (car alist) sigma))
))
```

We may implement the meaning of a loop instruction, which is defined in Appendix B by the following partial function:

$$M(Loop\ l,\ State\ \sigma) = M(l,\ M(l.\text{body},\ \sigma)) \qquad \text{if } M(l.\text{test},\ \sigma) \text{ is } true$$
$$= \sigma \qquad\qquad\qquad\qquad\qquad\quad \text{otherwise}$$

The Scheme implementation follows almost directly from this definition:

```
(define (m-loop statement sigma)
   (if (m-expression (car statement) sigma)
       (m-loop statement (m-statement (cdr statement) sigma))
       sigma
))
```

Finally, we consider the Scheme meaning function for Jay expression evaluation. To this end, we choose an appropriate list representation for an abstract Jay expression:

```
(value val), where val is either a number, #t, #f
(variable id), where id is a variable name
(operator term1 term2), where operator is one of:
    plus minus times div -- arithmetic
    lt, le, eq, ne, gt, ge -- relational
    and, or -- boolean
```

The meaning function for a Jay abstract expression is implemented as a case on the kind of expression. The meaning of a value expression is just the value itself. The meaning of a variable is the value associated with the variable in the current state. The meaning of a binary expression is obtained by applying the operator to the meanings of the operands:

```
(define (m-expression expr sigma)
   (case (car expr)
      ((value) (cadr expr))
      ((variable) (get (cadr expr) sigma)
      (else (applyBinary (car expr) (cadr expr)
                      (caddr expr) sigma))
))
```

The function applyBinary defined in Appendix B is easily implemented as a case on the operator. Here we show only the arithmetic operators, leaving the relational and Boolean operators as exercises:

```
(define (applyBinary op term1 term2 sigma)
   (case op
      ((plus)   (+ (m-expression term1 sigma)
                   (m-expression term2 sigma)))
      ((minus)  (- (m-expression term1 sigma)
                   (m-expression term2 sigma)))
      ((times)  (* (m-expression term1 sigma)
                   (m-expression term2 sigma)))
      ((div)    (/ (m-expression term1 sigma)
                   (m-expression term2 sigma)))
      (else #f)
))
```

Similarly, the implementation of relational and unary expressions involving the not operator, as well as the assignment statement itself, is left as an exercise.

As an application of the m-expression function to the expression y+2 in the state {<x,5>, <y,3>, <z,1>}, consider the following:

```
(m-expression '(plus (variable y) (value 2)) '((x 5) (y 3) (z 1)))
  = (applyBinary '(plus (variable y) (value 2)) '((x 5) (y 3) (z 1)))
  = (+ (m-expression '(variable y) '((x 5) (y 3) (z 1)))
      (m-expression '(value 2) '((x 5) (y 3) (z 1))))
  = (+ (gett 'y '((x 5) (y 3) (z 1)))
      (m-expression '(value 2) '((x 5) (y 3) (z 1))))
  = (+ 3
      (m-expression '(value 2) '((x 5) (y 3) (z 1))))
  = (+ 3 2)
  = 5
```

This development of even a small fraction of the formal semantics of Jay should be convincing that a full semantic model for an imperative language can be defined in Scheme. Thus, via interpretation, Scheme is capable of computing any function that can be programmed in an interpretative language. The converse is also true since modern RISC computers are fundamentally imperative in nature; since Scheme interpreters are implemented on RISC machines, any function programmed in Scheme can be computed by an imperative program. Thus, in theory, imperative languages and functional languages are equivalent in computational power.

8.4.2 Symbolic Differentiation

The utility of Scheme for symbol manipulation is widespread, as the previous example suggests. This next example further illustrates some of the power of Scheme by doing symbolic differentiation and simplification of simple calculus formulae. Some familiar rules for symbolic differentiation are given in Figure 8.2.

Figure 8.2 Symbolic Differentiation Rules

$$\frac{d}{dx}(c) = 0 \qquad c \text{ is a constant}$$

$$\frac{d}{dx}(x) = 1$$

$$\frac{d}{dx}(u + v) = \frac{du}{dx} + \frac{dv}{dx} \qquad u \text{ and } v \text{ are functions of } x$$

$$\frac{d}{dx}(u - v) = \frac{du}{dx} - \frac{dv}{dx}$$

$$\frac{d}{dx}(uv) = u\frac{dv}{dx} + v\frac{du}{dx}$$

$$\frac{d}{dx}\left(\frac{u}{v}\right) = \left(v\frac{du}{dx} - u\frac{dv}{dx}\right)\Big/v^2$$

For example, differentiating the function $2 \cdot x + 1$ with respect to x using these rules gives:

$$\frac{d(2 \cdot x + 1)}{dx} = \frac{d(2 \cdot x)}{dx} + \frac{d1}{dx}$$

$$= 2 \cdot \frac{dx}{dx} + x \cdot \frac{d2}{dx} + 0$$

$$= 2 \cdot 1 + x \cdot 0 + 0$$

which would ordinarily simplify to 2.

In Scheme it is convenient to represent expressions using prefix Polish notation:

```
(+ term1 term2)
(- term1 term2)
(* term1 term2)
(/ term1 term2)
```

The required function to do symbolic differentiation first tests to see if the expression is either a constant or the variable being differentiated, as in the first two rules above. Otherwise, the expression is a list starting with an operator, and the code applies one of the remaining four rules using a case on the operator. A let function has been used to make the Scheme code look as much like the rules in Figure 8.2 as possible.

```
(define (diff x expr)
  (if (atom? expr)
    (if (equal? x expr) 1 0)
    (let ((u (cadr expr)) (v (caddr expr)))
      (case (car expr)
        ((+) (list '+ (diff x u) (diff x v)))
        ((-) (list '- (diff x u) (diff x v)))
        ((*) (list '+
              (list '* u (diff x v))
              (list '* v (diff x u))))
        ((/) (list '/ (list '-
                      (list '* v (diff x u))
                      (list '* u (diff x v)))
                  (list '* v v)))
))))
```

An application of the diff function to the expression $2 \cdot x + 1$ gives:

```
(diff 'x '(+ (* 2 x) 1))
  = (list '+ (diff 'x '(* 2 x)) (diff 'x 1))
  = (list '+ (list '+ (list '* 2 (diff 'x 'x))
                      (list '* x (diff 'x 2)))
            (diff 'x 1))
```

```
= (list '+ (list '+ (list '* 2 1) (list '* x (diff 'x 2)))
        (diff 'x 1))
= (list '+ (list '+ '(* 2 1) (list '* x (diff 'x 2)))
        (diff 'x 1))
= (list '+ (list '+ '(* 2 1) (list '* x 0)) (diff 'x 1))
= (list '+ (list '+ '(* 2 1) '(* x 0)) (diff 'x 1))
= (list '+ '(+ '(* 2 1) '(* x 0)) (diff 'x 1))
= (list '+ '(+ '(* 2 1) '(* x 0)) 0)
```

or 2*1 + 0*x + 0. Writing an expression simplifier is left as an exercise.

8.4.3 Eight Queens

In Chapter 7, we developed an object-oriented version of Wirth's backtracking algorithm [Wirth 1976]. The general solution that Wirth presents is a recursive procedure that iterates through a series of trial moves. Each move is tested to see if it satisfies an appropriate *validity* criterion. If it does, the move is recorded, and if the problem is not yet solved, the procedure calls itself recursively to try the next level; if the recursive call fails, then the current move is undone and the next move is tried. The process of trying moves continues until either a completely successful solution is found or all the moves at the current level have been unsuccessfully tried.

The general iterative solution according to Wirth [1976, p. 136] and transliterated to a C-like notation is:

```
boolean try(Solution) {
  boolean successful = false;
  initialize moves;
  while (more moves && !successful) {
    select next move;
    if (move is valid) {
      record move in Solution;
      if (Solution not done) {
        successful = try(Solution);
        if (!successful)
          undo move in Solution;
      }
    }
  }
  return successful;
}
```

In this section we present a purely functional version of this algorithm and then specialize it to solve the eight queens problem. This solution is interesting because it shows some of the positive and negative aspects of functional programming, in contrast with imperative and object-oriented programming.

There are effectively two problems we must solve in converting this general, imperative solution to a purely functional one. The first problem is that the function try returns two results: the solution and whether or not it is successful. In the imperative outline given above, the function `try` returns `successful` as the value of the function. The *Solution* is a reference parameter: the commands *record* and *undo* are generalized assignments implemented as function calls. A purely functional language does not have reference parameters and assignments, nor can it return more than a single result.

The solution to this problem in Scheme is to simply `cons` the value of the variable `successful` onto the front of the solution whenever convenient. That solves the first problem.

The second problem is that Wirth's solution uses a while loop to iterate through a series of moves until either a completely successful solution is found or there are no more moves at this level. A direct Scheme encoding of this problem would use the imperative features of Scheme to essentially duplicate Wirth's algorithm. However, we want to present a purely functional equivalent to the imperative loop structure, which suggests that we use a recursive method instead.

We shall present our algorithm in bottom-up or inside-out fashion, depending on your point of view. This means that we shall attack the inner if statements first, then the while loop, and finally the overall function. Functions particular to the actual problem being solved, such as when the solution is done, when there are no more moves, and so forth, will be left unspecified for now.

The first function, denoted `tryone`, was developed to solve the *if move is valid* statement:

```
(define (tryone move soln)
  (let ((xsoln (cons move soln)))
    (if (valid move soln)
       (if (done xsoln)  (cons #t xsoln)
           (try  xsoln))
    (cons #f soln)
) ) )
```

The function `tryone` is only called if the variable `successful` is *false*; so the parameter `soln` does not have the value of `successful` on the front of the list. However, it returns a solution with the value of `successful` on the front of the list. Note that we used a `let` function as a functional shorthand to avoid computing the extended solution `xsoln` twice. The function first checks if the current move is valid given the current partial solution. If it is not valid, then it returns *false* for `successful` and the current solution via (`cons #f soln`). If the move is valid, then it checks to see if the extended solution solves the problem (function `done`). If yes, then it returns true for `successful` and the extended solution. Otherwise it recursively calls `try` with the extended solution to attempt to continue extending the solution.

Next we convert the while loop to a recursive function, noting that any imperative while loop of the form:

```
while (test) {
   body
}
```

can be converted to the recursive function:

```
(define (while test body sigma)
   (if (test sigma)
       (let ((onepass (body sigma)))
           (while test body onepass)
       )
       sigma
))
```

Here, the variable `onepass` delivers the state that results from executing the body of the while loop one time. So if the test is *true*, the while statement is reexecuted after making one pass on the body. Otherwise, the current state is returned.

Our program state for eight queens is a little more complicated, but this general conversion scheme produces the following function:

```
(define (trywh move soln)
   (if (and (hasmore move) (not (car soln)))
       (let ((atry (tryone move (cdr soln))))
           (if (car atry) atry (trywh (nextmove move) soln))
       )
       soln
))
```

Note that we use a `let` function as a functional shorthand to avoid writing the call on the `tryone` function twice. Note that the `trywh` function expects the value of the variable `successful` to be on the front of the list, while the `tryone` function does not, since `tryone` is called only when `successful` is *false*.

Finally, we implement the `try` function. It is called with a partial solution without the variable `successful`, and returns the `cons` of the variable `successful` and the solution found. It is responsible for getting the first move to initialize the while loop:

```
(define (try soln) (trywh (firstmove) (cons #f soln)))
```

To specialize this to a particular problem, we must implement a number of functions. The functions `firstmove`, `hasmore`, and `nextmove` are concerned with generating trial moves. The function `valid` is concerned with whether a trial move validly extends the current partial solution. The function `done` tests whether an extended solution solves the problem. We illustrate implementations of these functions by developing a solution to the eight queens problem.

A major issue in the eight queens problem is how to store the (row, column) position of each of the queens. Recall from Section 7.6 that we developed the solution a column at a time, storing the row position for each column using an array. In the solution developed here, we store the row position for each column using a list, but with one fundamental difference. We store the list in reverse order so that the most recently added row is at the head of the list at all times. For example, the board with three queens in the (row, column) positions shown in Figure 8.3 is represented as the following list:

```
(5 3 1)
```

Figure 8.3 Three Queens on an 8 × 8 Chess Board

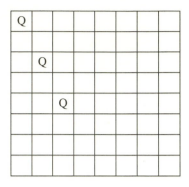

If a value for the variable N representing the number of rows and columns of the chess board has been defined, we can define the functions for generating moves as:

```
(define  (firstmove)  1)
(define  (hasmore  move)  (<= move N))
(define  (nextmove  move)  (+ move 1))
```

which generates row numbers in the sequence from 1 to N. Similarly, we can define a solution to be "done" in the following way:

```
(define (done soln) (>= (length soln) N))
```

Now all that remains is to define whether or not a trial row validly extends the current partial solution. Recall from Chapter 7 that three conditions must hold:

1 The trial row must not be occupied. This means that the trial row (or move) must not be a member of the current solution.
2 The southwest diagonal formed by the trial row and column must not be occupied. The southwest diagonal is the sum of the row and column numbers.
3 The southeast diagonal formed by the trial row and column must not be occupied. The southeast diagonal is the difference of the row and column numbers.

Given a row and column number the southwest and southeast diagonals are easily computed as:

```
(define (swDiag row col) (+ row col))
(define (seDiag row col) (- row col))
```

Now for a given solution all we have to do is convert the list of row positions into a list of southwest and southeast diagonal positions, where for a given soln the row position is (car soln) and the associated column number is (length soln). It is straightforward to write appropriate recursive functions to do this computation.

But Scheme provides the built-in function map1 to apply a function given as an argument recursively to each element of a list. Thus, our required functions can be defined as:

```
(define (diagonal f soln)
   (map1 (lambda (alist) (f (car alist) (length alist))) soln))
```

The function `diagonal` can be used to compute both diagonals by passing it the function `seDiag` for f in one case, and `swDiag` for f in the other.

Then the current trial move representing a row position validly extends the current partial solution, if the move (row) is not a member of the solution, and if the move (row position and associated column) is not a member of either the southeast or southwest diagonal:

```
(define (valid move soln)
  (let ((col (length (cons move soln))))
    (and (not (member move soln))
      (not (member (seDiag move col) (diagonal seDiag soln)))
      (not (member (swDiag move col) (diagonal swDiag soln)))
) ) )
```

This concludes our functional presentation of backtracking and the eight queens problem, which has been interesting for a number of reasons. On the positive side, it shows the power of functional programming, particularly the ability for an unevaluated function to be passed as a parameter.

On the negative side, our solution shows some of the weaknesses of functional programming. First, converting a program that has an iterative loop to a recursive function may be nontrivial. Even the simple act of embedding print statements in the code for debugging purposes is not purely functional. Second, using a list to return multiple values from a function is clumsy when compared to using reference parameters or returning an object with named instance variables. For these reasons (and also for the sake of efficiency), Scheme extends "pure Lisp" by including imperative features such as local variables, assignment statements, and iterative loops.

8.5 PROGRAM CORRECTNESS

Program correctness was briefly discussed in Chapter 3, where we introduced the idea of using axiomatic semantics as a basis for developing a proof that a program correctly implements its formal specifications. When examining the notion of program correctness in Scheme, we find that it is a much more straightforward process. That is, absent the notion of program state and assignment, we need not write Hoare triples to keep track of the state transformations that accompany a series of statements. Instead, we base correctness proofs for Scheme functions on the well-worn technique of mathematical induction.

For a simple example, consider again the Scheme function that computes the factorial of a nonnegative integer n:

```
(define  (factorial n)
    (if (= n 0)  1
        (* n (factorial (- n 1)))
))
```

Suppose we want to prove that this function computes the product of the first n non-negative integers, given n. That is, we want to prove that:

```
fact(0) = 1
fact(n) = 1 · 2 · ... · (n − 1) · n   if n>0
```

Recall that, for an inductive proof, we need to show both:

1 That the function computes the correct result for the "base case" (in this example, n = 0), and
2 That an "induction step" can be taken. That is, given the hypotheses that the function computes the correct result for some value, say n − 1, this leads to the conclusion that the function computes the correct result for the next value, n.

Since the function fact is recursively defined, its *if* function naturally delineates the base case from the induction step. That is, the base case is handled by the first line of the function definition and the induction step is addressed by the second. Thus, the function definition satisfies the base case by observation. That is, when n = 0 we have fact(0) = 1 from the first line.

For the induction hypothesis, suppose that n > 0 and fact(n-1) = 1 · 2 · ... · $(n − 1)$. Then the induction step can be proved by using the second line of the function definition and the hypothesis, followed by a simple algebraic simplification (using standard infix notation):

$$fact(n) = n*fact(n-1)$$
$$= n*(1 · 2 · ... · (n − 1))$$
$$= 1 · 2 · ... · (n − 1) · n$$

A similar strategy can be used for all Scheme functions that are defined recursively on lists.[5] For instance, consider the function defined for list reversal:

```
(define (reverse lst)
   (if (null? lst) ()
       (append (reverse (cdr lst)) (list (car lst)))
))
```

We will assume the basic definitions of the basic Scheme functions: car, cons, cdr, and list; proof of correctness of append is left as an exercise. We want to prove the following fact about reversing a list (using standard functional notation):

```
reverse(a1 ... an) = (an ... a1)
```

where only the top level elements are reversed; for instance:

```
(reverse '(a b (c d) e) = (e (c d) b a)
```

An induction proof begins with the base case and appeals to the definition of the reverse function based on the length of the list. That is, we first need to show that the

---

5. Induction on list-processing functions is often called *structural induction* because it reduces the structure (size) of a list as it defines the hypothesis and shows the validity of the induction step.

list is reversed when the length of the list is zero (i.e., the empty list):

```
reverse () = ()
```

But by the first line in the definition of reverse, we have

```
reverse () = (if (null? ()) () ...)
           = ()
```

The induction hypothesis for this proof is that the conclusion holds for a particular list xs whenever the length (xs) equals n. Now the induction step that needs to be proved uses a slightly longer (by 1) list (cons x xs) where xs is the list (x1 ... xn), as follows:

```
(reverse (cons x xs)) = ((reverse xs) x)
                      = (xn ... x1 x)
```

That is, the result is the list consisting of the reverse of the tail of the list followed by the first element of the list. So we now transform the left-hand side of this expression using our hypothesis and the second line in the definition of the function reverse (since the list is not the empty list), as follows:

```
(reverse (cons x xs)) = (append (reverse xs) (list x))
                      = (append (xn ... x1) (x))
                      = (xn ... x1 x)
```

Observant readers will notice that the second line in this derivation uses the inductive hypothesis, while the third line assumes the correctness of the append of two lists.

8.6 ADVANCES IN FUNCTIONAL PROGRAMMING: HASKELL

A number of recent developments in functional programming are not well-captured by the traditional languages, Common Lisp and Scheme. In this section, we introduce a more modern functional language, Haskell [Haskell 1999], whose features signal more clearly the present and future directions in functional programming research and applications. The distinct and salient features of Haskell include its lazy evaluation strategy and its type system. While Haskell is a strongly typed language (all type errors are identified), sometimes a type error is not detected until the program element that contains the error is actually executed.[6]

8.6.1 Expressions

Expressions in Haskell are normally written in infix notation, in which the operator or function appears between its operands, as in the example:

```
2+2                 -- compute the value 4
```

---

6. This is different from strongly typed languages like Java, where all type errors are detected at compile time, so that when execution begins the program is guaranteed to be free of type errors.

When this expression is presented to a Haskell interpreter, it computes the value 4. A double dash (--) starts a Haskell comment, which continues to the end of the line. The usual arithmetic and relational operators are provided in Haskell, and more complicated expressions can be built using parentheses and the built-in precedence relationships among these operators. Here, for instance, is a Haskell expression that computes the value 48.

```
5*(4+6)-2
```

which would be equivalent to the Scheme expression (- (* 5 (+ 4 6) 2)). Moreover, we may write Haskell expressions using prefix notation, provided that we parenthesize all operators and nonatomic operands. This is illustrated by the following expression (equivalent to the above infix expression).

```
(-) ((*) 5 ((+) 4 6)) 2
```

A more complete summary of the Haskell operators and their precedence relationships is given in Table 8.1.

Table 8.1

Summary of the Haskell Operators and Their Precedences

Precedence	Left-Associative	Non-Associative	Right-Associative
9	!, !!, //		.
8			**, ^, ^^
7	*, /, 'div', 'mod', 'rem', 'quot'		
6	+, -	:+	
5		\\	:, ++
4		/=, <, <=, ==, >, >=, 'elem', 'notElem'	
3			&&
2			||
1	>>, >>=	:=	
0			$, 'seq'

The right-associative operators are evaluated from right to left when they are adjacent in an expression at the same level of parenthesization; the left-associative operators are evaluated from left to right. For instance, the Haskell expression

```
2^3^4
```

denotes raising 2 to the 3^4 power (or 2^{81} or 2417851639229258349412352), rather than raising 2^3 to the 4th power (or 2^{12} or 4096). The non-associative operators cannot appear adjacent in an expression. That is, the expression a+b+c is permissible, but a<b<c is not. The meanings of many of these operators should be self-explanatory. Many of the others will be explained in the discussion below.[7]

8.6.2 Lists and List Comprehensions

Like Lisp and Scheme, the fundamental data structure of Haskell is the list. Lists are collections of elements with a given type. Lists can be defined by enumerating their elements, as shown in the following definitions for two small lists of numbers:

```
evens = [0, 2, 4, 6, 8]
odds = [1, 3 .. 9]
```

The list odds is defined by the familiar mathematical convention of using ellipses (..) to omit all the intermediate elements when the pattern is obvious. Pictorially, the list evens is represented in Figure 8.1.

Alternatively, a list can be defined using a so-called generator which takes the following form:

```
moreevens = [2*x | x <- [0..10]]
```

This literally says, "the list of all values 2*n such that n is an element in the list [0..10]." The operator <- represents the mathematical symbol $\in$, which denotes list membership.

A list *comprehension* can be defined using a generator, and the list it defines may be infinite. For instance, the following defines the infinite list containing all the even non-negative integers:

```
mostevens = [2*x | x <- [0,1 .. ]]
```

Here, the generator is the expression x <- [0,1 ..]. Alternatively, this infinite list could have been defined by:

```
mostevens = [0,2 .. ]
```

This example illustrates a strong departure of Haskell from the traditional functional languages. Infinite lists, and functions that compute values from them, are common in Haskell. They are possible because of Haskell's general commitment to *lazy evaluation,* which says simply to evaluate no argument to a function until the moment it is absolutely needed.[8] For infinite lists, this means that they are stored in unevaluated form; however the *n*th element, no matter how large the value of *n*, can be computed whenever it is needed.

---

7. Haskell also supports the definition of additional operators, provided that they are formed from the following symbols: # $ % * + . / < = > ? \ ^ | | : ~.

8. Recall the distinction between "eager" and "lazy" evaluation made in Chapter 5, where parameter passing was discussed. It should be clear that eager evaluation of arguments to a function would prohibit the definition of infinite lists or functions that operate on them.

The basic function for constructing a list is the infix operator : , which takes an element and a list as its two arguments.[9] Here are some examples, where [] denotes the empty list:

```
8:[]                    -- gives [8]
6:8:[]                  -- gives 6:[8] or [6,8]
4:[6,8]                 -- gives [4,6,8]
```

A Haskell list has two parts, the first element or the "head" of the list, and the list of remaining elements or its "tail." The functions head and tail return these two parts, respectively. Referring to the list evens pictured in Figure 8.1, the following examples illustrate these functions:

```
head evens              -- gives 0
tail evens              -- gives [2,4,6,8]
head (tail evens)       -- gives 2
tail (tail evens)       -- gives [4,6,8]
head [6,8]              -- gives 6
head 6:[8]              -- gives 6
tail [6,8]              -- gives [8]
tail [8]                -- gives []
```

The principal operator for putting lists together is ++.[10] This operator is illustrated by the following examples:

```
[1,2]++[3,4]++[5]       -- gives [1,2,3,4,5]
evens ++ odds           -- gives [0,2,4,6,8,1,3,5,7,9]
[1,2]++[]               -- gives [1,2]
[1,2]++3:[]             -- gives [1,2,3]
1++2                    -- error; wrong type of arguments for ++
```

Since Haskell was designed to process lists, it contains a number of special list processing functions. Because the need frequently arises, there is a special function null to test for an empty list:

```
null  []                -- gives True
null  evens             -- gives False
null  [1,2,3]           -- gives False
null  5                 -- error; wrong type of argument for null
```

Haskell contains functions for testing if one object is equal or equivalent to another. The main function is embodied in the infix operator ==, which is fairly general. This function returns True if the two objects have the same structure and content; otherwise

---

9. This operator is like the Scheme cons function.

10. This operator is like the Scheme append function.

it returns `False` or a type error:

```
5==5                -- returns True
5==1                -- returns False
[1,2]==[1,2]        -- returns True
5==[5]              -- error; mismatched argument types
[1,2,3]==[1,[2,3]]  -- error; mismatched argument types
[1,2]==[2,1]        -- returns False
[]==[]              -- returns True
```

List types can be defined and then later used in the construction of functions. To define a list type `IntList` of `Int` values, for instance, the following statement is used:

```
type IntList = [Int]
```

Notice that the use of brackets signals that the type being defined is a particular kind of list—one whose entries are of type `Int`.[11]

8.6.3 Elementary Types and Values

So far, all the values we have seen in Haskell are integers, predefined symbols (function names), and type names. Haskell supports various types of elementary values, including booleans (called `Bool`), integers (`Int` and `Integer`), characters (`Char`), character strings (`String`), and floating point numbers (`Float`).

As noted above, the boolean values are `True` and `False`. The `Int` type supports a finite range of values (-2^{31} through $2^{31} - 1$, the usual range for 32-bit representation). However, the `Integer` type supports integers of any size, and hence contains an infinite set of values.

Characters in Haskell are represented inside single quotes, as in `'a'`, and familiar escape conventions are used to identify special characters, like `'\n'` for newline, `'\t'` for tab, and so forth. Strings are represented either as series of characters inside double quotes (") or as lists of `Char` values. That is, the type `String` is equivalent to the type `[Char]`. So the list `['h','e','l','l','o']` is equivalent to the String `"hello"`. That is, the following type definition is implicit in Haskell:

```
type String = [Char]
```

Because of this equivalence, many String operators are the same as list operators. For instance, the expression

```
"hello " ++ "world"
```

represents string concatenation, and yields the result `"hello world"`.

---

11. Haskell type names are distinguished from other names by the fact that they begin with an upper-case letter.

Floating point values are written in either decimal notation or scientific notation. Each of the following represents the number 3.14.

```
3.14
0.000314e4
314e-2
```

Various functions are available for transforming floating point values in Haskell, including the following, whose meanings are fairly self-explanatory (arguments to trigonometric functions are expressed in radians):

```
abs acos atan ceiling floor cos sin
log logBase pi sqrt
```

8.6.4 Control Flow

The major control-flow constructs in Haskell are the guarded command and the if...then...else.[12] The guarded command is a generalization of a nested if...then...else, and can be written more briefly. For instance, suppose we want to find the maximum of three values, x, y, and z. Then we can express this as an if...then...else as follows:

```
if x >= y && x >= z then x
else if y >= x && y >= z then y
        else z
```

Alternatively, we can express this as a guarded command in the following way:

```
| x >= y && x >= z = x
| y >= x && y >= z = y
| otherwise = z
```

The guarded command is widely used when defining Haskell functions, as we shall see below.

8.6.5 Defining Functions

Haskell functions are defined in two parts. The first part identifies the function's name, domain, and range, and the second part describes the meaning of the function. That is, a function definition has the following form:

```
name :: Domain -> Range
name x y z
        | g1 = e1
        | g2 = e2
        :
        | otherwise = e
```

---

12. Haskell also has a case function, which is similar to the case in Ada and the switch in Java and C. However, this function seems to be relatively unimportant in Haskell programming, as its utility is subsumed by the guarded command.

Here, the body of the function is expressed as a guarded command, and the domain and range can be any types. For example, a maximum function for three integers can be defined as:

```
max3 :: Int -> Int -> Int -> Int
max3 x y z
    | x >= y && x >= z    = x
    | y >= x && y >= z    = y
    | otherwise           = z
```

The first line in a function definition can be omitted, in which case Haskell derives that line automatically, giving the function the broadest possible interpretation. When we omit the first line of the above function definition, Haskell derives the following for it:

```
max3 :: Ord a => a -> a -> a -> a
```

This notation means that if `a` is *any* ordered type (`Ord`), then the meaning of `max3` is explained by the above definition. An *ordered type* in Haskell is any type that carries the relational operators (==, !=, >=, >, <=, and <), which allow its individual values to be ordered. Thus, our `max3` function is now well-defined on arguments that are `Int`, `Float`, `String`, or any other type whose values are ordered, as illustrated by the following examples:

```
> max3 6 4 1
6
> max3 "alpha" "beta" "gamma"
"gamma"
```

This function `max3` is an example of a *polymorphic* function. A polymorphic function is one whose definition applies equally well to arguments of various types, within the constraints given by the first line of the function definition. For instance, an attempt to compute the maximum of a string and two integers gives the run-time type error:

```
> max3 "a" 2 3
ERROR: Illegal Haskell 98 class constraint in inferred type
*** Expression : max3 "a" 2 3
*** Type       : Num [Char] => [Char]
```

Functions in Haskell can be defined using recursion or iteration. Here is a recursive factorial function definition:

```
fact :: Integer -> Integer
fact n
    | n == 0    = 1
    | n > 0     = n*fact(n-1)
```

Here is its iterative counterpart (`product` is a built-in function);

```
fact n = product[1..n]
```

Here, the `product` function is a built-in function. Simple iterative tasks like summing a list of numbers can also be written recursively or iteratively in Haskell. The following function also illustrates how Haskell uses pattern matching to distinguish different list structures and parts.

```
mysum []      = 0
mysum (x:xs)  = x + mysum (xs)
```

The first line defines `mysum` for the special (base) case where the list is empty. The second line defines `mysum` for the other cases, where the list is nonempty—there, the expression `x:xs` defines a pattern that separates the head (`x`) from the rest (`xs`) of the list, so that they can be distinguished in the function definition. Thus, pattern-matching provides an alternative to writing a guarded statement or an if…then…else statement to distinguish alternative cases in the function definition.

This sum function is defined on any list of numerical values—`Int`, `Integer`, `Float`, `Double`, or `Long`. Here are some examples, with their results:

```
> mysum [3.5,5]
8.5
> mysum [3,3,4,2]
12
```

Haskell provides a number of list-transforming functions in its standard library called Prelude. A summary of these functions appears in Table 8.2.

Table 8.2

Some Common List Functions in Haskell

Function	Domain and Range	Explanation
:	a -> [a] -> [a]	Add an element at the front of a list
++	[a] -> [a] -> [a]	Join (concatenate) two lists together
!!	[a] -> Int -> a	x !! n returns the *n*th element of list x
length	[a] -> Int	Number of elements in a list
head	[a] -> a	First element in the list
tail	[a] -> [a]	All but the first element of the list
take	Int -> [a] -> [a]	Take n elements from the beginning of a list
drop	Int -> [a] -> [a]	Drop n elements from the beginning of a list
reverse	[a] -> [a]	Reverse the elements of a list
zip	[a] -> [b] -> [(a,b)]	Make a list of pairs*
unzip	[(a,b)] -> ([a],[b])	Make a pair of lists
sum	[Int] -> Int [Float] -> Float	Sum the elements of a list
product	[Int] -> Int [Float] -> Float	Multiply the elements of a list

*A "pair" is an example of a Haskell *tuple,* which is explained in Subsection 8.6.6.

In these and other function definitions, the notation a or b signifies "any type of value." That is, the various functions in Table 8.2 are polymorphic to the extent specified in their domain and range. For example, the element type of the list passed to the head function does not affect its meaning.

Another simple function is the member function which tests to see whether an element occurs as a member of a list and returns True or False accordingly. The definition starts with an empty list as the base case and returns False. Otherwise, it tests to see if the head of the list is equal to the element sought; if so, it returns True or otherwise it returns the result of recursively calling itself on the tail of the list.

```
member :: Eq a => a -> [a] -> Bool
member elt alist
    | alist == []        = False
    | elt == head alist = True
    | otherwise          = member elt (tail alist)
```

An alternative way to define functions in Haskell is to exploit its pattern-matching capabilities. Consider the following:

```
member elt []      = False
member elt (x:xs) = elt == x || member elt xs
```

This alternative definition is equivalent to the first. Its second line combines the last two lines of the first definition, taking advantage of the disjunction (||) function's lazy evaluation of its arguments.

In the above examples, the arguments to a function have been either simple values or lists. Haskell also allows a function to be an argument to another function being defined:

```
maphead :: (a -> b) -> [a] -> [b]
maphead fun alist = [ fun x | x <- alist ]
```

The maphead function has two parameters, a function fun and a list alist. It applies the function fun to each element x of alist, building a list from the results. As an example consider the function square:

```
square x = x*x
```

This function can be combined with maphead to square all the elements of a list:

```
maphead square [2,3,5,7,9]       -- returns [4,9,25,49,81]
maphead (\x -> x*x) [2,3,5,7,9] -- an alternative
```

In the first example, the first parameter is the name of a predefined function. In the second example, a nameless function is defined using lambda notation[13] and passed to the maphead function.

---

13. The symbol \ is used in Haskell to approximate the Greek symbol λ in forming a lambda expression. In general, the lambda expression $(\lambda x \cdot M)$ is written in Haskell as (\x->M).

8.6.6 Tuples

A Haskell *tuple* is a collection of values of different types,[14] enclosed in parentheses and separated by commas. Here is a tuple that contains a String and an Integer:

```
("Bob", 2771234)
```

Tuple values are defined in a way similar to list values, except they are enclosed in parentheses () rather than brackets [], and their size is inflexible. For instance, here is a definition for the type Entry, which may represent an entry in a phone book:

```
type Entry = (Person, Number)
type Person = String
type Number = Integer
```

This definition combines a person's name and his/her phone number as a tuple. The first and second members of a tuple can be selected using the built-in functions fst and snd, respectively. For instance:

```
fst ("Bob", 2771234) = "Bob"
snd ("Bob", 2771234) = 2771234
```

Continuing this example, it is natural to define a type Phonebook as a list of person-number pairs:

```
type Phonebook = [(Person, Number)]
```

Now we can define useful functions on this data type, such as the function find that returns all the phone numbers for a given person p:

```
find :: Phonebook -> Person -> [Number]
find pb p = [n | (person, n) <- pb, person == p]
```

This function returns the list of all numbers n in the phone book for which there is an entry (person,n) and person==p (the desired person). For example, if:

```
pb = [("Bob", 2771234), ("Allen", 2772345), ("Bob", 2770123)]
```

then the call

```
find pb "Bob"
```

returns the list:

```
[2771234, 2770123]
```

---

14. The analogue for a tuple in C/C++ is the struct.

Moreover, we can define functions that add and delete entries from a phone book:

```
addEntry :: Phonebook -> Person -> Number -> Phonebook
addEntry pb p n = [(p,n)] ++ pb

deleteEntry :: Phonebook -> Person -> Number -> Phonebook
deleteEntry pb p n = [entry | entry <- pb, entry /= (p, n)]
```

The Haskell type system is a more powerful tool than this example shows. It can be used to define new data types recursively, as we shall illustrate in the next section.

8.7 EXAMPLE: HASKELL APPLICATIONS

This section develops two interesting examples that illustrate some of the unique value of functional programming in Haskell. The first example revisits the semantics of Jay, which were originally discussed and implemented in Java. The second illustrates the use of correctness methods to verify Haskell functions.

8.7.1 Semantics of Jay

Recall that a key notion in the semantics of imperative languages is that of a state, which consists of a set of bindings of variables to their current values. Mathematically, these bindings are represented as pairs.

$$\sigma = \{\langle id_1, val_1 \rangle, \langle id_2, val_2 \rangle, \ldots, \langle id_m, val_m \rangle\}$$

In our Java implementation, this particular set was implemented as a hashtable in which the variable identifier was the key and the associated value was the current value of the variable (see Appendix B).

A starting point for the Haskell implementation is to represent a state as a list of pairs, with each pair representing the binding of a variable to its value. That is, the following type definitions apply:

```
type State = [(Variable, Value)]
type Variable = String
data Value = Intval Integer | Boolval Bool
             deriving (Eq, Ord, Show)
```

The third line in this definition is an example of an *algebraic type* definition in Haskell, where the new type `Value` is defined as either an `Integer` or a `Bool` value. The clause `deriving (Eq, Ord, Show)` asserts that this new type inherits the equality, ordering, and display characteristics of its component types `Integer` and `Bool`, thus allowing us to use equality (==), ordering (<), and display (`show`) functions on all of its values.

So the Jay state:

$$\{\langle x, 1 \rangle, \langle y, 5 \rangle\}$$

can be represented as the Haskell list:

```
[("x",(Intval 1)),("y",(Intval 5))]
```

Next we implement the state access functions `get` and `onion` (overriding union) from the Java implementation (see Appendix B).

Recall that the `get` function obtains the value of a variable from the current state. In Haskell the code needed is similar to the `member` function:

```
get :: Variable -> State -> Value
get var (s:ss)
    | var == (fst s) = snd s
    | otherwise      = get var ss
```

where the functions (`fst s`) and (`snd s`) return the first and second members of a tuple `s`, respectively. Since the Jay type system requires that all variables used in a program be declared, there cannot be a reference to a variable that is not in the state. Thus, the function `get` is simpler than the `member` function since the null-list case need not be tested.

An application of the `get` function is:

```
get "y" [("x",(Intval 1)),("y",(Intval 5)),("z",(Intval 4))]
    = get "y" [("y",(Intval 5)),("z",(Intval 4))]
    = (Intval, 5)
```

A good model for the `onion` (overriding union) function is the previously defined `subst` function, with one difference being the structure of the lists and the other being that there must be exactly one occurrence of each variable in the state:

```
onion :: Variable -> Value -> State -> State
onion var val (s:ss)
    | var == (fst s) = (var, val) : ss
    | otherwise      = s : (onion var val ss)
```

Again the `onion` function makes the simplifying assumption that the variable for which we are searching occurs within the state; hence, there is no need to check for a null list as the base case. The other simplifying assumption is that there is only a single occurrence of the variable within the state; hence, the `onion` function does not continue to recurse once it finds the first instance.

An application of the `onion` function is:

```
onion "y" (Intval 4) [("x",(Intval 1)),("y",(Intval 5))]
    = ("x",(Intval 1)) : onion "y" (Intval 4) [("y",(Intval 5))]
    = [("x",(Intval 1)),("y",(Intval 4))]
```

In our discussion of semantic functions for Jay, we assume that statements in Jay abstract syntax (see Appendix B) are represented as Haskell recursive data types in the following way:

```
data Statement = Skip |
                 Assignment Target Source |
                 Block |
                 Loop Test Body |
                 Conditional Test Thenbranch Elsebranch
                 deriving (Show)
type Target = Variable
type Source = Expression
data Block = Nil | Nonnil Statement Block
type Test = Expression
type Body = Statement
type Thenbranch = Statement
type Elsebranch = Statement
```

Now the meaning function for a Jay abstract statement can be written as the following overloaded[15] Haskell function m:

```
m :: Statement -> State -> State
```

The implementation of this meaning function follows directly from the mathematical definitions in Appendix B. For example, a *Skip* statement leaves the state unchanged, so the output state is a copy of the input state.

```
m (Skip) state = state
```

We may implement the meaning of a Jay *Loop*, which is defined in Appendix B by the following function:

$$M(Loop\ l,\ State\ \sigma) = M(l, M(l.\text{body}, \sigma)) \quad \text{if } M(l.\text{test}, \sigma) \text{ is } true$$
$$= \sigma \quad \text{otherwise}$$

The Haskell implementation follows almost directly from this definition:

```
m (Loop t b) state
  | (eval t state)==(Boolval True) = m(Loop t b)(m b state)
  | otherwise                      = state
```

The Haskell implementation of a Jay assignment statement utilizes the overriding union function alongside the meaning of *Assignment* defined in Appendix B.

```
m (Assignment target source) state
    = onion target (eval source state) state
```

---

15. An *overloaded* function is slightly different from a polymorphic function. The former refers to a function that has different definitions depending on the types of its arguments. The latter, as we have seen, has one definition that applies to all types of arguments.

Similarly, the meaning of a *Conditional* statement can be written directly from its formal definition in Appendix B, as follows:

```
m (Conditional test thenbranch elsebranch) state
   | (eval test state) == (Boolval True) = m thenbranch state
   | otherwise                           = m elsebranch state
```

Finally, we consider the Haskell meaning function `eval` for Jay expression evaluation. To this end, we choose an appropriate algebraic type definition for abstract Jay expressions:

```
data Expression = Var Variable |
                  Lit Value |
                  Binary Op Expression Expression
                  deriving (Eq, Ord, Show)
type Op = String
```

The meaning function for a Jay *Expression* can now be implemented in the following way:

```
eval :: Expression -> State -> Value
eval (Var v) state = get v state
eval (Lit v) state = v
```

We leave the Haskell definition of `eval` for expressions with arithmetic and relational operators as an exercise.

This development of a small fraction of the formal semantics of Jay should be convincing that a full semantic model for an imperative language can be readily defined in Haskell.

8.7.2 Program Correctness

Program correctness was briefly discussed in Chapter 3, where we introduced the idea of using axiomatic semantics as a basis for developing a proof that a program correctly implements its formal specifications. When examining the notion of program correctness in Haskell, we find that it is a much more straightforward process. That is, absent the notion of program state and assignment, we need not write Hoare triples to keep track of the state transformations that accompany a series of statements. Instead, we base correctness proofs for Haskell functions on the well-worn technique of mathematical induction.

For a simple example, consider again the Haskell function that computes the factorial of a nonnegative integer n:

```
fact n
   | n == 0   = 1
   | n > 0    = n*fact(n-1)
```

Suppose we want to prove that this function computes the product of the first n nonnegative integers, given n. That is, we want to prove that:

```
fact(0) = 1
```
$$\text{fact}(n) = 1 \cdot 2 \cdot \ldots \cdot (n-1) \cdot n \quad \text{if } n > 0$$

Recall that, for an inductive proof, we need to show both:

1 That the function computes the correct result for the "base case" (in this example, n = 0), and

2 That an "induction step" can be taken. That is, given the hypothesis that the function computes the correct result for some value, say n − 1, this leads to the conclusion that the function computes the correct result for the next value, n.

Since the function `fact` is recursively defined, its guarded commands naturally delineate the base case from the induction step. That is, the base case is handled by the first line of the function definition and the induction step is addressed by the second. Thus, the function definition satisfies the base case by observation. That is, when n = 0 we have fact(0) = 1 from the first line.

For the induction hypothesis, suppose that n > 0 and $fact(n-1) = 1 \cdot 2 \cdot \ldots \cdot (n − 1)$. Then the induction step can be proved by using the second line of the function definition and the hypothesis, followed by a simple algebraic simplification:

```
fact(n) = n*fact(n-1)
        = n*(1 · 2 · . . . · (n-1))
        = 1 · 2 · . . . · (n-1) · n
```

A similar strategy can be used for all Haskell functions that are defined recursively on lists.[16] For instance, consider the functions defined for concatenation and reversal:

```
[] ++ ys     = ys
(x:xs) ++ ys = x:(xs ++ ys)

reverse []     = []
reverse (x:xs) = reverse (xs) ++ x
```

Suppose we want to prove the following fact about concatenating and reversing two lists:

```
reverse(xs ++ ys) = reverse(ys) ++ reverse(xs)
```

For instance, if the two lists are "hello" and "world," then the following is true:

```
reverse("hello world") = reverse("world") ++ reverse("hello ")
                       = "dlrow olleh"
```

An induction proof begins with the base case and appeals to the definitions of these two functions. That is, we first need to show that:

```
reverse ([] ++ ys) = reverse (ys) ++ reverse ([])
```

But by the first line in each of the definitions of ++ and reverse, we have[17]

```
reverse([] ++ ys) = reverse (ys)
                  = reverse (ys) ++ []
                  = reverse (ys) ++ reverse ([])
```

---

16. Induction on list-processing functions is often called "structural induction" because it reduces the structure (size) of a list as it defines the hypothesis and shows the validity of the induction step.

17. This is *almost* true. Readers should note that this step also assumes ys++[]=ys for any list ys, and technically this needs to be proved as well.

The induction hypothesis for this proof is written by simply stating the conclusion for two particular lists xs and ys.

```
reverse(xs ++ ys) = reverse(ys) ++ reverse(xs)
```

Now the induction step that needs to be proved uses a slightly longer (by 1) list x:xs, as follows:

```
reverse((x:xs) ++ ys) = reverse (ys) ++ reverse (x:xs)
```

So we now transform the left-hand side of this expression using our hypothesis and the second lines in the definitions of the functions reverse and ++, as follows:

```
reverse ((x:xs) ++ ys) = reverse (x:(xs ++ ys))
                       = reverse (xs ++ ys) ++ [x]
                       = (reverse (ys) ++ reverse (xs)) ++ [x]
                       = reverse (ys) ++ (reverse (xs) ++ [x])
                       = reverse (ys) ++ reverse (x:xs)
```

Observant readers will notice that the fourth line in this derivation also assumes associativity for the operator ++, which can also be proved by induction.

In many ways, Haskell programs are more consistent with the properties of mathematical functions than are Scheme programs. Especially notable are Haskell's robust algebraic type system, its list continuations, and its lazy evaluation strategy. As a "pure" functional programming language, Haskell provides especially strong support for correctness proofs in large software systems.

EXERCISES

8.1 Evaluate the following lambda expressions using *eager* beta-reduction (use the standard interpretations for numbers and booleans wherever needed).
(a) $((\lambda x \cdot x*x)5)$
(b) $((\lambda y \cdot ((\lambda x \cdot x + y + z)3))2)$
(c) $(\lambda v \cdot (\lambda w \cdot w)((\lambda x \cdot x)y(\lambda z \cdot z)))$

8.2 Evaluate the expressions in Exercise 8.1 using *lazy* beta-reduction. Do you get the same results?

8.3 Evaluate the following expressions using your Scheme interpreter:
(a) `(null? ())`
(b) `(null? '(a b c d e))`
(c) `(car '(a (b c) d e))`
(d) `(cdr '(a (b c) d e))`
(e) `(cadr '(a (b c) d e))`

8.4 Evaluate the Scheme expression `(sum 1 2 3 4 5)`, showing all the steps in the expansion of the sum function given in this chapter.

8.5 Write a Scheme function named `elements` which counts the number of elements in a list; for example: `(elements '(1 (2 (3) 4) 5 6))` is 6, while the length of the same list is 4.

8.6 In the Jay interpreter of Section 8.4, manually trace:

```
(m-expression '(plus (times (variable a) (variable b))
                     (value 2)) '((a 2) (b 4)))
```

8.7 For the Jay interpreter discussed in this chapter, implement in Scheme the meaning of the relational and Boolean operators.

8.8 For the Jay interpreter discussed in this chapter, implement in Scheme the meaning of the assignment statement.

8.9 Add an implementation of the unary operator `not` to the Jay interpreter.

8.10 (Team Project) Rewrite the abstract syntax of Jay as Scheme lists. Then use these definitions to implement a type checker for Jay in Scheme using the Java implementation as a model.

8.11 (Team Project) Rewrite the abstract syntax of Jay as Scheme lists. Then use these definitions to implement the run-time semantics for Jay in Scheme using the Java implementation as a model.

8.12 Extend the symbolic differentiation program so that it differentiates functions with exponents as well as sums and products. This extension should rely on the following knowledge:

$$\frac{du^n}{dx} = nx^{n-1}\frac{du}{dx} \qquad \text{for integers } n > 0$$

8.13 Use your extended symbolic differentiation program to differentiate the following functions:
(a) $x^2 + 2x + 1$
(b) $(5x - 2y)/(x^2 + 1)$

8.14 Consider the problem of simplifying an algebraic expression, such as the result of symbolic differentiation. We know that mathematical identities like $x + 0 = x$ and $1 \cdot x = x$ are used in simplifying expressions.
(a) Design a set of rules for simplification, based on the properties of 0 and 1 when added or multiplied with another expression.
(b) Write a Scheme function that simplifies an arbitrary algebraic expression using these rules.
(c) Design a set of rules for simplification based on adding and multiplying constants.
(d) Write a Scheme function that simplifies an arbitrary algebraic expression using these rules.
(e) Extend the Scheme functions above so that the rules are applied repeatedly until no further simplification results. Hint: apply the simplifications and test to see if the "simpler" expression is different from the original.

8.15 Consider the eight queens backtracking problem. Turn on tracing for the functions `try`, `trywh`, and `tryone`.
(a) Show that there is no solution when N is 3.
(b) Show that when N is 5, the solution is found without backtracking.
(c) Is a solution found when N is 6? Is backtracking used?

8.16 Implement knight's tour in Scheme for a board of size 5 when the knight begins at square (1, 1). For a description of knight's tour, see Exercise 7.7.

8.17 Prove the correctness of the Scheme `length` function given in Subsection 8.2.6.

8.18 Prove the correctness of the following Scheme append function:

```
(define (append x y)
   (if (null? x)  y
        (cons (car x) (append (cdr x) y))
))
```

8.19 Evaluate the following expressions using your Haskell interpreter:
(a) `[1,2,3,4,5]!!2`
(b) `[1,2,3,4,5]!!5`
(c) `head [1,2,3,4,5]`
(d) `tail [1,2,3,4,5]`

8.20 For the phonebook example discussed in Section 8.6, evaluate the following functions assuming that the list pb has the initial values shown there.
(a) `addEntry pb "Jane" 1223345`
(b) `deleteEntry pb "Bob" 2770123`

8.21 Rewrite the `deleteEntry` function in Section 8.6 so that it deletes all entries for a given person. For example, if pb is as defined there, then the function

```
deleteEntry "Bob"
```

will delete *all* entries from pb for the person named "Bob" and not just one.

8.22 Write a Haskell function named `elements` which counts the number of elements in a list. It should produce the same results as the `length` function.

8.23 Implement the Haskell meaning function for a Jay *Block,* recalling its mathematical definition from Appendix B:

$$M(Block\ b,\ State\ \sigma) = \sigma \qquad\qquad\qquad \text{if } b = \varnothing$$
$$= M((Block)b_{2\ldots n}, M((Statement)b_1, \sigma)) \quad \text{if } b = b_1 b_2 \ldots b_n$$

8.24 In the Haskell interpreter discussed in Section 8.7, implement meaning functions for the Jay arithmetic, relational, and boolean operators.

8.25 Add an implementation of the unary operator `not` to the Haskell version of the Jay interpreter.

8.26 After completing the previous two exercises, derive all steps in the application of the Haskell function `eval` to the *Expression* y+2 in the state {<x,5>, <y,3>, <z,1>}. That is, show all steps in deriving the following result:

```
eval("+" y 2)[("x",(Intval 5)),
                 ("y",(Intval 3)),("z",(Intval 1)))]
= (Value 5)
```

8.27 Prove by induction that the Haskell operator ++ is associative, using its recursive definition given in this chapter. That is, show that for all lists xs, ys, and zs:

```
(xs ++ ys) ++ zs = xs ++ (ys ++ zs)
```

8.28 (a) Give a recursive definition of the Haskell function `length`, which computes the number of entries in a list.
(b) Prove by induction the following, given your definition of `length`:

```
length(xs ++ ys) = length(xs) + length(ys)
```

8.29 Consider the following (correct, but inefficient) Haskell implementation of the familiar Fibonacci function:

```
fibSlow n
    | n == 0  = 1
    | n == 1  = 1
    | n > 1   = fibSlow(n-1) + fibSlow(n-2)
```

The correctness of this function is apparent, since it is a direct encoding of the familiar mathematical definition discussed in Chapter 3:

$fib(0) = 1$
$fib(1) = 1$
$fib(n) = fib(n - 1) + fib(n - 2)$ if $n > 1$

(a) But the efficiency of this function is suspect. Try running `fibSlow(25)` and then `fibSlow(50)` on your system and see how long these computations take. What causes this inefficiency?

(b) An alternative definition of the *fib* function can be made in the following way. Define a function `fibPair` that generates a 2-element tuple that contains the *n*th Fibonacci number and its successor. Define another function `fibNext` that generates the next such tuple from the current one. Then the Fibonacci function itself, which we optimistically call `fibFast`, is defined by selecting the first member of the *n*th `fibPair`. In Haskell, this is written as follows:

```
fibPair n
    | n == 0   = (1,1)
    | n > 0    = fibNext(fibPair(n-1))
fibNext (m,n) = (n,m+n)
fibFast n = fst(fibPair(n))
```

Try running the function `fibFast` to compute the 25th and 50th Fibonacci numbers. It should be considerably more efficient than `fibSlow`. Explain.

(c) Prove by induction that $\forall n \geq 0$: *fibFast*(n) = *fibSlow*(n).

8.30 (Team Project) Rewrite the abstract syntax of Jay as Haskell lists. Then use these definitions to implement a type checker for Jay in Haskell using the Java implementation as a model.

8.31 (Team Project) Rewrite the abstract syntax of Jay as Haskell lists. Then use these definitions to implement the meaning functions for Jay in Haskell using the Java implementation as a model.

8.32 (Team Project) Develop a concrete and abstract syntax for a small subset of Scheme or Haskell. Then use these definitions to implement a run-time semantics for Scheme or Haskell using Java as the implementation language.

Logic Programming

9

"Q: How many legs does a dog have if you call its tail a leg?
A: Four. Calling a tail a leg doesn't make it one."
Abraham Lincoln

CHAPTER OUTLINE

Declarative programming emerged as a distinct paradigm in the 1970s. It is distinguished from the other paradigms because it requires the programmer to declare the goals of the computation, rather than the detailed algorithm by which these goals can be achieved.[1] Applications of declarative programming fall into two major domains: database design and artificial intelligence. In the database area, SQL has been a dominant declarative language, while in the artificial intelligence area, Prolog has been very influential.

---

1. The goals are expressed as a collection of assertions, or rules about the goals and constraints of the computation. For this reason, declarative programming is sometimes called *rule-based* programming.

One particular focus of declarative programming in artificial intelligence has been to express specifications for problem solutions in the form of expressions in mathematical logic. This so-called *logic programming* style was motivated by the needs of researchers in natural language processing and automatic theorem proving. Conventional programming languages had not been particularly well suited to these researchers' needs. However, writing down the specification of a theorem or a grammar (such as the BNF grammar used to define the syntax of Jay) as a formal logical expression provided an effective vehicle to study the process of theorem proving and natural language analysis in an experimental laboratory setting. We shall introduce some of these applications in this chapter.

Prolog is the principal language used in logic programming. The development of Prolog is based on two powerful principles discovered by Robinson [Robinson 1965] called *resolution* and *unification*. Prolog itself emerged in 1970, out of the work of Colmerauer, Rousseau, and Kowalski [Kowalski 1969], and has been the major logic programming language to the present day. Applications of logic programming are especially widespread in the areas of natural language processing, automatic reasoning and theorem proving, database search, and expert systems.

Two interesting features of logic programs that these application domains exploit are *nondeterminism* and *backtracking*. A nondeterministic logic program may find several solutions to a problem rather than just one, as would be the norm in other programming domains. Further, the backtracking mechanism which enables nondeterminism is built into the Prolog interpreter, and therefore is available to all Prolog programs. By contrast, using other languages to write backtracking programs requires the programmer to define the backtracking mechanism explicitly. We shall see the power of these two features throughout this chapter.

9.1 LOGIC, PREDICATES, AND HORN CLAUSES

Propositional logic provides the formal foundation for boolean expressions in programming languages. A *proposition* is formed according to the following rules:

- The constants *true* and *false* are propositions.

- The variables p, q, r, ..., which have values *true* or *false,* are propositions.

- The operators $\wedge$, $\vee$, $\supset$, $\equiv$, and $\neg$, which denote conjunction, disjunction, implication, equivalence, and negation, respectively, are used to form more complex propositions. That is, if P and Q are propositions, then so are $P \wedge Q$, $P \vee Q$, $P \supset Q$, $P \equiv Q$, and $\neg P$.

By convention, negation has highest precedence, followed by conjunction, disjunction, implication, and equivalence, in that order. Thus, the expression

$$p \vee q \wedge r \supset \neg s \vee t$$

is equivalent to

$$((p \vee (q \wedge r)) \supset ((\neg s) \vee t)).$$

Propositions provide symbolic representations for *logic expressions;* that is, statements that can be interpreted as either *true* or *false.* For example, if p represents the proposition "Mary speaks Russian" and q represents the proposition "Bob speaks Russian," then $p \wedge q$ represents the proposition "Mary and Bob both speak Russian," and $p \vee q$ represents "Either Mary or Bob speaks Russian." If, furthermore, r represents the proposition "Mary and Bob can communicate with each other," then the expression $p \wedge q \supset r$ represents "If Mary and Bob both speak Russian, then they can communicate with each other."

Predicate logic expressions include all propositions such as the above, and also include variables in various domains (integers, reals, etc.), boolean-valued functions with these variables, and quantifiers. A *predicate* is a proposition in which some of the boolean variables are replaced by

- Boolean-valued functions, and
- Quantified expressions.

A *boolean-valued function* is a function with one or more variables that delivers a boolean result, *true* or *false*. Here are some examples:

$prime(n)$—*true* if the integer value of n is a prime number; *false* otherwise.

$0 \leq x + y$—*true* if the real sum of x and y is nonnegative.

$speaks(x, y)$—*true* if person x speaks language y.

A predicate combines these kinds of functions using the operators of the propositional calculus and the quantifiers $\forall$ and $\exists$. Here are some examples:

$0 \leq x \wedge x \leq 1$—*true* if x is between 0 and 1, inclusive; otherwise *false*.

$speaks(x, Russian) \wedge speaks(y, Russian) \supset talkswith(x, y)$—*true* if the fact that both x and y speak Russian implies that x talks with y; otherwise *false*.

$\forall x(speaks(x, Russian))$—*true* if everyone on the planet speaks Russian; *false* otherwise.

$\exists x(speaks(x, Russian))$—*true* if at least one person on the planet speaks Russian; *false* otherwise.

$\forall x \exists y(speaks(x, y))$—*true* if every person x speaks some language y; *false* otherwise.

$\forall x(\neg literate(x) \supset (\neg writes(x) \wedge \neg \exists y(reads(x, y) \wedge book(y))))$—*true* if every illiterate person x does not write and has not read any book y.

Table 9.1 summarizes the meanings of the different kinds of expressions that can be used in propositional and predicate logic.[2]

Propositions that are true for all possible values of their variables are called *tautologies*. For instance, the proposition $q \vee \neg q$ is a tautology, since if q is true then so is $q \vee \neg q$. But if q is *false*, then $\neg q$ is *true*, making $q \vee \neg q$ *true* again.

Predicates that are *true* for some particular assignment of values to their variables are called *satisfiable*. Those that are *true* for all possible assignments of values to their variables are called *valid*.

---

2. We assume readers are familiar with propositional and predicate logic, perhaps from an earlier course in discrete mathematics. Thus, we give only a brief review treatment here.

Table 9.1

Summary of Predicate Logic Notation

Notation	Meaning	Notes/Examples
true, false	Boolean (truth) constants	
p, q, r, . . .	Boolean variables	
$\neg p$	Negation of *p*	*True* if *p* is *false*; otherwise *false*
$p \wedge q$	Conjunction of *p* and *q*	*True* if *p* and *q* are both *true*
$p \vee q$	Disjunction of *p* and *q*	*True* if either *p* or *q* (or both) is *true*
$p \supset q$	Implication: *p* implies *q*	Logically equivalent to $\neg p \vee q$
$p \equiv q$	Logical equivalence of *p* and *q*	*True* if *p* and *q* are both *true* or both *false*
$\forall x P(x)$	Universally quantified expression	Read "for all values of *x*, *P(x)* is *true*"
$\exists x P(x)$	Existentially quantified expression	Read "there is an *x* for which *P(x)* is *true*"
p is a tautology	Proposition *p* is always *true*	E.g., $q \vee \neg q$ is a tautology
p(x) is valid	Predicate *p(x)* is true for every value of *x*	E.g., $even(x) \vee odd(x)$ is valid

For example, the predicate *speaks*(*x*, *Russian*) is satisfiable (but not valid) since presumably at least one person on the planet speaks Russian (but there are some people who do not speak Russian). Similarly, the predicate $y \geq 0 \wedge n \geq 0 \wedge z = x(y - n)$ is satisfiable but not valid since different selections of values for *x*, *y*, *z*, and *n* can be found that make this predicate either *true* or *false*. On the other hand, the predicate *even*(*y*) ∨ *odd*(*y*) is valid since it is *true* for all integers *y*.

Predicates have various algebraic properties, which are often useful when we are analyzing and transforming logic expressions. A summary of these properties is given in Table 9.2.

The commutative, associative, distributive, and idempotence properties have straightforward interpretations. The identity property simply says that either a proposition

Table 9.2

Properties of Predicate Logic Expressions

Property	Meaning	
Commutativity	$p \vee q \equiv q \vee p$	$p \wedge q \equiv q \wedge p$
Associativity	$(p \vee q) \vee r \equiv p \vee (q \vee r)$	$(p \wedge q) \wedge r \equiv p \wedge (q \wedge r)$
Distributivity	$p \vee q \wedge r \equiv (p \vee q) \wedge (p \vee r)$	$p \wedge (q \vee r) \equiv p \wedge q \vee p \wedge r$
Idempotence	$p \vee p \equiv p$	$p \wedge p \equiv p$
Identity	$p \vee \neg p \equiv true$	$p \wedge \neg p \equiv false$
deMorgan	$\neg(p \vee q) \equiv \neg p \wedge \neg q$	$\neg(p \wedge q) \equiv \neg p \vee \neg q$
Implication	$p \supset q \equiv \neg p \vee q$	
Quantification	$\neg \forall x P(x) \equiv \exists x \neg P(x)$	$\neg \exists x P(x) \equiv \forall x \neg P(x)$

or its negation must always be *true*, but that both a proposition and its negation cannot simultaneously be *true*.

DeMorgan's property provides a convenient device for removing disjunction (or conjunction) from an expression without changing its meaning. For example, saying "it is not raining or snowing" is equivalent to saying "it is not raining and it is not snowing." Moreover, this property allows the equivalence of statements like "both John and Mary are not in school" and "either John or Mary is not in school."

Similarly, the implication and quantification properties provide vehicles for removing implications, universal, or existential quantifiers from an expression without changing its meaning. For example, saying "not every child can read" is equivalent to saying "there is at least one child who cannot read." Similarly, saying "There are no flies in my bookbag" is equivalent to "every fly is not in my bookbag" (thank goodness).

These properties are useful for simplifying and transforming expressions, as we shall see below.

9.1.1 Horn Clauses

A *Horn clause* has a head *h*, which is a predicate, and a body, which is a list of predicates $p_1, p_2, \ldots, p_n$, written as follows:

$$h \leftarrow p_1, p_2, \ldots, p_n$$

Interpreted, this means that *h* is *true* only if $p_1, p_2, \ldots,$ and p_n are simultaneously *true*.

For example, suppose we want to capture the idea that it is snowing in some city *C* only if there is precipitation in city *C* and the temperature in city *C* is freezing. We can write this as the following Horn clause:

$$snowing(C) \leftarrow precipitation(C), freezing(C)$$

There is a limited correspondence between Horn clauses and predicates. For instance, the above Horn clause can be written equivalently as the predicate:

$$precipitation(C) \land freezing(C) \supset snowing(C)$$

This, of course, is logically equivalent to either of the following predicates, using the properties in Table 9.2.

$$\neg(precipitation(C) \land freezing(C)) \lor snowing(C)$$
$$\neg precipitation(C) \lor \neg freezing(C) \lor snowing(C)$$

It should be clear that any Horn clause can be written equivalently as a predicate. Unfortunately, the converse is not true: not all predicates can be translated into Horn clauses. Below is a six-step procedure[3] that will, whenever possible, translate a predicate *p* into a Horn clause.

1 Eliminate implications from *p*, using the implication property in Table 9.2.
2 Move negation inward in *p*, using the deMorgan and quantification properties, so that only individual terms are negated.

---

3. This procedure is described in [Clocksin 1994] Chapter 10, and is based on the article "Eliminating the irrelevant from mechanical proofs" by Martin Davis (*Proceedings of a Symposium in Applied Mathematics* 15, American Mathematical Society, Providence, RI, 1963, pp. 15–30).

3 Eliminate existential quantifiers from p, using a technique called *skolemization*. Here, the existentially quantified variable is replaced by a unique constant. For example, the expression $\exists x P(x)$ is replaced by $P(c)$, where c is an arbitrarily chosen constant in the domain of x.

4 Move all universal quantifiers to the beginning of p; as long as there are no naming conflicts, this step does not change the meaning of p. Assuming that all variables are universally quantified, we can drop the quantifiers without changing the meaning of the predicate.

5 Use the Distributive, Associative, and Commutative properties in Table 9.2 to convert p to *conjunctive normal form*. In this form, the conjunction and disjunction operators are nested no more than two levels deep, with conjunctions at the highest level.

6 Convert the embedded disjunctions to implications, using the implication property. If each of these implications has a single term on its right, then each can be rewritten as a series of Horn clauses equivalent to p.

To illustrate this procedure, consider the transformation of the following predicate to conjunctive normal form:

$$\forall x(\neg literate(x) \supset (\neg writes(x) \land \neg\exists y(reads(x, y) \land book(y))))$$

Applying Step 1 removes the implication, leaving

$$\forall x(literate(x) \lor (\neg writes(x) \land \neg\exists y(reads(x, y) \land book(y))))$$

Step 2 moves negations so that they are adjacent to individual terms:

$$\forall x(literate(x) \lor (\neg writes(x) \land \forall y(\neg(reads(x, y) \land book(y)))))$$
$$= \forall x(literate(x) \lor (\neg writes(x) \land \forall y(\neg reads(x, y) \lor \neg book(y))))$$

Since there are no existential quantifiers, skolemization is not necessary. Step 4 moves all quantifiers to the left and then drops them, giving:

$$\forall x \forall y(literate(x) \lor (\neg writes(x) \land (\neg(reads(x, y) \land book(y)))))$$
$$= literate(x) \lor (\neg writes(x) \land (\neg reads(x, y) \lor \neg book(y)))$$

Now we convert this to conjunctive normal form as follows:

$$literate(x) \lor (\neg writes(x) \land (\neg reads(x, y) \lor \neg book(y)))$$
$$= (literate(x) \lor \neg writes(x)) \land (literate(x) \lor \neg reads(x, y) \lor \neg book(y))$$
$$= (\neg writes(x) \lor literate(x)) \land (\neg reads(x, y) \lor \neg book(y) \lor literate(x))$$

These two conjuncts now convert back to implications,

$$(\neg writes(x) \lor literate(x)) \land (\neg reads(x, y) \lor \neg book(y) \lor literate(x))$$
$$= (writes(x) \supset literate(x)) \land (\neg(\neg reads(x, y) \lor \neg book(y)) \supset literate(x))$$
$$= (writes(x) \supset literate(x)) \land ((reads(x, y) \land book(y)) \supset literate(x))$$

which are equivalent to the following Horn clauses:

$$literate(x) \leftarrow writes(x)$$
$$literate(x) \leftarrow reads(x, y), book(y)$$

Unfortunately, conversion of a predicate to conjunctive normal form does not always ensure a series of equivalent Horn clauses. Consider the following predicate, which represents the statement "Every literate person reads or writes."

$\forall x(literate(x) \supset reads(x) \lor writes(x))$

which reduces to the following clausal form:

$\neg literate(x) \lor reads(x) \lor writes(x)$

But this converts to the following implication

$literate(x) \supset reads(x) \lor writes(x)$

which does not have a single term on the right. Thus, there is no equivalent Horn clause for this predicate.

9.1.2 Resolution and Unification

Making a single inference from a pair of Horn clauses is called *resolution*. The resolution principle is similar to the idea of transitivity in algebra. When applied to Horn clauses, it says that if h is the head of a Horn clause and it matches with one of the terms of another Horn clause, then that term can be replaced by h. In other words, if we have the clauses

$h \leftarrow terms$
$t \leftarrow t_1, h, t_2$

then we can resolve the second clause to $t \leftarrow t_1, terms, t_2$. For instance, consider the following clauses:

$speaks(Mary, English)$
$talkswith(X, Y) \leftarrow speaks(X, L), speaks(Y, L), X \neq Y$

The first of these is a Horn clause with an empty list of terms, so it is unconditionally *true*. Thus, resolution allows us to deduce the following:

$talkswith(Mary, Y) \leftarrow speaks(Mary, English), speaks(Y, English), Mary \neq Y$

with the assumption that the variables X and L are assigned the values "Mary" and "English" in the second rule. Resolution thus helps to arrive at conclusions. The assignment of variables to values during resolution is called *instantiation*.

Unification is a pattern matching process that determines what particular instantiations can be made to variables during the process of making a series of simultaneous resolutions. Unification is recursive, so it eventually finds all possible instantiations for which resolutions can be made. We illustrate unification in more detail below.

9.2 PROLOG: FACTS, VARIABLES, AND QUERIES

Prolog programs are made from *terms,* which can be constants, variables, or structures. A *constant* is either an atom (like `the`, `zebra`, `'Bob'`, and `'.'`) or a nonnegative integer (like 24). A *variable* is a series of letters (A-Z, a-z, _) that must begin with a capital letter (like Bob).[4] A *structure* is a predicate with zero or more arguments, written in functional notation. For example, the following are Prolog structures:

```
n(zebra)
speaks(Who, russian)
np(X, Y)
```

The number of arguments is called the structure's *arity* (1, 2, and 2 in these examples).

Prolog facts and rules are realizations of the formal idea of Horn clauses, as introduced in the previous section. A *fact* is a term followed by a period (.) and is similar to a Horn clause without a right-hand side. A *rule* is a term followed by :- and a series of terms separated by commas and ended by a period (.). A rule has the following form:

```
term :- term₁, term₂, ..., termₙ.
```

Note that this is equivalent to the Horn clause *term* ← *term*$_1$, *term*$_2$, . . . , *term*$_n$.

Rules are interpreted as "only if" assertions, with the comma playing the role of the logical "and" operator. Thus, the above form asserts that `term` is *true* only if `term`$_1$, `term`$_2$, . . . , and `term`$_n$ are simultaneously *true*.

A Prolog program is a series of facts and rules. Here is an example:

```
speaks(allen, russian).
speaks(bob, english).
speaks(mary, russian).
speaks(mary, english).
talkswith(Person1, Person2) :- speaks(Person1,L), speaks(Person2,L),
                               Person1 \= Person2.
```

This program asserts four facts: that `allen` and `mary` speak `russian` and `bob` and `mary` speak `english`. It also has a rule that defines the relation `talkswith` between two persons, which is true exactly when they both speak the same language, denoted by the variable `L`, and they are different people.

A Prolog rule *succeeds* when there are instantiations (which are temporary assignments) of its variables for which all of the terms on the right of the :- operator simultaneously succeed for those assignments. Otherwise, the rule is said to *fail*. A fact always succeeds; that is, it is universally *true*. For example, the rule in the above example succeeds for the instantiations

```
Person1 = allen
Person2 = mary
```

since there is an instantiation of the variable L (=russian) for which the three predicates:

```
speaks(allen, L)
speaks(mary, L)
allen \= mary
```

---

4. A constant cannot begin with a capital letter unless it is enclosed in quotes.

simultaneously succeed. However, this rule fails for other instantiations, such as:

```
Person1 = allen
Person2 = bob
```

since they share no common instantiation of variable L.

To exercise a Prolog program, one writes *queries* in reply to the Prolog prompt ?-. Here is a simple query that asks the question "Who speaks Russian?"

```
?- speaks(Who, russian).
```

In reply, Prolog tries to satisfy a query by finding a fact or series of fact/rule applications that will answer the query; that is, one that will find an assignment of values to the variables in the query that causes a fact or rule to succeed, in the pattern-matching sense.

9.2.1 Loading and Executing Code

Loading files with Prolog function definitions has the same effect as typing them directly to the Prolog interpreter. For example, to load the file named `diff` that contains the function `d`, you should use the command:

```
?- consult(diff).
```

You typically type your Prolog facts and rules into a separate file, and then use this `consult` command to load that file into the interpreter, which asserts each of the facts and rules that are defined there. Once a program file is loaded, you can pose queries to the Prolog interpreter in the form of assertions containing variables, and the interpreter will try to find answers for you.

Here are some general guidelines for writing Prolog programs:

1 Identifiers that begin with a capital letter or an underscore characters are taken as variables; all other identifiers are treated as constants.
2 There must be no space between the name of the predicate and the left parenthesis that opens its argument list.
3 All facts, rules, and queries must end with a period.
4 Any code file consulted must end with a carriage return character.

For example, suppose we have the following Prolog program file called `speaks`:

```
speaks(allen, russian).
speaks(bob, english).
speaks(mary, russian).
speaks(mary, english).
talkswith(Person1, Person2) :-
        speaks(Person1, L), speaks(Person2, L), Person1 \= Person2.
```

Then we can do the following:

```
?- consult(speaks).
speaks compiled, 0.00 sec, 1,312 bytes.

Yes
```

The `Yes` reply says that Prolog has successfully syntax-checked and loaded the file, so we can now go ahead and pose queries.

9.2.2 Unification, Evaluation Order, and Backtracking

When searching for a solution, Prolog examines all the facts and rules that have a head that matches with the function mentioned in the query (in this case `speaks`). If there are more than one (in this case, there are four), it considers them in the order they appear in the program. Since `russian` is a constant, the only variable to be resolved is the variable `Who`. Using the first fact in the program, Prolog replies with:

```
Who = allen
```

since that assignment to the variable `Who` causes the first fact to succeed. At this point, the user may want to know if there are other ways of satisfying the same query, in which a semicolon (;) is typed. Prolog continues its search through the program, reporting the next success, if there is one. When there are no more successful instantiations for the variable `Who`, Prolog finally replies `No` and the process stops. Here is the complete interaction:

```
?- speaks(Who, russian).
Who = allen ;
Who = mary ;
No
```

Another sort of query that this program can handle is one that asks questions like "Does Bob talk with Allen?" or "Who talks with Allen?" or "Which persons talk with each other?" These can be written as the following Prolog queries, with the replies to the first two shown below them:

```
?- talkswith(bob, allen).
No
?- talkswith(Who, allen).
Who = mary ;
No
?- talkswith(P1, P2).
```

To see how these queries are satisfied, we need to see how the rule for `talkswith` is evaluated. Any query of the form `talkswith(X, Y)` appeals to that rule, which can be satisfied only if there is a common instantiation for the variables X, Y, and L for which `speaks(X, L)`, `speaks(Y, L)`, and `X\=Y` are simultaneously satisfied. These three terms are often called *subgoals* of the main goal `talkswith(X, Y)`.

Prolog tries to satisfy the subgoals in a rule from left to right, so that a search is first made for values of X and L for which `speaks(X, L)` is satisfied. Once such values are found, these same values are used wherever their variables appear in the search to satisfy additional subgoals for that rule, like `speaks(Y, L)` and `X\=Y`.

The process of trying to satisfy the first query above is diagrammed in the *search tree* shown in Figure 9.1.

Figure 9.1 Attempting to Satisfy the Query `talkswith(bob, allen)`

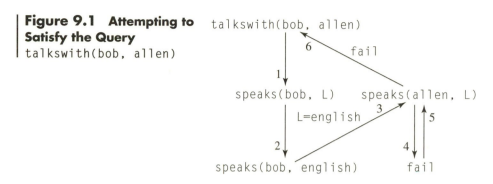

This process fails because the only instantiation of `L` that satisfies `speaks(bob, L)` does not simultaneously satisfy `speaks(allen, L)` for this program. The numbers assigned to the arrows in this diagram indicate the order in which subgoals are tried.

The response `no` indicates that Prolog can find no more solutions to a query. In general, Prolog operates under the so-called *closed world assumption,* which means that anything it has not been told is not *true.* In this example, the closed world contains only facts that have been stated about specific people speaking specific languages, and no others.

The process of satisfying the second query above is somewhat more complex. It first fails in the sequence shown in Figure 9.2.

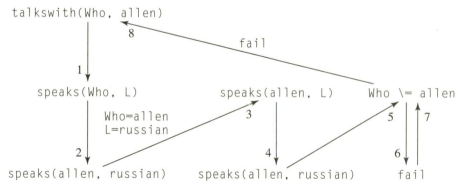

Figure 9.2 First Attempt to Satisfy the Query `talkswith(Who,allen)`

Although the subgoals `speaks(Who,L)` and `speaks(allen,L)` are satisfied by the instantiation `Who=allen`, the third subgoal fails, since `allen\=allen` fails.

Once this failure occurs, the process backtracks to the step labeled 2 in the figure and looks for other instantiations of `Who` and `L` that will satisfy all three of these subgoals simultaneously. Thus, the process eventually succeeds with the instantiations `Who=mary` and `L=russian`, but no others.

9.2.3 Database Searching—The Family Tree

It may be apparent that Prolog is well-suited to solving problems that require searching a database. In fact, the development of expert systems during the 1970s and 1980s was facilitated in large part by Prolog programs. The program in Subsection 9.2.1 can be viewed as a very simple database search program, where the first four facts represent the database and the rule represents the constraints upon which a successful search can occur. A slightly different example appears in Figure 9.3.

Figure 9.3 A Partial Family Tree

```
parent(A,B) :- father(A,B).
parent(A,B) :- mother(A,B).
grandparent(C,D) :- parent(C,E), parent(E,D).

mother(mary, sue).
mother(mary, bill).
mother(sue, nancy).
mother(sue, jeff).
mother(jane, ron).

father(john, sue).
father(john, bill).
father(bob, nancy).
father(bob, jeff).
father(bill, ron).
```

This program models a small group of people whose family "tree" is shown in Figure 9.4.[5] The diagram confirms that "parent" relates two people at adjacent levels in the tree and "grandparent" relates two people who are removed two levels from each other.

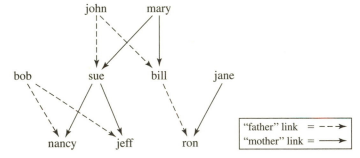

| **Figure 9.4 A Small Family "Tree"**

We can query this database in various ways to ask different questions. For instance, the question "Who is a grandparent of Ron" can be posed by:

```
?- grandparent(Who, ron).
```

Additional relationships can be defined to enable a wider variety of questions to be asked. For instance, the sibling relationship can be defined between two different

---

5. Strictly speaking, this isn't really a tree structure since some nodes have more than one parent and there is more than one potential "root" node. But it is a "family tree" in the colloquial sense.

people who share the same parent:

```
?- sibling(X, Y) :- parent(W, X), parent(W, Y), X \= Y.
```

9.3 LISTS

The basic data structure in Prolog programming is the list, which is written as a series of terms separated by commas and enclosed in brackets [and]. Sentences are usually represented as lists of atoms, as in the following example:

```
[the, giraffe, dreams]
```

The empty list is denoted by [], while a "don't care" entry in a list is represented by an underscore (_). The following denote lists of one, two, and three elements, respectively.

```
[X]
[X, Y]
[_, _, Z]
```

The head (first) element of a list is distinguished from its remaining elements by a vertical bar. Thus,

```
[X | Y]
```

denotes a list whose head is X and whose remaining elements form the list [Y].

Here is a simple Prolog function that defines the concatenation of two lists together to form one. The first two arguments for this function represent the two lists being concatenated, and the third represents the result.

```
append([], X, X).
append([H | T], Y, [H | Z]) :- append(T, Y, Z).
```

This rather odd-looking recursive definition has two parts. The "base case" is defined by the first line, which simply affirms that the empty list concatenated with any other list returns that other list as the result. The recursive case, defined by the second line, says that if Z is the result of concatenating lists T and Y, then concatenating any new list [H | T] with Y gives the result [H | Z].

It is important to understand the dynamics of execution for this function, since this form of recursive definition occurs often in Prolog. Consider the query

```
?- append([english, russian], [spanish], L).
```

which should yield the list L = [english, russian, spanish]. Figure 9.5 gives a partial search tree that traces the instantiations of H, T, X, Y, and Z as this result is developed.

The first two calls use the recursive rule, which strips the head H from the first argument and recalls append with a shorter list as first argument. The final call uses the

```
append([english, russian], [spanish], L).
```

H = english, T = [russian], Y = [spanish], L = [english | Z]

1

```
append([russian], [spanish], [Z]).
```

H = russian, T = [], Y = [spanish], [Z] = [russian | Z']

2

```
append([], [spanish], [Z']).
```

X = [spanish], Z' = spanish

3

```
append([], [spanish], [spanish]).
```

Figure 9.5 Partial Search Tree for append([english, russian], [spanish], L)

base case, which forces instantiation of the variable X = [spanish] and Z' = spanish.[6] Thus, the result [H | Z'] in the second call is resolved as [russian, spanish] and identified with the list Z in the first call. Finally, the list L is resolved to [english, russian, spanish], using this newly discovered value for Z as its tail.

Here are three more functions with lists that are very useful in Prolog programming. The first two, called *prefix* and *suffix*, mean exactly what their names suggest. X is a prefix of Z if there's a Y which we can append to X to make Z. The definition of Y as a suffix of Z is similar.

```
prefix(X, Z) :- append(X, Y, Z).
suffix(Y, Z) :- append(X, Y, Z).
```

The third useful function defines recursively the notion of membership in a list. X is a member of a list if it is identical to the first element or a member of the list's tail.

```
member(X, [X | _]).
member(X, [_ | Y]) :- member(X, Y).
```

Note here the use of the "don't care" notation in parts of the definition that don't affect the definition. In the first line, we don't care what the rest of the list looks like if X is identical with the first member. In the second, we don't care what's at the head of the list if X is a member of the tail.

---

6. The use of prime (') in this analysis helps to distinguish the use of a variable in a rule at one level of recursion from the use of the same variable at another level.

To illustrate, suppose we have the following list assignments in Prolog:

```
L = [my, dog, has, many, fleas]
M = [many, fleas, spoil, the, picnic]
```

Then the following Prolog queries cause the responses shown below them:

```
? - prefix(Answer, L).
Answer = [];
Answer = [my];
Answer = [my, dog];
...
Answer = [my, dog, has, many, fleas];
No
? - suffix(Answer, L), prefix(Answer, M).
Answer = [];
Answer = [many, fleas];
No
? - member(spoil, L).
No
? - member(spoil, M).
Yes
```

9.4 **PRACTICAL ASPECTS OF PROLOG**

Prolog is not, in practice, an altogether "pure" logic programming language. In particular, it has some features designed to make programming more efficient and practical. In this section, we discuss several prominent features, among them: the "cut," the `is` operator and arithmetic, and the `assert` function.

9.4.1 Tracing

Many Prolog implementations provide the predicates `trace` and `untrace`, which are used to turn on and off the tracing of other predicates. Because there can be different predicates with the same name and different arities (numbers of arguments), trace expects the name of a predicate to be followed by a slash and its arity. For example, consider the predicate `factorial` defined as follows:

```
factorial(0, 1).
factorial(N, Result) :- N > 0, M is N - 1,
                        factorial(M, SubRes), Result is N * SubRes.
```

This predicate defines the factorial function recursively, with the first line defining the base case ($0! = 1$) and the second and third lines defining the recursive case ($n! = n(n - 1)!$). Notice that we need to introduce the intermediate variable M to force the evaluation of $N - 1$ before the recursive call.

To trace this function, we can do this:

```
?- trace(factorial/2).
factorial/2: call redo exit fail

Yes
?- factorial(4, X).
Call: (  7) factorial(4, _G173)
Call: (  8) factorial(3, _L131)
Call: (  9) factorial(2, _L144)
Call: ( 10) factorial(1, _L157)
Call: ( 11) factorial(0, _L170)
Exit: ( 11) factorial(0, 1)
Exit: ( 10) factorial(1, 1)
Exit: (  9) factorial(2, 2)
Exit: (  8) factorial(3, 6)
Exit: (  7) factorial(4, 24)

X = 24
```

In the first call, the first argument is bound to 4, and the second is bound to an anonymous variable (_G173). This same pattern is repeated for each of the next four recursive calls, until the base case occurs and the second argument _L170 is finally assigned the value 1. Now the recursion unwinds, assigning intermediate values to the anonymous variables and doing the multiplications.

The predicate listing, as in listing(factorial/2) will display all the current facts and rules for the argument predicate:

```
?- listing(factorial/2).
factorial(0, 1).
factorial(A, B) :-
        A>0,
        C is A-1,
        factorial(C, D),
        B is A*D.
Yes
```

The predicate listing with no arguments lists *all* the functions of the currently consulted program.

9.4.2 The Cut and Negation

Prolog provides a special function called the *cut,* which forces the evaluation of a series of subgoals on the right-hand side of a rule not to be retried if the right-hand side succeeds once. The cut is written by inserting an exclamation mark (!) as a subgoal at the place where the interruption is to occur.

To illustrate, consider the following program that performs a bubble sort on a list.

```
bsort(L, S) :- append(U, [A, B | V], L),
               B < A, !,
               append(U, [B, A | V], M),
               bsort(M, S).
bsort(L, L).
```

This program first partitions a list L by finding two sublists U and [A, B | V] for which B < A is *true*. Once such a partition is found, the list M is formed by appending the sublists U and [B, A | V] and then recursively bubble-sorted to form the new list S.

This process repeats until no more partitions of L can be found: until there is no sublist [A, B | V] of L in which B < A. This is a terse way of saying that the list L is sorted. At that point, the only remaining applicable rule is bsort(L,L), which returns the sorted list as the answer. Figure 9.6 shows a trace of the program.

Figure 9.6 Trace of bsort for the List [5, 2, 3, 1].

```
?- bsort([5,2,3,1], Ans).
 Call:  (  7) bsort([5, 2, 3, 1], _G221)
 Call:  (  8) bsort([2, 5, 3, 1], _G221)
 Call:  (  9) bsort([2, 3, 5, 1], _G221)
 Call:  ( 10) bsort([2, 3, 1, 5], _G221)
 Call:  ( 11) bsort([2, 1, 3, 5], _G221)
 Call:  ( 12) bsort([1, 2, 3, 5], _G221)
 Redo:  ( 12) bsort([1, 2, 3, 5], _G221)
 Exit:  ( 12) bsort([1, 2, 3, 5], [1, 2, 3, 5])
 Exit:  ( 11) bsort([2, 1, 3, 5], [1, 2, 3, 5])
 Exit:  ( 10) bsort([2, 3, 1, 5], [1, 2, 3, 5])
 Exit:  (  9) bsort([2, 3, 5, 1], [1, 2, 3, 5])
 Exit:  (  8) bsort([2, 5, 3, 1], [1, 2, 3, 5])
 Exit:  (  7) bsort([5, 2, 3, 1], [1, 2, 3, 5])

Ans = [1, 2, 3, 5] ;

No
```

If the cut had not been present in this program, the search process would have continued with a Redo of the rule at level 11, since Prolog would be seeking all solutions:

```
Redo:  ( 11) bsort([2, 1, 3, 5], _G221)
```

and this would lead to the first of a series of incorrect answers. The cut is therefore useful when we want to cut off the search process after finding the first set of instantiations to the variables on the right that satisfy the rule, but no others.

9.4.3 The `is`, `not`, and Other Operators

The infix operator `is` can be used to force instantiation of a variable:

```
?- X is 3+7.
X = 10
yes
```

Prolog provides arithmetic $(+, -, *, /, \wedge)$ and relational operators $(<, >, =, =<, >=,$ and $\backslash=)$ with their usual interpretations. Note that, in order to keep $=>$ and $<=$ free for use as arrows, Prolog uses $=<$ for less-than-or-equal comparisons and $>=$ for greater-than-or-equal comparisons.

For example, consider the predicate `factorial` defined in Figure 9.7.

Figure 9.7 The Factorial Function in Prolog

```
factorial(0, 1).
factorial(N, Result) :- N > 0, M is N - 1,
                        factorial(M, P),
                        Result is N * P.
```

This predicate defines the factorial function recursively, with the first line defining the base case $(0! = 1)$ and the second and third lines defining the recursive case $(n! = n(n - 1)!$ when $n > 0)$. Notice that we need to introduce the intermediate variable M to force the evaluation of $N - 1$ before the recursive call. The `is` operator plays the role of an intermediate assignment operator by unifying a value with this variable.

A call to this function generates the series of assignments to different instantiations of the variables N, M, and P (shown with the aid of a trace output) in Figure 9.8.

```
?- factorial(4, X).              N   M   P      Result
Call:  (  7) factorial(4, _G173) 4   3   _G173  4*P
Call:  (  8) factorial(3, _L131) 3   2   _L131  3*P
Call:  (  9) factorial(2, _L144) 2   1   _L144  2*P
Call:  ( 10) factorial(1, _L157) 1   0   _L157  1*P
Call:  ( 11) factorial(0, _L170) 0       _L170
Exit:  ( 11) factorial(0, 1)                    1
Exit:  ( 10) factorial(1, 1)                    1*1 = 1
Exit:  (  9) factorial(2, 2)                    2*1 = 2
Exit:  (  8) factorial(3, 6)                    3*2 = 6
Exit:  (  7) factorial(4, 24)                   4*6 = 24
```

| Figure 9.8 Trace of Factorial (4)

The anonymous variables `_G173`, `_L131`, . . . are generated by the interpreter at each reinstantiation of the recursive rule in this definition. In the first call, the first argument is bound to 4, and the second is bound to an anonymous variable (`_G173`). This same pattern is repeated for each of the next four recursive calls, until the base case occurs and the second argument `_L170` is finally assigned the value 1. Now the recursion unwinds, assigning intermediate values to the anonymous variables and doing the multiplications.

The operator `not` is implemented in Prolog in terms of goal failure. That is, the clause `not(P)` succeeds when resolution of P fails. Thus, `not` can be used to define a function in place of the cut. Consider the following alternative definitions of the factorial function given in Figure 9.7.

```
factorial(N, 1) :- N < 1, !.
factorial(N, Result) :- M is N - 1,
                        factorial(M, P),
                        Result is N * P.
factorial(N, 1) :- N < 1.
factorial(N, Result) :- not(N < 1), M is N - 1,
                        factorial(M, P),
                        Result is N * P.
```

The first definition shows how the cut (!) can be used to delineate the base case from the recursive call. The second shows how `not` removes the need for using the cut (although at the expense of some efficiency, since it evaluates the clause N < 1 twice for every different value of N). Nevertheless, it is usually better programming style to use `not` in place of the cut, since it enhances readability.

It is important to point out that the `not` operator does not always act like logical negation. Sometimes, it will simply fail when one of the variables contained in its argument is uninstantiated.

9.4.4 The `assert` Function

Prolog applications often encounter situations where the program must "update" itself in response to the most recent query. For instance, in a database application like the one shown in Section 9.2.1 one might want to add a new member to the family tree and let that member play a role in the program's response to later queries. This can be done using the `assert` function, which essentially allows the program to dynamically alter itself by adding new facts and rules to the existing ones. For example, suppose we want to add the assertion to the program in Figure 9.3 that Jane is the mother of Joe. We would do this by the statement:

```
?- assert(mother(jane,joe)).
```

This fact is now added to all the others in that program, and will affect future queries such as the following:

```
?- mother(jane, X).

X = ron ;
X = joe ;
No
```

Moreover, the `assert` function can be added to the body of a function definition itself and dynamically add new facts and rules to the database. This kind of activity is important for programs that simulate learning in the sense that they can store new knowledge as they interact with the user.

9.5 EXAMPLE: PROLOG APPLICATIONS

In this section, we consider several example applications of Prolog in areas for which it is especially well-suited. These are symbolic differentiation, solving word puzzles, natural language processing, and the syntax and semantics of Jay.

9.5.1 Symbolic Differentiation

The use of Prolog for symbol manipulation and theorem proving is widespread. This example illustrates some of the natural deduction powers of Prolog in the area of logical reasoning by performing symbolic differentiation and simplification of simple calculus formulae. Figure 9.9 shows the familiar rules for differentiation

Figure 9.9 Symbolic Differentiation Rules

$$\frac{dc}{dx} = 0 \qquad c \text{ is a constant}$$

$$\frac{dx}{dx} = 1$$

$$\frac{d}{dx}(u + v) = \frac{du}{dx} + \frac{dv}{dx} \qquad u \text{ and } v \text{ are functions of } x$$

$$\frac{d}{dx}(u - v) = \frac{du}{dx} - \frac{dv}{dx}$$

$$\frac{d}{dx}(uv) = u\frac{dv}{dx} + v\frac{du}{dx}$$

$$\frac{d}{dx}\left(\frac{u}{v}\right) = \left(v\frac{du}{dx} - u\frac{dv}{dx}\right)\Big/v^2$$

For example, differentiating the function $2 \cdot x + 1$ using these rules leaves the (unsimplified) answer $2 \cdot 1 + x \cdot 0 + 0$, which simplifies to 2.

The Prolog solution mimics these rules one-for-one. They are intrinsically recursive, and so is the Prolog solution as shown in Figure 9.10.

```
d(X, U+V, DU+DV) :- d(X, U, DU), d(X, V, DV).
d(X, U-V, DU-DV) :- d(X, U, DU), d(X, V, DV).
d(X, U*V, U*DV + V*DU) :- d(X, U, DU), d(X, V, DV).
d(X, U/V, (V*DU - U*DV)/(V*V)) :- d(X, U, DU), d(X, V, DV).
d(X, C, 0) :- atomic(C), C\=X.
d(X, X, 1).
```

Figure 9.10 Prolog Symbolic Differentiator

The Prolog rules are written in this particular order so that the search process will analyze the expression recursively before getting down to the base case, where the individual terms and factors reside. A search tree for the query d(x, 2*x+1, Ans) is shown in Figure 9.11 (branches that lead to failure are not shown).

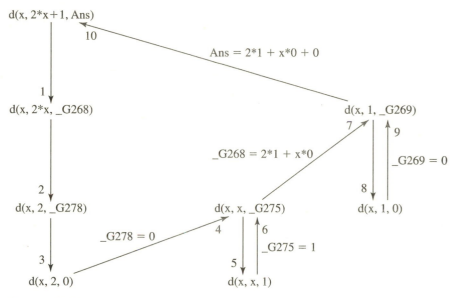

| Figure 9.11 Search Tree for the Query d(x, 2*x+1, Ans)

In this illustration, the temporary variables _G268, _G269, _G275, and _G278 represent anonymous variables generated by Prolog as it finds answers for the intermediate terms in the original expression.

Readers should note that the task of simplifying an algebraic expression is not covered by the rules for symbolic differentiation. For example, the following query

```
?- d(x, 2*x, 2).
```

fails to give the intuitive yes answer, since the symbolic result 2 * 1 + x * 0 + 0 is not obviously equivalent to 2. The task of simplification relies on identities like 1 * x = x and 0 + x = x, and so forth. An exercise at the end of the chapter provides an opportunity to extend the symbolic differentiation program in this way.

9.5.2 Solving Word Puzzles

Logic often asks us to solve problems that are word puzzles, which are series of assertions from which various inferences can be made and complex conclusions drawn. Here is a simple example:

> Baker, Cooper, Fletcher, Miller, and Smith live in a five-story building. Baker doesn't live on the 5th floor and Cooper doesn't live on the first. Fletcher doesn't live on the top or the bottom floor, and he is not on a floor adjacent to Smith or Cooper. Miller lives on some floor above Cooper. Who lives on what floors?

In Prolog, we can set up a list to solve this kind of problem, with one entry for each floor in the building. Since each floor has an occupant and a number, the function floor (Occupant, Number) can be used to characterize it. We can then fill in the facts that we do know for each floor using this particular list and function.

Figure 9.12 shows a solution for this problem.

```
floors([floor(_,5),floor(_,4),floor(_,3),floor(_,2),floor(_,1)]).
building(Floors) :- floors(Floors),
        member(floor(baker, B), Floors), B \= 5,
        member(floor(cooper, C), Floors), C \= 1,
        member(floor(fletcher, F), Floors), F \= 1, F \= 5,
        member(floor(miller, M), Floors), M > C,
        member(floor(smith, S), Floors), not(adjacent(S, F)),
        not(adjacent(F, C)),
        print_floors(Floors).
```

| Figure 9.12 Prolog Solution for the Building Problem

Each separate line in the Prolog rule contains subgoals that represent one of the sentences in the above problem statement; all of these subgoals must be satisfied simultaneously for the entire rule to succeed. The variables B, C, F, M, and S represent the different person's floor numbers, which the program seeks to instantiate. Their values are constrained to the integers 1 through 5 by the first statement.

The auxiliary function print_floors is a simple recursive routine to display the elements of a list on separate lines. All five persons live somewhere, so the member function is used to guarantee that.

```
print_floors([A | B]) :- write(A), nl, print_floors(B).
print_floors([]).

member(X, [X | _]).
member(X, [_ | Y]) :- member(X, Y).
```

The adjacent function succeeds whenever its two arguments X and Y differ by 1, so it defines what it means for two floors to be adjacent to each other.

```
adjacent(X, Y) :- X =:= Y+1.
adjacent(X, Y) :- X =:= Y-1.
```

The puzzle is solved by issuing the following query, which finds instantiations of the five variables that together satisfy all the constraints and assign a list of values to the array X.

```
? - building(X).
```

9.5.3 Natural Language Processing

We can write Prolog programs that are effectively BNF grammars which, when executed, will parse sentences in a natural language. An example of such a grammar along with a parse tree for the sentence "the giraffe dreams" is shown in Figure 9.13.

When using the list representation for sentences, we can write Prolog rules that partition a sentence into its grammatical categories, using the structure defined by the

Figure 9.13 A Simple BNF Grammar and Parse Tree for "The Giraffe Dreams"†

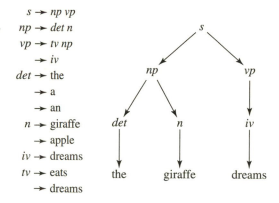

$s \rightarrow np\ vp$
$np \rightarrow det\ n$
$vp \rightarrow tv\ np$
$\rightarrow iv$
$det \rightarrow$ the
$\rightarrow$ a
$\rightarrow$ an
$n \rightarrow$ giraffe
$\rightarrow$ apple
$iv \rightarrow$ dreams
$tv \rightarrow$ eats
$\rightarrow$ dreams

grammar rules themselves. For example, consider the following BNF grammar rule, where s, np, and vp denote the notions "sentence," "noun phrase," and "verb phrase."

$s \rightarrow np\ vp$

A corresponding Prolog rule would be:

```
s(X, Y) :- np(X, U), vp(U, Y).
```

The variables in this rule represent lists. In particular, X denotes the list representation of the sentence being parsed, and Y represents the resulting tail of the list that will remain if this rule succeeds. The interpretation here mirrors that of the original grammar rule: "X is a sentence, leaving Y, if the beginning of X can be identified as a noun phrase, leaving U, and the beginning of U can be identified as a verb phrase, leaving Y."

The Prolog program for the grammar in Figure 9.13 is shown below:

```
s(X, Y) :- np(X, U), vp(U, Y).

np(X, Y) :- det(X, U), n(U, Y).

vp(X, Y) :- iv(X, Y).
vp(X, Y) :- tv(X, U), np(U, Y).

det([the | Y], Y).
det([a | Y], Y).

n([giraffe | Y], Y).
n([apple | Y], Y).

iv([dreams | Y], Y).

tv([dreams | Y], Y).
tv([eats | Y], Y).
```

† The grammatical categories shown here are: s = "sentence," np = "noun phrase," vp = "verb phrase," det = "determiner" (or "article"), n = "noun," iv = "intransitive verb," and tv = "transitive verb." Terminal symbols are denoted by nonitalicized words. Parsing proceeds for these kinds of grammars exactly as it does for grammars that represent the syntax of programming languages, as presented in Chapter 2.

Note that the facts identifying terminal symbols (giraffe, eats, etc.) effectively strip those symbols from the head of the list being passed through the grammar.

To see how this works, consider the following Prolog query, which asks whether or not "the giraffe dreams" is a sentence.

```
?- s([the, giraffe, dreams], [])
```

Here, X and Y are identified with the two lists given as arguments, and the task is to find a list U that will satisfy, in the order given, each of the following goals (using the right-hand side of the first rule in the program).

```
np([the, giraffe, dreams],U)  vp(U,[])
```

One way to see the dynamics of the entire parsing process is to run a trace on the query itself, which is shown in Figure 9.14.

```
?- s([the, giraffe, dreams],[]).
Call:  (  7) s([the, giraffe dreams], []) ?
Call:  (  8) np([the, giraffe, dreams], _L131) ?
Call:  (  9) det([the, giraffe, dreams], _L143) ?
Exit:  (  9) det([the, giraffe, dreams], [giraffe, dreams]) ?
Call:  (  9) n([giraffe, dreams], _L131) ?
Exit:  (  9) n([giraffe, dreams], [dreams]) ?
Exit:  (  8) np([the, giraffe, dreams], [dreams]) ?
Call:  (  8) vp([dreams], []) ?
Call:  (  9) iv([dreams], []) ?
Exit:  (  9) iv([dreams], []) ?
Exit:  (  8) vp([dreams], []) ?
Exit:  (  7) s([the, giraffe, dreams], []) ?

Yes
```

| Figure 9.14 Tracing Execution of a Prolog Query

From this trace, we can see that the variables U and Y are instantiated to [dreams] and [] respectively, to satisfy the right-hand side of the first grammar rule. Notice that, upon exit from each level of the trace, one or more words are removed from the head of the list. A careful reading of this trace reveals a direct correspondence between the successful calls (rule applications) and the nodes of the parse tree shown in Figure 9.13 for this sentence. So reading a trace can be helpful when developing a complex parse tree for a sentence.

Using Prolog to encode complex grammars in this way is often more cumbersome than helpful. For that reason, Prolog provides a very compact notation that directly mimics the notation of context-free grammar rules themselves. This notation is called a *Definite Clause Grammar* (DCG), and is very simple to assimilate.[7] The new Prolog

---

7. DCG's are in general LL(n) for arbitrary lookahead n. Thus, it is necessary to eliminate left recursion in the grammar rules, to avoid infinite looping during resolution.

operator - -> is substituted in place of the operator :- in each rule, and the list variables inside the rule are thus dropped. For instance, the rule

```
s(X, Y) :- np(X, U), vp(U, V).
```

can be replaced by the following equivalent simplified version:

```
s --> np, vp.
```

In making this transformation, it is important to emphasize that we are not changing either the arity of the function s (still 2) or the meaning of the original rule itself. This notation is introduced as a kind of "macro" which allows Prolog rules to be written almost identically to the BNF grammar rules which they represent. A complete rewriting of the Prolog program for the grammar in Figure 9.13 is shown below:

```
s --> np, vp.

np --> det, n.

vp --> iv.
vp --> tv, np.

det --> [the].
det --> [a].
n --> [giraffe].
n --> [apple].
iv --> [dreams].
tv --> [dreams].
tv --> [eats].
```

An additional refinement to the grammar-writing rules provides the capability to generate a parse tree directly from the grammar. That is, the above grammar can be modified so that a query gives not just a Yes or No answer, but a complete parse tree in functional form as a response. For instance, the functional form of the parse tree in Figure 9.13 is:

```
s(np(det(the), n(giraffe)), vp(iv(dreams)))
```

This modification is accomplished by adding an additional argument to the left-hand side of each rule, and appropriate variables to hold the intermediate values that are derived in the intermediate stages of execution. For instance, the first rule in the grammar above would be augmented as follows:

```
s(s(NP,VP)) --> np(NP), vp(VP).
```

This means that the query needs an extra argument, alongside the sentence to be parsed and the empty list. That argument, appearing first in the query, is a variable that will hold the resulting parse tree, as shown below:

```
?- s(Tree, [the, giraffe, dreams], []).
```

A complete revision of the above grammar that accommodates this refinement is left as an exercise.

It is very important to point out that Prolog is relational, in the sense that a program can be used to generate sentences as well as parse them. For example, consider applying the following general query to the above Prolog program (grammar):

```
? - s(Sentence, []).
```

This query, when initiated, asks the search process to find all instantiations of the variable Sentence that will succeed with this grammar. In the list of responses, we'll find the following as well as all others that can be generated by this grammar:

```
Sentence = [the, giraffe, dreams] ;
Sentence = [the, giraffe, eats, the, apple] ;
...
```

9.5.4 Syntax of Jay

Our formal treatment of Jay syntax and semantics in the first four chapters was implemented in Java. It is fair to ask whether or not a declarative language like Prolog can be used to specify the definition of Jay syntax, type system, and semantics in a more direct style. The answer is yes, but some of the details are awkward to implement in Prolog. Let us consider this question in two parts: syntax, and type checking and semantics.

The syntax of Jay can be defined in Prolog using a Definite Clause Grammar, provided that left recursion is avoided (owing to the depth-first nature of Prolog's search process). Figure 9.15 shows a Prolog grammar for expressions that is similar to the BNF definition of *Expression* in the concrete syntax of Appendix B.

Comparing the two grammars, we see three distinct differences. First, the semicolon (;) is used in Prolog instead of the bar (|) to separate alternatives on the right-hand

```
expression --> conjunction, ['||'], expression ; conjunction.
conjunction --> relation, [&&], conjunction ; relation.
relation --> addition, [<], relation ;
             addition, [<=], relation ;
             addition, [>], relation ;
             addition, [>=], relation ;
             addition, [==], relation ;
             addition, ['!='],relation ;
             addition.
addition --> term, [+], addition ;
             term, [-], addition ;
             term.
term --> factor, [*], term ;
         factor, [/], term ;
         factor.
factor --> ['('], expression, [')'] ; [id] ; [lit].
```

| Figure 9.15 Prolog DCG for the Syntax of Jay Expressions

side of a production rule. Second, none of the Prolog rules is left recursive, since left recursion results in infinite search loops as we noted earlier. Thus, Jay rules like

Relation → Relation < Addition

are rewritten in Prolog as:

```
relation --> addition, [<], relation.
```

Third, this Prolog grammar treats Jay expressions as lists of terminal symbols, including the terminals 'id' and 'lit' standing for the Jay grammatical categories *Identifier* and *Literal*. We could extend this Prolog grammar to include lexical analysis for these and other token types, but we would still need to add Prolog code to transform the individual characters in a Jay program into a list of tokens. That is, grammars like the one above are not in themselves adequate to specify the details of a lexical analyzer.

Nevertheless, what is impressive about this exercise is that Prolog definite clause grammars are very useful for formal experimentation with the concrete syntax of programming languages. In particular, a modest extension of the program in Figure 9.15 allows a query to generate a parse tree for a Jay expression. This is shown in Figure 9.16.

```
expression(expression(C, '||', E)) --> conjunction(C), ['||'],
                                        expression(E).
expression(expression(C)) --> conjunction(C).
conjunction(conjunction(R, &&, C)) --> relation(R), [&&],
                                        conjunction(C).
conjunction(conjunction(R)) --> relation(R).
relation(relation(A, <, R)) --> addition(A), [<], relation(R).
relation(relation(A, <=, R)) --> addition(A), [<=], relation(R).
relation(relation(A, >, R)) --> addition(A), [>], relation(R).
relation(relation(A, >=, R)) --> addition(A), [>=], relation(R).
relation(relation(A, ==, R)) --> addition(A), [==], relation(R).
relation(relation(A,'!=',R)) --> addition(A),['!='],relation(R).
relation(relation(A)) --> addition(A).

addition(addition(T, +, R)) --> term(T), [+], addition(R).
addition(addition(T, -, R)) --> term(T), [-], addition(R).
addition(addition(T)) --> term(T).

term(term(F, *, T)) --> factor(F), [*], term(T).
term(term(F, /, T)) --> factor(F), [/], term(T).
term(term(F)) --> factor(F).

factor(factor('(', E, ')')) --> ['('], expression(E), [')'].
factor(factor(I)) --> identifier(I).
factor(factor(Val)) --> literal(Val).

identifier(id) --> [id].
literal(val) --> [val].
```

| Figure 9.16 *Jay Expression Syntax Extended to Generate Parse Trees*

Now a Prolog query that will display a parse tree for an expression `id + val * id` can be written as follows, with the result shown below:

```
?- expression(Parse, [id,+,val,*,id], []).

Parse = expression(
            conjunction(
                relation(
                    addition(
                        term(factor(id)),
                        +,
                        addition(
                            term(
                                factor(val),
                                *,
                                term(factor(id))))))))
```

The layout of this result has been altered by hand to promote its readability. However, the content is an exact rendition of the output of the query. Turning this page on its side will help to reveal the tree-like structure of the parse.

Since Jay type checking and semantics are defined functionally, it is not difficult to implement a complete interpreter for Jay in Prolog. We would need to attach appropriate features to the syntax rules given above that would generate corresponding concrete syntactic structures. We would also need to define in Prolog a function for each of the type checking rules *V* and semantic rules *M* to complete the interpreter. In the next section we implement some of the semantic rules *M*. The type checking rules and the remaining semantic rules make an excellent team project, and we leave it as an exercise.

9.5.5 Semantics of Jay

In this section we implement much of the formal semantics of Jay using Prolog. Recall that a key notion in the semantics of imperative languages is that of a state, which consists of a set of bindings of variables to their current values. Mathematically, these bindings are represented as pairs.

$$\sigma = \{\langle id_1, val_1\rangle, \langle id_2, val_2\rangle, \ldots, \langle id_m, val_m\rangle\}$$

In our Java implementation, this particular set was implemented as a hashtable in which the variable identifier was the key and the associated value was the current value of the variable (see Appendix B). A state here is naturally represented as a list, with each element of the list being a pair representing the binding of a variable to its value. So the Jay state:

$$\{\langle x, 1\rangle, \langle y, 5\rangle\}$$

can be represented as the Prolog list:

```
[[x,1], [y,5]]
```

Next we implement the state access functions named `get` and `onion` (overriding union) from the Java implementation (see Appendix B).

Recall that the `get` function in Java was used to obtain the value of a variable from the current state. The `get` function takes an input variable and an input state and produces an output value.

```
/* get(var, inState, outValue) */
```

Since the Jay type system requires that all variables used in a program be declared, there cannot be a reference to a variable that is not in the state. The base case is that the variable-value pair occur at the front of the state list, in which case the value associated with the variable is the desired result value. Otherwise the search continues through the tail of the list.[8]

```
get(Var, [[Var, Val] | _], Val).
get(Var, [_ | Rest], Val) :- get(Var, Rest, Val).
```

An application of the `get` function is:

```
?- get(y, [[x, 5], [y, 3], [z, 1]], V).

V = 3.
```

The `onion` function takes an input variable, an input value, an input state and produces a new state with the value part of the matching variable-value pair replaced with the new value.

```
/* onion(var, val, inState, outState) */
```

Recall that the `onion` function is able to make the simplifying assumption that the variable for which we are searching occurs exactly once within the state. The base case is that the variable being matched occurs at the head of the list; the output state is just a new variable-value pair concatenated with the remainder of the input state. Otherwise the new state is constructed from the head concatenated with the output state resulting from the recursive application of `onion` on the tail of the input state.

```
onion(Var, Val, [[Var, _] | Rest], [[Var, Val] | Rest]).
onion(Var, Val, [Xvar | Rest], [Xvar | OState]) :-
   onion(Var, Val, Rest, OState).
```

An application of `onion` is:

```
?- onion(y, 4, [[x, 5], [y, 3], [z, 1]], S).
S = [[x, 5], [y, 4], [z, 1]].
```

Next, we consider the function for the meaning of a Jay expression. To this end, we choose an appropriate representation for a Jay expression in abstract syntax. One

---

8. An astute reader who has already read Chapter 8 may have noticed the similarity of this implementation to the Scheme implementation.

possibility is to use lists; instead, we prefer using structures:

```
value(val), where val is a number
variable(ident), where ident is a variable name
operator(term1, term2), where operator is one of:
    plus minus times div -- arithmetic
    lt, le, eq, ne, gt, ge -- relational
    and, or -- boolean
```

The meaning of a Jay abstract expression is implemented as a set of rules depending on the kind of expression. In Prolog, these rules take an input expression and an input state and return a value:

```
/* mexpression(expr, state, val) */
```

The meaning of a value expression is just the value itself.

```
mexpression(value(Val), _, Val).
```

The meaning of a variable is the value associated with the variable in the current state, obtained by applying the get function.

```
mexpression(variable(Var), State, Val) :-
    get(Var, State, Val).
```

The meaning of a binary expression is obtained by applying the operator to the meaning of the operands; below we show the meaning for plus:

```
mexpression(plus(Expr1, Expr2), State, Val) :-
    mexpression(Expr1, State, Val1),
    mexpression(Expr2, State, Val2),
    Val is Val1 + Val2.
```

This definition says first evaluate Expr1 in State giving Val1, then evaluate Expr2 in State giving Val2. Then add the two values giving the resulting value. The remaining binary operators are implemented similarly.

Finally, we need to pick a representation for the abstract syntax of Jay statements. Although we could use a list representation (as we did for Scheme), we prefer to use structures:

```
skip
assignment(target, source)
block([s1, ... sn])
loop(test, body)
conditional(test, thenbranch, elsebranch)
```

The meaning function for a Jay statement (or instruction) can be written as a sequence of Prolog rules. Recall that the meaning function for an instruction takes an input statement and an input state and computes an output state:

```
/* minstruction(statement, inState, outState) */
```

These meaning rules are straightforward and follow from the mathematical definitions in Appendix B. For example, a `skip` instruction leaves the state unchanged, so the output state is a copy of the input state.

```
minstruction(skip, State, State).
```

The meaning of an assignment is to evaluate the source expression in the current state, resulting in a value, and then use that value to produce an output state (using onion).

```
minstruction(assignment(Var, Expr), IState, OState) :-
    mexpression(Expr, IState, Val),
    onion(Var, Val. IState, OState).
```

The remaining meaning rules are left as an exercise. Note that this solution is fundamentally functional in nature. Nowhere did we require the automatic search ability of Prolog.[9]

This development of a small fraction of the formal semantics of Jay should be convincing that a full semantic model for an imperative language can be defined in Prolog. Thus, via interpretation, Prolog is capable of computing any function that can be programmed in an interpretative language. The converse is also true since modern RISC computers are fundamentally imperative in nature; since Prolog interpreters are implemented on RISC machines, any function programmed in Prolog can be computed by an imperative program. Thus, in theory, imperative languages and logic programming languages are equivalent in computational power.

9.6 CONSTRAINT LOGIC PROGRAMMING

A major generalization of the unification element of logic programming results in a refinement called *constraint logic programming*. Constraint logic programming extends the range of possibilities that come into play when backtracking is invoked, thus widening the range of problems that can be specified over that of logic programming.

To illustrate, consider the Prolog example that computes Fibonacci numbers:

```
fib(0, 1).
fib(1, 1).
fib(N, F) :- N1 is N-1,fib(N1,F1),N2 is N-2,fib(N2,F2),F is F1+F2.
```

Now this program can be used to answer queries like "What is the 8th Fibonacci number?" (Answer = 34). But it cannot be used to answer queries like "In what position is 34 in the Fibonacci sequence?" (Answer = 8). These two queries would be posed as follows:

```
? - fib(8, Answer).
? - fib(Answer, 34).
```

---

9. An astute reader who has read Chapter 8 may wish to compare this implementation to the Scheme implementation.

However, the second query will fail in Prolog. The first goal of the right-hand side of the rule, an assignment to N1, cannot be satisfied, since there is no initial instantiation of N.

Constraint logic programming allows this function to be rewritten as follows:

```
fib(0, 1).
fib(1, 1).
fib(N, F1+F2) :- N>=2, fib(N-1,F1), fib(N-2,F2).
```

Now the second query above will yield the correct result: Answer = 8. This result is accomplished by matching arguments and parameters to yield a series of equations to be solved that resolves the query. That is, the second query generates new variables F1 and F2 along with the following equations, or *constraints,* to be solved:

$$F1 + F2 = 34$$
$$N \geq 2$$

Each recursive call to fib generates new constraints that are added to these, yielding a system of equations whose solution finally resolves the query.

Many view constraint programming as a new paradigm that will enable solutions for a wide class of programs that have been hitherto unapproachable. In a 1995 *BYTE* magazine article, Pountain affirmed that constraint logic programming is the programming paradigm likely to gain most in commercial significance in the next five years. Moreover, several constraint logic programming languages have been developed by research groups since its emergence in the late 1980s. These include Prolog IV, CLP(R), and CHIP. For more complete information about constraint logic programming, see [Jaffar 1994; Bartak 1998] or visit the Web.

EXERCISES

9.1 Some of the operators in predicate logic expressions are redundant; that is, they can be replaced in the expressions by finding logically equivalent subexpressions. For example, an expression with the implication operator $p \supset q$ can be replaced by the equivalent expression $\neg p \vee q$. Find an equivalent expression, using only conjunction, disjunction, and negation, for the predicate $p \equiv q$.

9.2 Identify each of the clauses in the following statements by a logical variable, and then rewrite these statements as Horn clauses.
(a) If "Phantom" is being performed and ticket prices are reasonable, then we'll go to the theater.
(b) If the local economy is good or Webber is in town, then ticket prices will be reasonable.
(c) Webber is in town.

9.3 (a) Write the following statements as a series of Prolog facts and rules.

Mammals have four legs and no arms, or two arms and two legs. A cow is a mammal. A cow has no arms.

(b) Can Prolog derive the conclusion that a cow has four legs? Explain.

9.4 Consider the family tree defined in Figure 9.4. Draw a search tree, in the style of the one shown in Figure 9.2, for the query grandparent(Who, ron).

9.5 Reconsidering Figure 9.4, define a new relation "cousin" that defines the relationship between any two people whose parents are siblings. Write a query for this expanded program that will identify all people who are cousins of Ron.

9.6 Write a Prolog program to find the maximum, minimum, and range of the values in a list of numbers.

9.7 Write a Prolog program `remdup` that removes all duplicates from a list. For example, the query `remdup([a,b,a,a,c,b,b,a], X)` should return X = [a,b,c].

9.8 A call to the Prolog function `getO(C)` retrieves the next character typed by the user and unifies it with the variable C. The call `name(W, L)` associates any word W, which is an atom, with the list L of ASCII codes that represent its characters. Discuss the utility of these functions for a Prolog implementation of a Jay lexical analyzer.

9.9 Define a Prolog function `read_sent` that inputs a sentence typed by the user and stores it as a list of words.

9.10 Extend the symbolic differentiation program so that it differentiates functions with exponents as well as sums and products. This extension should rely on the following knowledge:

$$\frac{du^n}{dx} = nx^{n-1}\frac{du}{dx} \qquad \text{for integers } n > 0$$

In solving this problem, use the symbol ^ to denote exponentiation. That is, the expression x^2 would be typed x^2.

9.11 Use your extended symbolic differentiation program d to differentiate the following functions:
(a) $x^2 + 2x + 1$
(b) $(5x - 2y)/(x^2 + 1)$

9.12 Consider the problem of simplifying an algebraic expression, such as the result of symbolic differentiation. We know that identities like $x + 0 = x$ and $1 \cdot x = x$ are used in simplifying expressions.
(a) Design a set of rules for simplification, based on the properties of 0 and 1 when added or multiplied with another expression, and then write a Prolog recursive function `simp` that simplifies an arbitrary algebraic expression.
(b) Show how `simp` can be used to simplify the result of differentiating the expressions *a* and *b* in the previous question.

9.13 Considering the `append`, `prefix`, and `suffix` functions defined in this chapter, draw a search tree for each of the following Prolog queries:
(a) `suffix([a], L), prefix(L, [a, b, c]).`
(b) `suffix([b], L), prefix(L, [a, b, c]).`

9.14 Consider the Prolog program to find the factorial of a number n, given in Section 9.4. Draw the search tree of subgoals that Prolog uses to compute the factorial of 4.

9.15 Consider adding the following fact and rule to the Family Tree program discussed in Subsection 9.2.3

```
ancestor(X, X).
ancestor(X, Y) :- ancestor(Z, Y), parent(X, Z).
```

(a) Explain Prolog's response to the query `ancestor(bill, X)` using a search tree of subgoals.

(b) Describe the general circumstances under which an infinite loop can occur in a Prolog program.

(c) Suggest a slight revision of the fact and rule in Exercise 9.15 that will avoid the problem you discovered in part (a) of this question.

9.16   (a) While running the natural language processing program discussed in this chapter, determine whether or not each of the following is a valid sentence (instance of the nonterminal symbol s):

```
The giraffe eats the apple.
The apple eats the giraffe.
The giraffe eats.
```

(b) Suggest a small change in the program that would make all three of the above sentences valid.

9.17   Revise the Prolog grammar for Figure 9.13 so that it produces a complete parse tree for the query `s(Tree, [the, giraffe, eats, the, apple], [])`.

9.18   Consider the following Prolog grammar:

```
s -> np, vp.
np -> det, n.
np -> n.
np -> n, n.
vp -> tv, np.
vp -> iv, pp.
pp -> prep, np.
det -> [a].
det -> [an].
n -> [fruit].
n -> [apple].
n -> [flies].
iv -> [flies].
tv -> [like].
prep -> [like].
```

In this grammar, the category `prep` denotes a preposition (such as "like") and `pp` denotes a prepositional phrase (such as "like an apple"). Show that this grammar is ambiguous (recall the definition of *ambiguous* from Chapter 2) by finding two different parse trees for the sentence "fruit flies like an apple."

9.19   Consider the sentence "the woman saw the man on the hill with the telescope."

(a) Briefly discuss the different ways in which this ambiguous sentence can be interpreted (there are several different parses, depending on how the prepositional phrases are associated with the noun and verb phrases).

(b) Define an ambiguous BNF grammar which allows these different interpretations to be realized.

(c) Design a Prolog program that is equivalent to your grammar in part (b), and exercise it to be sure that all these parse trees occur.

9.20 Design Prolog functions that will display the output of a parse tree-generating grammar in a more readable fashion. That is, one function name would appear per line and different levels of the trees would be revealed by different indentations from the left-hand margin. For instance, the parse tree

```
s(np(det(the),n(giraffe)),vp(iv(dreams)))
```

would be displayed as follows:

```
s
    np
        det(the)
        n(giraffe)
    vp
        iv(dreams)
```

9.21 One way for a grammar to limit its acceptance of ungrammatical sentences is to require that the noun phrase and the verb phrase agree in number. That is, sentences like "the giraffe likes the fruit" should be accepted, but sentences like "the giraffe like the fruit" should not. To do this, we can augment the lexicon with a feature called `Number`, which can be `singular` or `plural` for each noun and verb. To support such a feature efficiently, Prolog provides the following syntactic convention:

```
lhs --> rhs , {conditions}.
```

in which the first part is an ordinary grammar rule and the second part can be any additional Prolog clauses that must also be satisfied for that grammar rule to apply. For example,

```
n(Number) --> [Word], {n(Word, Number)} .
```

along with a collection of lexical entries like

```
n(giraffe, singular).
n(giraffes, plural).
n(apple, singular).
```

describes a family of rules that are satisfied by noun-number pairs. A similar strategy can be used for encoding the number of verbs and determiners in the lexicon. Now a noun phrase can carry this number information as follows:

```
np(Number) --> det(Number), n(Number).
```

and so can a verb phrase:

```
vp(Number) --> iverb(Number).
```

Thus, we can force number agreement across a whole sentence by writing the following rule:

```
s(Number) --> np(Number), vp(Number).
```

This takes advantage of the idea that the only way to satisfy a Prolog rule is that a variable, like `Number`, must have the same instantiation (singular or plural) everywhere it appears in the rule. Make this refinement to the grammar you designed in Exercise 9.20. Convince yourself that it works correctly for each of the following sentences:

"The giraffe likes the fruit" (right)

"The giraffe like the fruit" (wrong)

9.22 Consider the Prolog grammar in Figure 9.16.

(a) Give a Prolog query that will assist you in discovering a parse tree for each of the following expressions:

```
id

(id + id) * id - id / val
```

(b) In what ways does this grammar differ from the entire syntax of Jay? Discuss what would be needed to extend this grammar so that it describes the entire syntax of Jay, including its statement types and lexical features.

9.23 Complete the Jay semantic functions begun in Subsection 9.5.5.

9.24 (Team project) Design a complete interpreter for Jay in Prolog, beginning with the concrete syntax and including Prolog rules for the functions *V* and *M* that define Jay's type system and semantics. Follow the specifications given in Appendix B for Jay.

9.25 Write a Prolog function "median" that finds the median element in a list (that is, the element whose value is in/near the middle position after the list is sorted). For example, the Prolog query

```
?- median([1, 3, 6, 4, 2], X).
```

should give the answer X = 3. To solve this problem, consider using other functions that are discussed in this chapter. Also, if the list has an even number of elements, consider its median to be the average of the two elements that are closest to the middle after the list is sorted. For instance, the median of the list [1,3,6,4,2,5] is 7/2.

9.26 Use Prolog to find all (zero or more) solutions to the following word puzzle: Mason, Alex, Steve, and Simon are standing in a police lineup. One of them is blond, handsome, and unscarred. Two of them who are not blond are standing on either side of Mason. Alex is the only one standing next to exactly one handsome man. Steve is the only one not standing next to exactly one scarred man. Who is blond, handsome, and unscarred?

9.27 Write a Prolog function "intersection" that returns a list containing only one instance of each atom that is a member of both of its two argument lists. For instance, the query:

```
?- intersection([a,b,a], [c,b,d,a])
```

should return the answer [b,a] or [a,b]. Hint: Consider using a member function and other functions you have written to assist with this problem.

9.28 Write a Prolog program that finds all solutions to the following problem. Your design should be similar to the building program discussed in this chapter.

Five runners named Harriet, Harvey, Larry, Paula, and Steve run marathons in five different towns (Brunswick, Quincy, Northhampton, Providence, and Williamsburg), wearing five different colored shirts (blue, green, purple, red, and yellow), and have five different last names (Dickerson, Gould, Kendrig, Simms, and Whitley). They have five different finishing times, ranging from 150 minutes to 170 minutes, in increments of 5 minutes. The following additional facts are known:

(a) Either Harriet or Dickerson has a finishing time of 155 minutes, and the other has a finishing time of 160 minutes.

(b) Dickerson does not wear a purple shirt.

(c) Harvey runs in Williamsburg.

     (d) Simms' finishing time is either 165 or 170 minutes, and Paula has a faster finishing time than Simms.

     (e) The runner in Quincy wears a red shirt.

     (f) The runner in Northhampton has the best finishing time, and Dickerson has a better finishing time than Steve.

     (g) The runner wearing a blue shirt has the second-best finishing time.

     (h) The runner in Providence is not Kendrig and does not have a finishing time of 165 minutes.

     (i) Each of the runners in Brunswick and Williamsburg wears a blue or a purple shirt.

     (j) Larry does not run in Northhampton, nor does he wear a green shirt.

     (k) Neither Gould nor the person wearing the green shirt has a finishing time better than 165 minutes.

     (l) The runner in Quincy does not finish in 160 minutes.

What is the first and last name, town, shirt color, and finishing time of each runner? How many solutions are there to this problem?

9.29 Suppose there are five houses, each of a different color, inhabited by people of different nationalities, with different pets, drinking preferences, and clothing preferences. From the following information, design a Prolog program that discovers who has the zebra as a pet. How many different solutions does this puzzle have?

     (a) The Finn lives in the red house.

     (b) The Spaniard owns a dog.

     (c) The coffee-drinker lives in a green house, which is next to an ivory house.

     (d) The Ukrainian drinks tea.

     (e) The person who has pet snails wears a skirt.

     (f) The person in the yellow house wears jeans and lives next to the horse.

     (g) Milk is drunk in the middle house.

     (h) The Norwegian lives in the first house, which is next to the blue house.

     (i) The person who wears slacks lives next to the fox.

     (j) The person who wears woolies drinks orange juice.

     (k) The Japanese person wears a vest.

     (l) Someone drinks vodka.

9.30 Discuss the basic differences between the object-oriented and logic programming paradigms. In what circumstances is each one particularly strong, and in what circumstances is each one particularly feeble?

9.31 Why is garbage collection important to logic programming languages? What garbage collection strategies are used in Prolog interpreters? Can you determine what strategies are used in the particular Prolog interpreter you are using?

9.32 If you have access to a constraint logic programming language, trace and run the `fib` function discussed in Section 9.6. What equations and inequalities are added to the group for each recursive call to `fib`? How and when are these solved?

9.33 (Team Project) Define and implement the concrete and abstract syntax, type system, and semantics of a small subset of Prolog using the functional notation and Java programming platform developed for Jay.

Event-Driven Programming

"Of all men's miseries the bitterest is this, to know so much and to have control over nothing."

Herodotus (484–432 B.C.)

CHAPTER OUTLINE

All the paradigms we've examined so far—imperative, object-oriented, functional, and logic programming—are based on a fundamental model of computation in which the program design predetermines what will occur when the program is run. Our imperative programming minds visualize a process in which the program controls the sequence of steps that occur at run time, and the input data play a relatively passive role in regulating how those steps are carried out. Moreover, in designing such a program, we visualize a process that will always terminate once its steps are completed.

The *event-driven* programming paradigm turns this world inside out. Event-driven programs do not predict the control sequence that will occur; they are written to react reasonably to any particular sequence of events that may occur once execution begins. In this model, the input data govern the particular sequence of control that is actually carried out by the program. Moreover, execution of an event-driven program does not typically terminate; such a program is designed to run for an arbitrary period of time, often indefinitely.

The most widespread example of an event-driven program is the GUI mouse- and windows-driven user interface found on most desktop and laptop computers in use today. Event-driven programs also drive web-based applications. For example, an online student registration system must be prepared to interact with a student no matter what her next action is: adding a course, dropping a course, determining the classroom where a course meets, and so forth. An online airline reservation system, similarly, must be prepared to respond to various sequences of user events, like changing the date of travel, the destination city, or the seating preference.

However, the event-driven programming paradigm has been in use much longer than the Web; it has only recently become prominent in the eyes of programmers because of the Web. Before the Web (if we can imagine such a time!), event-driven programs were found embedded in a variety of vehicles and devices, such as airplanes and home security systems. In these environments, the events that trigger programmed responses include a change in direction, wind speed, or temperature; by their nature these events also do not occur in any particular or predictable order.

To provide effective support for event-driven programming, some languages have developed some basic terminology and principles of design. Most recently, these principles have appeared in Java, though other languages like Visual Basic and Tcl/Tk also support event-driven programming. In this chapter, we use Java as the primary vehicle for illustrating the principles and practice of event-driven programming.

10.1 FOUNDATIONS: THE EVENT MODEL

The traditional programming paradigms have more clearly defined lineage than does the event-driven paradigm. For example, we have seen that functional programming has clear and traceable roots in lambda calculus, as does logic programming in Horn clause logic. However, event-driven programming is in an earlier stage of development, so its theoretical foundations are less clear and not as universally understood or accepted at this time.

One model, offered by Stein [1999, p. 1], explains event-driven programming by contrasting it with the traditional view of computation (which embodies the imperative, functional, and object-oriented paradigms):

> Computation is a function from its input to its output. It is made up of a sequence of functional steps that produce—at its end—some result as its goal. . . . These steps are combined by temporal sequencing.

Stein argues that modern computations are embedded in physical environments where the temporal sequencing of events is unpredictable and (potentially) without an end. In order to cope with this unpredictability, Stein claims that computation needs to be modeled as *interaction* [Stein 1999, p. 8]:

> Computation is a community of persistent entities coupled together by their ongoing interactive behavior. . . . Beginning and end, when present, are special cases that can often be ignored.

This view is well-supported by the wide range of applications for which computer programs are now designed, including robotics, video games, global positioning systems, and home security alarm systems.

A more extreme view is offered by Wegner [1997], who claims that interaction is a fundamentally more powerful metaphor than the traditional notion of algorithm (i.e., anything that can be modeled by a Turing machine). This view claims that there are interactive programs representative of a more powerful genre that cannot be systematically reduced to Turing machines. This claim has received considerable recent discussion in the literature, and Wegner has made efforts to further develop the underlying theory that would support it [Wegner 1999]. If successful, this work may have significant and long-lasting impact on our fundamental understandings about the theory of computing.

These concerns notwithstanding, the Wegner-Stein approach to describing computation as interaction provides a fairly rigorous foundation for modeling event-driven programming as it is practiced today.

10.2 THE EVENT-DRIVEN PROGRAMMING PARADIGM

The event-driven paradigm is different from the imperative paradigm, as summarized in Figure 10.1.

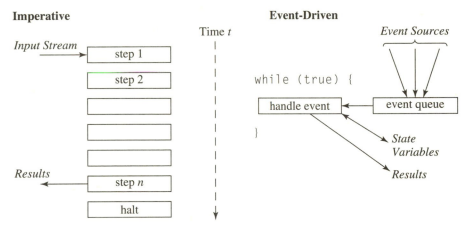

Imperative   **Event-Driven**

| Figure 10.1   Imperative and Event-Driven Paradigms Contrasted

Here, we see that the imperative paradigm models a computation as a series of steps that have a discrete beginning and ending in time. Input is generally gathered near the beginning of the time period, and results are generally emitted near the end. Some variations, of course, would have input and results continuously occurring, but nevertheless the process has a distinct ending time.

By contrast, the input to an event-driven program comes from different autonomous *event sources,* which may be sensors on a robot or buttons in an interactive frame in a web browser. These events occur asynchronously, and so each one enters an event queue whenever it occurs. As time passes, a simple control loop receives the next event by removing it from this queue and "handling" it. In the process of handling the event, the program may consult and/or change the value of a *state variable* or even produce intermediate *results.* Importantly, we see that the event-driven program is designed to run forever, with no predefined stopping point as is the case in an imperative program.

Java provides direct support for event-driven programming by providing certain classes and methods that can be used to design an interaction. When we design an interaction, our program needs to classify the events that can occur, associate those event occurrences with specific objects in the frame, and then handle each event effectively when it does occur.

The types of events that can occur in Java are defined by the subclasses of the predefined abstract class AWTEvent. These subclasses are summarized in Figure 10.2.

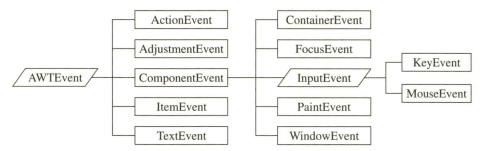

| Figure 10.2   Java Class AWTEvent and Its Subclasses*

Every event source in an interaction can generate an event that is a member of one of these classes. For instance, if a button is an event source, it generates events that are members of the ActionEvent class. We shall discuss the details of this relationship in Subsection 10.4.3.

The objects themselves that can be event sources are members of subclasses of the abstract class "Component." A summary of these classes is given in Figure 10.3. Here we see, for example, that any button that can be selected by the user in an interaction is declared as a variable in the Button class.

For a program to handle an event, it must be equipped with appropriate "listeners" that will recognize when a particular event, such as a click, has occurred on an object that is an event source. The EventListener class contains subclasses that play this role for each of the event classes identified above. These subclasses are summarized in Figure 10.4.

For example, to equip a button so that the program can "hear" an occurrence of that button's selection, the program needs to send it the message "addActionListener." If this is not done, button events will not be heard by the program. This will be more fully discussed in Subsection 10.4.3.

---

* In these class diagrams, abstract classes are enclosed in parallelograms, while nonabstract classes are enclosed in rectangles.

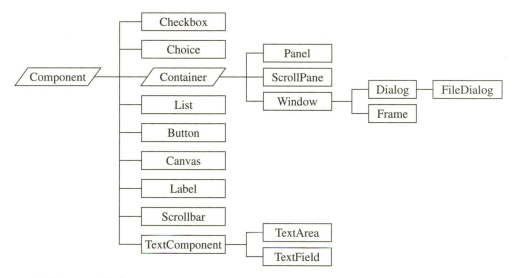

I **Figure 10.3   Subclasses of Component That Can Be Sources of Events**

Figure 10.4   Java EventListener Class Interface and Its Subclasses*

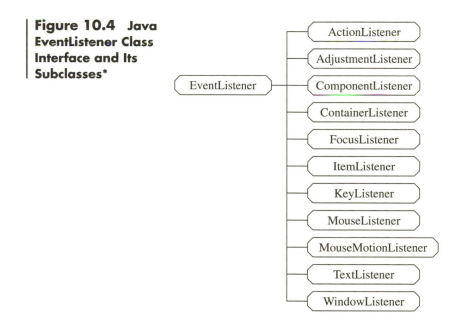

Finally, to respond to events initiated by objects in these classes, we need to implement special methods called *handlers*. Each class of events predefines the name(s) of the handler(s) that can be written for it. A summary of the handlers that are preidentified for button selections, choice (menu) selections, text typing, and mouse events is given in Figure 10.5.

---

* Enclosing a class in a hexagon distinguishes it as a class interface, rather than a regular class. Recall the distinction between classes and interfaces that was discussed in Chapter 7.

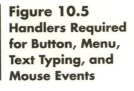

Figure 10.5 Handlers Required for Button, Menu, Text Typing, and Mouse Events

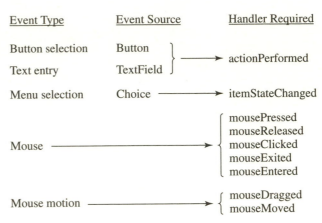

In the next section, we illustrate how these classes come together to support the event-driven design process in Java.

10.3 APPLETS

An *applet* is a Java program that runs inside a web browser. It provides a framework for programmers to design event-driven programs where the source of the events is the user interface.

Because they are designed to react to events rather than initiate them, applets have a slightly different structure than Java applications; this structure is sketched in Figure 10.6. The first three lines shown in this figure are necessary to provide access to the Java class libraries where the various event-driven programming classes are located.

```
import java.applet.*;
import java.awt.*;
import java.awt.event.*;
public class <classname> extends Applet
                    implements <listeners> {
   <state variable declarations>
   public void init () {
     <code to initialize the applet>
   }
   <event handlers>
}
```

| Figure 10.6 Overall Structure of a Java Applet

The <state variable declarations> define various objects that can be placed in the applet, as well as other values that help the program remember what has occurred so far. As with any other class, these variables collectively define the *state* of the interaction. They can be integers, floats, booleans, strings, and arrays, just as in Java application programs. Moreover, variables may also represent colors, buttons, menus, text fields, and other objects that have special functions as the program and the user interact.

An applet is different from other classes in that it has no constructor. Instead, when the applet begins executing, the `init` method is executed first. It has the responsibility of placing objects in the frame, such as buttons, choices, labels, and text fields. In this sense the `init` method takes the place of a constructor. The `init` method also attaches specific event listeners to different objects in the frame, so that these objects can be equipped with "ears" that recognize when they have been selected by the user. Event listeners are nothing more than objects which implement a particular interface; they can be either the applet itself as indicated above, or they can be separate classes. As we will see, such classes often need access to various applet methods, so they are commonly implemented as inner classes.

As a graphical user interface, an applet often has a paint method, which is invoked whenever the applet needs to repaint itself. This can occur for a number of reasons: a window partially obscures the applet for a time, the applet is first iconified and then de-iconified, and so forth. Components such as buttons, text fields, and so on will repaint themselves. However, anything done directly to the frame using Graphics methods will be lost during a repaint operation if not done in the paint method.

The other major applet methods, namely, start, stop, and destroy, are discussed in Appendix C.

For each specific kind of event (like a button selection, a mouse click, or a menu choice selection), the program must implement a special method called an `<event handler>`. The purpose of the handler is to change the state of the interaction so that it "remembers" that such an event has occurred. One handler is programmed to respond to the user pressing the mouse button, while another may respond to the user selecting a button in the frame. Whenever such an event actually occurs, its associated handler is executed one time.

The `<listeners>` that appear in the heading of the applet identify the *kinds* of events to which the applet is prepared to respond. Usually four different kinds of user-initiated events can be handled by an applet:

- Mouse motion events (handled by the `MouseMotionListener`).
- Mouse events (handled by the `MouseListener`).
- Button and text field selections (handled by the `ActionListener`).
- Selections from a menu of choices (handled by the `ItemListener`).

Importantly, the program cannot know, or predict, the order in which these different events will occur, or the number of times each one will be repeated; it has to be prepared for all possibilities. *That's the essence of event-driven programming—it's different from the other paradigms in this fundamental way.*

10.4 EVENT HANDLING

In this section we describe the basic Java programming considerations for responding to various types of user-initiated events that occur while an applet is running—mouse events, button selections, text areas, and choice (menu) selections.

10.4.1 Mouse Clicks

For the program to handle mouse clicks, the MouseListener interface must be implemented, either by the applet itself or by a mouse handler class. If the listener is being handled directly by the applet, then the applet must specify the listener in its `imple-ments` clause and activate the listener, usually inside the `init` method:

```
public class MyApplet extends Applet implements MouseListener {

    public void init( ) {
        ...
        addMouseListener(this);
        ...
    }
```

The alternative is to use a separate class to handle mouse clicks. Commonly, this class is an inner class to the applet, so that the mouse handler has access to all of the applet's methods, particularly the graphics context:

```
public class MyApplet extends Applet {

    public void init( ) {
        ...
        addMouseListener(new MouseHandler());
        ...
    }

    private class MouseHandler implements MouseListener {
        ...
    }
```

If an external class is used, it is common for the applet to pass itself in the call on the mouse handler constructor; the applet object can then be saved to an instance variable of the mouse handler class.

Whichever alternative is used, all of the following methods must be added to the class which implements the `MouseListener`, and at least one must have some statements that respond to the event that it represents:

```
public void mousePressed(MouseEvent e) { }
public void mouseReleased(MouseEvent e) { }
public void mouseClicked(MouseEvent e) { }
public void mouseExited(MouseEvent e) { }
public void mouseEntered(MouseEvent e) { }
```

An advantage to using a separate class is that Java provides a `MouseAdapter` class, which is precisely the trivial implementation of `MouseListener` given above. This means that the separate class can extend the `MouseAdapter` class (which an applet cannot do), overriding exactly the methods for which actions are to be provided. In most instances, this is usually only the `mouseClicked` method.

```
public class MyApplet extends Applet {

    public void init( ) {
      ...
      addMouseListener(new MouseHandler());
      ...
    }

    private class MouseHandler extends MouseAdapter {
        public void mouseClicked(MouseEvent e) {
            <action>
        }
    }
}
```

The typical response to a mouse event is to capture the x-y pixel coordinates where that event occurred on the frame. To do this, use the getX and getY methods of the MouseEvent class. For example, the following handler responds to a mouse click by storing the x-y coordinates of the click in the applet's instance variables x and y.

```
public void mouseClicked(MouseEvent e) {
    x = e.getX();
    y = e.getY();
}
```

10.4.2 Mouse Motion

Similar to mouse clicks, for the program to handle mouse motion, the MouseMotion-Listener interface must be implemented either by the applet itself or a mouse motion handler class. To activate the listener, the following calls must be placed inside the init method:

```
addMouseMotionListener(<listener>);
```

The class which implements the listener must implement all of the following methods; at least one must have some statements that respond to the event that the listener represents:

```
public void mouseDragged(MouseEvent e) { }
public void mouseMoved(MouseEvent e) { }
```

An advantage to using a separate class is that Java provides a MouseMotionAdapter class, which is precisely the trivial implementation of MouseMotionListener given above. This means that the separate class can extend the MouseMotionAdapter class (which an applet cannot do), overriding exactly the methods for which actions are to be provided. In most instances, this is usually only the mouseDragged method.

10.4.3 Buttons

A *button* is an object on the screen which is named and can be selected by a mouse click. Because any number of variables can be declared with class Button and placed in the applet, button handlers are usually implemented via a separate class, rather than by the applet itself. A button is declared and initialized as follows:

```
Button <variable> = new Button(<string>);
```

Here is an example:

```
Button clearButton = new Button("Clear");
```

A button is placed in the applet by including the following inside the init method in your program.

```
add(<variable>);
```

For example:

```
add(clearButton);
```

To be useful, a button needs to have a listener attached so that the button responds to mouse clicks. This is normally done by including the following inside the applet's init method:

```
<variable>.addActionListener(<listener>);
```

For example:

```
clearButton.addActionListener(new ClearButtonHandler());
```

The class which handles the user selecting the button must implement the Action-Listener interface. The listener class must implement an actionPerformed method to handle the button selection event:

```
public void actionPerformed (ActionEvent e) {
    if (e.getSource() == <variable>) {
        <action>
    }
}
```

Here, *<variable>* refers to the name of the Button variable as declared and initial-ized, and *<action>* defines what to do whenever that event occurs. If a unique handler is created for each button, the if test to determine which button was selected can be omit-ted; this is normally preferred. Following, for example, is a handler written as an inner class to the applet class that clears the screen whenever the `clearButton` is clicked by the user:

```
private class ClearButtonHandler implements ActionListener {
    public void actionPerformed(ActionEvent e) {
        repaint();
    }
}
```

Note that the `repaint` method is an applet method; thus, this class works as written only if it is an inner class to applet. Using an external class requires writing a constructor which takes the applet as an argument. Using our clear button as an example, the `addActionListener` code in applet's `init` method would appear as:

```
clearButton.addActionListener(new ClearButtonHandler(this));
```

The button handler class would then appear as:

```
public class ClearButtonHandler implements ActionListener {
    Applet applet;
    public ClearButtonHandler(Applet a) { applet = a; }
    public void actionPerformed(ActionEvent e) {
        applet.repaint();
    }
}
```

Note that using an external class makes it more difficult for a listener class to determine which button was selected since the buttons themselves are declared within the applet class.

10.4.4 Labels, TextAreas, and TextFields

A *Label* is an object whose string value can be placed inside a frame to label another object, such as a TextField. It can be added to the frame from within the `init` method. For example, the statement

```
add(new Label("Fahrenheit"));
```

would place the message "Fahrenheit" in the frame. Labels cannot have a listener attached to them.

A *TextArea* is an object on the screen which is named and can display text messages to the user. It is a scrollable object, so users have a complete record of the text output. A *TextField* is an object into which the user can type a single line of text from the keyboard; it raises an ActionEvent when the user types the return key at the end of the line. TextAreas and TextFields are declared as follows:

```
TextArea <variable>;
TextField <variable>;
```

For example:

```
TextArea echoArea;
TextField typing;
```

TextArea and TextField objects are normally placed in the applet as part of the init method in your program. Initialization requires the number of lines of text (for TextAreas) and the number of characters per line to be specified.

```
<variable1> = new TextArea(<lines>, <chars>);
add(<variable1>);
<variable2> = new TextField(<chars>);
add(<variable2>);
```

For example:

```
echoArea = new TextArea(5, 40);
add(echoArea);
typing = new TextField(40);
add(typing);
```

In this example, we declare and place a 5 line by 40 character TextArea and a 40-character TextField in the current frame.

When the user types in the TextField and hits the return key, the applet can handle that event by writing additional code in its actionPerformed event handler:

```
public void actionPerformed (actionEvent e) {
    if (e.getSource() == <variable>) {
      String s = <variable>.getText();
      <action>
    }
}
```

Here, *<variable>* refers to the name of the TextArea variable that was declared and placed in the frame by the init method, like typing in the example above. When the event occurs, the string value typed in the text area is assigned to the variable s and the *<action>* is then executed.

A better solution is to use an internal class that listens specifically to the TextField typing:

```
private class TextHandler implements ActionListener {
    public void actionPerformed (actionEvent e) {
      String s = <variable>.getText();
      <action>
    }
}
```

In this case, the handler need not check for the source of the triggering event; it must be the user pressing the return (or enter) key in the TextField `typing`.

As an example of an *<action>*, the user's typing can be immediately echoed in the TextArea by concatenating it with all the text that is already there. The `getText` and `setText` methods are useful for this purpose, as shown below:

```
echoArea.append(s + "\n");
```

If this line is added as the *<action>* in the above code, the user's typing will be echoed on a new line inside the TextArea object named `echoArea`.

10.4.5 Choices

A *choice* is an object on the screen that offers several options to be selected by the user; it is like a pull-down menu, but it can be placed anywhere within the applet, not just at the top. A choice is declared as follows:

```
Choice <variable> ;
```

For example:

```
Choice choice;
```

The choice is named and placed in the frame as part of the `init` method in your program. The different selections are assigned to the `Choice` variable using the `addItem` method, and interaction is triggered by adding a listener to the frame for the choice.

```
<variable> = new Choice();
<variable>.addItem(<string1>);
...
add(<variable>);
<variable>.addItemListener(<listener>);
```

For example:

```
choice = new Button();
choice.addItem("North");
choice.addItem("East");
choice.addItem("South");
choice.additem("West");
add(choice);
choice.addItemListener(new ChoiceHandler());
```

In the case above, an inner class to the applet itself is assumed to be handling the choice event. The applet or item listener event handler must implement `ItemListener`.

When the user selects one of the choices, the event is handled by an `itemStateChanged` method:

```
private class ChoiceHandler implements ItemListener {
  public void itemStateChanged (ItemEvent e) {
    String s = (String)e.getItem();
    if (s.equals(<string1>)) {
      <action1> in response to a selection of <string1>
    }
    else if (s.equals(<string2>)) {
      <action2> in response to a selection of <string2>
    }
    ...
  }
}
```

When the event of selecting a choice occurs, this handler is executed. The String `s` gets the value of the choice the user has selected, which is passed to the handler by way of the method call `e.getItem()`. This choice is used in a series of `if` statements to select the appropriate *<action>*.

10.5 EXAMPLE: A SIMPLE GUI INTERFACE

The process of event-driven program design involves anticipating the various states and state transitions that can occur as the program runs.

Consider the design of a simple interface, in which the user can draw rectangles and type texts in arbitrary locations of the frame. The user should be able to accomplish this as simply as possible, and so providing buttons, menus, and text typing areas, as well as handling mouse-click actions on the screen is essential. An initial frame design to support this activity is shown in Figure 10.7.

This frame has four objects; a clear Button, a Choice menu, a TextArea for communicating with the user as events are initiated, and a TextField in which the user can enter messages. Thus, we can begin our design by defining the state of the computation with the following objects and interpretations:

choice	User can select Nothing, Rectangle, or Message from this menu.
echoArea	TextArea for reporting the most recent event that has occurred.
typing	TextField for entering user input.

The button need not be part of the global state, since its function is merely to clear the screen, and this can be done completely within the event handler for the button. No other object or handler need be aware of the clear button.

The state of the computation for this problem must also keep track of all information that is relevant to the user accomplishing the next task, be it drawing a rectangle or locating a text somewhere in the frame. To draw a rectangle, the system must have two

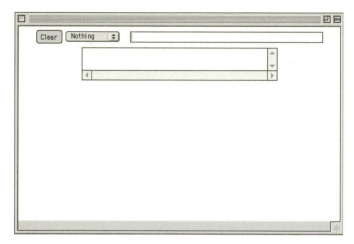

Figure 10.7   **Initial Frame Design for a Graphical Drawing Tool**

pieces of information, the x-y coordinates of the upper left-hand corner of the rectangle and the x-y coordinates of the lower right. These two points can be retrieved via a mouse event and the `mouseClicked` handler, but the first x-y coordinate pair must be stored globally within the applet's state. Furthermore, a count of the mouse clicks must also be stored globally so that the first click can be distinguished from the second in determining the corners of the rectangle. Thus, additional global state information includes:

```
lastX, lastY      X-y coordinates of last mouse click
clickNumber       The number of mouse clicks (odd or even)
```

The x and y coordinates of a mouse click are reported in the TextArea by the program whenever a mouse click event occurs. Informative messages to the user are also displayed there.

The code that defines the state is shown in Figure 10.8, and the code that initializes the interaction is shown in Figure 10.9.

```
// Variables used by the Applet -- this is the "state"
    int lastX = 0;               // first click's x-y coordinates
    int lastY = 0;
    int clickNumber = 0;       // most recent click; odd or even
    Choice choice;
    TextArea echoArea;
    TextField typing;
```

| Figure 10.8   **Code to Define the State for the Interaction**

```java
// Initialize the frame: establish the objects and their listeners
public void init() {
    // Set the background color and listen for the mouse
    setBackground(Color.white);
    addMouseListener(new MouseHandler());

    // Create a button and add it to the Frame.
    Button clearButton = new Button("Clear");
    clearButton.setForeground(Color.black);
    clearButton.setBackground(Color.lightGray);
    add(clearButton);
    clearButton.addActionListener(new ClearButtonHandler());

    // Create a menu of user choices and add it to the Frame.
    choice = new Choice();
    choice.addItem("Nothing");
    choice.addItem("Rectangle");
    choice.addItem("Message");
    add(choice);
    choice.addItemListener(new ChoiceHandler());

    // Create a TextField and a TextArea and add them to the Frame.
    typing = new TextField(40);
    add(typing);
    typing.addActionListener(new TextHandler());
    echoArea = new TextArea(2, 40);
    echoArea.setEditable(false);
    add(echoArea);

}
```

I Figure 10.9 Code to Initialize the Interaction

Designing the event handlers is a more intricate process. For each event that occurs, an appropriate handler must contain code to distinguish that event from the rest and then change the state and/or generate output into the frame appropriately. Consider the following scenario:

> The user first selects "Rectangle" from the choice menu. To properly handle that event, the system must store that selection and then prompt the user to click the mouse at the point where the upper left-hand corner of the rectangle should be drawn, as shown in Figure 10.10.

What code do we write to respond to this selection? We write code inside an `itemStateChanged` event handler of the `ChoiceHandler` class, since the object selected,

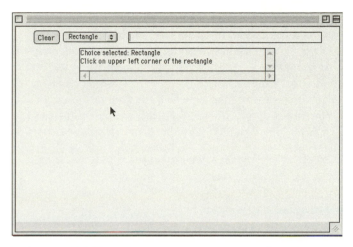

Figure 10.10 First Step in an Interaction: The User Selects Rectangle from the Menu

choice, is a `Choice`. The complete `itemStateChanged` handler for this problem is shown in Figure 10.11.

```
// Called when the user makes a Choice selection
private class ChoiceHandler implements ItemListener {
    public void itemStateChanged (ItemEvent e) {
        String currentChoice = (String) (e.getItem());
        echoArea.setText("Choice selected: " + currentChoice);
        clickNumber = 0;
            // prepare to handle first mouse click for this choice
        if (currentChoice.equals("Rectangle"))
          echoArea.append(
            "\nClick to set upper left corner of the rectangle");
        else if (currentChoice.equals("Message"))
          echoArea.append(
              "\nEnter a message in the text area");
    }
}
```

Figure 10.11 ItemStateChanged Handler for This Interaction

While this code is a bit obscure, it does reveal that the `itemStateChanged` handler must prepare for *any* menu event that can occur. It distinguishes among the possibilities by checking the parameter e for the item selected, which is assigned to the state variable `currentChoice`. If the choice is a `Rectangle`, the handler dutifully prompts the user to click to set the location where the upper left-hand corner of the rectangle should be located in the frame. If the choice is a `Message`, a different prompt goes to the user. In either case, this handler echoes the nature of this event in the `echoArea`.

Assuming that the user clicks the mouse in the frame, the system must respond by storing the x-y coordinates of that click in the applet's state variables lastX, lastY and prompt the user to click to set the lower right-hand corner of the desired rectangle. But that should be done *only* if the current choice is a Rectangle. By the time the mouse-click event happens, the only source of information about what event immediately preceded it comes from the applet's state. That is, the click could have been preceded by a different event, which should provoke a different response from the interaction. Where is this all sorted out? In the mouseClicked handler, as shown in Figure 10.12.

```
private class MouseHandler extends MouseAdapter {
    public void mouseClicked(MouseEvent e) {
        int x = e.getX();
        int y = e.getY();
        echoArea.setText("Mouse Clicked at " +
                            e.getX() + ", " + e.getY() + "\n");
        Graphics g = getGraphics();
        if (choice.getSelectedItem().equals("Rectangle")) {
            clickNumber = clickNumber + 1;
            // is it the first click?
            if (clickNumber % 2 == 1) {
                echoArea.setText
                    ("Click to set lower right corner of the rectangle");
                lastX = x;
                lastY = y;
            }
            // or the second?
            else g.drawRect(lastX, lastY, Math.abs(x-lastX),
                                            Math.abs(y-lastY));
        }
    // for a message, display it
        else if (choice.getSelectedItem().equals("Message"))
            g.drawString(currentMessage, x, y);
    }
}
```

Figure 10.12 Details of the mouseClicked Handler for This Interaction

This handler must also be prepared for anything, since it doesn't implicitly know what events occurred immediately before this particular mouse click. The state variable clickNumber helps sort things out, since its updated value will have an odd number for the first click of a pair and an even number for the second. Thus, the upper left-hand corner of a rectangle is indicated for odd values and the drawing of a complete rectangle, using the x and y coordinates of the current click together with the x and y coordinates of the previous click (stored in lastX and lastY), is indicated for even clicks.

The remainder of this event handler should be fairly readable. More details of the Graphics class and drawing methods are summarized in Appendix C. The effect of drawing a rectangle after the user has clicked twice is shown in Figure 10.13. Here, the

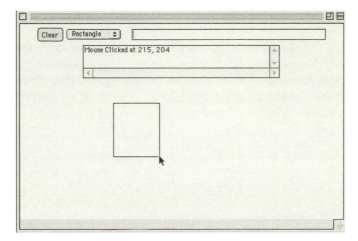

Figure 10.13 Effect of Selecting Rectangle Choice and Clicking the Mouse Twice

arrow in the figure shows the location of the second click, whose x and y coordinates are 215 and 204, respectively.

The next task in designing this interaction is to implement the event handler that responds to the user selecting the clear button or typing text in the typing area. The actionPerformed method for this event is shown in Figure 10.14. Note here the simplicity of attaching a unique handler to the clear button; it does not have to test what triggers the event (the button or the enter key in the typing area); it clears the screen via a repaint.

```
private class ClearButtonHandler implements ActionListener {
   public void actionPerformed (ActionEvent e) {
      echoArea.setText("Clear button selected ");
      repaint();
   }
}
```

Figure 10.14 ActionPerformed Handler for the Clear Button

Responding to a text typed by the user is straightforward; you need only to store the text for later use and prompt the user to click the mouse to locate the text in the frame, as shown in Figure 10.15.

```
private class TextHandler implements ActionListener {
   public void actionPerformed (ActionEvent e) {
      echoArea.setText("Text entered: " + typing.getText());
      if (choice.getSelectedItem().equals("Message"))
         echoArea.append("\nNow click to place this message");
   }
}
```

Figure 10.15 ActionPerformed Handler for the Enter Key in the Typing Area

Note that both the `TextHandler` and `ClearButtonHandler` classes implement the `ActionListener` interface and both have `actionPerformed` methods. Neither handler has to be aware of the other, as each is listening for separate events.

The net effect of typing text and clicking to locate it below the rectangle that had been placed in the frame is shown in Figure 10.16. There, the location of the mouse click is indicated by the arrow in the figure, which is at x-y coordinates 162 and 221.

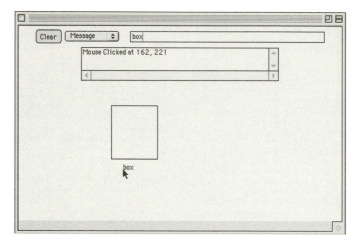

Figure 10.16   Net Effect of User Placing a Text in the Frame

This sketch provides a concrete example of the process of designing an event-driven program. The program runs indefinitely—the user can spend hours drawing rectangles, placing messages, and clearing the frame, and only the user decides what event sequence will occur at any particular point in time.

The observant reader will have noticed that this applet has no paint method. Thus, iconifying the window or overlaying another window on top of this window will eventually necessitate a repaint, causing all the rectangles and messages to disappear. If the applet needs to repaint what has been drawn to the screen, then the applet has to remember what it wrote to the screen. We will see examples of this in later programs.

10.6   EXAMPLE: EVENT-DRIVEN INTERACTIVE GAMES

Consider designing an event-driven program that monitors an interactive game between two persons. We develop an implementation of the tic-tac-toe game here, and discuss the implementation of the game of Nim, both as event-driven programs.

10.6.1 Tic-Tac-Toe

In the game tic-tac-toe, there is a 3 × 3 board and two players alternate turns. Each turn forces the board into a new state which differs from the old one by the contents of one square. A game is over when either the board is full or one of the players has placed three markers (X or O) in a row, either horizontally, vertically, or diagonally. The interaction should run indefinitely, so the players can clear the board and start a new game at any time. Thus, the *state* of a tic-tac-toe game naturally includes:

- The state of the board,
- Whose turn it is,
- Whether the game is over, and
- A "new game" button that clears the board and starts a new game.

An *event* in this setting is either a player move (clicking the mouse in an unoccupied square to place the next X or O) or a player selecting the "new game" button. The sequencing of these events is entirely unpredictable by the program—either one is equally likely while a game is going on.

The results displayed by the program are the board itself and a message area which is used to report whose turn it is, the winner, and other information as the game proceeds. Before continuing with our exploration of the game tic-tac-toe, we first consider some useful helper classes

10.6.2 The Grid and Cell Classes—Useful Assistants

Recognizing that many board games require a rectangular array, or "grid," of boxes or "cells" into which moves can be placed, the classes Grid and Cell are designed to support these activities. (A full implementation of the Grid and Cell classes is available at the website given in the Preface.) Let us consider the Cell class first.

A *cell* is basically a square that is capable of displaying itself on the screen. As such, it has x-y coordinates and a size; it can be implemented using the java.awt class Rectangle. A cell has a value; to accommodate a variety of games, the constant cell values include OFF (no value or empty), ON, EX (for tic-tac-toe), and OH (a simple circle). A cell can also have a color. These state variables are summarized in Figure 10.17.

```
final static char OFF = ' ', ON = '*', EX = 'X', OH = 'O';
Rectangle cell;
char value = OFF;
Color color = Color.black;
```

| Figure 10.17 State Variables for Class Cell

The class Cell has many methods but the designer of a game playing program need only be concerned with the methods that get/set the value of a cell and that get/set the color of a cell. The signature of these methods is given in Figure 10.18.

Figure 10.18
Important Methods
| in Class Cell

```
public char get( );
public void set(char value);
public Color getColor( );
public void setColor(Color c);
```

The remaining cell methods, including the constructors, are used primarily by the class Grid.

The important public variables and methods for the class Grid are summarized in Figure 10.19.

```
int row, col; // row and column of last mouse click in the grid
              // (-1, -1) means click was outside the grid
Grid (int rows, int cellSize, int offset);
void clear();
paint(Graphics g);
boolean contains(int x, int y);
Cell getCell(int row, int col);
```

| **Figure 10.19 Public Variables and Methods in Class Grid**

The following declaration creates a 5 × 5 rectangular grid and displays it the frame, as shown in Figure 10.20.

```
Grid board = new Grid(5, 15, 90);
```

This statement calls for the creation of a 5 × 5 grid whose cells are 15 pixels in size, and which is displaced 90 pixels horizontally and vertically away from the left and top edges of the frame. By convention, the rows and columns of this array are numbered from 0 to 4, reading vertically from the top and horizontally from the left.

**Figure 10.20
Creation of a
New Grid in a
Frame**

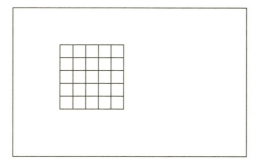

Any cell in the grid may be set by a single mouse click using a particular character from among the following alternatives:

EX: place an X in a cell.

OH: place an O in a cell.

OFF: clear a cell.

ON: fill a cell.

For example, suppose we want to place an X in row 4, column 1 of the grid board declared above, where the user has just made a mouse click in the pixel location given by integers x and y. This is illustrated in Figure 10.21.

The following conditional statement is used to accomplish this:

```
if (board.contains(x, y))
    board.getCell(board.row, board.col).set(Cell.EX);
```

**Figure 10.21
Placement of an
X in the Grid**

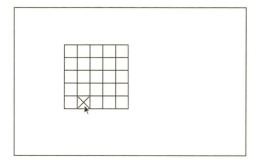

This statement sets the designated square to X, but only if the x-y pixel coordinates of the click are somewhere inside the boundaries of the grid in the frame. To accomplish this, the statement uses two Grid methods, `contains` and `getCell`, and one Cell method, `set`.

The `board.contains` method call does two things: it determines whether or not the coordinates of the pixel at the point (x, y) clicked by the user are inside the grid in the frame (returning a boolean result), and if so it translates that point to a corresponding row and column number for that point (given by `board.row` and `board.col`, respectively).

The `getCell` method gets the cell at the value of `board.row` and `board.col`. The cell returned is then set to a particular value, in this case X, as given by the argument `Cell.EX` (which is a static reference).

Having obtained a cell reference from the grid, the `Cell` method `get()` is used to obtain the value of a cell. This value (which is a `char`) should be set to one of the values: EX, OH, ON, or OFF. Consider the following statement which checks to see if the cell in a particular row and column of `board` is currently clear (OFF), and if so changes it to EX.

```
Cell c = board.getCell(board.row, board.col);
if (c.get() == Cell.OFF)
    c.set(Cell.EX);
```

10.6.3 Tic-Tac-Toe (continued)

Now with the `Grid` and `Cell` classes in hand, we can complete the design of the visual and event-handling parts of the tic-tac-toe program. The major visual design element is a 3 × 3 grid, as shown below:

Each player takes a turn by clicking the mouse to place an X or O on one of the unoccupied squares; player X goes first. The winner is the player who first places three X's or 3 O's in a row, either horizontally, vertically, or diagonally. A tie game occurs when the board is full, and no one has three X's or O's in a row.

The program uses a `TextArea` for displaying appropriate messages (for instance, when a player attempts to make an illegal move). It allows each player in turn to click on an empty square and replace that square with an X or an O. The program thus keeps track of whose turn it is and reports that information in the TextArea at the beginning of each turn. Thus, the state variables for this game include:

- A Grid variable for the 3 × 3 board.
- A TextArea variable for sending messages to the players.
- A variable that determines whose turn it is; that variable flips back and forth whenever a player has completed a legal move.

A sketch of the state variables and initialization for this game is shown in Figure 10.22.

```
public class TicTacToe extends Applet {
    // applet state variables
    TextArea echoArea;
    Grid board;                    // the Tic-tac-toe board
    char player = Cell.EX;  // Current player: EX or OH
    // Initializing the Frame
    public void init() {
        // listen for the mouse
        setBackground(Color.white);
        addMouseListener(new MouseHandler());

        // Create a button and add it to the Frame.
        Button b = new Button("New Game");
        b.setForeground(Color.black);
        b.setBackground(Color.lightGray);
        add(b);
        b.addActionListener(new NewGameHandler());

        // Create a TextArea and add it to the Frame
        echoArea = new TextArea(2, 40);
        echoArea.setEditable(false);
        add(echoArea);

        // Place a 3x3 grid in the frame
        board = new Grid(3, 20, 120);
    }
```

| Figure 10.22 Initial State for the Tic-Tac-Toe Interaction

The central event-driven code appears in the handler for mouse clicks. Some of these clicks reflect legal moves (i.e., a mouse click from a player on an unoccupied square of the board), and others reflect illegal moves (e.g., a mouse click outside the board). Another distinct event is the selection of the Button b to signal ending the game. These events can occur in any order, so the program must be equipped to sensibly handle them and change the state appropriately. A sketch of the mouseClicked handler for this problem is given in Figure 10.23.

```
private class MouseHandler extends MouseAdapter {
    public void mouseClicked(MouseEvent e) {
      if (board.contains(e.getX(), e.getY())) {
        Cell c = board.getCell(board.row, board.col);
        if (c.get() == Cell.OFF) {
            c.set(player);
            if (player == Cell.EX)
                player = Cell.OH;
            else player = Cell.EX;
            repaint();
            echoArea.setText("Player " + player + " make your move");
      }
      else echoArea.setText("Invalid move, try again");
  else echoArea.setText("Please click inside the board");
}
```

| Figure 10.23 **The mouseClicked Handler for Tic-Tac-Toe**

The update board is displayed, not by having a "display grid" method, but by invoking the applet's repaint method. This means that the applet should have a paint method (shown in Figure 10.24) that simply calls the board's paint method. This approach solves several problems. First, it gives the board, or grid, access to the applet's graphics context. Second, it insures that if the applet is iconified or even merely obscured by another window, the board will always be redrawn as needed.

```
public void paint(Graphics g) { board.paint(g); }
```

| Figure 10.24 **Tic-Tac-Toe's Paint Method**

Whenever the players decide to quit the current game, even perhaps before the game is over, the program should respond appropriately by clearing the board and changing the current player to X. The event handler must respond to a player's selection of the "new game" button whenever it occurs. It should initialize the board and set the current player to X. This event handler is given in Figure 10.25.

```
private class NewGameHandler implements ActionListener {
    public void actionPerformed (ActionEvent e) {
        echoArea.setText("New Game button selected ");
        board.clear();
        player = Cell.EX;
        repaint( );
    }
}
```

| Figure 10.25 **New Game Handler**

All of this code is available at the website given in the Preface. It contains what is presented here, which is basically the initialization of the applet and the event handling code. Completion of this program is left as an exercise.

To complete this game, it must be determined when the game is over (and whether anyone has won) and report that outcome in the TextArea. A method `GameOver` should determine whether or not the game is over (the board is full or there are 3 X's or 3 O's in a row). That method should be called at an appropriate time by the `mouseClicked` handler to tell whether or not to report the outcome or continue monitoring the next move.

10.6.4 Nim

Designing other interactive games involves similar considerations, whether the game be Othello, Connect-4, or Nim. Each one requires that the program keep track of the state of the game by defining appropriate variables and event handlers so that the state is altered in exactly the right way when each event occurs.

Consider the two-player game of Nim, which can be played on a board that has three rows of pebbles, as shown below:

Each player takes her turn by removing one or more pebbles from any one of the three rows. The winner is the player who picks up the last pebble. A Java program can monitor this game by using a 7×7 grid in which the first three rows contain O's in locations where the pebbles are initially placed, as shown below:

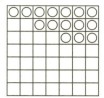

The program can conduct a dialogue with the two players using a TextArea for displaying appropriate messages. It should allow each player to click on the particular pebble(s) to be removed during that player's turn, but it should not allow a pebble to be picked up in two different rows in the same turn. To mark a "removed" pebble, the program can replace its O with a space (OFF) on the same position of the board.

To monitor this game, your program should be able to

1 Keep track of whose turn (Player 1 or Player 2) it is and report that information in the TextArea at the beginning of each turn;
2 Accept a series of mouse clicks that together constitute a legal move (the end of a player's move may be signaled by a mouse click outside the grid);
3 Determine when the game is over (and which of Player 1 or Player 2 is the winner) and report that event in the TextArea; and
4 Allow a new game to be started at any time, perhaps by providing a Choice or a Button that will cause a handler to restore the board to the state shown above.

The program should have a method `GameOver` that determines whether or not the game is over (the board contains only spaces). That method should be called by the `mouseClicked` handler to tell whether or not to report a winner.

The state of the program should include the following:

- A Grid variable for the 7 × 7 board.

- A TextArea variable for sending messages to the players.

- A variable that determines whose turn it is; that variable flips back and forth whenever a player has completed a legal move.

- A variable that records the row in which a player has picked up her first pebble for a single move (since all subsequent pebbles must be picked up from the same row).

Completion of the design of this interaction is left as an exercise.

10.7   OTHER EVENT-DRIVEN PROGRAMMING SITUATIONS

Event-driven programs occur in many other domains besides those which are Web-based. Here are three examples:

- An ATM machine.

- A home security system.

- A supermarket checkout station.

In this section, we briefly describe the first two of these interactions, focussing on their state variables and the kinds of events that should be handled in the event loop to maintain integrity among the state variables.

10.7.1   ATM Machine

An ATM machine is driven by a program that runs seven days a week and 24 hours a day. The program must be able to conduct transactions with a user. The essential elements of a typical ATM machine display are shown in Figure 10.26. (In practice, the details are different, but the elements shown here are adequate to characterize what happens during an ATM transaction).

Figure 10.26
Elements of a Typical ATM Machine Transaction User Interface

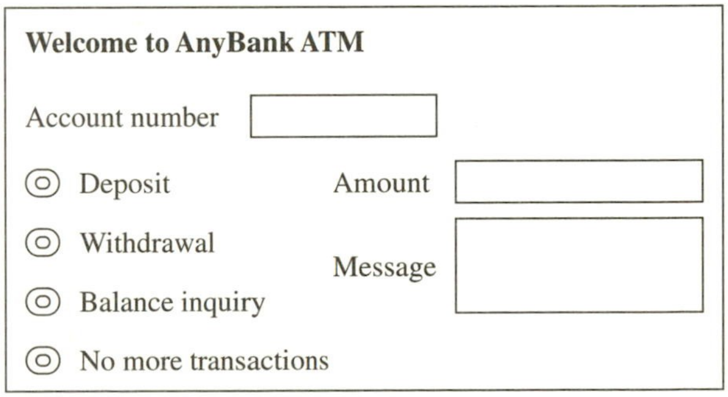

Welcome to AnyBank ATM

Account number [   ]

◎ Deposit   Amount [   ]

◎ Withdrawal
                    Message [   ]
◎ Balance inquiry

◎ No more transactions

The state of this interaction is captured partially by the objects in this display and partially by other information that relates to the particular user at the machine. A basic collection of state variables required for an ATM transaction includes:

- The user's account number—account.

- The type of transaction (deposit, withdrawal, etc.)—type.

- The amount of the transaction—amount.
- A message from the bank to the user—message.
- The user's available balance—balance.

The last variable in this list, the available balance, brings into play a new dimension that we haven't encountered in our other event-driven programming examples. In this case, the program must interact not only with the user but also with the bank's database of all its accounts and current balances. A program that interacts with such a database, which may reside on an entirely different computer, or "server," on the bank's network, is called a *client-server* application. Client-server applications exist in a wide variety of systems, including airline reservation systems, online textbook ordering systems, and inventory systems.

Returning to this example, we can now characterize the different events that can occur, together with how they should be handled (that is, the effect they should have on the state of the interaction).

> *Event:* User enters an account number (swipes her card).
> > *Handled by:* Program checks that account is a valid number, sets balance, and issues the message, "Choose a transaction."

> *Event:* User selects a button (deposit, withdrawal, etc.)
> > *Handled by:* Program checks to see that a valid account has been entered.
> > If so, save the type of button selected.
> > > If deposit or withdrawal, issue the message, "Enter an amount."
> > > If balance inquiry, display the balance.
> > > If no more transactions, clear the account.
> > If not, issue the message, "Enter an account number."

> *Event*: User enters an amount.
> > *Handled by:* Program checks that user has selected a deposit or withdrawal type.
> > If deposit, add the amount to the balance.
> > If withdrawal
> > > If balance is greater than amount, subtract amount from balance.
> > > Otherwise, issue the message, "Insufficient funds."
> > Otherwise, issue the message, "Select a transaction type (deposit or withdrawal)."

The key insight with this design is that the system does not anticipate the type of transaction or the order in which the events will occur. It responds to every different possibility and updates the state of the interaction appropriately.

10.7.2 Home Security System

Home security systems provide homeowners with a modest warning that an unwanted event, such as a break-in, fire, or flood, has occurred. These systems are programmed to react to sensors which can detect smoke, water, or motion and are placed strategically around the house. They can be programmed by homeowners so that their own motion about the house is not taken as an unwanted break-in. They also can be connected to the local fire and police stations so that notification of an unwanted event can receive immediate response.

The overall design for such a system is sketched in Figure 10.27.

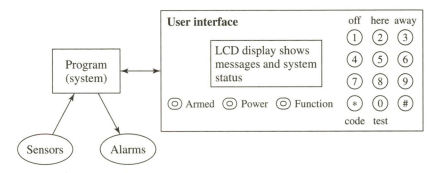

| **Figure 10.27   Overall Design of a Home Security System**

Here, sensors and the user interface supply events to the program, while alarms and the user interface receive responses from the program. Responses at the user interface are displayed on an LCD display. Since this system must be able to receive handle events in parallel (e.g., signals from two different sensors may occur simultaneously), the program must embody both the event-driven paradigm as discussed in this chapter and the concurrent programming paradigm (to be discussed in Chapter 11). We ignore the concurrent programming dimensions of this problem in the current discussion.

The state variables for this program are several:

- The user's password—password.
- The state of the user (here or away)—user.
- The state of the system (armed or unarmed)—armed.
- The state of each sensor (active or inactive)—sensors.
- The state of each alarm (active or inactive)—alarms.
- A message from the system to the control panel—message.

We have dramatically generalized this description in order to simplify the discussion and focus on the main ideas about event-driven programming that this problem evokes. In any case, here are some of the events that can reasonably occur, with a sketch of what should happen to the state in response to each event.

Event: User enters password.
> *Handled by:* Program checks that password is valid and displays message.

Event: User enters function "away."
> *Handled by:* Program checks password has been entered and changes the state of all sensors to "active," the state of the system to "armed," and displays message.

Event: Sensor receives signal.
> *Handled by:* If system is armed, program sends appropriate alarm and displays a message.

Event: User enters function "test."
> *Handled by:* Program disarms system.

Event: User enters function "here."
> *Handled by:* Program disables motion-detection sensors, enables all others, and changes state of the system to "armed."

EXERCISES

10.1 The TextArea variable happens to be scrollable, so that all actions in a run of this program can be echoed without a loss of information. How can you refine the interaction in Section 10.5 so that this happens? (Hint: replace the `setText` method with the string concatenation method `append` to affix a new message onto the tail end of an existing one.)

10.2 Augment the simple event-driven interaction given in Section 10.5 so that the menu of choices includes lines and ovals, in addition to rectangles and messages.

10.3 Consider augmenting this program again so that it has an erase function. Discuss the difference between erasing the most recently drawn shape on the screen and erasing objects in the reverse order in which they were drawn. What changes in the definition of the state of the program are needed to accomplish this more ambitious latter goal?

10.4 Considering the `Grid` variable g declared in this chapter, give a series of method calls that will achieve the following display of g.

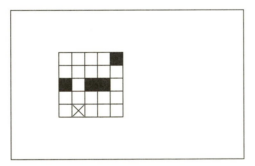

10.5 Consider the following tic-tac-toe board configuration.

Describe the sequence of events that should occur for this to be achieved, starting with an empty board. For each event, identify the handler that is called and the change that occurs among the state variables that are affected by that event.

10.6 Complete the tic-tac-toe event-driven program discussed in this chapter by:
(a) Writing a method `gameOver` that returns *true* or *false* depending on whether or not the game is over (that is, one player has won or the board is full).

(b) Altering the `mouseClicked` handler to take into account whether or not the game is over before accepting the next player's move and reporting that outcome in the TextArea (in the event that the game is really over).

10.7 Think of a strategy by which your program can support either a 2-player or a 1-player tic-tac-toe game. If the user chooses the one-player option (from, say, a menu), the program should assume the role of Player X and play a competitive game against the user—that is, Player X should never lose. (Do this part only after you have completed the previous question.)

10.8 Implement the Nim event-driven program by declaring the state variables and implementing the `init`, `mouseClicked`, `actionPerformed`, and `gameOver` methods.

10.9 (Hard) Think of a strategy by which your Nim program assumes the role of Player 1 and plays a competitive game of Nim. You may want to research this problem before beginning to write the code. (Do this problem only after you have completed the previous question.)

10.10 The game Connect-4 has two players who alternately place X's and O's on an 8 × 8 grid, like the one shown below.

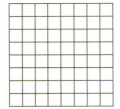

However, each move must be made at the bottom-most empty square of a column. The winner is the player who places four of her tokens (X or O) in a row, either horizontally, vertically, or diagonally. Design an event-driven interaction for this game. In doing this, start by designing the state variables, the objects in the frame, and finally the event-handlers that are required to effectively monitor the play of the game. Be sure to have a method that determines when the game is over (a player has placed four tokens in a row, or else the board has become full).

10.11 (Team project) Consider designing an event-driven interaction that demonstrates population growth. This interaction demonstrates a model of population growth and decay called the "Game of Life," which was designed by John Conway in 1970. It uses a grid to display a population of individuals in a single generation, such as the 8 × 8 grid shown below.

A square is filled in on the grid to indicate a living individual, and is left empty to indicate the absence of a living individual. Each square on the grid has up to eight immediate "neighbors," one on each side and one on each diagonal. For example, the eight neighbors of the cell at position (2, 3)—that is, row 2 and column 3—are the cells at positions (1, 2), (1, 3), (1, 4), (2, 2), (2, 4), (3, 2), (3, 3), and (3, 4).

The interaction tracks what happens to the grid from one generation to the next, over a series of generations. We start with an initial generation, such as the one shown above. To predict which cells will be living in the next generation, the following rules apply to each cell:

Survival. An individual survives into the next generation if it has two or three living neighbors in the current generation.

Birth. An individual is born in the next generation if (a) its cell is empty in the current generation, and (b) its cell has exactly three living neighbors in the current generation.

Death by loneliness. An individual dies in the next generation if it has fewer than two living neighbors in the current generation.

Death by overcrowding. An individual dies in the next generation if it has four or more living neighbors in the current generation.

The grid below shows the result of applying these four rules to each of the cells in the grid above.

As you can see, various cells have survived [e.g., the one in position (1, 1)], been born [e.g., the one in position (1, 0)], died of loneliness [e.g., the one in position (3, 5)], or died of overcrowding [e.g., the one in position (5, 4)]. Other cells have remained unoccupied from the first generation to the second.

Repeating this process over a series of generations gives some interesting patterns of population growth and decay. For instance, the pattern in the upper left-hand corner of the grid will repeat itself over a series of generations, while the one in the lower left-hand corner will completely disappear after the second generation. The pattern in the middle of the screen will change its shape and position in an interesting way across a series of generations.

To visualize these population changes, your interaction should provide two grids side-by-side on the board, and then ask the user to define the first generation by clicking on a series of squares in the left-hand grid. Completion of that activity may be signaled by the user clicking outside the grid, or perhaps selecting a different alternative in a Choice menu on the screen. Next, the user should be able to ask the program to compute and display the second generation on the right-hand grid, the third generation on the left-hand grid, the fourth on the right, and so on. The end of the simulation occurs with one of the following states:

1. The entire grid becomes empty (the whole generation has died);
2. Two successive generations are identical in their populations; or
3. The user selects a button that stops the simulation.

The user should also have the opportunity to start a new simulation; in this event, the program should clear both grids and allow the user to start a new game by selecting a different initial configuration in the left-hand grid.

10.12 Do some research on the Web and learn about the programming of a real home security alarm system. What programming language is used in implementing this system? How is the event-driven paradigm used in the program that drives this system?

Concurrent Programming

"Two roads diverged in a yellow wood,
And sorry I could not travel both ..."
Robert Frost, The Road Not Taken

CHAPTER OUTLINE

In Chapter 7 we saw that a good way to think of an object-oriented program is as a collection of interacting objects that communicate via *message passing*. In effect, each object can be thought of as a separate machine consisting of both data and operations on that data. Multiple objects can be instances of the same class; in this case, although the operations are the same, the data is distinct. Using a stack class as an example, the program can contain multiple instances of stacks, each with its own collection of data.

In this chapter we take that model one step further. In the object-oriented paradigm, at most one machine can be executing at a time. With the introduction of concurrent threads, or processes, it is possible for each object to be executing simultaneously, awaiting messages and responding appropriately. However, as we shall see, there are good reasons for limiting the number of threads.

As always, the major reason for investigating concurrent programming is that it provides a distinct way of conceptualizing the solution to a problem. A second reason is to take advantage of parallelism in the underlying hardware to achieve a significant speedup.

A good example of a concurrent program is the modern web browser. An example of concurrency in a web browser occurs when the browser begins to render a page, even though it may still be downloading various image or graphics files. The page being rendered is a shared resource which must be cooperatively managed among the various threads involved in downloading all aspects of a page. The various threads cannot all write to the screen simultaneously, especially if the image or graphic downloaded causes the space allocated for the display of the image to be resized, thus affecting the text layout. While doing all this, various buttons are still active and can be clicked, particularly the Stop button.

In this chapter we look at the use of threads cooperating to accomplish a task such as web page rendering. We will see that threads, or processes, must at times have exclusive access to a shared resource, such as the display, to prevent themselves from interfering with one another.

11.1 CONCEPTS

Conceptually, a sequential program specifies the execution of a sequence of statements that comprise the program. A *process* is a program in execution. As such, each process has its own state independent of the state of any other process or program, including operating system processes. A process also has attached resources, such as files, memory, and so on. Part of the state of a process includes not only memory, as we have seen in Chapters 3–5, but also the location of the current instruction being executed. Such an extended state is termed an *execution context*.

A *concurrent program* is a program designed to have two or more execution contexts. Such a program is said to be *multithreaded,* since it has more than one execution context. A *parallel program* is a concurrent program in which more than one execution context, or thread, is active simultaneously. From a semantic point of view, there is no difference between a concurrent program and a parallel one.

A *distributed program* is a system of programs designed to be executed simultaneously on a network of autonomous processors that do not share main memory, with each program on its own separate processor.

In a multiprocessing operating system the same program can be executed by multiple processes, each resulting in its own state or execution context, separate from the other processes. An example would be the editing of documents or program files, with each instance of the editor having been invoked separately and running in its own window. This is distinctly different from a multithreaded program in which some of the data resides simultaneously in each execution context.

Thus the term *concurrency* is a generic one used to denote a single program in which more than one execution context can be active simultaneously. The programs we have seen until now have had a single execution context, and thus are called *single-threaded*. A program with multiple execution contexts is called *multi-threaded*. In a multi-threaded program, part of the program state is shared among the threads, while part of the state including the flow of control is unique to each thread.

Concurrent execution of a program can either occur using separate processors or be logically interleaved on a single processor using time slicing. Early computers often had a single main processor and several other smaller processors for doing input and output separately. Programs on these early machines were executed in batch mode, with each program being executed to completion before the next program was executed. Later, multiprogramming was introduced to increase efficiency; several programs would be loaded into memory and executed in an interleaved fashion, with a *scheduler* being used to quickly switch from one program to another. As the cost of computing decreased relative to the cost of labor, the concept of *interactive time-sharing* was introduced. This meant that two or more people could use keyboards and monitors to simultaneously communicate with a computer. The Unix operating system, of which Linux is a variant, was developed in the late 1960s to support time-shared operation on relatively inexpensive computers.

Originally, concurrent programming was used in early operating systems to support parallelism in the underlying hardware and to support multiprogramming and time-sharing. But for a long time, concurrent programming was felt to be too difficult and error prone to be used by ordinary applications. However, both our understanding of concurrent programming and the programming language methods we use to support it have evolved so that many modern applications are multithreaded. On computers with two or more processors, such applications can have each thread executed by a separate processor, thus achieving a significant speedup.

If two or more pieces of communicating software run concurrently, the result is a concurrent program when the pieces form a conceptual whole. Otherwise, the situation is viewed as two programs that might communicate through an agreed protocol such as a file system or network protocol. If the programs do communicate, then they form a concurrent system.

In both Java and Ada, separate threads are applied to functions or methods, rather than being at the operation or statement level. However, starting a thread is distinct from merely calling a function. First, the invoking thread does not wait for the new thread to complete, but immediately continues executing. Second, when the new thread terminates, control does not return to the invoking thread.

A thread can be found in any one of the following states:

1 Created: the thread has been created, but is not yet ready to run.
2 Runnable or ready: the thread is ready to run, but awaits getting a processor to run on.
3 Running: the thread is actually executing on a processor.
4 Blocked or waiting: the thread is either waiting on gaining access to a critical section or has voluntarily given up the processor.
5 Terminated: the thread has been stopped and will not execute again.

These states and the transitions between them are pictured in Figure 11.1.

In the next section we consider how threads communicate. As we shall see, this is a very important question.

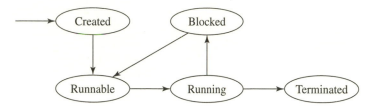

| **Figure 11.1** **States of a Thread**

11.2 COMMUNICATION

All concurrent programs involve interthread communication or interaction. This occurs for the following reasons:

1 Threads (and even processes) compete for exclusive access to shared resources, such as physical devices, files, or data.
2 Threads communicate to exchange data.

In both cases it is necessary for threads to synchronize their execution to avoid conflict when acquiring resources, or to make contact when exchanging data. A thread can communicate with other threads through:

1 Nonlocal shared variables: this is the primary mechanism used by Java, and it can also be used by Ada.
2 Message passing: this is the primary mechanism used by Ada.[1]
3 Parameters: this is used by Ada in conjunction with message passing.

Threads normally cooperate with one another to solve a problem. Thus, even in the simplest cases, communication between threads is essential. It is unusual for a thread not to communicate with other threads. However, it is highly desirable to keep communication between threads to a minimum; this makes the code easier to understand and allows each thread to run at its own speed, without being slowed down by the coordination of communication.

The fundamental problem in sharing access to a variable is termed a *race condition*. This occurs when the function computed by a program depends on the order in which operations occur. Consider, for example, two threads both trying to execute the statement:

```
c = c + 1;
```

On a single address machine, the sequence of instructions actually executed might look like:

```
1.  load   c
2.  add    1
3.  store  c
```

1. Ada uses an interthread communication mechanism known as a *rendezvous*. Design of this mechanism was heavily influenced by Hoare's work on Communicating Sequential Processes (CSP) [Hoare 1978; Hoare 1985]. CSP provides a theory of concurrency; there is currently ongoing work to support CSP style programming in Java.

Assume that each of the above instructions is atomic; that is, each instruction runs to completion without being stopped or interrupted. However, a thread can be stopped between any two instructions.

If the initial value of c is 0, then, depending on the order of instructions executed by the two threads, either of the final values 1 or 2 is possible. Imagine the following sequence of events: thread A executes instructions 1 and 2; next thread B executes 1 and 2; then thread A executes instruction 3; and finally thread B executes instruction 3:

	--- Thread A ---		--- Thread B ---		
	Next		Next		C
Executing	Instr	Register	Instr	Register	Memory
initial	1	?	1	?	0
A	2	0	1	?	0
A	3	1	1	?	0
B	3	1	2	0	0
B	3	1	3	1	0
A	4	1	3	1	1
B	4	1	4	1	1

As the number of threads trying to execute this code increases, the number of distinct answers varies between 1 and the number of threads.

A thread wishing to acquire a *shared resource* such as a file or shared variable must first acquire access to the resource; that is, obtain permission to access it. When the resource is no longer required, the resource is released and the thread relinquishes its access rights.

In the presence of such nondeterminism, faults in a concurrent program may appear as *transient errors*. The error may or may not occur, even for the same data, depending on the execution paths of the various threads. Finding a transient error can be extremely difficult because the events that precede the occurrence of the fault may not be known precisely; unlike sequential programming, rerunning the same program on the same data may not reproduce the fault. Inserting debugging output may alter the behavior of the concurrent program so as to prevent the fault from occurring. Thus, a great skill in designing a concurrent program is the ability to express it in a form that guarantees correct program behavior in the presence of nondeterminism.

If a thread is unable to acquire a resource, its execution is normally suspended until the resource becomes available. Resource acquisition should normally be administered so that no thread is unduly delayed.

Code that accesses a shared variable or other resource is termed a *critical section*. For a thread to safely execute a critical section, there needs to be a locking mechanism such that it can test and set a lock as a single atomic instruction. Such a mechanism is used to ensure that only a single thread is executing a critical section at a time; this eliminates the race condition we saw earlier. In Section 11.4, we examine the use of such a mechanism, termed a *semaphore*.

First, however, we consider other design considerations, such as waiting for an event that will never happen.

11.3 **DEADLOCK AND UNFAIRNESS**

A thread is said to be in a state of *deadlock* if it is waiting for an event that will never happen. Deadlock normally involves several threads, each waiting for resources held by others. A deadlock can occur whenever two or more threads compete for resources; there are four necessary conditions for a deadlock to exist [Coffman 1971]:

1 Threads must claim exclusive rights to resources.
2 Threads must hold some resources while waiting for others; that is, they acquire resources piecemeal rather than all at once.
3 Resources may not be removed from waiting threads (no preemption).
4 A circular chain of threads exists in which each thread holds one or more resources required by the next thread in the chain.

Techniques for avoiding or recovering from deadlocks rely on negating at least one of these conditions. One of the best techniques, although largely impractical, for avoiding deadlock is the Banker's Algorithm [Dijkstra 1968]. Dijkstra has also posed a classic illustrative problem in this field, known as the Dining Philosophers problem [Dijkstra 1971]; this problem is given as an exercise.

A thread is said to be *indefinitely postponed* if it is delayed awaiting an event that may never occur. Such a situation can occur if the algorithm that allocates resources to requesting threads makes no allowance for the waiting time of a thread. Allocating resources on a first-in-first-out basis is a simple solution that eliminates indefinite postponement.

Analogous to indefinite postponement is the concept of *unfairness*. In such a case no attempt is made to ensure that threads of equal status make equal progress in acquiring resources. Fairness in a concurrent system should be considered at the design level. A simple fairness criterion is that when an open choice of action is to be made, any action should be equally likely. A neglect of fairness in designing a concurrent system may lead to indefinite postponement, thereby rendering the system incorrect.

11.4 **SEMAPHORES**

Semaphores were originally defined by Dijkstra [1968]. Basically, a semaphore is an integer variable and an associated thread queueing mechanism. Two atomic operations are defined on semaphores, P and V:

- P(s)—if s > 0 then set s = s - 1 else the thread that called P is blocked (enqueued).
- V(s)—if a thread T is blocked on the semaphore s, then wake up T, else set s = s + 1.

If the value of the semaphore only takes on the values 0 and 1, the semaphore is a *binary* semaphore. A semaphore that can take on arbitrary nonnegative values is termed a *counting semaphore*.

One use of a binary semaphore occurs when two tasks use semaphores to signal each other when there is work for the other to do; this process is sometimes termed *cooperative synchronization*. A classic example occurs in the case of producer-consumer cooperation, where the single producer task produces information for the single consumer task to consume. The producer thread waits (via a P) for the buffer to be empty, deposits information, then signals (via a V) that the buffer is full. The consumer thread waits (via a P) for the buffer to be full, then removes the information from the buffer, and signals (via a V) that the buffer is empty. Code for this example in Concurrent Pascal is given in Figure 11.2.

Figure 11.2 Simple Producer-Consumer Cooperation Using Semaphores

```
program SimpleProducerConsumer;
var buffer : string;
    full : semaphore = 0;
    empty : semaphore = 1;

procedure Producer;
var tmp : string
begin
    while (true) do begin
        produce(tmp);
        P(empty);  { begin critical section }
        buffer := tmp;
        V(full);   { end critical section }
    end;
end;

procedure Consumer;
var tmp : string
begin
    while (true) do begin
        P(full);   { begin critical section }
        tmp := buffer;
        V(empty);  { end critical section }
        consume(tmp);
    end;
end;

begin
    cobegin
        Producer; Consumer;
    coend;
end.
```

A more complicated case occurs when you have both multiple producers and multiple consumers sharing a buffer of finite size. In this case, it is insufficient, for example, for a producer to know that the buffer is not full. It must also lock out other producers while it is depositing information. The usual protocol for this is given in Figure 11.3, in which the producer first tests (via a P) that the buffer is not full and then locks the critical section (via another P on the lock semaphore). If the producer were to do the operations in the opposite order, it would produce a *deadlock,* a situation in which all threads would be blocked from running. Note that the nonfull, nonempty semaphores are general counting semaphores, while the lock semaphore is a binary semaphore.

Figure 11.3 Multiple Producers-Consumers

```
program ProducerConsumer;
const size = 5;
var buffer : array[1..size] of string;
    in      : integer = 0;
    out     : integer = 0;
    lock    : semaphore = 1;
    nonfull : semaphore = size;
    nonempty : semaphore = 0;

procedure Producer;
var tmp : string
begin
    while (true) do begin
        produce(tmp);
        P(nonfull);
        P(lock);    { begin critical section }
        in := in mod size + 1;
        buffer[in] := tmp;
        V(lock);    { end critical section }
        V(nonempty);
    end;
end;

procedure Consumer;
var tmp : string
begin
    while (true) do begin
        P(nonempty);
        P(lock);    { begin critical section }
        out = out mod size + 1;
        tmp := buffer[out];
        V(lock);    { end critical section }
        V(nonfull);
        consume(tmp);
    end;
end;
```

The producer first produces information locally. Then it ensures that the buffer is not full by doing a P operation on the nonfull semaphore; if the buffer is not full, one or more producers will continue. Next the producer needs exclusive access to the shared-buffer variables. To gain this access the producer performs a P operation on the binary lock semaphore. Getting past this point ensures exclusive access to the various shared-buffer variables. The producer deposits its information and exits the critical section by performing a V operation on the lock semaphore. Finally, the producer signals the consumer threads that the buffer is not empty via a V operation on the nonempty semaphore. The code for the consumer is similar.

While the semaphore is an elegant, low-level mechanism for synchronization control, you would not want to build a large, multitasking system, such as an operating system, using semaphores. This results from the fact that omission of a single P or V operation could bring on catastrophe. In Section 11.5 we consider a higher level mechanism.

11.5 MONITORS

Monitors [Hoare 1974] provide the basis for synchronization in Java. The concept of a monitor is based on the monitor or kernel of early operating systems, which were used as a method of communication between operating system threads. These early monitors ran in privileged mode and were uninterruptible.

The monitor proposed by Hoare is a decentralized version of early operating system monitors. Its purpose is to encapsulate a shared variable and operations on the variable. This encapsulation is combined with an automatic locking mechanism on the operations so that at most one thread can be executing an operation at one time.

A bounded buffer example given as a monitor is presented in Figure 11.4. The critical section lock of the semaphore version is provided automatically by the monitor on

**Figure 11.4
Producer-Consumer
Monitor**

```
monitor Buffer;
const size = 5;
var buffer : array[1..size] of string;
    in      : integer = 0;
    out     : integer = 0;
    count   : integer = 0;
    nonfull : condition;
    nonempty : condition;

procedure put(s : string);
begin
    if (count = size) then
        wait(nonfull);
    in := in mod size + 1;
    buffer[in] := tmp;
    count := count + 1;
    V(nonempty);
end;

function get : string;
var tmp : string
begin
    if (count = 0) then
        wait(nonempty);
    out = out mod size + 1;
    tmp := buffer[out];
    count := count - 1;
    signal(nonfull);
    get := tmp;
end;
end;
```

each function or procedure. This means that a producer has to attempt a `put` operation before it can determine whether or not there is space in the buffer. In this case, after entering the `put` procedure, a producer must check the value of the variable `count` which keeps track of the number of portions of the buffer in use. If the buffer is full, then the producer thread waits on the condition `nonfull`. Thus, the previous general counting semaphore is now an integer variable and a condition. The changes to the function `get` are similar. Note that when a thread is forced to wait on a condition, the lock on the monitor is released.

The actual code for the producer and consumer threads is not given in Figure 11.4, only the operations used that are associated with the shared buffer. Monitors and semaphores are equivalent mechanisms in power in that you can implement a monitor using semaphores [Hoare 1974] and implement a semaphore using a monitor [Ben-Ari 1982].

Before examining this example in Java (Section 11.9), we first describe the process of creating and starting a thread in Java.

11.6 JAVA THREADS

Recall from Section 11.1 that a thread can be in one of five states: created, runnable, running, blocked, or terminated. In this section and the next one, we discuss how a thread makes transitions from one state to another, largely ignoring the transition from the runnable state to running, since this is handled by the underlying Java virtual machine.

In Java, as with everything else, a thread is a class. So the simplest way to create a thread is to create a class that inherits from the `Thread` class:

```
public class MyThread extends Thread {
   public MyThread( ) { ... }
   ...
}
```

and do a *new* operation to create an instance of a `Thread`:

```
Thread thread = new MyThread( );
```

To make a created thread runnable, you merely invoke its `start` method:

```
thread.start( );
```

After some overhead, the newly runnable thread has control transferred to its `run` method. Each class that extends the `Thread` class must provide its own `run` method, but does not provide a `start` method, relying instead on the `start` method provided by the `Thread` class.

The `run` method of a thread normally contains a loop, since exiting the `run` method terminates the thread. In a graphics animation, for example, the `run` method would repeatedly move the graphics objects, repaint the screen, and then sleep (to slow the animation down). Thus, a typical graphics animation might appear as:

```
public void run () {
    while (true) {
        moveObjects( );
        repaint( );
        try { Thread.sleep(50);
        } catch (InterruptedException exc) { }
    }
}
```

Note that the method `sleep` potentially throws an `InterruptedException`, which must be caught in a `try-catch` statement.

Calling the `sleep` method moves the thread from the running state to a blocked state, where the thread awaits an interval timer interrupt. Sleeping is often done in visual applications to prevent the visualization from proceeding too quickly. Other forms of blocking involving access to shared variables are discussed in Section 11.7.

The only state remaining to be discussed is the terminated state. One way to achieve a terminated state, already noted, is merely to have the thread exit its `run` method, which after some cleanup delay will terminate the thread. Prior to Java 1.2, you could also terminate a thread by calling its `stop` method; however, for complicated reasons this turned out to be problematic and the `stop` method in the class `Thread` was deprecated in Java 1.2. A simpler way to accomplish the same goal is merely to set a boolean which is used by the thread's `run` method to continue looping; for example:

```
public void run () {
    while (continue) {
        moveObjects( );
        repaint( );
        try { Thread.sleep(50);
        } catch (InterruptedException exc) { }
    }
}
```

To stop the above thread, another thread merely calls a method to set the value of the instance variable `continue` to *false*. Such a variable is not regarded as shared and any potential race condition can safely be ignored, since at worst it merely causes an extra iteration of the loop.

Sometimes it is inconvenient to subclass the `Thread` class; for example, you may want your applet class to be a separate thread. In such cases, a class merely has to implement the `Runnable` interface; that is, implement a `run` method. The outline of such a class is:

```
public class MyClass extends SomeClass implements Runnable {
    ...
    public void run( ) { ... }
}
```

Making an instance of `MyClass` into a thread is accomplished using:

```
MyClass obj = new MyClass();
Thread thread = new Thread(obj);
thread.start( );
```

Here again we see an instance where Java's use of interfaces obviates the need for multiple inheritance.

Figure 11.5 summarizes the states of a Java Thread and the transitions between them.

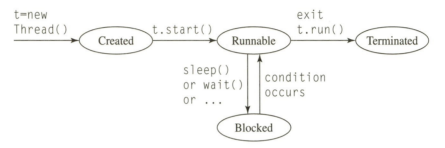

I Figure 11.5 **States of a Java Thread**

In Section 11.7 we consider the issue of shared variables in Java using synchronization.

11.7 SYNCHRONIZATION IN JAVA

Basically, Java implements the monitor concept fairly closely by associating a lock with each object. To implement a shared variable, you create a shared variable class and denote each method (other than the constructor) as synchronized:

```
public class SharedVariable ... {
    public SharedVariable (...) { ... }

    public synchronized ... method1 (...) { ... }
    public synchronized ... method2 (...) { ... }
    ...
}
```

To actually share a variable, you have to create an instance of the class and make it accessible to the separate threads. One way of accomplishing this would be to pass the shared object as a parameter to the constructor for each thread. In the case of a producer-consumer shared variable, this might appear as:

```
SharedVariable shared = new SharedVariable( );
Thread producer = new Producer(shared);
Thread consumer = new Consumer(shared);
```

where it is assumed that both `Producer` and `Consumer` extend `Thread`. The complete bounded buffer example is done in Java in Section 11.9.

However, we first present a simple animation example using a thread without synchronization.

11.8   **EXAMPLE: BOUNCING BALLS**

In this example, we consider the simple case of using a thread to run an animation. The problem is to animate one or more balls bouncing around a window. When a ball reaches the edge of a window, it reverses direction; however, no attempt is made to be physically realistic.

Initially, we construct two classes, one which encapsulates the ball and the other the application itself. Let us consider the class `Ball` first.

What information must be kept about a ball in motion? If a ball is painted on the screen as a circle, then we should know:

- Its location, as an (x, y) coordinate pair within the animation window or frame.
- Its direction and velocity (*delta*), as a change in the (x, y) coordinates (dx, dy).
- Its size, as a diameter in pixels.
- Its color (to make the animation more fun).

Other than a constructor, two methods are provided:

- A `move` method, which moves the ball one step (*delta*). If the ball collides with the edge of the window frame, then its direction is reversed.
- A `paint` method, which draws the ball on the screen.

The constructor is passed only the initial position of the ball on the screen. The velocity and direction of motion and color are chosen as simple pseudo-random functions of these coordinates. The diameter is fixed; all balls are the same size. The complete code for the ball class is given in Figure 11.6.

Construction of an initial version of the application class, called `BouncingBalls`, is equally simple. Recall from Chapter 10 that a graphical application class should inherit from the class `Applet`. In this initial version, two methods are provided:

- The `init` method, which does some housekeeping by setting the width and height of the frame and places a single ball in the frame.
- A `paint` method, which asks the ball to paint itself, in typical object-oriented fashion.

This simple, unanimated version is shown in Figure 11.7.

Two problems remain: adding motion and adding more balls. There are a variety of ways to add more balls to the screen. One can randomly generate balls at random coordinates. An equally simple, and more fun, alternative is to insert a ball using a mouse click. However additional balls are added, each ball has to be recorded and the `paint` method revised to ask each ball to paint itself. A solution is to insert each ball into a `Vector`.

The standard way of adding motion to computer graphics is to use a thread. One approach is to make each ball a separate thread whose `run` method moves and paints the ball. However, to make the move visible on the screen, the ball must call the application's

```java
import java.awt.*;

public class Ball {

    int x, y;
    int dx, dy;
    int diameter = 10;
    Color color = Color.red;

    public Ball (int ix, int iy) {
        x = ix;
        y = iy;
        color = new Color(x % 256, y % 256, (x+y) % 256);
        dx = x % 10 + 1;
        dy = y % 10 + 1;
    }
    public void move ( ) {
        x += dx;
        y += dy;
        if (x < 0 || x >= BouncingBalls.width)
          dx = - dx;
        if (y < 0 || y >= BouncingBalls.height)
          dy = - dy;
    }

    public void paint (Graphics g) {
        g.setColor(color);
        g.fillOval(x, y, diameter, diameter);
    }
} // Ball
```

| Figure 11.6   Ball Class

```java
import java.awt.*;
import java.applet.*;

public class BouncingBalls extends Applet {

    public static int width;
    public static int height;

    Ball ball = new Ball(128, 127);

    public void init ( ) {
        width = getBounds().width;
        height = getBounds().height;
    } // init

    public void paint(Graphics g) { ball.paint(g); }
} // BouncingBalls
```

| Figure 11.7   Initial Application Class

repaint method. Upon reflection it seems excessive to require a repaint of the entire application after the movement of each ball.

A better approach is to have a thread class whose `run` method moves each ball one step and only then repaints the screen. This class is an inner class to the application itself. In order to make the movement of the balls more visible on a fast processor, the thread sleeps after each repaint.

The expanded set of instance variables and associated init method for this revised bouncing balls applet is given in Figure 11.8.

Figure 11.8 Final Bouncing Balls init Method

```
public int width;
public int height;
private Vector balls = new Vector();

public void init ( ) {
    height = getBounds().height;
    width = getBounds().width;
    addMouseListener(new MouseHandler());
    Ball b = new Ball(128, 127);
    balls.addElement(b);
    Thread t = new BallThread();
    t.start( );
} // init
```

Since the balls are now all in a vector, the `paint` method (shown in Figure 11.9) must be revised. Instead of merely painting a single ball, we must iterate over all the objects in the vector `balls`, asking each ball to paint itself.

Figure 11.9 Final Bouncing Balls paint Method

```
public void paint(Graphics g) {
    Enumeration e = balls.elements();
    while (e.hasMoreElements()) {
        Ball b = (Ball)(e.nextElement());
        b.paint(g);
    }
}
```

The application class also contains a `MouseHandler` inner class (shown in Figure 11.10) whose `mousePressed` method is invoked when a mouse click is detected. This method creates a new ball at the (x, y) coordinates of the click and inserts the ball into the vector.

```
private class MouseHandler extends MouseAdapter {
    public void mousePressed(MouseEvent e) {
        balls.addElement(new Ball(e.getX(), e.getY()));
    }  // mousePressed
} // MouseHandler
```

Figure 11.10 Bouncing Balls Mouse Handler

Finally, the `BallThread` class is shown in Figure 11.11. This class consists of only a run method, which loops forever. On each iteration of the loop, each ball is moved, the entire frame repainted, and then the thread sleeps (to slow down the animation).

```
private class BallThread extends Thread {
    public void run( ) {
        while (true) {
            Enumeration e = balls.elements();
            while (e.hasMoreElements()) {
                Ball b = (Ball)(e.nextElement());
                b.move();
            }
            repaint( );
            try { Thread.sleep(50);
            } catch (InterruptedException exc) { }
        }
    }
}
```

| Figure 11.11   Bouncing Balls Thread

An observant reader of the material earlier in this chapter should be concerned about possible race conditions. In this simple application a race condition is unlikely to occur but may, depending on the implementation of the class `Vector`. It is theoretically possible that the implementation of Vector's `addElement` method creates an empty element in the vector and then inserts the appropriate information into the element. A check of the Java API for the class `Vector` shows that the `addElement` method is synchronized, thus locking the object from access by another thread (e.g., the thread that calls `paint`).

Several additional imports must now be added to the header of this class:

```
import java.awt.*;
import java.awt.event.*;
import java.applet.*;
import java.util.*;

public class BouncingBalls extends Applet {
    ...
```

A variety of possible modifications to this class are given as exercises.

11.9 EXAMPLE: BOUNDED BUFFER

In this section we revisit the bounded buffer example, only this time in Java. Recall that we have at least two threads, a producer and a consumer. However, our solution will accommodate multiple producers and multiple consumers.

Recall from Section 11.5 that the producer and consumer communicate via a shared buffer of finite size. The buffer is effectively placed inside a monitor by declaring each of its public methods as synchronized. In this case Java creates a lock associated with each instance or object of the Buffer class; only a single thread is allowed to be executing any synchronized method for a given object.

Both the producer and the consumer access the buffer in a circular fashion. The producer deposits information (in this example, date strings) using a put method, while the consumer removes information via a get method.

In the monitor version, after entry into the method, the producer may have to wait (relinquish the monitor) on the condition nonfull, while the consumer may have to wait on the condition nonempty. In both cases, after depositing/receiving information the producer/consumer has to signal the other. Java provides for both waiting (method wait()) and signaling (method notify()), but not on a specific condition. A notify() signals a waiting thread, which can be either a producer or a consumer. Thus, the simple if statements of the monitor solution become while loops in Java. Otherwise the code for the Buffer class given in Figure 11.12 mimics the monitor solution fairly closely.

```java
class Buffer {
    private String[] buffer;
    private int in = -1;
    private int out = -1;
    private int count = 0;

    public Buffer(int size) { buffer = new String[size]; }

    public synchronized void put(String s) {
        while (count >= buffer.length)
            try{ wait(); } catch(InterruptedException e) { };
        count++;
        buffer[++in % buffer.length] = s;
        notify();
    }

    public synchronized String get() {
        while (count == 0)
            try{ wait(); } catch(InterruptedException e) { };
        count--;
        String s = buffer[++out % buffer.length];
        notify();
        return s;
    }
} // Buffer
```

| Figure 11.12 Buffer Class

The producer and consumer are quite similar in construction. Both classes are subclasses of Thread, and take three arguments: an instance of the shared buffer, an integer telling the thread how long to sleep, and an iteration limit. Each class consists of only a constructor and a `run` method which are given in Figure 11.13 and Figure 11.14, respectively.

Figure 11.13
Producer Class

```
import java.util.Date;

public class Producer extends Thread {
    private Buffer buffer;
    private int millisecs;
    private int iterations;

    public Producer(Buffer b, int s, int n) {
        super(); buffer = b;
        millisecs = s; iterations = n;
    }

    public void run() {
        try {
            for (int i = 0; i<iterations; i++) {
                buffer.put(new Date().toString());
                Thread.sleep(millisecs);
            }
        } catch(InterruptedException e) { };
    }
} // Producer
```

Figure 11.14
Consumer Class

```
public class Consumer extends Thread {
    private Buffer buffer;
    private int millisecs;
    private int iterations;

    public Consumer(Buffer b, int s, int n) {
        super(); buffer = b;
        millisecs = s; iterations = n;
    }

    public void run() {
        try {
            for (int i = 0; i<iterations; i++) {
                System.out.println(buffer.get());
                Thread.sleep(millisecs);
            }
        } catch(InterruptedException e) { };
    }
} // Consumer
```

The main application (see Figure 11.15) is quite simple. It first constructs a buffer, then a producer and a consumer. The buffer is passed as an argument to the two threads, together with a time in milliseconds and an iteration count. In this example, the producer is set to produce a time stamp every second, but the consumer consumes the message only every three seconds. Because the buffer is finite in size, eventually the producer is slowed down to the rate of the consumer.

```
public class BoundedBuffer {

    public static void main(String[] arg) {
        Buffer buffer = new Buffer(5);
        Producer producer = new Producer(buffer, 1000, 20);
        producer.start();
        Consumer consumer = new Consumer(buffer, 3000, 20);
        consumer.start();
    }
} // BoundedBuffer
```

| **Figure 11.15 Bounded Buffer Class**

11.10 EXAMPLE: SIEVE OF ERATOSTHENES

An area of increasing importance in concurrent/parallel programming is scientific computing. The idea is to take numerical algorithms and reformulate them so that portions of the problem can be solved in parallel. The advent of inexpensive but powerful workstations has made this approach very appealing to solve such "grand challenge" problems as structural analysis of aircraft, fluid dynamics, weather modeling, and so on.

In this example we compute all the prime numbers less than a given input using the *Sieve of Eratosthenes*. Using sets, the abstract sequential algorithm works as follows:

```
Set s = {2..N}; // initialize s to all numbers from 2 to N
while (|s| > 0) { // s is not empty
  int p = x in s  // x is the minimum value in s;
  print(p); // p is prime
  for (int i = p; i <= N; i += p) // forall multiples of p
    s = s - {i}; // delete multiple from s
}
```

We initialize a set s to all the integers from 2 to N (our input value). Then while the set s is not empty, we first select the minimum value of s and call it p. The value p must be prime, so we output it. Then we remove from the set s all multiples of p, including p itself.

In converting this sequential algorithm to a concurrent one, we first note that the filtering of multiples of a given prime from the set can be done concurrently. Second, we note that the set itself can be implicit rather than explicit. That is each filter can pass whatever numbers are not eliminated from the set via a buffer to the next filter. Provided that the numbers are kept in numerical order, the first number sent to each concurrent thread must have passed all the previous filters and must be prime.

Our solution to the Sieve of Eratosthenes as a concurrent program appears in Figure 11.16.[2]

Figure 11.16 Sieve of Eratosthenes

```
class Sieve implements Runnable {
  Buffer in;

  public Sieve(Buffer b) { in = b; }

  public void run( ) {
    int p = in.get( );
    if (p < 0) return;
    System.out.println(p);
    Buffer out = new Buffer(5);
    Thread t = new Thread(new Sieve(out));
    t.start();
    while (true) {
      int num = in.get();
      if (num < 0) {
        out.put(num);
        return;
      }
      if (num % p != 0)
        out.put(num);
    }
  }
}
```

In this solution the end of the sequence of numbers is marked with a negative number, say −1. All communication is through a Buffer object that we adapted from Figure 11.12 to accommodate integers rather than strings. The first number received through the input buffer is checked to see if it is less than 0; if so, the sequence is now empty and the process of filtering should cease.

Otherwise the number is remembered in the variable p; as noted earlier, p must be prime so it is printed. An output buffer is created and passed to a new Sieve, started as a thread; hereafter, all communication to the thread started is through the output buffer.

Then we repeatedly get another number out of the input buffer. If the number is less than 0, then it marks the end of the sequence. In this case, the end marker is copied to the output buffer, and the thread terminates itself by exiting its run method. Otherwise the number is checked to see if it is a multiple of p; if it is not a multiple, then the number is passed through the sieve via the output buffer.

All that remains is to create a test driver (see Figure 11.17). In this test driver, the input number N is obtained from the command line. Then a buffer is created and passed to a sieve filter started as a thread. Then all the numbers from 2 to N are passed to the sieve filter via the buffer. Finally, the end of the number sequence is indicated by passing a negative one through the buffer.

---

2. Dershem and Jipping [1990, p. 210] present a solution to this problem in Ada.

```
public static void main (String[] arg) {
  if (arg.length < 1) {
    System.out.println("Usage: java Sieve number");
    System.exit(1);
  }
  try {
    int N = Integer.parseInt(arg[0]);
    Buffer out = new Buffer(5);
    Thread t = new Thread(new Sieve(out));
    t.start();
    for (int i = 2; i <= N; i++)
      out.put(i);
    out.put(-1);
  } (catch NumberFormatException e) {
    System.out.println("Illegal number: " + arg[0]);
    System.exit(1);
  }
}
```

| Figure 11.17   Test Driver for Sieve of Eratosthenes

As with our previous concurrent programs, this one assumes a shared memory through which the threads communicate. Without multiple processors, this program would run slower than the sequential version. With some effort, this program could be converted into a distributed program. In this case, the buffer would need to be replaced by a network socket, and the code that starts a new thread would be replaced by code that obtains a network address of a waiting process. In the case of a distributed program, there is also the problem of reassembling the output into a coherent whole. However, the basic strategy of the program would remain intact.

EXERCISES

11.1   Use [Hoare 1974] to convert the bounded buffer monitor to a semaphore solution; you may ignore conditions.

11.2   Add semaphores as needed to the solution of Exercise 11.1 to implement conditions.

11.3   Consider the bouncing balls example. Make it more realistic by making the following modifications:
   (a) Change the ball's move method so that a ball reverses direction as soon as it touches the window frame.
   (b) Make the *reverse direction* more physically realistic (e.g., add gravity).
   (c) Make the *delta* and color of a ball more truly random by using the low order bits of the time of day clock.
   (d) Try removing the vector of balls, making each ball a Component. Can you now merely *add* each ball into the frame? Speculate as to what is truly happening based on other examples.
   (e) Modify the example so that it can be run either as an application or as an applet.

11.4 In the bouncing balls example, remove the `BallThread`, and instead have the application implement the `Runnable` interface. Adjust the rest of the application as needed. Which is better?

11.5 Modify the bouncing balls example to use an array of size 5 instead of a `Vector`. Without any other changes, can you introduce a race condition? Demonstrate it.

11.6 Modify the bouncing balls example so that it will run either as an application or as an applet.

11.7 The bouncing balls applet is not well behaved in the sense that the animation continues to run, even when the browser is iconified or moves away from the page. Fix this problem by adding `start` and `stop` methods to the applet; in the former invoke the thread's `start` method. In the applet's `stop` method, use the ideas outlined in Section 11.6 to stop the thread. Have the applet's `start` and `stop` methods write the number of balls started/stopped (i.e., the size of the vector) to `System.out`.

11.8 Compile and run the bounded buffer example of Section 11.9. How many messages does it take before the producer slows down to the speed of the consumer?

11.9 Add a second producer and a second consumer to the bounded buffer example using the same parameters. Modify the messages so that it is clear which producer produced the date message, and which consumer is printing it. How many messages does it take before the producer slows down to the speed of the consumer?

11.10 In the multiple producer-consumer bounded buffer of Exercise 11.9, modify the code for the `put` method replacing the `while` with an `if`. Does this produce a race condition? Are you able to show it with experiments?

11.11 Modify the parameters of one of the consumers of Exercise 11.9 so that it only sleeps for two seconds and repeat the experiment.

11.12 Modify the stopping condition for the consumers of Exercise 11.9 so that each stops when there are no more messages. Can a race condition occur? Explain. If a race condition can occur, run the experiment 50 times to see if it actually ever occurs.

11.13 Modify the Sieve of Eratosthenes example so that all printing is done by a printserver; that is, a thread that loops through a buffer accepting prime numbers and printing them. Like the other threads, it should terminate when it receives a negative number.

11.14 (Dining Philosopher's Problem [Dijkstra 1971]) Five philosophers wish to philosophize together. They each go through alternating periods of philosophizing and eating. Five bowls and five forks are arranged around a circular table, with each philosopher having her own place at the table. In the center is a large bowl of spaghetti, which is continually replenished. To eat, each philosopher needs both the fork on her left and the fork on her right. A fork may be used by only one philosopher at a time. The problem is to coordinate the use of the forks so that no philosopher dies of starvation.

This problem nicely exemplifies many problems and solutions found in concurrent programming. Deadlock can easily occur if each philosopher takes her left fork and refuses to relinquish it until she has eaten. Starvation can occur if two philosophers conspire against a third. Exclusive access to a fork embodies the usual mutual exclusion/synchronization problem.

11.15 (The Sleepy Barber Problem [Dijkstra 1965]) A barbershop consists of a waiting room with n chairs and a barber room containing the barber chair. If there are no customers to be served, the barber goes to sleep. If a customer enters the barbershop and finds the barber asleep, he wakes him up. Write a program to coordinate the barber and the customers.

11.16 (Cigarette Smokers Problem [Patil 1971]) Consider a system with three smoker threads and one agent thread. Each smoker makes a cigarette and smokes it. To make a cigarette, three ingredients are needed: tobacco, paper, and matches. One of the smokers has tobacco, one has paper, and one has matches. The agent has an infinite supply of all three. The agent places two of the ingredients on the table. The smoker who has the third ingredient can then make and smoke a cigarette, signalling the agent upon completion. The agent then puts out two of the three ingredients, and the cycle repeats. Write a program to synchronize the agent and the smokers.

The notation used in this text is summarized below. Much of it comes from discrete mathematics and should be familiar. Some comes from formal language theory, and is more fully discussed in Chapters 2 and 3.

A.1 FUNCTIONS AND SETS

Functions define mappings between sets. *Sets* are collections of objects, often of the same type. Here is a summary of the functional and set notation used in this text.

Table A.1

Functional Notation

Notation	Meaning	Notes/Examples
$f: X \to Y$ $f(x) = y$	Function f is a mapping between sets X and Y, called the *domain* and *range* of f, in which every element $x \in X$ has a corresponding element $y \in Y$ such that $y = f(x)$.	$Square: I \to N$ $Square(x) = x^2$ $M : Program \to \Sigma$ $M(p) = M(p.body, \varnothing)$
S^*	The function that maps characters from the set S to strings of those characters. (ε denotes the empty string.)	$\{a, b\}^* = \{\varepsilon, a, b, aa, ab, \ldots\}$

Table A.2

Set Notation

Notation	Meaning	Notes/Examples
$\varnothing$	The empty set.	$\varnothing$ is sometimes written as { }.
$\{e_1, e_2, \ldots, e_n\}$	The set whose elements are $e_1, e_2, \ldots,$ and e_n (and there are no duplicates).	$\{1, 3, 6, 7\}$ $\{(x, 1), (y, 6), (z, 7)\}$
$x \in S$	The element x is a member of the set S.	$3 \in \{1, 3, 6, 7\}$
$x \notin S$	x is not a member of S.	$4 \notin \{1, 3, 6, 7\}$
$S \subset T$	S is a subset of T; every element of S is an element of T.	$\{1, 6\} \subset (1, 3, 6, 7)$
$S = T$	Equivalence of S and T; they have the same elements.	$\{1, 6\} = (1, 6)$
$S \cup T$	Union of S and T: the set of all elements that are in S or T or both.	$\{1, 6\} \cup \{3, 6, 7\} = \{1, 3, 6, 7\}$

Continued

Table A.2

Continued

Notation	Meaning	Notes/Examples
$S \cap T$	Intersection of S and T: the set of all elements that are in both S and T.	$\{1, 6\} \cap \{3, 6, 7\} = \{6\}$
$S \times T$	Cross-product of S and T: all pairs of elements (s, t) for which $s \in S$ and $t \in T$.	$\{1, 6\} \times \{3, 6, 7\} = \begin{Bmatrix} (1, 3), (6, 3), \\ (1, 6), (6, 6), \\ (1, 7), (6, 7) \end{Bmatrix}$
$S - T$	Difference of S and T; if S and T are sets of pairs, all pairs whose first member is in S but not in T.	$\{\langle x, 1 \rangle, \langle y, 2 \rangle\} - \{\langle y, 9 \rangle, \langle w, 4 \rangle\}$ $= \{(x, 1)\}$
$S \otimes T$	Natural join of S and T; if S and T are sets of pairs, all pairs whose first member is in both S and T.	$\{\langle x, 1 \rangle, \langle y, 2 \rangle\} \otimes \{\langle y, 9 \rangle, \langle w, 4 \rangle\}$ $= \{\langle y, 2 \rangle, \langle y, 9 \rangle\}$
$S \overline{\cup} T$	Overriding union of S and T; equivalent to $(S - (S \otimes T)) \cup T$	$\{\langle x, 1 \rangle, \langle y, 2 \rangle\} \overline{\cup} \{\langle y, 9 \rangle, \langle w, 4 \rangle\}$ $= \{\langle x, 1 \rangle, \langle y, 9 \rangle, \langle w, 9 \rangle\}$
R	The real (decimal) numbers.	
I	The integers.	Abbreviates $\{ \dots, -2, -1, 0, 1, 2, \dots \}$
N	The natural numbers.	Abbreviates $\{0, 1, 2, \dots\}$
B	The boolean constants.	Abbreviates $\{true, false\}$

A.2 PREDICATE LOGIC

Logical expressions occur in a variety of settings in programming language design. Here is a summary of the language of predicate logic that we use in this text.

Table A.3

Predicate Logic

Notation	Meaning	Notes/Examples
true, false	boolean (truth) constants	
p, q, r	truth variables	
$\neg p$	negation of p	*true* if p is *false*; otherwise *false*
$p \wedge q$	conjunction of p and q	*true* if p and q are both *true*
$p \vee q$	disjunction of p and q	*true* if either p or q (or both) is *true*
$p \supset q$	implication: p implies q	logically equivalent to $\neg p \vee q$
$p \equiv q$	logical equivalence of p and q	*true* if p and q are both *true* or both *false*
$\forall x P(x)$	universally quantified expression	read "for all x, $P(x)$ is *true*"
$\exists x P(x)$	existentially quantified expression	read "there is an x for which $P(x)$ is *true*"
p is a tautology	p is always *true*	e.g., $q \vee \neg q$ is a tautology.
$p [a \backslash b]$	substitution	read "replace all occurrences of b by a in P."

A.3 **SYNTAX AND SEMANTICS**

Table A.4

BNF Notation

Notation	Meaning	Notes/Examples
N	A finite set of nonterminal symbols.	These denote the grammatical categories in a language.
Σ	A finite set of terminal symbols.	These denote the alphabet of a language (e.g., the ASCII set or the Unicode set).
$A \rightarrow \omega$	A BNF grammatical rule, for which $A \in N$ and $\omega \in (N \cup \Sigma)^*$.	E.g., *Term → Term ∗ Factor*
$A \rightarrow \omega_1\|\omega_2\|...\|\omega_n$	Abbreviation for a list of grammatical rules of the form: $A \rightarrow \omega_1$ $A \rightarrow \omega_2$ . . . $A \rightarrow \omega_n$	E.g., *Term → Factor | Term ∗ Factor* *Statements → ε | Statements Statement*
$S \Rightarrow \alpha_1 \Rightarrow \cdots \Rightarrow \alpha_n$	Derivation of the string α_n from the start symbol S in a grammar.	E.g., *Integer ⇒ Digit ⇒ 3*

Table A.5

Semantic Notation

Notation	Meaning	Notes/Examples
$\{P\}s\{Q\}$	Execution of statement *s* from a state that satisfies *P* results in state *Q*, provided that *s* halts.	Basic form of a "Hoare triple" used in axiomatic semantics.
$\dfrac{\textit{premise}}{\textit{conclusion}}$	If *premise* is valid, then *conclusion* is valid.	Basic form of a proof rule used in axiomatic and operational semantics.
$M: Class \times \Sigma \rightarrow \Sigma$	The denotational semantics of an abstract *Class* in a state is a new state.	E.g., $M: Assignment \times \Sigma \rightarrow \Sigma$

The hypothetical imperative programming language Jay is defined by its lexical syntax, concrete syntax, abstract syntax, static type checking functions, and semantic functions. These five definitions are given formally, using BNF and functional notation, in this appendix. Some of these definitions are supplemented by their implementations as Java classes and methods. Electronic copies of these Java classes are available at the book website given in the Preface.

B.1 LEXICAL SYNTAX OF JAY

InputElement → *WhiteSpace* | *Comment* | *Token*
WhiteSpace → space | \t | \r | \n | \f | \r\n
Comment → // any string ended by \r \n or \r\n
Token → *Identifier* | *Keyword* | *Literal* |
     Separator | *Operator*
Identifier → *Letter* | *Identifier Letter* | *Identifier Digit*
Letter → a | b | ... | z | A | B | ... | Z
Digit → 0 | 1 | 2 | ... | 9
Keyword → boolean | else | if | int |
     main | void | while
Literal → *Boolean* | *Integer*
Boolean → true | false
Integer → *Digit* | *Integer Digit*
Separator → (|) | { | } | ; | ,
Operator → = | + | − | * | / | < | <= |
     > | >= | == | != | && | || | !

The tokens that can appear in a Jay program are formally defined by the above grammar. They fall into five classes: *Identifier, Keyword, Literal, Separator,* and *Operator.* Every input element that is not a *Token*—that is, every instance of *Whitespace* or *Comment*—is bypassed during the lexical analysis of a Jay program.

B.2 REMAINING CONCRETE SYNTAX OF JAY

The remaining rules that complete the concrete syntax of Jay are given below in both EBNF and BNF versions.

B.2.1 EBNF Version

Program → void main ( ) '{' *Declarations Statements* '}'
Declarations → { *Declaration* }*
Declaration → *Type Identifiers*;

$$Type \rightarrow \text{int} \mid \text{boolean}$$

$$Identifiers \rightarrow Identifier \{ , Identifier \}*$$

$$Statements \rightarrow \{ \ Statement \ \}*$$

$$Statement \rightarrow ; \mid Block \mid Assignment \mid IfStatement \mid WhileStatement$$

$$Block \rightarrow \text{'\{'} Statements \text{'\}'}$$

$$Assignment \rightarrow Identifier = Expression ;$$

$$IfStatement \rightarrow \text{if} (Expression) Statement \{\text{else } Statement \}_{opt}$$

$$WhileStatement \rightarrow \text{while} (Expression) Statement$$

$$Expression \rightarrow Conjunction \{ \mid\mid Conjunction \}*$$

$$Conjunction \rightarrow Relation \{ \&\& Relation\}*$$

$$Relation \rightarrow Addition \{[< \mid <= \mid > \mid >= \mid == \mid !=] Addition \} *$$

$$Addition \rightarrow Term \{[+ \mid -] Term \}*$$

$$Term \rightarrow Negation \{['* \mid /] Negation \}*$$

$$Negation \rightarrow \{ ! \}_{opt} Factor$$

$$Factor \rightarrow Identifier \mid Literal \mid (Expression)$$

B.2.2 BNF Version

$$Program \rightarrow \text{void main} ( ) \{ Declarations \ Statements \}$$

$$Declarations \rightarrow \varepsilon \mid Declarations \ Declaration$$

$$Declaration \rightarrow Type \ Identifiers;$$

$$Type \rightarrow \text{int} \mid \text{boolean}$$

$$Identifiers \rightarrow Identifier \mid Identifiers, Identifier$$

$$Statements \rightarrow \varepsilon \mid Statements \ Statement$$

$$Statement \rightarrow ; \mid Block \mid Assignment \mid IfStatement \mid WhileStatement$$

$$Block \rightarrow \{ Statements \}$$

$$Assignment \rightarrow Identifier = Expression ;$$

$$IfStatement \rightarrow \text{if} (Expression) Statement \mid$$
$$\text{if} (Expression) Statement \text{ else } Statement$$

$$WhileStatement \rightarrow \text{while} (Expression) Statement$$

$$Expression \rightarrow Conjunction \mid Expression \mid\mid Conjunction$$

$$Conjunction \rightarrow Relation \mid$$
$$Conjunction \&\& Relation$$

$$Relation \rightarrow Addition \mid$$
$$Relation < Addition \mid$$
$$Relation <= Addition \mid$$
$$Relation > Addition \mid$$
$$Relation >= Addition \mid$$
$$Relation == Addition \mid$$
$$Relation != Addition$$

$$Addition \rightarrow Term \mid$$
$$Addition + Term \mid$$
$$Addition - Term$$

$$Term \rightarrow Negation \mid$$
$$Term * Negation \mid$$
$$Term / Negation$$

$$Negation \rightarrow Factor \mid ! Factor$$

$$Factor \rightarrow Identifier \mid Literal \mid (Expression)$$

The EBNF version is related most directly to the design of the recursive descent parser discussed in Chapters 2 and 4. In that version, the Jay symbols {, }, and * are enclosed in quotes ('), so they will not be confused with the same symbols when they are used to describe EBNF expressions. For instance, '*' denotes a Jay arithmetic operator, while * denotes "0 or more occurrences" of an EBNF expression.

Jay programs have a syntax similar to C/C++, but they have only integer and boolean types and expressions, assignment statements, if statements, and while statements. Various extensions to this basic language are suggested in the discussions and exercises throughout the first five chapters.

B.3 ABSTRACT SYNTAX OF JAY

$$
\begin{aligned}
\textit{Program} &= \textit{Declarations} \text{ decpart; } \textit{Block} \text{ body} \\
\textit{Declarations} &= \textit{Declaration}* \\
\textit{Declaration} &= \textit{Variable} \text{ v; } \textit{Type} \text{ t} \\
\textit{Type} &= \text{int} \mid \text{boolean} \mid \text{undef} \\
\textit{Statement} &= \textit{Skip} \mid \textit{Block} \mid \textit{Assignment} \mid \textit{Conditional} \mid \textit{Loop} \\
\textit{Block} &= \textit{Statement}* \\
\textit{Assignment} &= \textit{Variable} \text{ target; } \textit{Expression} \text{ source} \\
\textit{Conditional} &= \textit{Expression} \text{ test; } \textit{Statement} \text{ thenbranch, elsebranch} \\
\textit{Loop} &= \textit{Expression} \text{ test; } \textit{Statement} \text{ body} \\
\textit{Expression} &= \textit{Variable} \mid \textit{Value} \mid \textit{Binary} \mid \textit{Unary} \\
\textit{Variable} &= \textit{String} \text{ id} \\
\textit{Value} &= \textit{int} \text{ intValue} \mid \textit{boolean} \text{ boolValue} \\
\textit{Binary} &= \textit{Operator} \text{ op; } \textit{Expression} \text{ term1, term2} \\
\textit{Unary} &= \textit{UnaryOp} \text{ op; } \textit{Expression} \text{ term} \\
\textit{Operator} &= \textit{BooleanOp} \mid \textit{RelationalOp} \mid \textit{ArithmeticOp} \mid \textit{UnaryOp} \\
\textit{BooleanOp} &= \text{\&\&} \mid \mid \mid \\
\textit{RelationalOp} &= < \mid <= \mid == \mid != \mid > \mid >= \\
\textit{ArithmeticOp} &= + \mid - \mid * \mid / \\
\textit{UnaryOp} &= !
\end{aligned}
$$

The abstract syntax defines the structure of all abstract syntax trees for Jay programs. Abstract syntax provides a target representation for the parsing, and a source representation for the type checking and semantic interpretation of Jay programs.

B.3.1 Java Implementation

Below is a Java implementation for the Jay abstract syntax. This provides a set of names for the abstract representation of Jay program elements, and thus serves as a basis for defining and implementing the syntactic analysis, type checking, and semantic analysis (interpretation) of Jay programs.

```
class Program {
// Program = Declarations decpart ; Block body
  Declarations decpart;
  Block body;
}
```

```
class Declarations extends Vector {
// Declarations = Declaration *
//      (a Vector of declarations d1, d2, ..., dn)
}

class Declaration {
// Declaration = Variable v; Type t
  Variable v;
  Type t;
}

class Type {
// Type = int | boolean | undef
  final static String INTEGER = "int";
  final static String BOOLEAN = "boolean";
  final static String UNDEFINED = "undef";
  String id;

  Type (String t) { id = t; }

  public boolean isBoolean ( ) { return id.equals(BOOLEAN); }
  public boolean isInteger ( ) { return id.equals(INTEGER); }
  public boolean isUndefined ( ) { return id.equals(UNDEFINED); }
}

class Statement {
// Statement = Skip | Block | Assignment | Conditional | Loop
}

class Skip extends Statement { }

class Block extends Statement {
// Block = Statement *
//         (a Vector of members)
  public Vector members = new Vector();
}

class Assignment extends Statement {
// Assignment = Variable target; Expression source
  Variable target;
  Expression source;
}

class Conditional extends Statement {
// Conditional = Expression test; Statement thenbranch, elsebranch
  Expression test;
  Statement thenbranch, elsebranch;
            // elsebranch == null means "if... then"
}
```

```
class Loop extends Statement {
// Loop = Expression test; Statement body
  Expression test;
  Statement body;
}


class Expression {
// Expression = Variable | Value | Binary | Unary
}


class Variable extends Expression {
// Variable = String id
  String id;

  public boolean equals (Object obj) {
    String s = ((Variable) obj).id;
    return id.equalsIgnoreCase(s); // case-insensitive identifiers
  }

  public int hashCode ( ) { return id.hashCode( ); }
}

class Value extends Expression {
// Value = int intValue | boolean boolValue
  Type type;
  int intValue; boolean boolValue;

  Value (int i)     { type = new Type(Type.INTEGER); intValue = i; }
  Value (boolean b) {
    type = new Type(Type.BOOLEAN); boolValue = b;
  }
  Value ( )  { type = new Type(Type.UNDEFINED); }
}

class Binary extends Expression {
// Binary = Operator op; Expression term1, term2
  Operator op;
  Expression term1, term2;
}


class Unary extends Expression {
// Unary = Operator op; Expression term
  Operator op;
  Expression term;
}
```

```
class Operator {
// Operator = BooleanOp | RelationalOp | ArithmeticOp | UnaryOp
// BooleanOp = && | ||
  final static String AND = "&&";
  final static String OR  = "||";
// RelationalOp = < | <= | == | != | >= | >
  final static String LT = "<";

  final static String LE = "<=";
  final static String EQ = "==";
  final static String NE = "!=";
  final static String GT = ">";
  final static String GE = ">=";
// ArithmeticOp = + | - | * | /
  final static String PLUS = "+";
  final static String MINUS = "-";
  final static String TIMES = "*";
  final static String DIV = "/";
// UnaryOp = !
  final static String NOT = "!";

  String val;

  Operator (String s) { val = s; }

  boolean BooleanOp ( ) {
    return val.equals(AND) || val.equals(OR);
  }
  boolean RelationalOp ( ) {
    return val.equals(LT) || val.equals(LE) || val.equals(EQ)
        || val.equals(NE) || val.equals(GT) || val.equals(GE);
  }
  boolean ArithmeticOp ( ) {
    return val.equals(PLUS) || val.equals(MINUS)
        || val.equals(TIMES) || val.equals(DIV);
  }
  boolean UnaryOp ( ) { return val.equals(NOT); }
}
```

B.4 TYPE CHECKING FUNCTIONS FOR JAY

Below are the static type checking rules for Jay, formally defined. Implementations of these functions as a collection of Java methods are also shown. Together, these functions provide a full specification for a static type checker for abstract Jay programs.

The "type map" of a *Program* is a set of pairs, each of which is a *Variable v* and its declared *Type t*.

$$tm = \{\langle v_1, t_1\rangle, \langle v_2, t_2\rangle, \ldots, \langle v_n, t_n\rangle\}$$

```
class TypeMap extends Hashtable {
    // TypeMap is implemented as a Java Hashtable
}
```

The function *typing* creates a *TypeMap* from a series of *Declarations*. The Java implementation of *TypeMap* is a hashtable; since identifiers are mutually unique the method `put` ensures that all declared variables and their types are represented in the hashtable.

typing: *Declarations* → *TypeMap*

$$typing(Declarations\ \text{d}) = \bigcup_{i \in \{1,\dots,\,n\}} \langle d_i \cdot v, d_i \cdot t \rangle$$

```
private TypeMap typing (Declarations d) {
    TypeMap map = new TypeMap();
    for (int i=0; i<d.size(); i++) {
        map.put (((Declaration)(d.elementAt(i))).v,
                    ((Declaration)(d.elementAt(i))).t);
    }
    return map;
}
```

A series of *Declarations* is valid if its variable names are mutually unique. Note that the Java implementation has a more efficient nested loop than that which is suggested by a strict encoding of the functional definition.

V: *Declarations* → **B**
$V(Declarations\ \text{d}) = \forall i,j \in \{1, \dots, n\}: (i \neq j \supset d_i \cdot v \neq d_j \cdot v)$

```
public boolean V (Declarations d) {
    for (int i=0; i<d.size() - 1; i++)
        for (int j=i+1; j<d.size(); j++)
            if ((((Declaration)(d.elementAt(i))).v).equals
                (((Declaration)(d.elementAt(j))).v))
            return false;
    return true;
}
```

A program is valid if its *Declarations* are valid and its *Block* is valid for the *TypeMap* defined by those *Declarations*.

V: *Program* → **B**
$V(Program\ \text{p}) = V(\text{p.decpart}) \wedge V(\text{p.body}, typing(\text{p.decpart}))$

```
public boolean V (Program p) {
    return V(p.decpart) && V(p.body, typing (p.decpart));
}
```

The auxiliary function *typeOf* defines the type of an *Expression*. Here, the expression *tm(e)* means to retrieve the type of variable *e* from the type map.

typeOf: Expression × *TypeMap* → *Type*
typeOf(Expression e, TypeMap tm)

= *e*. type	if *e* is a *Value*
= *e* ∈ tm ⊃ tm(*e*)	if *e* is a *Variable*
= *e. op* ∈ {*ArithmeticOp*} ⊃ int	if *e* is a *Binary*
= *e. op* ∈ {*BooleanOp, RelationalOp*} ⊃ boolean	
= *e. op* ∈ {*UnaryOp*} ⊃ boolean	if *e* is a *Unary*

```
public Type typeOf (Expression e, TypeMap tm) {
  if (e instanceof Value) return ((Value)e).type;
  if (e instanceof Variable) {
    Variable v = (Variable)e;
    if (!tm.containsKey(v))
      return new Type(Type.UNDEFINED);
    else return (Type) tm.get(v);
  }
  if (e instanceof Binary) {
    Binary b = (Binary)e;
    if (b.op.ArithmeticOp( ))
      return new Type(Type.INTEGER);
    if (b.op.RelationalOp( ) ||
        b.op.BooleanOp( ))
    return new Type(Type.BOOLEAN);
  }
  if (e instanceof Unary) {
    Unary u = (Unary)e;
    if (u.op.UnaryOp( ))
      return new Type(Type.BOOLEAN);
  }
  return null;
}
```

An *Expression* is valid if it is a *Value,* a *Variable* in the program's type map, or a *Binary* or *Unary* whose operands satisfy additional constraints. A *Binary* whose operands are both integers must have an *ArithmeticOp* or *RelationalOp* as its operator, while a *Binary* whose operands are both boolean must have a *BooleanOp* as its operator. A *Unary* must have a boolean operand and a *UnaryOp* as its operator. Other combinations of operand types and operators are invalid *Expression*s.

V: Expression × *TypeMap* → **B**
V(Expression e, TypeMap tm)

= *true*	if *e* is a *Value*
= *e* ∈ tm	if *e* is a *Variable*
= *V(e.*term1, *tm*) ∧ *V(e.*term2, *tm*)	

∧ *typeOf(e.*term1, tm) = int ∧ *typeOf(e.*term2, tm) = int
                    if *e* is a *Binary* ∧ *e. op* ∈ {*ArithmeticOp, RelationalOp*}

$$= V(e.\text{term1}, tm) \wedge V(e.\text{term2}, tm)$$
$$\wedge \; typeOf(e.\text{term1}, tm) = \text{boolean} \wedge typeOf(e.\text{term2}, tm) = \text{boolean}$$
$$\text{if } e \text{ is a } Binary \wedge e. \, op \in \{BooleanOp\}$$
$$= V(e.\text{term}, tm) \wedge typeOf(e.\text{term}, tm) = \text{boolean} \wedge e.\text{op} = \,!$$
$$\text{if } e \text{ is a } Unary$$

```
public boolean V (Expression e, TypeMap tm) {
  if (e instanceof Value) {
    return true;
  }
  if (e instanceof Variable) {
    return tm.containsKey((Variable)e);
  }
  if (e instanceof Binary) {
      Type typ1 = typeOf(((Binary)e).term1, tm);
      Type typ2 = typeOf(((Binary)e).term2, tm);
      if (! V (((Binary)e).term1, tm)) return false;
      if (! V (((Binary)e).term2, tm)) return false;
      if (((Binary)e).op.ArithmeticOp( ) ||
        ((Binary)e).op.RelationalOp( ))
        return typ1.isInteger() && typ2.isInteger();
      if (((Binary)e).op.BooleanOp( ))
        return typ1.isBoolean() && typ2.isBoolean();
  }
  if (e instanceof Unary) {
      Type typ1 = typeOf(((Unary)e).term, tm);
      return typ1.isBoolean() && V(((Unary)e).term, tm) &&
        (((Unary)e).op.val).equals("!") ;
  }
  return false;
}
```

A *Statement* is valid if its constituent parts are individually valid. Different kinds of statements have different parts. (In the Java method *V* for *Statement,* the null statement is also valid, since it occurs whenever the elsebranch of a *Conditional* is not present.)

V: Statement $\times$ *TypeMap* $\rightarrow$ **B**
V(*Statement s, TypeMap* tm)

$= true$	if s is a *Skip*
$= s.\text{target} \in tm \wedge V(s.\text{source}, tm) \wedge tm(s.\text{target}) = typeOf(s.\text{source}, tm)$	
	if s is an *Assignment*
$= V(s.\text{test}, tm) \wedge typeOf(s.\text{test}, tm) = \text{boolean} \wedge V(s.\text{thenbranch}, tm)$	
$\wedge V(s.\text{elsebranch}, tm)$	if s is a *Conditional*
$= V(s.\text{test}, tm) \wedge typeOf(s.\text{test}, tm) = \text{boolean} \wedge V(s.\text{body}, tm)$	
	if s is a *Loop*
$= V(b_1, tm) \wedge V(b_2, tm) \wedge \ldots \wedge V(b_n, tm)$	if s is a *Block* $= b_1 b_2 \ldots b_n \wedge n \geq 0$

```
public boolean V (Statement s, TypeMap tm) {
  if (s instanceof Skip || s==null) return true;
  if (s instanceof Assignment) {
     boolean b1 = tm.containsKey(((Assignment)s).target);
     boolean b2 = V(((Assignment)s).source, tm);
     if (b1 && b2)
        return ((Type)tm.get(((Assignment)s).target)).id.equals
               (typeOf(((Assignment)s).source, tm).id);
     else return false;
  }
  if (s instanceof Conditional)
     return V (((Conditional)s).test, tm) &&
        typeOf(((Conditional)s).test, tm).isBoolean() &&
        V (((Conditional)s).thenbranch, tm) &&
        V (((Conditional)s).elsebranch, tm);
  if (s instanceof Loop)
     return V (((Loop)s).test, tm) &&
        typeOf(((Loop)s).test, tm).isBoolean() &&
        V (((Loop)s).body, tm);
  if (s instanceof Block) {
     for (int j=0; j < ((Block)s).members.size(); j++)
        if (! V((Statement)(((Block)s).members.elementAt(j)), tm))
           return false;
     return true;
  }
  return false;
}
```

B.5 SEMANTICS OF JAY

Below is the semantics of Jay programs, formally defined. These functions collectively represent the behavior of a run-time interpreter for abstract Jay programs.

The state of a *Program* is a set of pairs, each of which is a *Variable* and its currently assigned value. This is naturally implemented as a Java Hashtable, since *Variable*s are mutually unique in a Jay program. The overriding union operator, discussed in the text, is implemented as the method onion in the class State.

$$\sigma = \{\langle v_1, val_1 \rangle, \langle v_2, val_2 \rangle, \ldots, \langle v_m, val_m \rangle\}$$

```
class State extends Hashtable {
// State is implemented as a Java Hashtable

public State onion (State t) {
   for (Enumeration e = t.keys(); e.hasMoreElements(); ) {
     Variable key = (Variable)e.nextElement();
     put(key, t.get(key));
```

```
        }
    return this;
    }
}
```

Values in Jay all come from the set $\mathbf{I} \cup \mathbf{B} \cup \{undef\}$, where $\mathbf{I}$ and $\mathbf{B}$ are the integer and boolean semantic domains with their usual mathematical operators. The special value *undef* marks the value of an uninitialized variable.

The meaning of a *Program* is the meaning of its body starting with an initial state containing each of the program's *m* declared variables with undefined values.

$M : Program \rightarrow \Sigma$
$M(Program\ \mathrm{p}) = M(\mathrm{p.body}, \{\langle v_1, undef \rangle, \langle v_2, undef \rangle, \ldots, \langle v_m, undef \rangle\})$

```
    State M (Program p) }
        return M (p.body, initialState(p.decpart));
    }

    State initialState (Declarations d) {
      State sigma = new State();
      Value undef = new Value();
      for (int i = 0; i < d.size(); i++)
        sigma.put(((Declaration)(d.elementAt(i))).v, undef);
      return sigma;
    }
```

The function *ApplyBinary* (or *ApplyUnary*) computes a *Value* when given a binary (or unary) *Operator* and two (or one) *Value*s that are its operands. It assumes that the operators $+, -, \ldots$ carry their usual meanings in the semantic domains of integers $\mathbf{I}$ and booleans $\mathbf{B}$. Note the definition of the operator / is a complicated, mathematical way of specifying the integer division of $v1$ divided by $v2$, although the Java implementation is straightforward (actually simpler to express).

$ApplyBinary : Operator \times Value \times Value \rightarrow Value$
$ApplyBinary(Operator\ op,\ Value\ v1,\ Value\ v2)$

$$
\begin{aligned}
&= v1 + v2 & &\text{if } op = + \\
&= v1 - v2 & &\text{if } op = - \\
&= v1 \times v2 & &\text{if } op = * \\
&= floor\left(\left|\frac{v1}{v2}\right|\right) \times sign(v1 \times v2) & &\text{if } op = / \\
&= v1 < v2 & &\text{if } op = < \\
&= v1 \leq v2 & &\text{if } op = <= \\
&= v1 = v2 & &\text{if } op = == \\
&= v1 \neq v2 & &\text{if } op = != \\
&= v1 \geq v2 & &\text{if } op = >= \\
&= v1 > v2 & &\text{if } op = > \\
&= v1 \wedge v2 & &\text{if } op = \&\& \\
&= v1 \vee v2 & &\text{if } op = \|
\end{aligned}
$$

```
Value applyBinary (Operator op, Value v1, Value v2) {
  if (v1.type.isUndefined() || v2.type.isUndefined()) {
    return new Value();
  }
  else if (op.ArithmeticOp( )) {
    if (op.val.equals(Operator.PLUS))
      return new Value(v1.intValue + v2.intValue);
    if (op.val.equals(Operator.MINUS))
      return new Value(v1.intValue - v2.intValue);
    if (op.val.equals(Operator.TIMES))
      return new Value(v1.intValue * v2.intValue);
    if (op.val.equals(Operator.DIV))
      return new Value(v1.intValue / v2.intValue);
  }
  else if (op.RelationalOp( )) {
    if (op.val.equals(Operator.LT))
      return new Value(v1.intValue < v2.intValue);
    if (op.val.equals(Operator.LE))
      return new Value(v1.intValue <= v2.intValue);
    if (op.val.equals(Operator.EQ))
      return new Value(v1.intValue == v2.intValue);
    if (op.val.equals(Operator.NE))
      return new Value(v1.intValue != v2.intValue);
    if (op.val.equals(Operator.GE))
      return new Value(v1.intValue >= v2.intValue);
    if (op.val.equals(Operator.GT))
      return new Value(v1.intValue > v2.intValue);
  }
  else if (op.BooleanOp( )) {
    if (op.val.equals(Operator.AND))
      return new Value(v1.boolValue && v2.boolValue);
    if (op.val.equals(Operator.OR))
      return new Value(v1.boolValue || v2.boolValue);
  }
  return null;
}
```

$ApplyUnary : \text{Operator} \times Value \rightarrow Value$
$ApplyUnary\ (\text{Operator}\ op,\ Value\ v) = \neg v \qquad \text{if } op = !$

```
Value applyUnary (Operator op, Value v) {
  if (v.type.isUndefined()) return new Value();
  else if (op.val.equals("!")) return new Value(!v.boolValue);
  return null;
}
```

The meaning of an *Expression* is either a *Value,* the value of a *Variable* in the current state, or the result of applying a binary or unary operator to the meanings of its operands in the current state.

M : Expression $\times \Sigma \rightarrow$ *Value*
M(Expression e, State σ)

$= e$	if *e* is a *Value*
$= \sigma(e)$	if *e* is a *Variable*
$= ApplyBinary(e.\text{op}, M(e.\text{term1}, \sigma), M(e.\text{term2}, \sigma))$	if *e* is a *Binary*
$= ApplyUnary(e.\text{op}, M(e(.\text{term}, \sigma)))$	if *e* is a *Unary*

```
Value M (Expression e, State sigma) {
  if (e instanceof Value)
    return (Value)e;
  if (e instanceof Variable)
    return (Value)(sigma.get((Variable)e));
  if (e instanceof Binary)
    return applyBinary (((Binary)e).op,
                        M(((Binary)e).term1, sigma),
                        M(((Binary)e).term2, sigma));
  if (e instanceof Unary)
    return applyUnary(((Unary)e).op, M(((Unary)e).term, sigma));
  return null;
}
```

The meaning of a statement is, in turn, the meaning of the particular type of statement that it represents.

M : Statement $\times \Sigma \rightarrow \Sigma$
M(Statement s, State σ) $= M((Skip)s, \sigma)$ if *s* is a *Skip*

$= M((Assignment)s, \sigma)$	if *s* is an *Assignment*
$= M((Conditional)s, \sigma)$	if *s* is a *Conditional*
$= M((Loop)s, \sigma)$	if *s* is a *Loop*
$= M((Block)s, \sigma)$	if *s* is a *Block*

```
State M (Statement s, State sigma) {
  if (s instanceof Skip) return M((Skip)s, sigma);
  if (s instanceof Assignment)  return M((Assignment)s, sigma);
  if (s instanceof Conditional)  return M((Conditional)s, sigma);
  if (s instanceof Loop)  return M((Loop)s, sigma);
  if (s instanceof Block)  return M((Block)s, sigma);
  return null;
}
```

The meaning of a *Skip* statement is effectively the identity function, since it does not change the current state of the computation.

$$M\ (Skip\ \text{s},\ State\ \sigma) = \sigma$$

```
State M (Skip s, State sigma) {
  return sigma;
}
```

The meaning of an *Assignment* is the overriding union of the current state and a new pair formed by the *Variable* that is the target of the *Assignment* and the meaning of the *Expression* that is the source.

$$M : Assignment \times \Sigma \rightarrow \Sigma$$
$$M(Assignment\ \text{a},\ State\ \sigma) = \sigma\ \overline{U}\ \{\langle \text{a.target},\ M(\text{a.source},\ \sigma)\rangle\}$$

```
State M (Assignment a, State sigma) {
  return sigma.onion(new State(a.target, M (a.source, sigma)));
}
```

The meaning of a *Block* is either the identity function (if it has no statements), or the meaning of the rest of the *Block* applied to the new state achieved by executing the first statement of the *Block*. This can be implemented with either a `for` loop or a recursive method.

$$M(Block\ \text{b},\ State\ \sigma) = \sigma \qquad\qquad\qquad\qquad\qquad \text{if b} = \varnothing$$
$$= M((Block)\text{b}_{2\ldots n},\ M((Statement)\text{b}_1,\ \sigma)) \quad \text{if b} = b_1 b_2 \ldots b_n$$

```
State M (Block b, State sigma) {
  for (int i=0; i<b.members.size(); i++) {
    sigma = M ((Statement)(b.members.elementAt(i)), sigma);
  }
  return sigma;
}
```

The meaning of a *Conditional* is the meaning of one or the other of its branches, depending on whether the test is *true* or not.

$$M(Conditional\ c,\ State\ \sigma) = M(c.\text{thenbranch},\ \sigma) \quad \text{if } M(c.\text{test},\ \sigma) \text{ is true}$$
$$= M(c.\text{elsebranch},\ \sigma) \quad \text{otherwise}$$

```
State M (Conditional c, State sigma) {
  if (M (c.test, sigma).boolValue)
    return M (c.thenbranch, sigma);
  else
    return M (c.elsebranch, sigma);
}
```

The meaning of a *Loop* is either the identity function (if the test is not *true*) or the meaning of the same loop when applied to the state resulting from executing its body one time. This is a recursive definition, which can be implemented either recursively (shown below) or as a loop (not shown).

$$M(Loop\ l,\ State\ \sigma) = M(l, M(l.\text{body}, \sigma)) \qquad \text{if } M(l.\text{test}, \sigma) \text{ is } true$$
$$= \sigma \qquad\qquad\qquad\qquad \text{otherwise}$$

```
State M  (Loop l, State sigma) {
  if (M (l.test, sigma).boolValue)
    return M(l, M (l.body, sigma));
  else return sigma;
}
```

Java is a "simple, object-oriented, distributed, interpreted, robust, secure, architecture neutral, portable, high-performance, multi-threaded, and dynamic language" [Gosling 1996a]. Java is implemented on most platforms, including Mac, Windows, and Linux. This tutorial provides a quick introduction to Java if you have some Pascal (or C/C++) programming experience, and is based on a Linux implementation.

C.1 RUNNING JAVA PROGRAMS

A Java program is written as a *public class,* which may be compiled and run as a standalone application, or else compiled and run as an "applet." The Java program file in either event is identified by the suffix ".java". The compiled class always carries the suffix ".class". Below is a Java "Hello World" program that can be compiled and run as a standalone program.

```
public class HelloWorld {
  public static void main (String[] args) {
    System.out.println("Hello World!");
  }
}
```

To compile this program, assuming it has been stored as the file HelloWorld.java, the following shell command should be issued:

```
$ javac HelloWorld.java
```

This step produces the executable file HelloWorld.class. To run this program, the following command should be issued:

```
$ java HelloWorld
```

This step should produce the familiar "Hello World!" message on the screen.

C.2 BASIC JAVA SYNTAX

Java syntax is similar to C/C++ syntax, though Java is more consistent in many ways. Below is a brief summary of its main features, with examples.

A Java program is called a *class*. Some Java programs are written for use in an interactive environment, while others are written as standalone applications. We shall discuss the structure of programs for interactive environments in Section C.5.

A Java program designed as a standalone application has a basic structure much like that of a Pascal, C, or C++ program. The program has a series of statements embedded in a method (function) called *main,* a collection of auxiliary method declarations, and a collection of global variable declarations used by the statements in the program. The method main is the first to be executed when the program begins running. The syntax of a complete standalone Java application program is as follows:

```
import java.io.*;
public class <classname> {
   <variable declarations>
   <method declarations>

   public static void main (String[] args) {
     <statements to execute when the program begins running>
   }
}
```

The *import* statements at the beginning of the program indicate specific libraries (called *packages*) which supply many useful functions, or methods, to the program. The import statement here suggests that most Java application programs use some of the stream/file input and output methods from the "java.io" package. (Java uses the term *method* as a synonym for the term *function* or *procedure.*) In addition, the Java program may declare its own methods to supplement those provided by these libraries.

C.2.1 The Standard Java Packages

The predefined Java classes are grouped into a small number of standard packages. For instance, input and output operations are performed through classes in the java.io package, which is summarized in Section C.3. Here's an overview of the major packages in the Java API (application programming interface):

java.applet—a small superclass of all applets, which are programs that run inside Web browsers.

java.awt—abstract windowing toolkit; contains classes for graphics and GUI interfaces.

java.io—stream and file I/O classes. Unfortunately, Java I/O does not support automatic conversion of stream input values from their text representation to their internal numerical (int or float) representation. Thus, simple input functions in Java are a bit more tedious than their counterparts in Pascal or C/C++.

java.lang—core language classes (implicitly imported by all programs), like Object, Math, String, Thread, and Throwable (for defining and handling exceptions).

java.net—classes for networking, including URL, Socket, DatagramSocket, and InetAddress.

java.util—some useful general classes, like Date, Random, Vector, and Stack.

C.2.2 Declarations

The scope of a declaration in a Java program is the range of statements that may reference the declared variable or method. The scope of the variables and methods identified in the declarations above includes the entire class. As we shall see, all methods (including the method main) and statements may declare additional variables for local use, in which case their scope is limited to the body of the method or statement in which they are declared.

Variable names must be unique within the scope for which they are declared. Moreover, variable names are case sensitive, so that (for instance) the names "sum," "Sum," and "SUM" refer to distinct variables.

Unlike Pascal (and like C/C++), Java method declarations may not be nested. Thus, the structure of a Java program is relatively flat. When two variables have the same name, their scopes must be mutually exclusive. Thus, if a variable declared locally within a method has the same name as another variable declared among the <variable declarations>, all references to that name from within that method are treated as references to that local variable. In general, no two variables declared within a single method should have the same name.

C.2.3 Data Types and Variable Declarations

There are two types of variables in Java, *primitive types* and *reference types*. When used in an assignment statement, primitive values are copied just as in Pascal, C, and C++. However, reference values are actually pointers and an assignment statement merely copies the pointer value; this is called *reference semantics*. Consider the following assignment statement, where a and b are both of reference type:

```
a = b;
b.change();
```

After executing the assignment statement, both a and b point to the same object. A change to either a or b also changes the other; hence, the change to b in the second statement also changes a.

Table C.1 summarizes the primitive data types in Java.

Table C.1

Primitive Types in Java

Type	Values	Comments (Examples)
boolean	true, false	not 0, 1 as in C/C++
char	16-bit Unicode character	\u0000 (ASCII is a subset of the Unicode character set.)
byte, short, int, long	8- 16- 32- and 64-bit signed integers	0, −17, 3500
float, double	32- and 64-bit floating point numbers	0.0, 3e−5, 0.00003, 3.14159

Variables declared with each of these types are assigned initial "default" values, normally the zero bit pattern.

The Unicode character set is a 16-bit representation for characters, which includes the ASCII characters. Most of these are typed into a Java string as they appear on the keyboard; the following characters have escape sequences when they are typed as part of a Java string:

Table C.2

Characters and Their Escape Codes

Character	Coding
backspace	\b
tab	\t
new line	\n
form feed	\f
carriage return	\r
double quote	\"
single quote	\'
backslash	\\

C.2.4 Variable Declarations

Here are some example Java variable declarations, alongside their Pascal counterparts:

```
Java            Pascal

char a;         a : character;
int b;          b : integer;
float c;        c : real;
boolean d;      d : Boolean;
```

C.2.5 Expressions and Operators

Operators in Java mirror those in C/C++, except that + applies to String values as well as numbers, and the dereferencing and referencing operators * and & are not available in Java (since there are no pointers).

Reference types in Java are arrays and *objects*. The idea of an object is similar to the idea of a variable—an object has a state (i.e., a value) and an associated set of operations that can be performed on that value. A String variable in Java is an example of an object. A String's state is its current value (i.e., its sequence of characters between quotes), to which certain string operations (e.g., concatenation, selecting a substring, etc.), called *methods,* can be applied. Declaring an array or String variable in Java is somewhat more general than in Pascal, as the following examples show.

```
Java                                Pascal
--------------------------          --------------------------------
int[] A = new int[5];               var A: array[1..5] of integer;
float[] B = {3, 6, 9, 2};
String s = "Hello World!";          var s: string;
                                    ... s := 'Hello World';
String t;
```

The first line declares an array A, which in Java is indexed from 0 to 4 (not 1 to 5, as in Pascal). So the reference A[0] refers to the first element in A, and A[4] refers to the last. The second line shows how in Java a declaration can initialize the values in a variable or array. The third line illustrates the declaration of a String variable in Java, along with an initial value assignment.

While standard Pascal doesn't formally support strings, most of its implementations do, as shown in the example on the right. In Java, objects are *reference types*. Thus, like the array A, the String s is created as a reference to a dynamically allocated block of storage in a memory area called the *heap*. If passed as an argument to a method, the array A or the String s will be passed by reference.

The default value for reference types is null. For instance, the String variable t declared above, with no initial value, is initially a null reference. Later, when the string is assigned a value, that value will be dynamically created in the heap and t will reference, or "point to," that value.

If you are beginning to suspect that Java references are something like pointers in Pascal or C/C++, you're exactly right. But you're not allowed to declare pointers in Java. Moreover, while all arrays and objects (all reference types) are dynamically allocated at run time, they cannot be explicitly deallocated by the programmer. That is, Java provides "automatic garbage collection," which prevents programs from explicitly disposing blocks of dynamic storage. In the long run, this strategy promotes more reliable and painless programming without any loss of generality. More discussion of objects, classes, and reference types appears in Subsection C.2.9.

C.2.6 Statements

Java statement types include expressions (including assignments), loops, conditionals, switch, break, and continue statements. Their syntax follows their counterparts in C/C++.

Assignments. The assignment operator is = (which, by the way, should not be used as a comparison operator).

```
Java                            Pascal
-----------------------         --------------------
i = i + 1;                      i := i + 1;
i++;
```

Note that the second example is a commonly used variation of the first. That is, the ++ operator in Java is often used to increment a variable by 1.

Other Expressions, Operators, and Mathematical Functions. Operators in Java mirror those in C/C++, except that + applies to String values (for concatenation) as well as numbers, and the dereferencing and referencing operators * and & are not available. Table C.3 shows a summary of the principal Java operators, in order from highest to lowest precedence.

Note that == is the equality comparison operator in Java, not = (which is assignment). Also, note that / gives an integer quotient when both operands are integers, and a decimal quotient otherwise; so it acts sometimes like div in Pascal.

Table C.3

Operators in Java
and Pascal

Java	Pascal
++ -- + - ! (<type>)	n/a n/a + - not n/a
* / %	* / div mod
+ -	+ -
<= >= < >	<= >= < >
== !=	= <>
&&	and
||	or
= (assignment)	:=

Mathematical functions are available through Java's library `java.lang.Math`, along with some others. When using any of these, the program must have the statement `import java.lang.Math;` at its beginning, and prefix the method call by the qualifier `Math`. Here is an incomplete summary of these functions:

```
abs atan cos exp log
acos asin ceil floor
max min pow random
rint round
sin sqrt tan
```

C.2.7 Loops and Conditionals
These are generally like C/C++ loops and conditionals.

```
for (<initialization> ; <condition> ; <increment>)
   <statement>

if (<condition>)
   <statement>
else
   <statement>
```

The else part is optional, and braces { } should be used when *<statement>* needs to be more than one statement. Here's how the syntax compares with that of loops in Pascal.

```
Java                            Pascal
----------------------          --------------------------
for (i=1; i<=n; i++) {          for i:=1 to n do begin
   <statements>                    <statements>
}                               end
while ( <expression> ) {        while <expression> do begin
   <statements>                    <statements>
}                               end
```

Usually, Java loops run from 0 to $n-1$, rather than from 1 to n, due to the fact that arrays and other linear structures (Vectors and Strings) index their entries beginning at 0. This is a direct outcome of the C/C++ influence on Java's design.

C.2.8 Switch and Break

```
Java                                  Pascal
-----------------------------         ---------------------------
switch ( <expression> ) {             case <expression> of
  case <value1>: <statement1> ;          <value1>: <statement1> ;
       break;
  case <value2>: <statement2> ;          <value2>: <statement2> ;
       break;

  ...                                      ...
}                                     end
```

Note that the `break` statement must explicitly end each of the case alternatives in the Java code if the same meaning is to be conveyed as in the Pascal version. Leaving out the `break` statement between two cases is sometimes useful when a different effect is needed.

C.2.9 Classes and Methods (Functions and Procedures)

A Java program is a special case of a class declaration, which has the following general structure.

```
public class <CLASSNAME> [extends <CLASSNAME>]opt {
   <declarations of variables for objects in this class>
   <declarations of methods for objects in this class>
}
```

Here, the optional "extends" clause is used when the program is written as an extension, or subclass, of an existing class.

A Java method is similar to a C/C++ function, or a Pascal function or procedure, except that it is always defined inside a class declaration. Methods that are designed to be called from other classes should also be prefixed by the keyword "public."

```
Java                                  Pascal
-----------------------------         ------------------------------
<type> <name> (<params>) {            function <name> (<params>): <type>
   <local variable declarations>         <local variable declarations>
                                      begin
   <statements>                          <statements>
   return <expression> ;                 <name> := <expression>
}                                     end;
```

The `<type>` returned by a method may be any primitive or reference type, or else void. A method with a `void` return type is comparable to a Pascal procedure. If the return type is not `void`, the "return" statement must be used to send the returned value back to the call. As shown above, this is similar to a Pascal function, in which the result is returned by making an assignment to the function's <name>.

All parameters with primitive types are passed by value in a method call, while all parameters with reference types (arrays and objects) are passed by reference. Thus, Pascal's var parameter can partially be simulated in Java by using a parameter with a reference type.

As in C++, a Java constructor is a method that is called to create and initialize an object of a class. Below is an example of a constructor called to initialize a new object in the class Button.

```
Button clear_button = new Button("Clear");
```

However, unlike C++, Java has no destructors. All objects are dynamically allocated, and reclamation of memory used by unreferenced objects at run time is done by automatic garbage collection.

A method may be called in one of two different ways; in the conventional way or in "dot" notation. The conventional call is like an ordinary function call in Pascal or C/C++. For instance, the call

```
myMethod(x)
```

returns some value computed by myMethod using the argument x. On the other hand, the call to the String method equals

```
s.equals("Hello World!")
```

where s is a String, returns the boolean value *true* or *false* depending on whether the current value of s is identically "Hello World!".

A general rule of thumb for whether or not to use the dot notation is guided by whether or not the called method is a member of the same class where the call appears. In the second example, the dot notation is used because the variable s is a member of the String class, which exports the method equals.

C.3   STREAM INPUT AND OUTPUT

Input and output are supported in various ways by Java. In this section, we summarize the basic facilities for reading and displaying values in the standard input and output streams, System.in and System.out. We then present and illustrate a simplified stream input facility that is easier to use than the standard fare.

The Java class System has a number of predefined variables, including the following:

System.in—standard input stream.

System.out—standard output stream.

System.err—standard error log.

In Unix Java applications, these streams appear in the same window that is used for compiling and running Java programs. In CodeWarrior applications, two new windows appear when running a program that uses System.in and System.out, one for each stream. This is a bit of a "kluge," since the familiar practice of seeing input typing echoed in the output window (when alternating readln and writeln statements in Pascal) is lost, but it is workable.

To display output in Java, either of the statements

```
System.out.print( <expression> );
System.out.println( <expression> );
```

is used, where <expression> can be any String, integer, real, or other value or expression. The second statement differs from the first only by placing a line-feed at the end of the value displayed.

To read input, a program has four options:

1 Obtain input through the args parameter in the main method.
2 Obtain input through a file or System.in using readLine() to obtain a String and explicitly converting the string to the target type.
3 Use a StreamTokenizer to process a file or System.in.
4 Use an auxiliary class like ReadStream or Keyboard,[1] which provides Pascal-like stream input (the conversions are performed automatically).

To obtain input from the args parameter in the main function, that input must be listed on the same line as the run-time command for the program. However, if the web browser in which this applet is running is moved to another page and back (or equivalently, iconified and then re-opened), the "Hello Web" message disappears. For instance,

```
% java MyProgram a b c
```

calls for a run of the program MyProgram.class by the Java interpreter, passing the values a b and c as arguments. In turn, the program should have a main method that accommodates these values, such as

```
public static void main (String args[])) ...
```

Now the String array args will have the following values for use when this program is run:

```
args[0] == "a"
args[1] == "b"
args[2] == "c"
```

The second, more flexible option for reading input is reminiscent of Pascal or C/C++ programming, but is also somewhat tedious because the program must convert

---

1. The class ReadStream was developed by Duane Bailey at Williams College. The class Keyboard was developed by Kamin and Reingold at the University of Illinois.

each input read to the desired type. First, a variable of class `BufferedReader` should be declared and initialized to point to System.in.

```
static BufferedReader MyInput = new BufferedReader(
                              new InputStreamReader(System.in));
```

To read an ordinary double, int, float, . . . value from the input stream, you can read a complete line of input as a String (called inputLine below); then convert it to a Double (which is the class corresponding to the simple type double, called dValue below); and finally convert it to an ordinary double value using the method doubleValue() before assigning it to the variable delta_x. Wow!

```
try {
    System.out.println("Enter x distance to move: ");
    String inputLine = MyInput.readLine();
    Double dValue = new Double(inputLine);
    double delta_x = dValue.doubleValue();
}
catch (IOException e) {
    System.out.println("I/O exception"); }
catch (NumberFormatException e) {
    System.out.println("Invalid number entered");
}
```

The third option uses a StreamTokenizer to break an input file into values delimited by whitespace. As such, it is very similar to C++ stream input. First, a variable of type StreamTokenizer should be declared and initialized similar to the code above:

```
static StreamTokenizer MyInput = new StreamTokenizer(
        new BufferedReader(new InputStreamReader(System.in));
```

To read the next value, you merely obtain the next token from the stream. Adapting the code from the above example and adding error checking, we get:

```
System.out.println("Enter x distance to move: ");
MyInput.nextToken();
if (MyInput.ttype == MyInput.TT_NUMBER)
    double delta_x = MyInput.nval;
else // error
```

The fourth option for reading input is similar to Pascal or C/C++ stream input. To use it, you must use a nonstandard class, such as Keyboard [Kamin 1997]. To do this, your program must import the Keyboard class.

The statements that can be used to read individual input values from the keyboard are of the form:

```
<variable> = Keyboard.<method>();
```

where <method> is chosen from the following list in accordance with the type of the <variable> on the left.

```
String readString()
    // reads next input line as a string
int readInt()
    // reads next value as an int
double readDouble()
    // reads next value as a double
```

For instance, to read the next line from the input stream r and assign it to the String variable s, you would use a statement of the form:

```
s = Keyboard.readString();
```

This corresponds to the Pascal statement readln(s), where the conversion of the input line to a string value and assignment to the variable s is implicit.

The following additional method

```
boolean eof()
```

returns `true` when the most recent read operation caused end of file (indicated when the user enters ctrl-D on the keyboard in Unix).

C.4 EXAMPLE: MAKING AN APPLICATION

Here is a standalone Java program that inputs a number and displays a countdown from that number to 1 followed by the message "Welcome to Java!"

```
public class MyFirst {
  public static void main(String args[]) {
    System.out.println( "Enter an integer in the System.in window");
    int n = Keyboard.readInt();    // read an input integer
    for (int i=n; i>0; i--)
        System.out.println(i);
    System.out.println( "Welcome to Java!" );
  }
}
```

Note that the int variable n can be declared at the point where it is first used, in the input statement. We could have declared and initialized n outside the main method altogether, in which case it would be globally accessible to all methods inside the program (if there were others).

A roughly equivalent Pascal program for this problem is shown below, so that other correspondences and differences between Java and Pascal can be identified.

```
program myfirst (input, output);
var i, n: integer;
begin
        writeln('Enter an integer:');
        readln(n);                      { read an input integer}
        for i := n downto 1 do
            writeln(i);
        writeln('Welcome to Pascal!');
end.
```

C.5 JAVA APPLETS

An *applet* is a Java program that runs inside a web browser. It provides users with a *graphical user interface* (or *GUI*) for interaction while the program is running. Applets have a slightly different structure than Java applications, since they are designed to run within a web browser. An applet extends the class `Applet`; as such, it has neither a `main` method as discussed in Section C.4, nor a constructor.

An applet is actually a GUI container that allows it to be embedded in another GUI environment such as a web browser. As such there are four parts to an applet's life cycle, which are depicted in Figure C.1.

The `Applet` class provides four methods to guide it through its life cycle:

- `init()`—invoked when the applet is first started. It is called only once and takes the place of a constructor.
- `start()`—invoked each time the applet becomes visible. Within a web browser, `start` is invoked each time the web page is visited. The normal use of this method is to start any threads (e.g., animation threads) used by the applet. Threads are discussed in more detail in Chapter 11.
- `stop()`—invoked each time the applet becomes invisible. Within a web browser, `stop` is called each time the web page is left. The normal use of this method is to stop any threads used by the applet, since the web page is no longer visible. The methods `start` and `stop` are always called in sequence and may be called many times in the lifetime of an applet.
- `destroy()`—invoked when the applet is about to be terminated. The method is used to release any resources that the applet may be holding.

| Figure C.1   The Life Cycle of an Applet

In addition to these methods an applet is a subclass of the class `Component`; as such, it has a method:

```
public void paint(Graphics g)
```

which is invoked whenever the applet needs to repaint itself. In particular, any use of the Graphics drawing methods, such as drawString, drawLine, and so forth, would normally appear in the paint method.

Thus, a typical applet without animation or other threads has the following overall structure:

```
import java.applet.*;
import java.awt.*;
import java.awt.event.*;

public class <classname> extends Applet implements <listeners> {
    <instance variable declarations>

    public void init() {
      <code to initialize the applet>
    }

    public void paint (Graphics g) {
       <code to draw using graphics methods>
    }

    <event handlers>
}
```

The instance variable declarations create various objects that can be placed in the applet, as well as other class values that represent the state of the applet. Variables may be integers, floats, booleans, Strings, arrays or other objects, just like in application programs. Variables may also represent colors, buttons, menus, and text fields that have special interactive roles inside the frame while the applet is running. Examples of these will be shown later.

A minimal applet analogous to the "Hello World" program is:

```
import java.awt.*;
import java.applet.*;

public class Hello extends Applet {
    public void paint(Graphics g) {
       g.drawString("Hello Web", 100, 100);
    }
}
```

This program, when invoked from a web page, simply displays the message "Hello Web" at coordinates 100, 100. It has no init() method because it has no instance variables to be initialized. Similarly, it does not implement any event handlers.

A web page needed to invoke the compiled version of this applet is:

```
<html>
<header>
<title>Hello Web</title>
</header>
<body>
<applet code="Hello.class" width=300 height=300>
</applet>
</body>
</html>
```

As far as applets are concerned, the important part of the web page is the *applet tag,* which specifies the name of the class file to be executed, and the height and width of the frame in which the applet is to run. In this particular example, the class file must reside in the same directory as the web page. The web page would be referenced by the browser in the usual way.

The init method is executed first, when the applet begins executing. It has the responsibility of initializing all instance variables and placing specific objects in the frame, such as buttons, choices, labels, and text fields. The init method also adds specific event listeners to the frame, one for each kind of event that can occur.

Widgets such as buttons, choices, labels, and text fields inherit from the Java AWT (Abstract Windowing Toolkit) class Component, which includes a paint method. So these widgets need not be explicitly repainted by the applet once added to the frame. However, any information written to the screen by the applet, usually using the Graphics class methods, must normally appear in the applet's paint method. Otherwise, if the window is iconified or hidden by another window, the information written will be erased (more properly, not rewritten).

Consider, for example, the slightly revised version of the Hello program:

```
import java.awt.*;
import java.applet.*;

public class Hello extends Applet {
   public void init( ) {
      Graphics g = getGraphics( );
      g.drawString("Hello Web", 100, 100);
   }
}
```

When compiled and run, this version appears to work identically as the previous one. However, in the web browser in which this applet is running (or moved to another page and back), the "Hello Web" message disappears. The web browser signals the applet to repaint itself, but the nonexistent paint method is effectively empty. So the message is not rewritten. Using the first option, input can be passed to the *main* function via the *args* parameter by listing the input on the command line for the program.

An applet's start method is invoked each time the web page on which the applet is running is visited. Correspondingly, the stop method is invoked when the web page is left. So start and stop form a sequence pair. The normal use of these methods is to start any needed threads from the applet's start method and stop them in the applet's stop method. The topic of threads is explored in Chapter 11.

C.6 EVENTS AND LISTENERS

An applet normally identifies the kinds of events to which the applet is prepared to respond. Some events that can be handled include:

- Mouse events (the MouseListener interface), such as mouse clicks.
- Mouse motion events (the MouseMotionListener interface), such as dragging the mouse.
- Button clicks (the ActionListener interface).
- Typing characters into a text field (the ActionListener interface).
- Choice selections (the ItemListener interface), using the mouse.

For each specific kind of event (like a button selection, mouse click, menu choice selection, or mouse drag) that can occur, the program must define a special method called an *event handler*. One handler is programmed to respond to the user pressing the mouse button, another may respond to the user dragging the mouse while the button is pressed, and still another may respond to the user selecting a button on the screen. Whenever such an event actually occurs, the appropriate handler is executed.

An event handler is nothing more than a class that implements the appropriate listener interface. For a simple applet that has only a few listeners, the applet itself might implement the listeners directly. More commonly, inner classes are used which implement the appropriate listener interface. In an applet with many buttons, for example, an appropriate handler can be attached to each button; this obviates the need for the handler to test to see which button was clicked. Examples of both types of handlers are given in the subsections that follow.

The program cannot know, or predict, the order in which events will occur, or the number of times each one is repeated; it has to be prepared for all possibilities. That is the essence of event-driven programming, which differs from procedural programming in this fundamental way.

The following sections illustrate the principal Java programming considerations for defining listeners and event handlers in an applet.

C.6.1 Mouse Clicks

For the program to handle mouse clicks, the MouseListener interface must be implemented, either by the applet itself or by a mouse handler class. If the listener is being handled directly by the applet, then the applet must specify the listener in its implements clause and activate the listener, usually inside the init method:

```
public class MyApplet extends Applet implements MouseListener {

    public void init( ) {
        ...
        addMouseListener(this);
        ...
    }
```

The alternative is to use a separate class to handle mouse clicks. Commonly, this class is an inner class to the applet, so that the mouse handler has access to all of the applet's methods, particularly the graphics context:

```
public class MyApplet extends Applet {

    public void init( ) {
        ...
        addMouseListener(new MouseHandler());
        ...
    }

    private class MouseHandler implements MouseListener {
        ...
    }
}
```

If an external class is used, it is common for the applet to pass itself in the call on the `mouseHandler` constructor; the applet object can then be saved to an instance variable of the `mouseHandler` class.

Whichever alternative is used, all of the following methods must be added to the class which implements the `MouseListener`, and at least one must have some statements that respond to the event that it represents:

```
public void mousePressed(MouseEvent e) { }
public void mouseReleased(MouseEvent e) { }
public void mouseClicked(MouseEvent e) { }
public void mouseExited(MouseEvent e) { }
public void mouseEntered(MouseEvent e) { }
```

An advantage to using a separate class is that Java provides a `MouseAdapter` class which is precisely the trivial implementation of `MouseListener` given above. This means that the separate class can extend the `MouseAdapter` class (which an applet cannot do), overriding exactly the methods for which actions are to be provided. In most instances, this is usually only the `mouseClicked` method.

For instance, the typical response to a mouse event is to capture the x-y pixel coordinates where that event occurred on the frame. To do this, use the `getX` and `getY` methods of the `MouseEvent` class. For example, the following handler responds to a mouse click by storing the x-y coordinates of the click in the instance variables x and y.

```
public void mouseClicked(MouseEvent e) {
    x = e.getX();
    y = e.getY();
}
```

C.6.2 Mouse Motion

Similar to mouse clicks, for the program to handle mouse motion, the `MouseMotionListener` interface must be implemented either by the applet itself or a mouse motion handler class. To activate the listener, the following calls must be placed inside the `init` method:

```
addMouseMotionListener(<listener>);
```

The class which implements the listener must implement both of the following methods; at least one must have some statements that respond to the event that it represents:

```
public void mouseDragged(MouseEvent e) { }
public void mouseMoved(MouseEvent e) { }
```

An advantage to using a separate class is that Java provides a `MouseMotionAdapter` class which is precisely the trivial implementation of `MouseMotionListener` given above. This means that the separate class can extend the `MouseMotionAdapter` class (which an applet cannot do), overriding exactly the methods for which actions are to be provided. In most instances, this is usually only the `mouseDragged` method.

C.6.3 Buttons

A *Button* is an object on the screen that is named and can be selected by a mouse click. Any number of variables can be declared with class `Button` and placed in the applet. Because of this, button handlers are usually implemented via a separate class, rather than by the applet itself. A button is declared and initialized as follows:

```
Button <variable> = new Button(<string>);
```

Here is an example:

```
Button clearButton = new Button("Clear");
```

A button is placed in the applet by including the following inside the `init` method in your program.

```
add(<variable>);
```

For example:

```
add(clearButton);
```

To be useful, a button needs to have a listener attached so that the button responds to mouse clicks. This is normally done by including the following inside the applet's `init` method:

```
<variable>.addActionListener(<listener>);
```

For example:

```
clearButton.addActionListener(new ClearButtonHandler());
```

The class which handles the user selecting the button must implement the ActionListener interface. The listener class must implement an actionPerformed method to handle the button selection event:

```
public void actionPerformed (ActionEvent e) {
    if (e.getSource() == <variable>) {
        <statements>
    }
}
```

Here, the *<variable>* refers to the name of the Button variable as declared and initialized, and *<statements>* define what to do whenever that event occurs. If unique handlers are created for each button, the if test to determine which button was selected can be omitted; this is normally preferred. Below, for example, is a handler written as an inner class to the applet class that clears the screen whenever the clearButton is clicked by the user:

```
private class ClearButtonHandler implements ActionListener {
    public void actionPerformed(ActionEvent e) {
        repaint();
    }
}
```

Note that the repaint method is an applet method; thus, this class works as written only if it is an inner class to applet. Using an external class requires writing a constructor which takes the applet as an argument. Using our clear button as an example, the addActionListener code in applet's init method would appear as:

```
clearButton.addActionListener(new ClearButtonHandler(this));
```

The button handler class would then appear as:

```
public class ClearButtonHandler implements ActionListener {
    Applet applet;
    public ClearButtonHandler(Applet a) { applet = a; }
    public void actionPerformed(ActionEvent e) {
        applet.repaint();
    }
}
```

Note that using an external class makes it more difficult for a listener class to determine which button was selected since the buttons themselves are declared within the applet class.

C.6.4 Labels, TextAreas, and TextFields

A *Label* is an object whose string value can be placed inside a frame to label another object, such as a TextField. It can be added to the frame from within the init method. For example, the statement

```
add(new Label("Fahrenheit"));
```

would place the message "Fahrenheit" in the frame. Labels cannot have a listener attached to them.

A *TextArea* is an object on the screen that is named and can display text messages to the user. It is a scrollable object, so users have a complete record of the text output. A *TextField* is an object into which the user can type a single line of text from the keyboard; it raises an ActionEvent when the user types the return key at the end of the line. TextAreas and TextFields are declared as follows:

```
TextArea <variable> ;
TextField <variable> ;
```

For example:

```
TextArea echoArea;
TextField typing;
```

`TextArea` and `TextField` objects are normally placed in the applet as part of the `init` method in your program. Initialization requires the number of lines of text (for TextAreas) and the number of characters per line to be specified.

```
<variable1> = new TextArea(<lines>, <chars>);
add(<variable1>);
<variable2> = new TextField(<chars>);
add(<variable2>);
```

For example:

```
echoArea = new TextArea(5, 40);
add(echoArea);
typing = new TextField(40);
add(typing);
```

In these examples, we have declared and placed a 5 line by 40 character TextArea and a 40-character TextField in the current frame.

When the user types in the TextField and hits the return key, the applet can handle that event by writing additional code in its `actionPerformed` event handler.

```
public void actionPerformed (actionEvent e) {
   if (e.getSource() == <variable>) {
      String s = <variable>.getText();
      <action>
   }
}
```

Here, *<variable>* refers to the name of the TextArea variable that was declared and placed in the frame by the `init` method, like `typing` in the example above. When the event occurs, the string value of the user's typing in the text area is assigned to the variable s and the *<action>* is then executed.

A better solution is to use an internal class that listens specifically for only the user entering a line in the TextField:

```
private class TextHandler implements ActionListener {
    public void actionPerformed (actionEvent e) {
        String s = <variable>.getText();
        <action>
    }
}
```

In this case, the handler need not check for the triggering event; it must be the user pressing the return (or enter) key.

As an example of an *<action>*, the user's typing can be immediately echoed in the TextArea by concatenating it with all the text that is already there. The getText and setText methods are useful for this purpose, as shown below:

```
echoArea.setText(echoArea.getText() + s + "\n");
```

If this line is added as the *<action>* in the above code, the user's typing will be echoed on a new line inside the TextArea object named `echoArea`.

C.6.5 Choices

A *choice* is an object on the screen that offers several options to be selected by the user; it is like a pull-down menu, but it can be placed anywhere within the applet, not just at the top. A choice is declared as follows:

```
Choice <variable> ;
```

For example:

```
Choice choice;
```

The choice is named and placed in the frame as part of the init method in your program. The different selections are assigned to the Choice variable using the `addItem` method, and interaction is triggered by adding a listener to the frame for the choice.

```
<variable> = new Choice();
<variable>.addItem(<string1>);
...
add(<variable>);
<variable>.addItemListener(<listener>);
```

For example:

```
choice = new Button();
choice.addItem("North");
choice.addItem("East");
choice.addItem("South");
choice.additem("West");
add(choice);
choice.addItemListener(this);
```

In the case above, the applet itself is assumed to be handling the choice event. The applet or item listener event handler must implement ItemListener. When the user selects one of the choices, the event is handled by an itemStateChanged method:

```
public void itemStateChanged (ItemEvent e) {
    String s = (String)e.getItem();
    if (s.equals(<string1>) {
      <action1> in response to a selection of <string1>
    }
    else if (s.equals(<string2>) {
      <action2> in response to a selection of <string2>
    }
    ...
}
```

Here, the *<variable>* refers to the name of the Choice variable as declared and initialized, like the variable choice in the example above. When the event occurs, the *<action>* specified in this handler is executed. The String s has the value of the choice the user selected, which is passed to the handler by way of the method call e.getItem().

C.6.6 Summary of Components and Their Event Handlers

In the table below we summarize for quick reference the various components discussed, usually denoted widgets, and their event handlers. Java provides many other components that we have not discussed. See www.java.sun.com for more complete information.

For each widget, three things must usually be done:

1 Create the widget (except where the widget column is empty, i.e., mouse and mouse motion) by invoking the constructor for the class.
2 Insert the widget into the frame (except where the widget column is empty), via add (w), where w is the widget created by the constructor. In the event of a repaint, the paint method of each widget is automatically invoked by virtue of its having been inserted into the frame. So the applet is not responsible for repainting the widgets.
3 Attach an object listener to the widget, via

```
w.addXListener(<listener>);
```

Table C.4

Components and
Their Event Handlers

Widget	Implements Listener	Interface Methods	Event Source
Button Choice Label	ActionListener ItemListener	actionPerformed(ActionEvent e) itemStateChanged(ItemEvent e)	e.getSource() (String) e.getItem()
	MouseListener	mouseClicked(MouseEvent e) mouseEntered(MouseEvent e) mouseExited(MouseEvent e) mousePressed(MouseEvent e) mouseReleased(MouseEvent e)	e.getX() e.getY()
	MouseMotion– Listener	mouseDragged(MouseEvent e) mouseMoved(MouseEvent e)	e.getX() e.getY()
TextArea	ActionListener	actionPerformed(ActionEvent e)	e.getSource()
TextField	ActionListener	actionPerformed(ActionEvent e)	e.getSource()

where X is either Action, Mouse, MouseMotion, or Item, as appropriate, and
<listener> is an object that implements the appropriate listener interface. Note
that the Label widget has no listener.

C.7 **COLORS**

Colors and graphical methods are well-supported in Java. Specifically, *Color* is a distinct class, and we can declare variables of class Color. For instance:

```
Color c = new Color(Color.green);
```

declares the variable C to have color green, which is one of the "constants" available for
class `Color` (just like 1, 2, 3, etc. are the constants available for the type `int` in Java).

We can also declare an array of colors and initialize it with four different color constants, as follows:

```
Colors a[] = {Color.green, Color.red, Color.blue, Color.yellow};
```

Now `a[0]==Color.green`, `a[1]==Color.red`, and so forth.

The following two commands can be used to set the foreground and background
colors of the current applet. These settings affect the color of lines and text drawn in the
applet.

```
setForeground( <color> );    // sets the foreground color
                             // normally Color.black
setBackground( <color> );    // sets the background color
                             // normally Color.gray
```

C.8 **THE GRAPHICS ENVIRONMENT**

When an event handler is called, it often must do something inside the frame, like draw a line, display a text, or clear the entire frame. To accomplish this, the handler must retrieve the graphics environment associated with the frame where the event occurred. This is done by the following statement:

```
Graphics g = getGraphics();
```

Literally, this statement says to retrieve the graphics environment and assign it to the local variable g. Now, all the usual Graphics methods may be called to draw information inside the frame. For instance, the example in the previous section uses the Graphics methods setColor and fillRect to change all the pixels inside the frame to match the background color, effectively erasing whatever had been there.

The graphical drawing environment of the current applet can be obtained by the following declarations and assignments:

```
Graphics g = getGraphics();
Rectangle r = getBounds();
```

This declares the variable g as type Graphics and initializes its value to the window where the current Java applet is running. The rectangle r is a variable that has four fields— r.x, r.y, r.width, and r.height—which are assigned the values 0, 0, 500, and 300 (assuming that the width and height of the applet in which the program is running are 500 and 300). This variable g, since it is of type Graphics, has the following features and available methods (functions):

```
g.setColor( <color> );  // sets the foreground "color" for drawing
                        // and filling shapes in the graphics area
g.fillRect(x,y,width,height); // fills rectangular area at
                        // corner location (x, y), width, height
g.drawRect(x, y, width, height);  // draws that rectangle
g.fillOval(x, y, width, height); // fills that oval
g.drawOval(x, y, width, height); // draws that oval
g.drawLine(x, y, z, w); // draws a straight line from
                        // (x, y) to (z, w)
g.drawString(s, x, y); // displays the String s, starting at (x, y)
```

C.9 **PLACEMENT OF OBJECTS IN THE FRAME**

By default, objects are placed in a frame in the order in which they are added within the init method. This placement proceeds horizontally from left to right across the top of the frame. If not all the objects fit across the top, then a second row is created, and so forth.

Whenever the frame is resized, the objects are replaced to fit the new size. This can happen any time while the applet is running. However, the original order of objects is not rearranged when the frame is resized.

You may exercise more control over the placement of objects in the frame by selecting a different "layout manager." There are three kinds of layout managers available, FlowLayout (the default), GridLayout (where you divide the frame into a rectangular array of locations), and BorderLayout (where you place objects either on the north, east, south, west, or center of the frame). More information about these options can be found in the Java API documentation at the website java.sun.com/products/jdk/1.2/docs/api/overview-summary.html.

C.10 KEY JAVA CLASSES

This section summarizes the methods in some of the key Java classes used in this book, and with which you should be familiar.

C.10.1 The Object Class

Object is the root class in Java; as part of the package java.lang, it is automatically imported into every Java source file. All classes are subclasses of Object and thus have access to all public and protected methods of Object. The class Object is abstract; objects are always elements of a subclass of the Object class, never elements of the Object class itself.

Here we discuss only the most useful methods:

```
public boolean equals(Object o);
public final native Class getClass();
public native int hashcode();
public String toString();
protected native Object clone()
    throws CloneNotSupportedException;
```

The `equals` method is used to test whether or not two objects contain the same value. As implemented in Object, this is a byte-for-byte comparison. Some subclasses provide their own implementation when this interpretation is inadequate.

The method `getClass` can be used to obtain the actual class of an object. It is often used with the `instanceof` operator. It cannot be overridden by a subclass (nor would you want to).

The method `hashcode` computes a hashcode for an object so that it can be placed into a hashtable. Subclasses that override `equals` commonly override `hashcode` as well.

The method `toString` is used in string concatenation and in the print methods of PrintStream and PrintWriter. Almost all subclasses want to provide their own `toString` method; it is invaluable in debugging and should be implemented early.

The method `clone` provides a byte-for-byte copy for subclasses that implement the Cloneable interface. Subclasses that override the `equals` method should also provide their own `clone` method.

C.10.2 The Math Class

The Math class is also part of the package java.lang and is automatically imported into every Java compilation. The class defines constants for the mathematical values *e* and Π and static methods for many common mathematical functions, including trigonometry, exponentiation, and so forth. In this sense it is analogous to the C library <math.h>.

Again, we only show the most useful methods;

```
public static final double E;
public static final double PI;
public static int abs(int i);
public static long abs(long l);
public static float abs(float f);
public static double abs(double d);
public static native double acos(double d);
public static native double asin(double d);
public static native double atan(double d);
public static native double atan2(double d, double e);
public static native double cell(double d);
public static native double cos(double d);
public static native double exp(double d);
public static native double floor(double d);
public static native double log(double d);
public static int max(int i, int j);
public static long max(long l, long m);
public static float max(float f, float g);
public static double max(double d, double e);
public static int min(int i, int j);
public static long min(long l, long m);
public static float min(float f, float g);
public static double min(double d, double e);
public static native double pow(double d, double e);
public static synchronized double random();
public static native double rint(double d);
public static int round(float a);
public static int round(float a);
public static native double sin(double d);
public static native double sqrt(double d);
public static native double tan(double d);
```

C.10.3 The Integer and Float Classes

The primary purpose of the Integer class (in package java.lang) is to provide a wrapper for the primitive type int. In this way, primitive int values can then be stored in the various collection classes. Secondarily, the Integer class provides the parseInt method for converting strings representing an integer to a primitive int value.

A Long Class provides similar methods for wrapping long integers and converting strings to long integers. The most useful Integer methods are:

```
public Integer(int value);
public Integer(String s) throws NumberFormatException;
public int intValue();
public int parseInt(String s) throws NumberFormatException;
public int parseInt(String s, int radix)
    throws NumberFormatException;
public String toString();
```

The primary purpose of the Float class (in package java.lang) is to provide a wrapper for the primitive type float. In this way a primitive float value can then be stored in the various collection classes. The most useful methods are:

```
public Float(float value);
public Float(String s) throws NumberFormatException;
public float floatValue();
public String toString();
```

A Double Class provides similar methods for wrapping long floating point values and converting strings to long floating point values.

C.10.4 The String Class

Character strings are implemented in Java by way of the String class. The plus sign (+) is used to denote the concatenation of two strings into one, while the method equals is used instead of == to test for equality between two String variables or expressions. The == and != relations are used to see if two objects have identical pointer values; this is stricter than equals, which is used to determine equality in the underlying type. Here are a few examples of the major actions on strings.

```
Function                            Example
------------------------------      ------------------------------------
Declaration                         String s;
Declaration and initialization      String s = "Hello!";
Assignment                          s = "Goodbye!";
Comparison -- equal                 if (s.equals("Goodbye!")) ...
           -- less than             if (s.compareTo("Goodbye!") < 0) ...
           -- greater than          if (s.compareTo("Goodbye!") > 0) ...
Concatenation                       s = "Goodbye Cruel" + " World!";
Length                              s.length()  returns 20 for s
Search for a substring              s.indexOf(" ") returns the position
                                        of the first blank in s, or 7.
                                        NB the first character is at
                                        position 0!
Substring selection                 s.substring(8, 13) returns "Cruel"
```

While Pascal does not have a standard string type, most of its implementations support strings and a few common functions. Here is a quick summary of the differences between Java and Pascal string functions:

```
Java                              Pascal
-----------------------           -----------------------
"Hello World!"                    'Hello World!'
String s = "Hello World!";        var s, t: string;
                                  ... s := 'Hello World!';

String t = "Hello " + s;          t := concat('Hello ', s);
i = t.length();                   i := length(t);
i = s.indexOf(" ");               i := pos(s, ' ');
t = s.substring(6, 11);           t := copy(s, 7, 5);
```

C.10.5 The Vector Class

The Vector class (in package java.util) effectively provides an array of objects that grows in size as needed. As such, it is useful whenever you need to sequentially store objects, but do not know in advance how large the collection will be. The most useful methods are;

```
public Vector();
public final synchronized void addElement(Object o);
public synchronized clone();
public final boolean contains(Object o);
public final synchronized void copyInto(Object[] array);
public final synchronized Object elementAt(int index);
public final synchronized Enumeration elements();
public final synchronized Object firstElement();
public final int indexOf(Object o);
public final synchronized void insertElementAt(Object o, int index);
public final synchronized Object lastElement();
public final int lastIndexOf(Object o);
public final boolean removeElement(Object o);
public final void removeElementAt(int index);
public final synchronized void setElementAt(Object o, int index);
public final int size();
public final synchronized String toString();
```

Methods are provided for adding elements to the end of the Vector (addElement) and at an arbitrary index (insertElementAt), and for conveniently accessing the first (firstElement) and last (lastElement) elements.

Like arrays, Vector indexing starts at zero and runs through size-1. A method is also provided for accessing an element by position (elementAt) and for replacing an element by specifying its index (setElementAt). A number of methods are provided for finding a specific object within the Vector: contains, indexOf, lastIndexOf. The latter two return the value −1 if the object is not found. Elements can be removed either by searching for the specific object (removeElement) or by position (removeElementAt).

C.10.6 The Hashtable Class

The Hashtable class (in package java.util) is an implementation of the Dictionary abstract class and provides an associative array, in which the keys can be any object. Thus, it provides a key to value mapping, implemented as a hashtable.

The primary methods are:

```
public Hashtable();
public synchronized Object clone();
public synchronized boolean contains(Object value);
public synchronized boolean containsKey(Object key);
public synchronized Enumeration elements();
public synchronized Object get(Object key);
public synchronized Enumeration keys();
public synchronized Object put(Object key, Object value);
public synchronized Object remove(Object key);
public final int size();
public final synchronized String toString();
```

The primary methods for accessing a hashtable are get, put, and remove. The put method enters a key-value pair into the hashtable, while the get method, given a key, returns the value associated with the key (or null if the key is not in the hashtable). The remove method removes a key from the hashtable, returning its associated value.

Two boolean methods are provided for searching the hashtable; containsKey returns *true* if its argument is a key, while contains returns *true* if its argument is a value (for some key). Also, methods are provided for enumerating the set of keys (keys) and for enumerating the set of values (elements).

C.10.7 The PrintStream and PrintWriter Classes

The PrintStream and PrintWriter classes are quite similar; the former was developed in Java 1.0 for ASCII text output, while the latter was developed in Java 1.1 for Unicode output. The output console files System.out and System.err (corresponding to cout and cerr in C++) are variables of type PrintStream.

If you are creating an output file, you should normally use the PrintWriter class. File creation would normally be accomplished using:

```
PrintWriter out = new PrintWriter(new BufferedWriter(
        new FileWriter(s)));
```

where s is a string giving the output file name. The FileWriter connects to the file system, while the BufferedWriter provides buffering for the sake of efficiency. Note that the BufferedWriter could also be connected just as easily to a pipe, a socket, or even a URL.

Both PrintStream and PrintWriter provide a wealth of `print` methods, essentially one for each primitive type, one for Strings, and one for Objects. The latter accomplishes printing by using the object's `toString` method:

```
public void print(boolean b);
public void print(char c);
public void print(int i);
public void print(long l);
public void print(float f);
public void print(double d);
public void print(char[] ca);
public void print(String s);
public void print(Object o);
public void println( );
```

There are also `println` methods analogous to the `print` methods shown above. This makes simple unformatted text output fairly convenient for both PrintStreams and PrintWriters.

C.10.8 The Graphics Class

This class defines a device-independent interface for drawing on the screen, including line drawing, area filling, image painting, and graphics output clipping. It is an abstract class, which means that a `Graphics` object cannot be created via a constructor. The usual way of getting a `Graphics` object is through an applet or other component's `getGraphics()` method. Specific subclasses of `Graphics` are implemented for different computer platforms and different output devices. `Graphics` must be imported from `java.awt`.

The primary methods are:

```
public void clearRect(int x, int y, int width, int height);
public void clipRect(int x, int y, int width, int height);
public void drawArc(int x, int y, int width, int height,
    int startAngle, int arcAngle);
public void drawLine(int x1, int y1, int x2, int y2);
public void drawOval(int x, int y, int width, int height);
public void drawRect(int x, int y, int width, int height);
public void drawRoundRect(int x, int y, int width, int height);
public void drawString(String s, int x, int y);
public void fillArc(int x, int y, int width, int height,
    int startAngle, int arcAngle);
public void fillLine(int x1, int y1, int x2, int y2);
public void fillOval(int x, int y, int width, int height);
public void fillRect(int x, int y, int width, int height);
public void fillRoundRect(int x, int y, int width, int height);
public Color getColor();
public void setColor();
```

Although not indicated, all of the above methods are abstract.

Bibliography

Ada [1983]. *Military Standard Ada Programming Language.* ANSI/MIL-STD-1815A, Feb. 1983.

Adams, Jeanne C., et al. [1997]. *Fortran 95 HandBook: Complete ISO/ANSI Reference.* MIT Press.

Aho, Alfred V.; Ravi Sethi; and Jeffrey D. Ullman [1986]. *Compilers, Principles, Techniques, and Tools.* Addison-Wesley.

Alves-Foss, J. (ed.) [1999]. *Formal Syntax and Semantics of Java.* Lecture Notes in Computer Science, 1523. Springer.

Andrews, G. R, and R. A. Olsson [1993]. *The SR Programming Language.* Benjamin Cummings.

Appel, Andrew W. [1998]. *Modern Compiler Implementation in Java.* Cambridge University Press.

Backus, J., et al. [1954]. "Preliminary Report: Specifications for the IBM Mathematical FORmula TRANslating System, FORTRAN." IBM Corporation.

Bartak, R. [1998] "Guide to Constraint Programming." http://kti.ms.mff.cuni.cz/~bartak/constraints/intro.html.

Ben-Ari, M. [1982]. *Principles of Concurrent Programming.* Prentice-Hall International.

Booch, Grady [1994]. *Object-Oriented Analysis and Design with Applications.* 2nd ed. Benjamin/Cummings.

Budd, Timothy A. [1994]. *Classic Data Structures in C++.* Addison-Wesley.

Budd, T. [1995]. *Multiparadigm Programming in Leda.* Addison-Wesley.

Budd, Timothy A. [2000]. *Understanding Object-Oriented Programming with Java.* Addison-Wesley.

Carrano, Frank M.; Paul Helman; and Robert Veroff [1998]. *Data Abstraction and Problem Solving with C++.* 2nd ed. Addison-Wesley.

Chamberland, Luc [1995]. *Fortran 90: A Reference Guide.* Addison-Wesley.

Chomsky, N. [1957]. *Syntactic Structures.* Mouton.

Church, Alonzo [1941]. *The Calculi of Lambda Conversion.* Princeton University Press.

Clocksin and Mellish [1997]. *Programming in Prolog.* 4th ed. Springer.

Coffman, E. G.; M. J. Elphnick; and A. Shosani [1971]. "System deadlocks." *Computing Surveys* 3 (June 1971), pp. 67–78.

Cohen, N. H. [1996]. *Ada As a Second Language.* 2nd ed. McGraw-Hill.

Davis, Martin [1963]. "Eliminating the irrelevant from mechanical proofs." *Proceedings of a Symposium in Applied Mathematics* 15, American Mathematical Society, Providence, RI, pp. 15–30.

De Millo, Richard A.; Richard J. Lipton; and Alan J. Perlis [1979]. "Social processes and proofs of theorems and programs." *Communications of ACM* 22 (May 1979), pp. 271–280.

Dershem, Herbert L., and Michael J. Jipping [1990]. *Programming Languages: Structures and Models.* Wadsworth.

Dijkstra, Edsger W. [1968a] "Cooperating sequential processes." In *Programming Languages,* ed. F. Genuys. Academic Press, pp. 43–112.

Dijkstra, Edsger W. [1968b]. "Go to statement considered harmful." *Communications of ACM* 11 (March 1968), pp. 147–148.

Dijkstra, Edsger W. [1971]. "Hierarchical ordering of sequential processes." *Acta Informatica* 1, pp. 115–138.

Dijkstra, Edsger W. [1972]. "Notes on structured programming." *Structured Programming.* O. J. Dahl, E. W. Dijkstra, and C. A. R. Hoare, eds. Academic Press.

Dijkstra, Edsger W. [1972]. "The humble programmer." *Communications of ACM* 15 (October 1972), pp. 859–866.

Dybvig, R. Kent [1996]. *The Scheme Programming Language, ANSI Scheme.* Prentice-Hall.

Fowler, Martin [2000]. *Refactoring: Improving the Design of Existing Code.* Addison-Wesley.

Gamma, Erich; Richard Helm; Ralph Johnson; and John Vlissides [1995]. *Design Patterns.* Addison-Wesley.

Goldberg, Adele, and David Robson [1989]. *Smalltalk-80: The Language.* Addison-Wesley.

Goldberg, David [1991]. "What every computer scientist should know about floating-point arithmetic." *Computing Surveys* 23 (March 1991), pp. 5–48.

Gosling, J.; B. Joy; and G. Steele [1996]. *The Java Language Specification.* Addison-Wesley.

Gosling, James, and Henry McGilton [1996a]. "The Java Language Environment: A White Paper." http://java.sun.com/docs/white/langenv.

Gries, David [1981]. *The Science of Programming.* Springer.

Guttag, John [1977]. "Abstract data types and the development of data structures." *Communications of ACM* 20 (June 1977), pp. 396–404.

Guttag, John, and J. J. Horning [1978]. "The algebraic specification of abstract data types." *Acta Informatica* 10, pp. 27–52.

Guttag, John [1980]. "Notes on type abstraction." *IEEE Transactions on Software Engineering,* SE-6, 1 (January 1980), pp. 13–23.

Hennessy, John, and David A. Patterson [1998]. *Computer Organization and Design: The Hardware/Software Interface.* Morgan Kaufmann.

Hoare, C.A.R. [1969]. "An Axiomatic Basis for Computer Programming." *Communications of ACM* 12 (October 1969), pp. 576–580, 583.

Hoare, C.A.R. [1978]. "Communicating sequential processes." *Communications of ACM* 21 (August 1978), pp. 666–677.

Hoare, C.A.R. [1985]. *Communicating Sequential Processes.* Prentice-Hall International.

Hughes, John [1989]. "Why functional programming matters." *The Computer Journal* 32, 2, pp. 98–107.

Jaffar, J., and M. Maher [1994]. "Constraint logic programming, a survey." *Journal of Logic Programming* 19/20, pp. 503–581.

Jones, R. Richard, and Rafael Lins [1996]. *Garbage Collection.* John Wiley.

Kelsey, Richard; William Clinger; and Jonathan Rees, eds. [1998]. "Revised report on the algorithmic language Scheme." *SIGPLAN Notices* 33, 9, pp. 26–76.

Kernighan, B., and D. Ritchie [1988]. *The C Programming Language.* 2nd ed. Prentice-Hall.

Landin, P. [1966]. "A lambda calculus approach to computer programming." In *Advances in Programming and Non-Numerical Computation,* ed. L. Fox. Pergamon Press, Oxford, pp. 97–141.

Liskov, B. H., and A. Snyder [1979]. "Exception handling in CLU." *IEEE Transactions on Software Engineering,* SE-5, 6, pp. 546–558.

Liskov, B. H., et al. [1981]. *CLU Reference Manual.* Springer-Verlag.

Matthews, Clive [1998]. *An Introduction to Natural Language Processing through Prolog,* Longman.

McCarthy, John [1960]. "Recursive functions of symbolic expressions and their computation by machine." *Communications of the ACM* 3, 4, pp. 184–195.

McCarthy, John, et al. [1965]. *Lisp 1.5 Programmer's Manual.* MIT Press.

Meyer, Bertrand [1988]. *Object-Oriented Software Construction.* Prentice-Hall.

Meyer, Bertrand [1990]. *Introduction to the Theory of Programming.* Prentice-Hall.

Meyer, Bertrand [1997]. *Object-Oriented Software Construction.* 2nd ed. Prentice-Hall.

Mills, Harlan [1975]. "The new math of computer programming." *Communications of the ACM* 18, 1, pp. 43–48.

Mitchell, J. G.; W. Maybury; and R. Sweet [1979]. *Mesa Language Manual, Version 5.* Xerox Palo Alto Research Center.

Naur, P. (ed), et al. [1963]. "Revised report on the algorithmic language Algol 60." *Communications of ACM* 6, 1, 1–23.

Noonan, Robert E. [2000]. "An object-oriented view of backtracking." *Proceedings of the Thirty-first SIGCSE Technical Symposium on Computer Science Education,* pp. 362–366.

Patil, S. [1971]. Limitations and capabilities of Dijkstra's semaphore primitives for coordination among processes. Technical report, MIT (February 1971).

Steele, G. L. [1990]. *Common Lisp—The Language.* 2nd ed. Digital Press, Cambridge, MA.

Stein, L. A. [1999]. "Challenging the computational metaphor: implications for how we think." *Cybernetics and Systems* 30, 6.

Stroustrup, Bjarne [1991]. *The C++ Programming Language.* 2nd ed. Addison-Wesley.

Unicode Consortium [2000]. *The Unicode Standard Version 3.0.* Addison-Wesley. See also http://www.unicode.org for more information about the Unicode standard.

Walker, Henry M., and G. Michael Schneider [1996]. "Revised model curriculum for a liberal arts degree in Computer Science." *Communications of the ACM* 39, pp. 85–95.

Wegner, Peter [1997]. "Why interaction is more powerful than algorithms." *Communications of the ACM* 40, 5.

Wegner, Peter, and D. Goldin [1999]. Interaction, computability, and Church's thesis. Unpublished manuscript (June 1999); see http://www.cs.brown.edu/~pw.

Wirth, Nicklaus [1973]. *Systematic Programming: an Introduction.* Prentice-Hall.

Wirth, Nicklaus [1974]. On the design of programming languages. *Proceedings of IFIP Congress* 74, pp. 386–393.

Wirth, Nicklaus [1976]. *Algorithms + Data Structures = Programs.* Prentice-Hall.

Index